SITING OF MAJOR FACILITIES
A Practical Approach

EDWARD A. WILLIAMS
and
ALISON K. MASSA

in association with
David H. Blau
and
Herbert R. Schaal
Sponsored by
EDAW inc.

McGraw-Hill Book Company
New York St. Louis San Francisco Auckland Bogotá
Hamburg Johannesburg London Madrid Mexico Montreal New Delhi
Panama Paris São Paulo Singapore Sydney Tokyo Toronto

Library of Congress Cataloging in Publication Data

Williams, Edward A.
  Siting of major facilities.

  Bibliography: p.
  Include index.
  1. Building sites.   2.   Environmental protection.
3.   Landscape architecture.   I.   Massa, Alison K.
II. Title.
TH375.W54   338.6′042′0973   82-7774
ISBN 0-07-070420-1   AACR2

338.6 = organization of production

1 2 3 4 5 6 7 8 9 0   HDHD   8 9 8 7 6 5 4 3 2

ISBN 0-07-070420-1

The editors for this book were Joan Zseleczky and Beatrice E.
Eckes, the designer was Elliot Epstein, and the production
supervisor was Paul A. Malchow. It was set in Optima by
Progressive Typographers.

Printed and bound by Halliday Lithograph.

CONTENTS

Preface, v

Illustration Credits, vi

Introduction, 1

PART ONE 7

1
SITE SELECTION:
AN HISTORICAL PERSPECTIVE 9
The Hetch Hetchy Case, 9
The Evolution of Environmental Consciousness, 9
Some Freeway Issues, 11
Some Power Plant Efforts, 13
The Everglades Jetport, 16
The Second Campus, 17
Project Seafarer, 18
A Petrochemical Complex, 19

2
THE NEED FOR A
SITE-SELECTION PROCESS 23
Lessons from the Past, 23
Requirements for Successful Site Selection, 25

3
THE OVERALL SITING PROCESS 29
The Structure of the Process, 29
The Attributes of the Process, 30
The Evolution and Application of the Process, 31

4
PROJECT GOALS AND OBJECTIVES 35
The Need for Goals, 35

Identifying the Mission of an Organization, 36
Defining Organizational Goals, 36
Defining Organizational Objectives, 37
Defining the Project Goal, 38
Defining Project Objectives, 38

5
PROJECT DEFINITION 43
The Purpose of Defining the Project, 43
When Is the Project Defined? 44
Defining the Physical Characteristics of the Facility, 49
What Is an Appropriate Format? 50
Graphic Presentation Methods, 55

6
PROJECT-ENVIRONMENTAL
RELATIONSHIPS 59
Purpose, 59
Approaches to Environmental Analysis, 59
The Preferred Organization of the Environmental Study, 61
Identification of Siting Requirements, 62
Identification of Effects, 64
Refinement of Objectives and Environmental Criteria, 71
Identification of Issues, 77

7
THE SCREENING PROCESS 79
Introduction, 79
Design of the Screening Process, 79
Identification of Site-Screening Factors, 83
The Classification of Factors, 85
Weighting Systems, 103
Identification of Candidate Area, 128
Identification of Candidate Site, 128

8
THE SITE-EVALUATION PROCESS 131
Introduction, 131
Site Verification, 131
Preparation of Conceptual Layouts and Cost Estimates, 131
Review of Agency and Public Concerns, 133
Establishing the Framework for Site Evaluation, 133
The Site-Evaluation Summary, 142
Site Ranking, 142
Conclusion, 151

9
DATA NEEDS AND ANALYSIS 153
The Need for a Data Plan, 153
Considerations in Identifying Data Needs, 153
The Data Plan, 161
Methods and Sources of Data Collection, 161
Data Analysis and Organization, 168
Methods of Organizing Mapped Data, 168
Conclusion, 179

10
CITIZEN PARTICIPATION 181
The Purpose of Citizen Participation, 181
Design of the Program, 182
Selection of Participants and Timing of Participation, 182
Site-Screening and Site-Evaluation Participation Techniques, 183
Conclusion, 192

PART TWO   193

Case Study 1
THE WEST OAHU COLLEGE SITE EVALUATION   194

Case Study 2
THE TYRONE ENERGY PARK TRANSMISSION LINE STUDY   205

Case Study 3
PROJECT SEAFARER   229
The Upper Michigan Site-Selection Study, 237

Case Study 4
THE DAVENPORT SITING STUDIES   247
Land-Use Study, 247
Power Plant Siting Study, 254
Findings and Recommendations, 257
Transmission Routing Study, 259

Case Study 5
SWAN FALLS–GUFFEY HYDROELECTRIC PROJECT   273

Case Study 6
DULUTH FREEWAY ROUTING STUDY   277

Case Study 7
COAL-FIRED POWER PLANT SITING STUDY   289
History and Scope of This Study, 289
The Siting Process, 289
Statewide Analysis Phase, 289
Statewide Siting Data Base Breakdown, 290
Preferred Candidate Area Analysis Phase, 296
Preferred Candidate Area Data Base Breakdown, 296
Preferred Candidate Site Identification and Analysis Phase, 299
Candidate Site Data Summaries, 299

References Cited, 303
Selected Bibliography, 305
Index, 309

PREFACE

This book describes a systematic and comprehensive process for selecting sites for major facilities. From freeways to power plants and petrochemical plants, major facilities have rarely met with a smooth passage from concept to construction. Poor siting decisions have far-reaching effects on the natural environment, on individuals and communities, and on the economy. The planning and landscape architectural firm of EDAW inc. has been assisting government agencies and industry with site selection for over a decade. Toward the end of the 1970s, we recognized a need to make our experience and techniques more widely available, and so the concept of presenting one structured and broadly applicable process in this book came into being.

The goal of this book is to improve site-selection decision making. It is more possible today than it was 10 or 15 years ago to cite cases that illustrate the use of systematic siting methods. Nevertheless, the need for a more widespread understanding of the comprehensive nature and impacts of the process on the part of industry, government, and the affected or interested public remains clear.

We are indebted to our fellow principals of EDAW who patiently accommodated this effort and whose thoughtful contributions both to the manuscript and through the conduct of individual site-selection studies made this book possible. In addition, we want to acknowledge the work of Victor Viets, a former member of the firm, in the field of power plant siting. We would also like to thank the several individuals involved in typing the manuscript, Beverly Cubbage for editing it, Cindy Schafer for research and graphics assistance, and Bonnie Ng for her outstanding work in preparing and editing the graphics.

The business of locating major facilities is likely to become increasingly challenging as we gain a better understanding of their effects and as the space in which to accommodate them shrinks. We believe the methods we present will provide the means for making all major siting decisions more rationally, more quickly, and more economically.

Edward A. Williams
Alison K. Massa

ILLUSTRATION CREDITS

Introduction title page: The San Onofre nuclear generating station under construction. [*Southern California Edison Company. Reprinted by permission.*]

Chapter 1 title page: The Comanche Peak nuclear power plant. [*Gibbs and Hill. Reprinted by permission.*]

Chapter 2 title page: Tellico Dam, Georgia. [*Source: Tennessee Valley Authority. Reprinted by permission.*]

Chapter 3 title page: Morrow Bay fossil-fueled power plant, California. [*Source: Pacific Gas and Electric Company. Reprinted by permission.*]

Chapter 4 title page: Refineries: bulk aerial view. [*Courtesy of Cities Service Company and American Petroleum Institute Photographic and Film Services. Reprinted by permission.*]

Chapter 5 title page: Refining bulk equipment catalytic crackers (Phillips), Boiger, Texas. [*Courtesy of American Petroleum Institute Photographic and Film Services. Reprinted by permission.*]

Chapter 6 title page: Electric power transmission tower installation. [*Courtesy of Tennessee Valley Authority. Reprinted by permission.*]
Overhead electric power transmission. [*Courtesy of Tennessee Valley Authority. Reprinted by permission.*]

Chapter 7 title page: PASNY power plant. [*Courtesy of JAF. Reprinted by permission.*]

Chapter 8 title page: A section of the Tennessee Valley Authority's national fertilizer development center at Muscle Shoals, Alabama. [*Source: Tennessee Valley Authority. Reprinted by permission.*]

Chapter 9 title page: Completed section of Trans-Alaska pipeline, 1977. [*Courtesy of Alaska Pipeline Service Company and American Petroleum Institute Photo Library. Reprinted by permission.*]

Chapter 10 title page: Norris Dam, Tennessee. [*Courtesy of Tennessee Valley Authority. Reprinted by permission.*]

Case Study 1 title page: Puu Kapuai, one of the sites considered for location of West Oahu College.

Case Study 5 title page: The existing Swan Falls–Guffey Dam on the Snake River, Idaho.

Those figures not otherwise acknowledged are from EDAW sources.

INTRODUCTION

If the revolution in land-use controls preceding the National Environmental Policy Act (NEPA) of 1969 was, in the now familiar phrase, "a quiet one" (Bosselman and Callies, 1971), many of the battles along the way were noisy, costly, and often lengthy.

This revolution in land-use controls has affected the way in which all kinds of land-use decisions are made, from small residential developments to major public and industrial facilities. While the cumulative impacts of small developments have a fundamental influence on the fabric of our environment, large-scale development has provided the primary impetus of much of the state legislation in the late 1960s which culminated in NEPA. Isolated conflicts earlier in the century, such as the damming of Hetch Hetchy in California and the freeway location battles of the 1960s, were merely warm-ups for more to come. Increased recognition of the potential direct impacts of key facilities and the often irresistible growth pressures surrounding them grew out of battles over such projects as the Cross-Florida Barge Canal and the proposed Everglades Jetport (Blackwelder, 1972).

Since NEPA, however, the battles have continued to rage. While they have perhaps raged less fiercely in the public mind until recently, they have made severe demands on the times and financial resources of both the sponsors of major public and private projects and the public agencies and private organizations that watchdog those projects. NEPA has indeed revolutionized notions of what it takes to get a proposed major facility approved, but it has not on the whole revolutionized the manner in which facilities are conceived and planned. Impact statements are still too frequently prepared after the fact of a siting decision. They tend to be viewed by project sponsors as troublesome obstacles and by environmentalist opponents as often inadequate substitutes for responsible planning which only rarely result in modification or curtailment of inappropriate projects.

The battle lines are thus being redrawn. On one hand we have industrialists calling for more public education, "presenting the problems associated with overly restrictive land use controls, environmental controls, no-growth concepts and other damaging restrictions that will prohibit sound industrial expansion" (Seelig, 1976:13–14). The proliferation of regulatory agencies, permit requirements, and impact evaluation guidelines is viewed with increasing concern not only by industrialists but also more frequently now by economists. They see related development costs fueling inflation and the curtailment of development opportunities potentially affecting the economic health of the nation as well as that of individual industries. As labor, land, energy, and raw-material costs become increasingly severe problems for economic development, the already surfacing backlash against what Bernard Frieden (1979) has called "environmental elitism" can be expected to solidify.

On the other hand, the backlash can already be seen to be rekindling the determination of environmentally minded individuals and organizations, which celebrated a remarkable advance in environmental consciousness in the 1960s and 1970s. More ammunition is continually being stacked by our expanding scientific understanding of the potential health and environmental impacts of our actions and by what seems to be steady procession of alarming events and horror stories.

But as the two sides retrench, the general public stands in the middle, confused and divided. It hears of a chemical company which has dumped the by-products of fertilizer manufacture on uncontrolled sites, polluting groundwater and surface water for some 20 years. But the plant means jobs, fertilizers provide a contribution to the control of food costs and maintaining exports, while the cost of cleanup means tax dollars. Those for whom the problem cannot be dismissed as out of sight and mind, who must live with the scare of impaired health and birth defects but who cannot afford to move because of the diminished value of homes that lie on poisoned land, may find the temptation to rationalize even greater. The public also hears of a nuclear power plant failure and of people being evacuated from its vicinity. But the evacuees move back, out of economic necessity and because the area is home; and, after all, nuclear power may be the only short-run chance of maintaining our living standards. Should similar plants be shut down? No, said the supervisors of Yolo County, next door to California's Rancho Seco plant, shortly after the Three Mile Island accident in mid-1979; it means jobs and in-come. Yes, say the growing number of antinuclear activists.

The public, caught in these dilemmas, includes the professional protagonists as well as those directly affected and the disinterested lay public. We are all to some degree affected by our actions in designing and locating the paraphernalia of civilization. Some mistakes can be recognized only in hindsight and should be excused and accepted or amended. Others made by sponsors with open eyes and selfish motivation, but without

"Good evening, sir. As you may know, the soaring costs of recent environmental-protection legislation have forced us to pass part of this burden along to the consumer. Your share comes to $171,947.65."

[*Drawing by Lorenz; copyright 1979, The New Yorker Magazine, Inc.*]

public scrutiny or scruples, cannot. In this book we are examining ways to avoid the mistakes of siting facilities in inappropriate locations (socially, economically, and environmentally). Anticipating all the potential impacts may be impossible. For example, we do not know the effects of the as yet incompletely understood and little-publicized fine-particulate emissions on tomato crops downwind from a coal-fired power plant. But we do have the capability to make the best judgment based on available knowledge. What is also clear is that virtually no major factility can now be located anywhere in the United States without close public scrutiny, public participation, and a large measure of public acceptance of the result.

Increased public awareness and the myriad of federal, state, and local regulations and reviews to be satisfied may on the whole be resulting in better siting decisions. If so, it is only at the continued expense of enormous outlays of money, time, and effort due to delays, replanning, junked plans, construction halts, and unfinished projects. For example, it has been estimated that prior to the Three Mile Island incident the time required to get a nuclear power plant built in the United States was almost 10 years, twice as long as in Europe. Although costs are lower, the time from initiation to operation of a coal-fired power plant is now almost as long. In both cases, delays involve serious increases in development costs due to interest, inflated building costs, and continued use of oil, costs that are passed on in consumer rate increases.

The list of projects stymied late in their planning or even during or after construction is a long one. Well-publicized recent examples, some of which have been permanently scuttled, include numerous dams (Tellico, Tocks Island, Hell's Canyon, Dickey-Lincoln, Bonneville, Warm Springs, and Auburn); power plants (Kaiparowits

"I wish I knew how to break this gently. They killed it."

[*Drawing by Calvin Grondahl for the* Deseret News; *copyright 1979.*]

in Utah, Storm King on the Hudson River, and California's Humboldt Bay, Point Arena, and Diablo Canyon nuclear plants); the Cross-Florida Barge Canal; the Tennessee-Tombigbee Waterway; Dow Chemical Company's Montezuma Hills chemical plant; and a deepwater port and oil refinery off the coast of Maine. The list also includes some major urban projects, such as San Francisco's Yerba Buena (renamed George Moscone) Convention Center, as well as numerous freeway, sewer plant, or airport expansions. Some of these projects, together with older pre-NEPA examples, are described in Chapter 1 because they provide valuable insight into past siting failures.

In the files of industry and government there are now reports and working papers describing various methods of site selection. Understanding of the relative importance of factors in site selection has become more sophisticated and more industry-specific. Drawing on the work of management specialists and of academic regional location theorists such as Isard (1960), what can almost be described as a new discipline has grown up. Articles and texts devoted principally to the technical and economic aspects of industrial location are now readily available. Such apparent details as proximity to postal facilities and distribution facilities and the degree of unionization and skill of the labor force have been recognized as highly significant to the success or failure of sites for certain industries. However, environmental and social concerns are often dealt with in industry publications in the form of lists of regulatory agencies and requirements rather than in discussions of appropriately prioritized siting criteria. Industrial plant locators have become more adept at working with or avoiding the regulators, a procedure which has not always worked out as expected. The history of the Dow Chemical plant proposal in California's Solano County, which is described in Chapter 1, is just one such case.

Some of the site-selection techniques now prescribed by industry and consultants are so complex and sophisticated that they tend to create suspicion and frustration. Lay persons find it difficult to trust a conclusion made on the basis of a highly technical formula that they cannot understand, but they may be equally suspicious of a technician's intuitive opinion—they want to be shown why certain conclusions are drawn and what factors have been considered. The suspicion has turned into hostility in cases in which government and business have been proved wrong in their judgments.

Despite the growth in site-selection theory as it affects the operating success of an industry, the authors know of

almost nothing published to date that brings together all the environmental, social, economic, and technical factors of concern to the wide public as well as to industry and explains how they fit into and can be weighted in their proper proportion in the decision-making process. The process of selecting sites remains primarily an adversarial one.

Environmental groups that were once predominantly lay have been forced to become more technically and legally oriented. Many organizations, such as the Natural Resources Defense Council, Inc., the Sierra Club, and the Environmental Defense Fund, support staffs of scientists, lawyers, and lobbyists in specialized fields. Countering the expansion of public-interest legal activism is the National Legal Center for the Public Interest, created by California business leaders in 1973 to preserve the values of free enterprise, private property, and citizens' rights (*Industrial Development,* May–June 1978).

So, with growing lay concern, increasingly difficult technical material to comprehend, and an adversarial rather than a cooperative relationship between project sponsors and environmentalists, siting decisions have increasingly ended in the courts or never-never land.

It may be argued that court decisions in difficult siting cases are both appropriate and inevitable. Certainly the importance of the judiciary in bringing about social, economic, and environmental change cannot be disputed. But litigation is time-consuming and costly, adding to already heavy burdens of industry, government, environmental organizations, and, ultimately, the taxpayer and consumer. In the words of the report on the National Coal Policy Project, an extraordinary example of industry-environmentalist voluntary cooperation:

[T]raditionally this task [of finding solutions to difficult industry-environmental problems] has been accomplished through the adversary process, whereby opposing groups meet at legislative hearings or in the courts to assert their positions. Advocates are forced by the nature of this process to present their cases in the starkest terms in order to "win" a favorable decision. This precludes the search for a mutually agreeable outcome. Further, it can lead to additional delays and costs that are in no one's best interest (National Coal Policy Project, 1977:4).

The dual trends evident over the past decade—the entry of the general public as "authorities" into decision making on a large scale and the reaction against adversary proceedings and complex permit and approvals processes—have prompted both the search for alternative methods of making decisions and a change in the role of the planner.

The planner is no longer a quasi decision maker, acknowledging conflicts, stating assumptions, recommending a course of action, and awaiting the outcome. In some instances, the planner is now a negotiator. Malcolm Rivkin has described efforts to negotiate development of relatively small-scale types of projects. But he notes that "atomic power plants, major industrial facilities and large scale public projects . . . which have profound impacts on the environment are still inherently explosive matters" (Rivkin, 1977:2) and are less amenable to relatively unstructured negotiation. In such cases as these, the planner needs to be the facilitator of public decisions. As such, he or she must anticipate issues, structure problem statements, and provide data in a way that permits the public or its representatives to make the decisions.

This book, therefore, is the result of a perceived need shared by industry, government, and citizens alike for a comprehensive, mutually acceptable, commonly understood, and dependable framework for dealing with the many issues that arise in connection with the location of a major industrial plant or public facility. What is presented here is a process that brings divergent interests together to resolve issues and participate in cooperative, orderly site selection. The concerns, methods, and techniques we describe are the result of our own experience in successful (and, in some cases, unsuccessful) siting efforts under contract to both business and government. The methods have been developed during the course of helping to locate such diverse facilities as power plants, pipelines, a college campus, freeways, and power transmission routes. With appropriate adaptation, they can be used for other major facilities, such as ports, airports, refineries, and waste disposal sites.

The book is divided into two parts, the first describing

"I brought you up here today, son, because I wanted you to get a feel for the scope of this damned thing."

[Drawing by Ziegler; copyright 1979, The New Yorker Magazine, Inc.]

the need for a site-selection process and the process itself and the second presenting some actual case studies to illustrate the process in operation.

Part One begins with a number of historical cases which are described to demonstrate the changes that have occurred in the way in which site selectors need to approach the location of major facilities. The lessons that can be drawn from these cases are discussed and translated into requirements for more successful site selection in Chapter 2. Chapter 3 summarizes the overall process of site selection that we recommend and shows how it responds to the requirements.

Each of the next five chapters deals in detail with one of the five phases of the recommended process: identification of goals and objectives, definition of the project, identification of environmental conditions necessary to or likely to be affected by the project, identification of and selection among candidate areas and candidate sites, and, finally, comparative evaluation of candidate sites.

The two concluding chapters in Part One discuss approaches to data collection and analysis and to citizen participation. These two activities are dealt with separately not because they are considered separate steps in the process; rather, they are fundamental components of the site-selection process in all or most of its five phases.

Part Two presents a number of case studies that illustrate various aspects of the recommended process in greater depth. The particular studies, all performed by EDAW, have been chosen to represent the application of the process to a range of typical site-selection problems.

Application of the recommended methods requires adaptation to meeting needs that vary widely among different types of siting studies and are often unique to specific cases. However, a few caveats about what the book does and does not offer should be borne in mind.

First, the book should not be viewed as a manual or "cookbook" on how to conduct a siting study. It deals primarily with methods for handling environmental concerns, social issues, economics, and technical requirements, for organizing information, opinions, and judgments on these subjects, and for combining many individual conclusions in an order of priority so that a final decision can be reached. Application of the recommended methods to specific cases requires adaptation to

meet widely varying and often unique needs. Most siting studies involve collection and analysis of highly detailed technical data, which we have chosen to omit in order to avoid lengthy lists and explanation. It should also be recognized that the state of the art in techniques for recording and manipulating spatial and other site-selection data is changing rapidly. The book is not an attempt to present the full state of the art. Rather, it aims to broaden awareness of the range and interrelationships of relevant considerations.

Second, we have given very limited consideration to the broad political environment which will influence many siting decisions in the final analysis. An intrinsic characteristic of the process we recommend is the ability to incorporate local and even state-level values and political opinion, to the extent that they are clearly expressed. In some instances, however, the outcome of the process may be overridden by questions of national security or obscured by political controversy.

A related point is that we have chosen to omit specific discussion of nuclear energy facilities. The site-selection process we describe is intrinsically able to respond to differing values, but it cannot resolve far-reaching controversies. We believe that the differences of scientific judgment, emotional or philosophical attitude, and political response surrounding nuclear power plants are currently so great as to make inclusion of the subject both distracting and subject to misunderstanding.

Finally, we must emphasize that the methods we present cannot be a cure-all for badly conceived projects. Nor can they be seen as the savior of siting proposals that are opposed by the public for reasons that may not be entirely sound. It has been shown, however, that the comprehensive and democratic siting process we describe can and (albeit not without exception) does work. For example, one utility company using the open siting process in a very sensitive area was able to complete a power plant on schedule for the first time in a decade (Comstock, 1975).

It is hoped that by setting forth the entire process from beginning to end, new levels of understanding of the need for a methodical approach will be reached before further expensive commitments to unproductive or environmentally inappropriate sites are made.

ONE

1 | SITE SELECTION: AN HISTORICAL PERSPECTIVE

The industrial era, both in Europe and in the United States, was characterized by an almost universal and rarely questioned faith in progress and mastery of the environment. As we have moved on through the technological age into one of supertechnology, decisions made in the name of progress have been questioned with increasing frequency and insistence. As a people, we are now divided and confused in our attitudes toward major developments and our ability to combine human activities with a fragile and already degraded environment. Depending upon our varying vested interests and degree of direct involvement, our approach to such developments may be alarmist, complacent, or optimistic. But regardless of viewpoint, the public spotlight is now focused on major-facility siting decisions and requires a process for making them which is more open, thoughtful, and efficient.

How did we arrive at this point, and what lessons have we learned that can be applied to an improved process for siting major facilities? The historical transition from almost automatic approval of major projects to equally automatic public scrutiny and reaction which has taken place essentially over the past 20 years provides valuable insights.

THE HETCH HETCHY CASE

At the beginning of the twentieth century in California, in an isolated preview of later controversies, the youthful conservation movement led by John Muir and the Sierra Club fought a 12-year battle to prevent Hetch Hetchy Valley from being turned into a lake. San Francisco officials had decided, in 1901, to use the site for a reservoir for water supply and the generation of hydroelectric power. Hetch Hetchy Valley on the Tuolumne River, which in Muir's words was "an exact counterpart of the Merced Yosemite," lay within the boundaries of Yosemite Na-

tional Park. Figure 1-1 shows the valley as it looked at that time. Muir and his supporters felt that no national park—or even any other public park—would be safe from development if Hetch Hetchy could be so abused. The issue found two old friends taking opposite sides. Congressman William Kent, who had purchased and given Muir Woods to the nation in tribute to Muir, led the movement for damming the valley.

It was late in 1913 before Congress finally passed legislation authorizing the dam. The vote was based on the finding of a U.S. Army Corps of Engineers advisory board that the dam would be cheaper to build and would generate more power than other sites considered. A view of the valley after construction of the dam can be seen in Figure 1-2. It is interesting that this early case involved the comparison of alternative sites, a procedure which is now required by law. Whether San Francisco, which now benefits functionally and financially from the dam, could have done so at less cost to the nation is still a matter of debate, since the factors and criteria used in the comparison do not appear to have been spelled out explicitly.

THE EVOLUTION OF ENVIRONMENTAL CONSCIOUSNESS

It was almost half a century later before conservationists, industry, and government again became embroiled in such a serious conflict. The Hetch Hetchy battle took place during the administration of Theodore Roosevelt, a champion of conservation of land as a planned public resource as opposed to private freedom to use or alter the land for profit. That philosophy held sway in varying degrees for four decades, during which dams continued to be built together with industrial and power plants, freeways, airports, and expanding urban areas.

The years following World War II, in particular, brought a dramatic population increase accompanied by

FIGURE 1-1   The Hetch Hetchy Valley, California, as it looked before damming. The proposal to dam Hetch Hetchy, considered by John Muir the exact counterpart of Yosemite Valley, sparked one of the earliest facility-siting controversies. [*Source: San Francisco Public Library.*]

a movement of people into the cities and into the western states. New suburban communities mushroomed, and people's ability to travel and to spend increased sharply.

For industry, business, and government, the growth occurring during this period had a special meaning. Rapid growth became quite predictable in the short term and was confidently expected to continue beyond that; the problem was to keep up with needs. The major concern was to plan new land uses and facilities, select sites, and acquire and develop them faster than had ever been required before. Planning for growth, which had occurred since colonization on a small scale and in a simple and manageable fashion, became a way of life, a monstrous addiction for business and government.

Site selection had historically been, and continued to be, based almost exclusively on technical aspects of the needed facilities and on short-term economic considerations, the objective being to deliver a product or a service in the most cost-efficient manner. Social, environmental, and aesthetic matters, if they were considered, were secondary. The emphasis tended to be placed on how well social and environmental conditions filled the sponsor's goals rather than on how they might be affected by the project.

By the early 1960s, it was becoming apparent to a growing number of people that what was happening was in direct contradiction to the national dream. There was no longer an unspoiled frontier. New urban and industrial development was bringing with it air, water, noise, and visual pollution and leaving behind blighted central cities. The renewal of conflict was not an isolated occurrence like the Hetch Hetchy case but a series of protests across the country in reaction to uncontrolled growth and the facilities that were seen as related, directly and indirectly, to growth and environmental degradation. The new movement has been traced back to the Hawaiian Legislature's passage of that state's land-use law in 1961. It was the threat represented by growing residential and recreational use of land and water to agriculture, the mainstay of the islands' economy, and not a response to a single facility, that prompted this historic law. But the law's passage was perhaps the first indication of a change in mood and awareness on the part of the public.

The new mood found expression in two forms: growing interest in outdoor recreation and wilderness protection in general and reaction to specific projects and activities which threatened valued environments. Public perception was sharpened by the writings of scientists, sociologists, conservationists, planners, and de-

FIGURE 1-2   The Hetch Hetchy Valley today. Authorization of the proposed dam was finally obtained after a 12-year battle between supporters and conservationists. Before passage, Congress required a cost comparison with other sites, a procedure that is now a matter of course. [*Source: San Francisco Public Library.*]

signers. In some instances, such as the gradual and almost imperceptible destruction of San Francisco Bay by filling, it was the press that alerted the public to environmental changes.

Broad coalitions of often diverse interests formed to take on particular threats, such as San Francisco Bay fill, freeway construction or extension, and other attempts by both industry and government agencies to site large facilities with little attention to important issues and publicly held values. Legislation aimed at increasing scrutiny of development proposals began to be passed in several states, and finally, in 1969, Congress decided also to set the federal house in order. It endeavored to do so by passing the National Environmental Policy Act (NEPA). Subsequent regulations of the Environmental Protection Agency (EPA) specified that no federal or federally financed project could be carried out until an environmental impact statement (EIS) had been filed and made publicly available.

NEPA and similar legislation relating to state, local, and privately financed developments later passed in at least eighteen states have notably changed siting procedures. However, public concern and skepticism remain such that development proposals that would once have been welcomed for their economic spin-offs can meet, as often as not, with mass protests. Industry and government must now deal with new dimensions, in addition to impact evaluation, in their siting and development studies.

Examination of a selection of cases from across the nation suggests that any one of a wide range of problems and situations can result in the failure of a siting study. It also appears that the longer a controversy continues, the more new points of contention tend to arise. The examples that follow are intended only to illustrate the way in which studies were handled. Whether or not the success or failure of a particular proposal was appropriate, in view of the spectrum of environmental, economic, and social factors, is not at issue in this historical review.

SOME FREEWAY ISSUES[1]

Most siting failures involving adequately financed and otherwise thoroughly thought-out facility proposals have

---

[1] Information about the San Francisco freeways is drawn from memory of events and reports, part from personal experience in public meetings and hearings and part from office files.

Information about the Duluth Freeway and the "second campus" study is taken from personal and secondhand experience and from office files.

resulted from overlooking public attitudes, at least in part. Notable examples can be found in many of the early battles over proposals for freeways, highly visible features that disrupted existing neighborhoods and made sprawling new developments possible. Both in urban and in rural areas, highway engineers had been building the United States interstate system of freeways virtually unopposed for 20 years. By the mid-1960s, they were no longer unchallenged, particularly when urban connections were proposed. But, unable to comprehend or to accept the change in public attitude, the planners pressed on, becoming more frequently the object of angry opposition. San Francisco offers two instances of freeway projects, considered by the state of California as the final and vital connecting links to existing freeway systems, which have not been and probably never will be constructed. The proposed Panhandle Freeway, so named because its route in part coincided with the narrow ten-block-long portion of Golden Gate Park known as the Panhandle, was initiated in the early 1960s. Its design required taking some of the city's precious park for an interchange (see Figure 1-3). State officials were already aware that one of the objections to urban freeways was a lack of sensitivity to urban design. So they retained an eminent urban design firm to assist in routing and design. But good design could not overcome public reaction to the loss of highly valued parkland and the disruption of neighborhoods. After a series of emotion-filled public hearings, the San Francisco Board of Supervisors turned down the state's proposal.

Shortly thereafter the design of the proposed Golden

FIGURE 1-3 Model illustrating a part of the area potentially affected by the proposed Panhandle Freeway.

Gate Freeway along the city's northern waterfront was approached, in light of the previous experience, with unusual care. EDAW was retained to assist the state engineers in design of the freeway. Tunnels were planned to avoid neighborhood and park disruption, and for the first time the state agreed to the restoration of disturbed areas in the air rights over the freeway. As additional enticements, new park areas and replacement of obsolete docks with an expanded yacht harbor were proposed, all carefully designed to blend with their surroundings. As they were developed, the preliminary plans were presented to public officials, civic groups, and other key individuals with requests for comments. All seemed to be going smoothly in these small private meetings.

Only when the design was nearing final form was it officially presented at public meetings. The public protest was awesome. Neighborhood groups all along the route, supported by other citizen groups, organized in opposition. The opposition's efforts included producing and showing a film depicting the negative aspects of local freeways, complete with a sound track of freeway noise.

Politicians who had been quietly supporting the state turned against the proposal, and it was defeated even more resoundingly than the Panhandle proposal had been. The state planners had attempted to discover what the public would accept by talking to elected officials and other influential people and had tried hard to provide the acceptable approach. Despite all the effort, it was found that public attitudes could neither be safely assumed nor be accurately anticipated without talking to the people directly.

Unlike the Southern Freeway, which was being planned uneventfully at the same time through an unpopulated industrial area, the Panhandle and especially the Golden Gate route traversed some of the most populous and politically effective areas of the city. Even more important, numerous special interests were affected in addition to the residents, who had no wish to be displaced or to trade adjacent park space for a freeway. These interests included the people of the Marina and Telegraph Hill districts, who were concerned about their views of the waterfront, and real estate developers, who were embarking on an ambitious Fisherman's Wharf project and were firmly set against a project that would leave them landless.

Instead of a homogeneous "public" to be placated, the state faced individual complaints on the part of all those affected, and it was the sum of those individual complaints that became overwhelming. At that time the state had no theory or method for dealing with such a sit-

FIGURE 1-4 The Embarcadero Freeway stub end in San Francisco. Once intended to connect with the proposed Golden Gate Freeway, the uncompleted elevated structure still stands as a reminder of the power of public opinion.

uation and therefore no alternative to giving up the project. As a result the Embarcadero Freeway, with which the Golden Gate Freeway would have connected, remains incomplete; moreover, demolition of the elevated structure, whose stub end is shown in Figure 1-4, is now being considered.

Similar stories can be found throughout the country, from New York's Westway (Interstate 478), Los Angeles's Century Freeway (I-105), and Interstate 95 in Boston to the West Valley Freeway in the Salt Lake City area and numerous minor expressway proposals. Comparison of the failures with the successes such as Interstate 90 in Seattle and Interstate 35 in Duluth, achieved in equally sensitive situations, is instructive.

In Seattle, mediators from the University of Washington's Office of Environmental Mediation negotiated a successful settlement between parties that were at an impasse over plans for Interstate 90. In Duluth, a team of consultants working closely and openly with a broadly based citizens' advisory committee arrived at an acceptable route and design for Interstate 35 through the eastern half of Duluth. It should be clear that public opinion, if effectively translated into action, is a crucial element in making or breaking projects.

SOME POWER PLANT EFFORTS

In the early 1960s, two power plant siting conflicts crowded the headlines across the country, one on each coast. The Pacific coast fight involved the siting of a nuclear plant at Bodega Head, north of San Francisco. The Atlantic coast battle was over the proposed Cornwall hydroelectric plant at Storm King Mountain on the Hudson River, 40 miles north of New York City. In each case, the sponsors had not realized either the degree of concern or the specific concerns of significant sectors of the public.

In the case of the Bodega Head plant, to be sited on a beautiful oceanside promontory near the San Andreas earthquake fault, a widely representative opposition was led by conservationists supported by biological scientists from across the country. The main issues were scenic beauty, preservation (the state legislature had authorized purchase of the site for a state park), and safety. The public became thoroughly confused on the subject of safety when well-known marine biologists argued on both sides of the radioactive-contamination issue; but Pacific Gas and Electric Company, the sponsoring company, settled the contest by withdrawing its proposal in 1964, when its detailed geological investigations revealed that the plant would be located on an active earthquake fault subsidiary to the major San Andreas fault. As Figure 1-5 indicates, construction was well under way by the time of the decision.

An interesting follow-up to the Bodega Head case was the next siting attempt by the same company. In 1966, it selected and bought property for a nuclear plant at Nipomo Dunes, about halfway between San Francisco and Los Angeles on the oceanfront. Again conservationists, fresh from the Bodega Bay struggles, were alerted. This time the site had previously been designated by the National Park Service as being one of unexcelled scenic quality that should be acquired for public recreation. Before a full-scale conflict started, the company consulted with the opposition-leading Sierra Club and a special task force set up by the California Resources Agency. Negotiations resulted in the plant's being shifted to a site about 20 miles away at Diablo Canyon.

The Diablo Canyon plant was completed in 1979 (see Figure 1-6), but at the time of this writing it still has not gone into operation. While the plant was under construction, geologists discovered an earthquake fault less than 3 miles off the coast from the facility. In the aftermath of the Three Mile Island nuclear plant failure in Pennsylva-

nia, this information brought growing anxiety and opposition. In mid-1980, the Sierra Club and the League of Women Voters, supported by a varied group of local citizens, petitioned the California Public Utilities Commission to reopen consideration of the interim certificate of public convenience and necessity originally issued in 1970. The petition called for new evidence on the cost of operating the facility as a nuclear plant and a study of the feasibility of converting it to nonnuclear operation.

After review of this plant's safety features in light of the new seismic information, the Nuclear Regulatory Commission (NRC) issued a low-power operating license in September 1981, amid protests and demonstrations at the plant. However, discovery of design errors that could affect the safety of the plant caused the NRC to withdraw the license 3 months later and to halt fuel loading. Reissuance of the license awaits completion of studies to verify design corrections, but in view of several pending lawsuits and administrative actions the outlook for the plant remains obscure.

The Storm King Mountain hydroelectric plant is called the Cornwall project by its sponsor, Consolidated Edison Company of New York, because of its location near the village of Cornwall on the Hudson River. The company first filed for a Federal Power Commission (FPC) license

FIGURE 1-5   The reactor site at Bodega Head. A proposal to construct a nuclear power plant at Bodega Head, authorized for purchase as a state park, was withdrawn in 1964 after the presence of an active earthquake fault was revealed. [*Source: San Francisco Public Library.*]

FIGURE 1-6 The Diablo Canyon power plant. An earthquake fault was found close to the Diablo Canyon nuclear power plant during its construction. Completed in 1979, the unopened plant faces an uncertain future. [*Source: California Department of Water Resources.*]

in January 1963. However, at this writing completion remains uncertain.

Early protests centered on visual concerns, later expanded to include even earthquake hazards. The initial protest was led by people across the river from the proposed plant whose views would be altered and by people who had second homes in the area of the plant and were concerned with the growth that might accompany it. They organized the Scenic Hudson Preservation Conference, which was supported by major conservation organizations. A public relations firm was hired, and the conflict turned into a national issue. The Hudson River Fishermen's Association joined the fray, and the principal points of contention became impacts on scenic and historic qualities, growth inducement, possible fish kills, public safety, and need for the project. The site had also been considered for inclusion in a state park. The FPC granted a license for the plant in the spring of 1965 but was promptly taken to court by the opposition. The Second Circuit Court remanded the license in December with the judgment that the FPC had not compiled an adequate hearing record, that aesthetic, conservation, and recreational aspects had to be protected in power development cases, and that a conservation organization could sue to protect public interest in the environment under the Federal Power Act.

The FPC reopened hearings in 1966, and in 1970 it reissued the license to build the power plant. Originally proposed with an aboveground powerhouse, to soften the opposition the project was redesigned to place its powerhouse completely underground so as not to detract from the appearance of the mountain. Likewise, transmission lines from the plant were designed to run underwater and underground to an inland point on the opposite side of the river. Another appeal by Scenic Hudson, this time to set the license aside, was turned down by the court. In 1972 the Supreme Court refused to hear Scenic Hudson's appeal of this decision, clearing the last legal hurdle to construction after 9 years of litigation.

Construction began in March 1974 but was suspended 4 months later following issuance of a United States circuit court decision that further hearings should be held by the FPC to examine the Cornwall project's effect on fish life in the Hudson River. In February 1977, Con Ed submitted an 1100-page ecological report on the Hudson River to the FPC. The report summarized the findings of 10 years and $20 million worth of ecological studies related to Hudson River power plants. Though the future of this plant is still uncertain, well-publicized demonstrations and citizen actions led to a legal decision of far-reaching importance. The Second Circuit Court's decision of 1965 encouraged citizen's suits against other federal agencies and helped lay the basis for NEPA.

Meanwhile, an approach somewhat different from those just described was being tried in the midwest. In a talk given before the Westinghouse International School of Environmental Management in July 1975, R. W. Comstock, vice president for communications of Northern States Power Company (NSP), described two successful "open planning" efforts. The first of these, because of its originality and experimental quality, was approached apprehensively by the utility. As will be seen, the second effort, though somewhat different, seems to have reaffirmed the experience of the first.

The initial effort occurred in early 1970, when NSP decided to try to share decision making relative to a needed site for a new power plant. The company contacted some thirty conservation groups and asked them to send representatives to a plant-siting task force being formed by NSP. None of the groups refused to meet with the company, though many were suspicious that they were being "used" by the company. The governor's environmental cabinet also accepted an invitation. In March 1970 weekly company-conducted meetings were started. The first goal was for the task force to make a recommendation to the company on the location of its next generating plant, scheduled for service in 1976. The second goal was for the task force to develop environmental criteria to assist the company in future site-selection and utility studies.

The early meetings, which were devoted to educating members about the nature of the utility business, were marked with suspicion and hostility as critics of the company unloaded complaints about almost every phase of the business. However, at about the sixth week the hostility began to wane as some members voiced concern about the challenge to do something constructive with the problems at hand.

The results of this first effort were two site recommendations, one by the citizens' task force and another by the governor's environmental cabinet. The company subsequently elected to accept the citizens' task force site

recommendation and later proceeded, without interruption, with licensing and construction, for the first time in 10 years.

The second effort of NSP began in the spring of 1972 to select a site for a unit to go into service in 1980. By this time, the Minnesota Environmental Quality Council (MEQC) had been formed as an advisory body to the governor, so the company asked that the council act as convener. This being agreed to, the governor appointed a broadly based siting task force consisting of representatives from environmental groups, universities, labor, and other public interests to work with MEQC. The company's role was to supply information and function in a staff capacity. The task force met for many months and also held public hearings in local communities near potential sites. The final report of the task force recommended three alternative sites, each ranked in terms of preference. The MEQC selected the second-ranked site, which was subsequently accepted by NSP. The entire process took less than a year. At the time of Mr. Comstock's talk, the company was proceeding with purchasing the property and preliminary engineering designs. Some organized opposition had surfaced at the location of the site, but Mr. Comstock voiced confidence about the final outcome.

THE EVERGLADES JETPORT

Ground was broken in the Big Cypress Swamp of southern Florida on September 18, 1968, for what was touted as "the world's first all-new jetport for the supersonic age." Now called the Everglades Jetport, it is an abandoned project and concept except for a training runway, also to be abandoned at some time in the future. The proposed 39-square-mile development, to include four to six runways up to 6 miles long, was sponsored by the Dade County Port Authority. It had the approval of the Federal Aviation Administration, Dade and Collier counties, the Florida Board of Conservation, the flood control district, and the Florida Game and Fresh Water Fish Commission and had the tacit approval of the National Park Service. Five weeks after the ground breaking, with construction on the training runway proceeding rapidly, opposition began to develop almost by accident. The chairman of the flood control district discovered that part of the land under its jurisdiction and/or part of Everglades National Park would have to be taken, in violation of federal law, for a road connecting the jetport to Miami. Previous assurances given to the flood control district on this part of the plan had helped to gain its approval of the jetport. Eventually this initial right-of-way question snowballed from a local into a full-scale national issue which because of its magnitude has, like the Cross-Florida Barge Canal, been claimed to be partially responsible for passage of NEPA in 1969.

A hearing called by the flood control district in February 1969 turned up an admission by the port authority that environmental considerations had not been a part of the site-selection evaluations. By mid-April an Everglades Coalition of twenty-one national environmental groups and two trade unions had been formed and was demanding that the United States secretary of transportation halt construction. On a trip to Everglades National Park, Secretary of the Interior Walter J. Hickel became aware of the problems and asked for information. The U.S. Senate Interior Committee under Sen. Henry M. Jackson held hearings in June, and virtually simultaneously the Departments of the Interior and Transportation decided to undertake a crash joint environmental impact study. The study, done in a matter of months, concluded that in the absence of adequate land-use regulation the eastern Big Cypress would suffer drainage, pollution, and other adverse effects from the proposed development. Neither the state nor the counties had any history of such regulation. Subsequently, on January 15, 1970, the Everglades Jetport Pact was signed by local, state, and federal officials. This cleared the way for a new site-selection study and, it was hoped, resolution of the problem.

A site-selection review team was retained and undertook the work of identifying alternative candidate sites and gathering information about them. Thirty-six candidate sites were initially graded into three categories of acceptance, and work began on detailed studies of the most promising. Criteria to guide the selection were stipulated to Dade County by the secretary of the interior and the secretary of transportation. After a year and a half of intensive analysis, the list was reduced to three sites.

Finally, in July 1973, or 5 years after the first ground breaking, a new site of 23 square miles (Site 14), in north Dade County approximately 25 miles east of the original site, was recommended and approved by the county commissioners. In the meantime, the statewide Florida Aviation System Plan and additional information and forecasts resulted in changing the original concept from a regional airport to a smaller one that would be but one in a constellation of airports.

The intervening years to 1977 were filled by a losing at-

tempt at an antiairport referendum, draft EIS issuance and comments, and applications for site acquisition and runway construction to replace the present training runway at the Big Cypress location.

At the present time, the issue is before Congress. Under terms of the jetport pact of 1970, upon congressional approval and authorization of $69.6 million, the new site will be acquired, the new training facility built, and the present 39-square-mile site conveyed to the federal government to become part of Big Cypress National Preserve.

And what became of the original dream of the world's first all-new jetport for the supersonic age? The passage of time since 1968 has seen a fuel shortage seriously affect air travel to Florida and upset previous growth calculations, and it has seen a decrease in airline training at the Everglades Jetport owing to increasing operational costs and the more widespread use of flight simulators. But time has also permitted the proposed jetport program to be related to the statewide Florida Aviation System Plan, the Miami Urban Area Transportation System Plan, and the Dade County Comprehensive Land Use Plan, with the subsequent assurance that it will fit as an integrated element of those plans.

In summary, it was a single factor, probably the port authority's lack of concern with the effect of taking land for the connecting highway, that decided the fate of the project, for this is what brought a virtually accomplished fact out into the open. As it developed later, the lack of environmental impact studies, the sheer size of the facility, and the lack of land-use controls for surrounding areas all contributed to the need for further studies. The general public must also take some of the responsibility for the fact that the project proceeded as far as it did, because at the time there was relatively little awareness of and care for the values and fragility of the Everglades and Big Cypress.

THE SECOND CAMPUS

In some cases a siting study becomes an inappropriate and expensive means of determining basic policy questions that should be settled before site-selection studies are begun. For instance, the just discussed jetport program was scaled down during the second site-selection cycle as a result of state plans which recommended that it become but one in a constellation of airports. However, a more clear-cut case on the other side of the nation and an ocean away was occurring in Hawaii at about the same time. West Oahu College was the name given by the University of Hawaii Board of Regents to a scaled-down version of a proposed major "second campus" after public protest and the state legislature had forced it to take another look at the selection of a site.

The second-campus issue began in 1964, when the University of Hawaii Academic Plan set a 25,000-student limit on its main campus at Manoa. In 1967, a consulting firm, on the basis of demographic projections, recommended that a site of at least 500 acres be obtained in central Oahu for a campus to accommodate 25,000 students, with land acquisition and development of plans as the highest priority.

In 1969, the University Academic Development Plan II reiterated the need for a second Oahu campus by 1974–1975; and representatives from Bishop Estate, Campbell Estate, and Mililani Town, Inc., made land offers to the legislature and the board of regents. A preliminary site-selection study was undertaken by the University Land Study Bureau. The study focused on six sites and favored the Campbell Estate lands.

In 1970, dissatisfied with that report, the board of regents retained a consultant, who reviewed fifteen sites, finding six of them essentially suitable. The consultant recommended the Bishop Estate site, which the board of regents agreed to adopt in principle. Under severe public pressure, because both the campus and the surrounding urban development which it would attract would displace sugarcane lands valuable to the economy of Hawaii, the university agreed to limit the campus to no more than 15,000 students. Under continued pressure, this figure was subsequently dropped to 8000 and then to 7000.

During the 1971 session of the state legislature, both houses conducted hearings on university growth and the need for additional campuses. While both houses agreed that the university should proceed with plans for a second campus on Oahu, the House Committee on Higher Education recommended that the board of regents reconsider its decision to adopt the Bishop Estate site.

The university was also requested by the legislature to develop its plans for the second campus within the framework of a comprehensive system of higher education, involving community groups and other governmental agencies in the formation of these plans. Subsequently, the Site-Selection Advisory Committee, consisting of representatives from community groups, governmental agencies, university faculty, and students, was established. The committee developed criteria for site selection and met with university officials and site-evaluation consultants during the site-selection process. As a result of that process, which is described in Part Two of this book (Eckbo, Dean, Austin & Williams, October 1972), a site area on Campbell Estate lands finally was officially selected in 1973, subject to later negotiations with the owners on exact boundaries. A state revenue crisis resulting from the general nationwide recession has made it impossible to construct the new West Oahu College. The college is presently (1982) open and educating students in rented space in the general area of the new campus, but because of lack of anticipated enrollment at the Manoa campus many wonder if West Oahu College will ever be needed.

PROJECT SEAFARER

This next siting case is an unusual one because it involves a major military installation. In light of the highly publicized saga of the MX missile system, however, it is not unique. When it was originally proposed some 20 years ago, the U.S. Navy's designation for its proposed extremely low-frequency radio communication system was Shelf. Because of technical design changes made in the system in the early and mid-1970s, the name was changed twice, first to Project Sanguine and then to Project Seafarer (EDAW Inc., April 1976). For the uninitiated, the system was virtually the same: a buried grid of cables requiring a land area of from 2500 to 5000 square miles, depending on a number of factors. It was designed to be capable of communicating with submarines underwater anywhere in the world and was proposed as a deterrent to nuclear attack because it could, under such a circumstance, signal retaliation. For efficient operation and maximum economy, the underground geologic structure has to be of low conductivity (such as granite). This factor was one of the principal considerations in locating potential sites during a search that covered areas in Wisconsin, Michigan, Texas, and federally controlled land in numerous western states. Final site location, however, was hampered for years by public protests.

The protests were based on a number of concerns, including the environmental consequences related to burying the cables, fear of adverse health effects from the electromagnetic field generated, disagreement with the opinion that the system would be a deterrent, and fear that the system would be a primary target in a nuclear war. The Navy responded to protests over possible environmental and health effects by undertaking a number of scientific studies to provide the basis for discussion in the federal EIS. Protests based on the deterrent and target factors, however, appear not to have been adequately anticipated or factored into the site-selection process.

Essentially, for over 10 years Seafarer was a system looking for a site where the public would accept it rather than a site that was most satisfactory from all viewpoints. By early 1980, under a fourth name, ELF (for extremely low frequency), the project seemed to have found at least a temporary home on the Upper Michigan Peninsula, the location that received the majority of attention in the draft EIS. The Upper Mighican Peninsula was one of the best sites because of its geology. However, the original choices, sites in Wisconsin and central Texas, were larger and allowed greater siting flexibility. In October 1981, several months after the Navy had abandoned the project, President Reagan ordered it reactivated in a vastly reduced and altered form. As now proposed, 56 miles of buried antenna (instead of 6000) are to be located in Michigan and Wisconsin, providing more limited submarine communications capability (*The New York Times,* October 9, 1981).

Public protest drove Seafarer out of both Wisconsin and Texas. Presumably, public protest could have driven Seafarer out of any of the states under consideration. What would Congress have done then? It seems, for in-

stance, that Congress deemed the system essential for national security when it began appropriating funds for its development many years ago. Under such circumstances would Congress decide to abandon the program? Or would it exert its influence or power to locate the system in spite of the protests? Though it is not productive to pursue answers to these particular "What if?" questions, it would be productive to develop methods for resolving similar questions at both federal and state levels because as time goes on and as experience to date with the MX missile system suggests, similar standoff situations surely will arise. As land resources are depleted and as the number of facilities that no one wants in his or her own backyard increases, choices are continually being narrowed.

A PETROCHEMICAL COMPLEX

The examples we have considered thus far originated prior to passage of NEPA and similar state environmental impact legislation, although several were subsequently affected by the new requirements during the protracted battles. This last case is particularly interesting for having taken place entirely within the post-NEPA years.

In January 1975, Dow Chemical Company publicly announced plans to construct a petrochemical complex in

FIGURE 1-7 Dow Chemical Company's Pittsburg site. [*Source: J. B. Gilbert and Associates.*]

FIGURE 1-8   Existing Montezuma view from the Sacramento River. Dow Chemical company's proposed Montezuma Hills site, a 2800-acre area purchased for the construction of a petrochemical complex, was relinquished after failure to obtain project approval. [*Source: J. B. Gilbert and Associates.*]

northern California. The rationale for building in California, which has no basic petrochemical facilities, was to serve the west coast with products manufactured from oil shipped from Alaska and other Pacific basin sources. Providing an alternative to shipping the oil to the gulf coast and transporting products back to the west coast seemed logical. Freight savings alone were estimated at $56 million per year.

Unable to consider the area with the largest market, Los Angeles (an air basin not in compliance with Clean Air Act standards), the company settled on the next-best choice, the San Francisco Bay area. Dow already had a small production facility on the southern bank of the confluence of the San Joaquin and Sacramento rivers at Pittsburg, shown in Figure 1-7. Across the river at Montezuma Hills in Solano County was rolling dry farmland, remote from urban development and offering adequate rail and road access, water frontage, and availability of naphtha, one of the major feedstocks, from neighboring refineries. Most important, the area was shown for industrial use on the County General Plan and appropriately zoned. Figures 1-8 and 1-9 show eye-level views of the site in its existing state and as it would look after development.

Knowing that California's laws and regulations were more stringent than most, the company states that it set extremely tight environmental goals for the thirteen units proposed for the complex. Air emissions were to be restricted to 25 percent of permitted standards, no water effluents would be produced, and little if any solid wastes were to leave the sites.

Dow optioned a 2800-acre site and then set about studying the requirements and regulations of the array of nineteen local, county, regional, state, and federal agencies that had jurisdiction. A total of sixty-five permits and decisions had to be obtained before construction could start, an obstacle course which Dow points out might have seemed insurmountable to a smaller company. Members of the Dow team spent almost 6 months in meeting with the affected agencies before making any public announcement.

The purpose, scope, and environmental impacts of the proposed project were reviewed in considerable detail with representatives of various environmental organizations as well as with the affected jurisdictions and government agencies. The suggestions of these groups were solicited and received. Detailed studies and recommendations of planning and environmental consultants had been carefully designed into the project to avoid damage to the environment and the communities involved. With the encouragement of those involved in the advance briefings, Dow had high hopes by the time of the public announcement. Dow believed that the plant would provide an unmatched standard of environmental excellence

FIGURE 1-9 Future Montezuma view from the Sacramento River. [*Source: J. B. Gilbert and Associates.*]

and a major contribution to the state's economic health. In the opinion of the environmental consultant and the director of the EPA's regional office, this assessment was essentially justified.

The first official requirement after the announcement was to obtain an approved state-level environmental impact report (EIR). Public hearings on the preliminary draft some 6 months later were attended by only about fifty people representing the Sierra Club and various other environmental groups. Their comments were incorporated in the final EIR, and, having received no adverse comments from the state reviewing agencies, the Solano Board of Supervisors certified the adequacy of the EIR 1 year after the public announcement.

All appeared to be running smoothly. Dow exercised its option to acquire the site and completed the process design of the first unit, a styrene plant. Suddenly, the atmosphere changed. State agencies complained of inadequate time to review the EIR, and the Sierra Club filed suit against the county for approving an inadequate EIR and removing farmland under tax protection from production. Dow at this point was working on obtaining the necessary approvals from regional, state, and federal agencies. These included the U.S. Army Corps of Engineers (the lead agency preparing the federal EIS) and the Bay Area Air Pollution Control District (BAAPCD).

Following the first public hearing on the draft EIS, the Corps was requested by the state not to issue any permits until the state had resolved all its concerns about the Dow project. At about the same time, having generally been encouraged by discussions with the BAAPCD technical staff, the company was informed by another section of the agency that the proposed site in Solano County did not meet primary ambient-air quality standards. The BAAPCD decision to permit the styrene plant now required proof that the plant not only would meet emissions standards but would not cause significant deterioration of air quality. The decision hinged on definition of the word *significant,* which changed several times, according to Dow, over the next few months.

The BAAPCD's final determination was that the permit application should be denied on the ground of detectable air pollution. Dow asserted that the calculations represented summing individual emissions below the minimum sensitivity of monitoring instruments at various sources on a worst-case basis and appealed the decision. The Sierra Club also appealed to the BAAPCD for denial of the entire project, although only two of twenty-six permits had been applied for.

The hearing board, presented with simultaneous appeals for and against the project, was unable to reach a decision before the subject became moot. The state requested that hearings before other state permit-issuing agencies be held jointly. It thus became clear that the state intended to rewrite the approved EIR. Having spent 2 years and $4 million in effort, in addition to $6 million for a site, Dow decided in January 1977 to withdraw its plans.

To a large extent this was a case of a well-thought-out project lost among the conflicting values, standards, and sometimes political motivations of a forest of local, state, and federal agencies and environmental organizations. No clear structure existed for resolving local issues first and then submitting remaining conflicts involving broader concerns to higher authority, although this was the approach that EPA attempted to adopt. As a result, both the local issues of tax revenue and service or environmental cost inequities between affected counties and the state and federal issues of air pollution, protection of a critical marsh, and economic benefits were considered fair game for anyone with an ax to grind.

2 | THE NEED FOR A SITE-SELECTION PROCESS

LESSONS FROM THE PAST

Several conclusions can be summarized from the cases described in Chapter 1. First, perhaps the most common cause of conflict and failure is misjudgment of public attitudes on the part of the project sponsor. During the past two decades, understandably the area of misjudgment has generally centered on attitudes related to impacts on the natural and social environments.

Freeways have been opposed for a number of reasons, including concern about visual, air, and noise pollution, neighborhood disruption, growth inducement, and violation of recreational, scenic, or historic areas. Unable to provide sufficient justification of freeways (because of questions about future use of automobiles versus rapid transit) and cope with public disapproval of standard engineering route-selection methods, highway departments have abandoned freeway projects all over the country, leaving stub ends of structures as permanent reminders of broken plans.

Power plants have been and are still being opposed because of the public's concerns for the environment. Bodega Head and Storm King were early examples of how widely separated public attitudes and sponsors' attitudes have become. A number of states have intervened by setting up means for reconciling the competitive demands characteristically involved. Two such methods, one established by Minnesota and one by California, will be discussed later.

The public attitude toward facilities considered to be growth-inducing has been an effective deterrent in certain areas of the country for a number of years. This attitude has principally affected residential, commercial, and industrial development, but it has also affected plans for highways, resort development, airports, and other facilities. However characterized, public attitudes in some areas of the country have changed in the past few decades from progrowth and support of "progress" to advo-

cacy of controlled growth or "antidevelopment." How long-lasting such attitudes may be remains to be seen, but in any case they are a factor that has to be taken into account in any siting procedure at present.

A second point, which is closely related to the basic source of conflict we have just discussed, is the project sponsors' frequent lack of consideration for environmental and social factors on an "equal" basis with economic and technical factors. The original Everglades Jetport proposal was one such case. Typically, few factors are really given equal consideration in site selection; rather, they are given weighted consideration, each being assigned a degree of importance relative to others. The term *equal* therefore means "on an acceptably weighted basis." The key question here is: Who does the weighting and whose values are used? When siting conflicts occur, it is generally the public conservation opposition that insists on recognition of its values and on its participation in the weighting of judgmental factors. We will deal at length with factor weighting and public participation in the weighting process in later discussions.

Thirdly, lack of information in critical areas can be the cause of failure or, at least, embarrassment. The Bodega Head and Diablo Canyon cases demonstrate how extremely difficult it can be to know everything about a site's geology and also how essential it is to be assured of this kind of basic information before proceeding with subsequent plans. Other categories of environmental information can, from time to time, also assume such critical importance. In the case of the Storm King Mountain power plant, if the question of fish kills had been given high priority in early studies, the last series of delays probably would have been avoided.

Withholding or concealing important information can also lead to trouble, as was the case when the Florida jetport sponsors withheld information about their highway-widening needs. There may be disagreement over the question of what is essential, important, and legitimate information. However, what is and is not essential is decided by the review agencies, the public, and, in the final analysis, the courts rather than by the project sponsor. Ideally, as we will emphasize elsewhere, it should be decided by the sponsor, the public, and affected agencies together. Adequate guidelines should be set by the agency with final review powers so as to permit nothing significant to be overlooked during the siting process.

A fourth point is that a degree of programmatic flexibility can be useful in some siting and routing programs. If the area of flexibility makes it possible to negotiate a successful solution, the sponsors' purpose and the public purpose will have been served. As a case in point, the ability of Consolidated Edison Company to place the Cornwall power plant and its principal transmission lines underground led to its approval from the visual standpoint. However, there is a point at which flexibility becomes vacillation—a sign of uncertainty. At this point credibility is challenged, and avoidable conflict arises. When the regents of the University of Hawaii, for instance, vacillated on the projected size of West Oahu College, they invited the criticism of the state legislature and probably lost some legislative and public support.

Fifth, complicated permit procedures are the cause of considerable difficulty and effort. However, they must be factored into the location processes just as other constraining factors must be taken into account.

A number of years ago, in recognition of the fact that agency regulation had proliferated to a staggering degree, the problem became the subject of study by a special committee of the American Bar Association. The committee's review draft, published in 1973, essentially recommended that each state establish an industrial siting council to exercise jurisdiction in all areas of statewide concern and that similar measures be established at the federal level to cover those areas under federal jurisdiction or cases in which the federal government should preempt state decisions.

However, the Dow Chemical Company case points to the fact that consideration of a range of environmental factors, integration of permit procedures into the location process, and flexibility in handling suggestions for design changes do not necessarily guarantee success. Openness with the public as well as all affected agencies at an earlier stage might have created a more receptive atmosphere within the state and regional agencies. In addition, as the company itself admits, acquisition of the site was premature. Retaining an option until all permits had been secured would have made better financial sense and might have reinforced the public image of good faith.

This brings us to the sixth and last point. In some of the cases recounted above problems were created, and in some instances programs failed, because of the lack of a plan to involve all the rightfully concerned interests in the decision-making process. Failure has also often been due to the fact that the agency which must give final approval, whether it is Congress, the Federal Energy Regulatory Commission, the state, or a local agency, has not been *directly* involved in the site-selection process. There have been enough experiences involving wide public and agency representation in site selection to show that such an approach can work.

Clearly then, while it is sometimes a single overlooked item that results in failure, more often than not it is several factors in common. In the following pages we shall identify and begin to organize the components necessary to a successful siting effort.

REQUIREMENTS FOR SUCCESSFUL SITE SELECTION

Accountability to the Public

We have stressed the now inescapable fact that any siting program must be prepared for review by numerous public-interest groups and government agencies. Often, the best way to provide an understanding of siting decisions is to include the public in the decisions and the steps leading up to them. So in many cases programs will also involve some form of active public participation throughout their course.

The involvement of outside representatives either as reviewers or in working roles is related to several other requirements of the successful study. To foster genuine participation the site-selection process itself must be comprehensive, clearly laid out, and presented in understandable language and concepts. Although it may seem to be demanding and time-consuming, attempts to circumvent such an open forum have often come to grief. The risk of protracted battles or of nonapproval is far more costly than the time spent to plan in the open. But there is another very practical rationale. Following logical, comprehensive, and open procedures may well produce more satisfactory results for the sponsor as well as for the public.

A Logically Sequenced and Organized Approach

Naturally when an industry or a government agency approaches a site-selection project, it aims to achieve its objectives with a minimum of wasted time, effort, and money. It will often take shortcuts. These may be based on trained, intuitive judgment or on formulas developed from experience.

In an open siting effort, the basis for each assumption and the process leading to each conclusion must be spelled out. It is hard to defend a decision reached on the basis of intuition, rules of thumb, or an ill-structured process. It is also unreasonable to expect a cooperative response from observers or committee members who cannot follow the logical progression of investigation. Problems of public understanding and indefensible procedures can be overcome best by defining a clear-cut step-by-step path which explains when and how goals and assumptions are developed, information analyzed, and key decisions made. Setting out this process in diagram form provides a good basis for early understanding of how the program will be run. Such a diagram will identify each phase of the program, each major decision point, the responsibilities of the various groups of participants, and the time schedule. However, this demands that the process itself be logically structured.

Writers on industrial location, such as Soderman (1975) and Stafford (1979), point out that many project sponsors lack experience in making locational decisions because they make them very rarely. Location selection therefore often proceeds without the benefit of logical programs or routines.

To some extent, according to both writers, the lack of programmed location decisions is also due to the large number of factors involved. Complex relationships exist among these factors, and critical factors may vary from one locational problem to another. Some choices may vary between alternatives. Others may involve merely acceptance or rejection of a single course of action. One decision may rest on relative costs, while others may be based entirely on qualitative factors.

Clear Identification of Goals

For organizations which practice a more carefully programmed and reasoned approach, optimum results may still not be achieved. One reason may lie in the fact that it is merely assumed that a certain type of facility in a certain kind of location is desirable. The end product is not clearly thought through. Thus the assumed goals of the project may be inappropriate, either from the standpoint of the organization's welfare or from that of the general social, economic, and natural environment.

In fact, we are not talking about an either-or situation. Any decision stemming from goals that are not entirely rational from the organization's viewpoint will have very broad public repercussions as well. Similarly, a decision based on internally rational goals that ignores broader public-interest considerations will engender public distrust and eventually affect the organization even if it succeeds in being approved.

A good siting study must therefore begin with carefully identified goals for the facility in terms of the profit to be made, the market to be served, and the efficient use of the organization's present and future resources and technology. It must also take account of goals that society deems important: protection of natural systems such as air, water, plant, and animal life; attention to existing land uses, visual quality, and noise levels; and provision of products, services, and jobs.

As they are stated initially, these goals may often be in apparent conflict. Some means for deciding which are the most critical goals in relation both to a particular project and to particular locations is needed but is not often in evidence in siting studies. As Stafford (1979) indicates, it is often difficult enough to resolve conflicts over goals merely within an organization.

Establishment of Environmental Performance Standards

The fourth requirement is that the site-selection process establish performance standards relating to the project's effects on the environment. This requirement follows naturally from the previous one in that it is one of the objectives of the program to fulfill environmental goals, and these can best be met by setting specific targets. It is usually possible to design and manage an installation so that it can be operated within tolerable environmental limits in certain, although not all, locations. This is the approach taken to meet air quality standards and can be used in the other areas of environmental concern. So as not to be surprised by the cost of modifications to meet such standards or perhaps by the inability to meet them at all in a desired location, the standards must be recognized early in the program. Following are just some of the areas in which performance standards can be established, depending on the type of facility planned:

· Surface-water and groundwater quality and quantity

· Air quality

· Noise

· Terrestrial ecology (flora and fauna)

· Marine or aquatic ecology

· Visual quality

- Public facilities and services
- Socioeconomic change
- Archaeology and history
- Radiology
- Agriculture
- Recreation
- Transportation

The sponsor's approach should be to identify what is required so that the facility can be designed to allow modifications to meet those standards in a given location. Costs attached to these modifications can be estimated and used in making decisions among alternatives as well as in arriving at the final decision.

The approach frequently taken, particularly in relatively footloose industries, is to avoid areas with particularly stringent standards. Lists of review and regulatory agencies are published as one component of some "location guides," such as the 1978 *Site Selection Handbook*. There is a danger, however, of giving up a location with more advantageous characteristics than another simply on the ground of potential hassles over environmental standards.

It may be argued that when a sponsor puts locational advantage ahead of regulatory stringency in selecting a site and tries to anticipate requirements, as Dow Chemical Company did at Montezuma Hills, it still may not be successful. As we have suggested previously, it is probably impossible to second-guess the causes of failure in that particular case. However, if public and regulatory agency participation in setting environmental standards is sought early in the project, the chances of establishing mutual trust are greatly improved.

A Comprehensive Approach

A frequent charge leveled at siting studies is that they have not thoroughly considered all possible locations or taken account of all the factors affecting the suitability of a site. Lack of comprehensiveness with respect to locational factors is often the result of inadequate attention to goals and performance standards. But even when goals and standards are established well enough to permit the right types of information to be sought, the information has to be handled carefully. A comprehensive approach demands knowledge and experience of the way in which natural and social systems behave and interact. For example, merely finding a site that has adequate groundwater for needed wells is not sufficient. Is the

groundwater being mined? Will there continue to be an adequate supply for this facility? What effect will the proposed withdrawal have on other users?

In other words, a siting study requires a holistic approach. The conditions or actions occurring in other geographic areas which may influence or be influenced by the proposed facility must be taken into account. It may be possible to reduce or avoid a particular environmental impact by widening the geographic scope of study or by use of different technology. Finally, it is important not only to consider existing regulations and standards but also to try to anticipate those that may be instituted in the future. Of course, the pitfall of covering too many factors or dealing prematurely with those useful only in final comparison of suitable sites has to be avoided. But the maxim should be "When in doubt, do not exclude a factor or an area from consideration."

Lack of geographic comprehensiveness is a frequent characteristic of siting studies. It is clear from observation and from site-selection case histories in the literature that an inventory of sites is often arrived at very informally. Selection of an area or areas of search may be made on the basis of a very limited number of factors. Actual sites available in that area are then identified by visual inspection or by contacts with real estate brokers for later comparison.

The informal approach has several weaknesses that make it inefficient and hard to defend. Because it depends on discovery rather than selection, suitable sites may be overlooked. Sites that are not discovered cannot be evaluated. Second, it is unnecessarily time-consuming to evaluate available sites which may be inherently unsuitable. Third, even though the final selection may seem to be a good one in later rationalization, there is no way to prove that it is in fact the best site. It is merely the best of those examined.

Lack of comprehensiveness can also result from inadequate representation of interest groups whose views on what comprises a comprehensive approach may vary. It is not necessary for participants to share the same view. Exposure to a wide range of subjects and ideas tends to raise the level of participation from one of contention to one in which many areas of agreement may be found.

Clear Presentation of Information

A site-selection program involving public review and participation has to be carried out and documented in easily understood language. Sophisticated formulas and methods, such as *decision analysis,* and unexplained technical terms have their value in communications between technologists, planners, and management within industry. Inability to understand the terms and concepts used by the sponsors of a facility impedes communication with the general public and even with well-educated lay representatives of the public and public agencies. It also generates suspicion that the real reasoning behind the siting decision is being obscured by jargon.

Another reason for avoiding technical language, if one is needed, is that the impact report or statement that will follow the siting decision is required by law to be written in lay language. The preparation of that document can be speeded up if an effort has already been made to use simple language and explain technical terms and concepts when necessary.

Graphic presentation methods and photographs can also quickly convey an understanding of how the facility will work, what it will look like, and how locational conditions are analyzed. Such techniques are also essential components of a comprehensive, logically organized site-selection process from the sponsor's point of view.

Distinction of Fact from Judgment

A final point with reference both to communication per se and to the conduct of a logical and defensible site-selection study is the need to distinguish fact from judgment.

As we shall see in later chapters, considerable judgment is involved in a siting decision. It cannot be presumed that just because factual information is observable and measurable it will not be subject to argument. In a comprehensive siting study we are dealing with competing *facts*. Whether a power plant will contribute a measurable quantity of pollutants to the air is a matter of fact. So are the quantity of water that it will require and the changes in water quality that it may cause. Which fact is the most important in the abstract and in relation to a given site is a matter of judgment.

Some facts will also have to be weighed against other considerations which in themselves are judgments. Measurable facts about the direct impact of a facility on the air and water quality of a site must be compared with less easily quantifiable judgments about the indirect or secondary impacts of future growth that may be induced in the area of the site.

Finally, the facts and judgments about the environmental effects, direct and indirect, of a major facility have to be weighed against the facts and judgments about the need for the facility, which takes us back to the requirement that project goals and their rationale be identified clearly and openly (Brooks, 1976).

In the days before active public involvement, siting decisions were made on the basis of fact and the sponsor's judgment. That judgment, as we have seen, was frequently later challenged. Today, a siting study must handle the problem of public judgment during the siting study. The public is, of course, made up of numerous interest groups with differing values and areas of knowledge. The site-selection process must therefore provide a means both for making judgments on the relative importance of facts and for resolving disagreements when values become an issue.

In Chapter 3 we will present a summary of the entire site-selection process that we recommend and show how it meets the requirements that we have just identified.

3 | THE OVERALL SITING PROCESS

THE STRUCTURE OF THE PROCESS

The site-selection process described in detail in the following chapters is the result of our own evolving response to changing client needs and environmental understanding. It contains means for meeting all the requirements discussed in Chapter 2 and has been applied, generally with success, in site-selection studies of widely varying type and scope.

The process has five clearly identifiable phases; each is discussed in a separate chapter. The phases (goal identification, project definition, project-environmental relationships, site screening, and site evaluation) are shown in simplified sequence in Figure 3-1.

Goal identification requires the project sponsor to think through what the major facility, the end product of the site-selection process, should be and what it should achieve under optimum circumstances. The product should satisfy, as far as is possible, the sponsor's profit, service, and environmental goals. To ensure that this occurs, the specific need to be met and the specific requirements for the facility have to be stated.

Project definition requires that the physical and technological characteristics of the facility be described. The description must be as thorough as necessary to allow identification of an appropriate environment for the facility.

Project-environmental relationship identification is concerned primarily with the potential and permissible effects of the facility on environmental conditions. It examines the characteristics and environmental requirements of the proposed facility in order to identify the conditions that may be affected and the criteria to be used in determining environmental suitability.

The *site-screening phase* is the most complex of the five. It begins with identifying a geographic study area on the basis of project goals. The sponsor's siting requirements and the potential environmental effects are trans-

lated into factors which allow smaller areas within the study area to be screened out or retained for further examination. Conflicts between the varying values of project planners and citizen or review agency participants regarding siting and environmental criteria are examined and discussed at this stage. Techniques such as the Delphi process (discussed in Chapter 7) may be used to resolve or reduce conflicts. A prioritized (or weighted) composite list of factors can then be compiled and used in a finer screening of the remaining candidate areas to identify several suitable sites.

The *site-evaluation phase* requires each candidate site to be examined in detail so that a conceptual plan for the facility on each site can be drawn up. The sites may then be rated or numerically ranked according to their ability to meet each of a list of specific weighted site-evaluation criteria.

The process follows in its most basic outline the logical sequence of analysis, synthesis, and evaluation phases common to other planning, design, and decision-making projects. That is, it begins with analysis of the project and what needs to be known in order to understand and solve the problem. The goals and objectives, project definition, and project-environmental relationship steps generally correspond to the analysis phase.

In the synthesis phase of most programs, data are gathered and manipulated to generate alternative solutions to the problem, using the goals and information needs identified in the analysis phase. In the site-selection process, synthesis is carried out by examining the spatial distribution of site-selection conditions or factors of varying importance within a geographic area. This occurs in the site-screening phase.

In the evaluation phase, alternative solutions are tested against established criteria, trade-offs are made, and preferred solutions are compared to reach a final decision. This corresponds very closely to our site-evaluation phase.

Many sponsors of major facilities now follow a general process of analysis, synthesis, and evaluation, but many may not be finding an improvement in their success rate. The reason lies in the thoroughness with which the process is carried out and documented.

THE ATTRIBUTES OF THE PROCESS

What distinguishes the site-selection process we describe from other planning efforts is the ability to handle, in an orderly and understandable manner, an extremely comprehensive set of information. The preferred approach involves a progressive narrowing of the study's scope from a very broad geographic area and range of factors to a few small sites and highly specific evaluation criteria. Its major advantages are:

· Its ability to consider all possible locations within a large study area and to identify and document the reasons for elimination or selection of any of them

· Its ability to integrate the lay public into the process at every stage for highly visible decision making

· Its ability to consider all significant factors including environ-

mental feasibility, safety, and economic and social requirements and effects

· Its provision for interaction among management, technical, engineering, and other professional specialists both within and outside the sponsoring agency

· Its ability to handle the differing values placed on the large number of siting factors by project participants through the use of weighted criteria

· Its use of maps and other graphic displays for easily understood communication of criteria, data, and site-selection decisions

The process laid out in Figure 3-1 is, as the diagram suggests, a rather clear-cut linear progression. It does, of course, permit a second iteration of any phase through so-called feedback loops, although these are not indicated in this diagram or in the more detailed flowcharts in later chapters. Findings in each phase not only affect subsequent phases but can also affect previously accomplished phases. New information or new situations requiring review of earlier assumptions or decisions can arise. However, since the site-selection process is one of narrowing down rather than building up, the need for recycling is not as common as it is in some other types of planning.

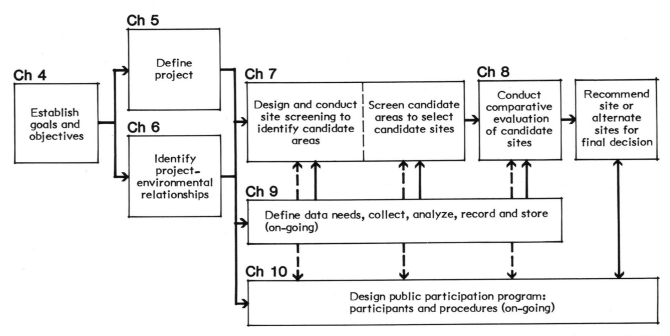

FIGURE 3-1 The overall siting process. This diagram summarizes the entire siting process. Each major step is shown in greater detail in diagrams in Chapters 4 through 8.

As a contrasting example, development of a general plan or a new community design tends to go through several iterations because understanding of the problem to be solved is generally less clear-cut than in the case of site selection. The process for this kind of planning is sometimes shown diagrammatically in the form of a spiral as in Figure 3-2. The size of the spiral at each iteration indicates the expanding scope of inquiry at each stage.

The narrowing linear progression of the site-selection process places particularly heavy reliance on thorough and accurate establishment of project goals and objectives, project definition, and environmental ground rules at the outset. Changes in project definition or in environmental regulations may unavoidably occur during the course of the study. But recycling is costly because the process is more highly structured than the general planning or design processes. It is the high degree of structure that makes it effective.

Possible changes in the ground rules must therefore be anticipated. Allowance for them must be built in as alternative or optional criteria, technical features, or environmental factors and kept under consideration as long as possible (bearing in mind the "When in doubt, leave it in" maxim expressed in Chapter 2). It requires several years to take a proposed power plant from initial conception to approval. During that time many potentially significant changes can and probably will occur in the technology for scrubbing stack emissions, in air quality regulations, or in fuel transportation costs. For this reason, it may be valuable to select alternative sites that represent both existing and possible future preferences. This may mean that one or more alternative sites (three are required under California law) should be selected in relatively remote areas where the visual, air quality, and other adverse effects of existing technology can be minimized. One site may be selected closer to a growth area on the assumption that stack emissions may be reduced by development of more efficient scrubbing technology. If that occurs before final site selection, the more urban site may become the most desirable option because it reduces fuel transportation and power transmission costs. It may also offer opportunities for clustering industry around the plant, an increasingly desirable concept because of its energy and land-use efficiency.

Openness to changing environmental values, land-use concepts, and changes in technology is an essential attribute of a major-facility siting study. Very close coordination with existing or proposed land-use planning programs and policies is also essential. Major facilities have great potential for influencing land-use allocation.

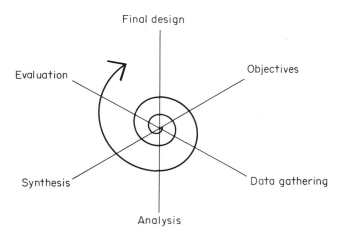

FIGURE 3-2   Typical planning process.

They can promote or preempt valuable and perhaps unique land uses. They can also induce growth at a pace or in a direction that may or may not be desired. For example, the direct and supporting labor force associated with constructing and operating a large facility in a small community can produce financially and environmentally unmanageable demands for housing and services. Conversely, location of major facilities such as government centers, sports complexes, or industrial and office centers in depressed or redevelopment areas can be a major stimulus to revitalization.

THE EVOLUTION AND APPLICATION OF THE PROCESS

We will digress at this point from discussion of the process to consider how it has evolved. What we describe may appear rather clear-cut and is indeed intended to be universally applicable. Obviously, however, adaptations are necessary to meet the special circumstances of particular site-selection studies. In the following chapters we will draw on our own experience to illustrate steps in the process and specific techniques.

By employing those projects with which we are most familiar, we are best able to make recommendations or express caveats regarding the use of particular techniques. To assist the reader both in following the process and in adapting it to specific needs, it will be useful to gain some familiarity with the scope and objectives of the projects to which we refer. Some of these projects are therefore summarized in Part Two.

The examples we have chosen span a 9-year period, from 1971 to 1980. Two of the studies from which we draw several times involved the development of a site-selection process rather than the selection of specific sites. The first of these is the study of the environmental impacts of underground electric power transmission systems which EDAW (1975a) prepared for the Electric Power Research Institute (EPRI) and the former Energy Research and Development Administration (ERDA). This study provided a handbook for utility companies and public planners concerned with route selection for cable systems. The second is a study that provided the California Energy Resources Conservation and Development Commission (ERCDC; now the California Energy Commission) with a methodology for use by utility companies for selecting and ranking power plant sites (EDAW Inc., 1977).

The remaining projects have been directed to the selection of an actual facility site or route. The types of facility with which we have been concerned have changed over the 9 years, although the preponderance of them has been in some way energy-related. To some extent, this is reflective of changing funding priorities. No recent freeway-routing study is included, for example. The Duluth Corridor Study (Eckbo, Dean, Austin & Williams, 1972) described in Part Two was conducted in 1971. Current projects involving hydroelectric power, such as the Swan Falls–Guffey project (EDAW Inc., 1979a), also described in Part Two, and surface mining suggest today's altered emphasis. In the future, attention is likely to focus increasingly on selection of sites for production of synthetic fuels and for disposal of hazardous wastes.

To some degree the projects we cite as examples also reflect changes in public awareness of potential impacts and in the state of the art of site selection. After we conducted numerous power transmission routing studies in the early 1970s, there was a shift in emphasis to statewide or regional energy generation siting studies. Many years ago transmission lines were recognized by conservationists as potentially damaging intrusions into the landscape (see Crowe's *The Landscape of Power*, 1958, for example). As the conservation movement evolved into the environmental movement, concerns about social and economic disruption, cost, and impacts on vegetation, wildlife, and other natural systems were added to the once paramount aesthetic considerations.

The routing of transmission lines provided siting specialists, including ourselves, with many opportunities for developing and refining graphic analysis and other siting techniques, sometimes for tens of thousands of square miles. Since the mid-1970s, there has been a dramatic in-

crease in concern for the complex and perplexing siting issues surrounding power plants. "Out of sight, out of mind" is a phrase that is no longer operative. In Minnesota in 1975 and in California in 1976, the primary concerns were with public safety, protection of wilderness and recreation areas, and effects on water supply and water quality (EDAW Inc., 1975b; February 1977).

In Colorado later in 1976, a regional power plant siting proposal raised the issue of land-value impacts in the region (EDAW Inc., 1978). This local concern is typical of the change in public receptivity to a project as soon as it begins to impinge on identifiable properties. Nevertheless, in this case the issue was raised at the regional level before specific sites were considered. It seems to illustrate a transition in understanding and concern from the more purely technological and environmental issues to as yet less well articulated concerns about overall land-use planning.

In a siting study (EDAW Inc., 1980) for the California Department of Water Resources (DWR), air quality, reflecting nationwide thinking and regulation, emerged as the paramount consideration. The evolution continues, and recognition of the complexity of issues in major-facility siting expands. The federal Clean Air Act, as it stands as of 1982, virtually confines fossil-fuel power plants to rural areas. However, it is apparent that there is increasing concern about growth inducement beyond already sprawling urban areas and alteration of more and more of the nation's highly valued natural environments.

Awareness of the impending economic impacts of scarce energy is also producing suggestions for *energy parks*, to which we alluded earlier. Locating industries close to power sources can minimize transmission losses, make use of waste heat, and perhaps move homes closer to work to cut transportation costs. Will these changes in public values result in a switch from remote to urban areas for future generating facilities? Will additional pressure for advances in emissions technology alter current air quality constraints? Will compatibility with adjacent industrial and other development be required of the power plant sites of the future? We cannot tell at present, but certainly the regulations and values associated with siting power plants and all other types of major facilities can be expected to change over time.

In various ways all the projects from which we draw for examples reflect limitations in the state of the art as well as its evolution, even though all or most have been deemed successful in terms of original project objectives. Further, they are all necessarily tailored to particular projects. None represents, in content or in organization, a structure that is immediately applicable to any future major-facility siting study.

The process we present is nevertheless a universal one. The essential steps are equally applicable to routing freeways, pipelines, and power transmission lines and to siting airports, colleges, petrochemical plants, power plants, synfuel plants, and hazardous waste disposal sites. The context, the criteria, and the issues will be unique to each and will demand selective evaluation of the usefulness of the techniques presented.

The process spans the length of a project from conception of goals to final selection of the site but can be begun at any point. For example, the site-evaluation process has been applied in a recent project in Idaho (the Swan Falls–Guffey project) to select from among three hydropower plant sites on the Snake River which were originally identified more than a decade ago.

The Idaho case also illustrates another attribute of the process. It is applicable not only to site-selection studies in which the field is, as it were, wide open but also to evaluating preselected sites. For example, we can fore-

see increasing applications of the process to selection of mining locations. Mining operations, like dam sites, have strict engineering and resource requirements which immediately limit the investigation to a few candidate sites.

Finally, before we move on to discussion of the process in detail, we should make mention of the close relationship between the site-selection process and land-use suitability analysis. Both employ many of the same types of data and techniques for data manipulation. EDAW, like other landscape architectural consultants, has also played a role in the evolution of land-use constraint and suitability overlay mapping first developed by British geographers. There is a fundamental difference between the two types of study, however. In land-use suitability analysis, we first look at what the land tells us and then select appropriate uses. In site selection, we first determine the characteristics of the proposed use and then select an appropriate site. With this in mind, it is possible to envision application of the process to an almost unlimited variety of project types even though they may not be mentioned here.

4 | PROJECT GOALS AND OBJECTIVES

THE NEED FOR GOALS

Goals are frequently emphasized as the essential foundation for any planning endeavor whether it is a personal career, a community plan, or a corporation's growth and facility strategy that is being discussed. Like keeping a journal or making New Year resolutions, goal setting is generally acknowledged to be a good idea but is rarely undertaken or completed.

The formulation of *goals*, toward which efforts and resources are directed, and *objectives*, the more precise and measurable steps need to achieve the goals, can make the difference between wasted effort and success. In planning a major facility, the articulation of goals and objectives permits the identification of specific areas of concern and of *criteria* by which to measure the ability of a site to meet them.

In a discussion of facility strategy, Mathey (March–April 1979) observes that because most companies do not have a facility strategy, not only is there often no orderly approach to developing a strategy but even the concept is unclear. He identifies at least two dozen basic forces that influence a single industrial facility decision prior to site selection, many of which conflict. If the conflicts are not recognized and resolved in a prioritized fashion, the organization may end up with a less than optimal project for its needs. In addition, when the close connections among goals, objectives, information, criteria, and subsequent planning activities are not recognized, the site selection itself will tend to be a hit-or-miss effort. Unarticulated or poorly articulated goals and objectives lead to confusion and misunderstandings among project observers and participants and impair the sponsor's ability to respond to critical review and comment. Without clearly established goals and objectives, information needs and methods of analysis cannot be efficiently and appropriately determined. This can result in collecting too many data or not enough. For example, there is no need to consider water transportation if there is no material supply or product distribution objective requiring water transportation to meet market or profit goals.

The three terms *goals, objectives,* and *criteria* are commonly encountered both in general and in planning contexts. It must be noted, though, that they are often rather loosely applied. In some cases, they may be used almost synonymously. More often, objectives alone appear, the goals from which they derive being unspoken. This may occur because they seem so obvious that they do not need to be stated. In other cases, only the most fundamental goals are stated without being translated into objectives and criteria. In either case, the project is immediately in danger of pursuing the wrong direction.

A simple analogy to the business of house hunting may help to clarify the hierarchy. Let us say that one's goal, in its most basic terms, is a larger house to accommodate a growing family. After some thought and family discussion, it is possible to refine the goal. Three bedrooms are essential, though four would be preferable; the price must be in a defined range but, naturally, less if possible; a garden is desirable, and the location should be close to work and to particular schools.

It is now possible to determine more precisely the steps you will take to achieve this goal. These steps, or objectives, may include the way in which you intend to finance the move, how you can obtain cash for the down payment, when you will be ready to buy, and how much work you can put into fixing up a house yourself.

You are now in the position to begin considering the factors that are of greatest concern. Is it more essential to be close to your work or to the children's schools? Is a garden essential, or would a condominium with community open space be acceptable? Would a three-bedroom house be acceptable if it offered opportunity for future expansion? If firm selections can be made, these then become additional objectives, measured by criteria related specifically to them that specify, for example,

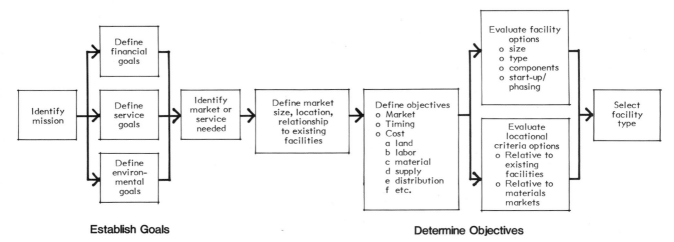

FIGURE 4-1 Project goals and objectives. Several important steps need to be taken by the project sponsor or the general public before a project goal can be identified.

minimum square footage, maximum price and monthly payments, and maximum commuting time. If alternative solutions are equally acceptable, these must be recognized as options. After a look through the Sunday real estate advertisements, you may be forced to consider some other options, change objectives, or relax criteria. A condominium apartment or smaller square footage may become realistic and acceptable objectives. It then becomes possible to develop a list of criteria thorough enough with which to begin a concerted search.

In reality, probably relatively few home purchases are made in this fashion. Exploring open houses can be a diverting activity. If you were being paid to find a house, however, clearly it would be a most inefficient approach. This is why it is critical to establish and refine the goal, the objectives to be met if the goal is to be realized, and the criteria that precisely define the objectives.

For the purpose of major-facility siting, Figure 4-1 sets out the hierarchy of goals, objectives, and criteria and outlines the sequence of decisions at this stage. The organization's mission, goals, and objectives are included to show their relationship to the object of a site-selection study. Ideally, they should be established and regularly reevaluated prior to a facility-siting study, but as we shall see, this can by no means be assumed. The formulation of an overall organizational strategy is not part of the scope of this book, but without it there is no firm basis for developing project goals, objectives, and criteria.

In the remainder of this chapter we will follow through the series of decisions in Figure 4-1, discussing

some of the quite complex considerations involved at each step.

IDENTIFYING THE MISSION OF AN ORGANIZATION

This is not necessarily, as it seems on first examination, the clearest and most generally accepted component of this stage of the overall siting process. For a manufacturing company, the *raison d'être* is to make money; for a utility company, it is to provide a service and also to make money; but for a transportation agency, established originally to plan and fund highway construction, the mission may now be much less clear. Should the agency be using road tax funds to assist in developing other forms of transportation? The California Department of Transportation has been the subject of attack because of varying opinions regarding its proper mission. Unless there is general agreement on this fundamental point, a project sponsor will be subject to challenge at every point in the process of siting a facility.

DEFINING ORGANIZATIONAL GOALS

The identification of an organization's overall goal or mission results in recognition of needs as the organization and the society in which it operates evolve. But the needs tend to be perceived differently by individuals with varying roles and personalities within the organization's management. There may thus be internal conflict over any decision that involves articulation of organizational goals.

One of the characteristics of organizational goals is that they are not always tightly defined. They tend to be assumed, and the assumptions tend to change over time. Another characteristic is that they can exhibit confusing contradictions. There are goals proclaimed for image purposes, made public in advertising and annual reports; and there are those by which the organization really operates, unwritten and subtle, but fairly well understood by top management.

But even those unwritten goals may involve internal inconsistencies when it comes to translating them into actions. Stafford gives four examples of possible motivations behind a goal of expanding or diversifying product investment:

· Make more money (increase profit return on investment)
· Have a larger firm (and increase total revenues, prestige, employees, and assets)
· Work less (and reduce "executive inconvenience")
· Reduce risk and uncertainty (conservative behavior)

Stafford suggests that while locational analyses and rationalizations usually stress the first motive, "Make more money," several or all of these motives are likely to be at work simultaneously. Depending on which is deemed most crucial, quite different investment strategies can result (Stafford, 1979:15).

One of the particular problems facing corporations and service agencies alike is the frequent dichotomy between the primary mission and external social, economic, and environmental goals. A corporation's essential and primary purpose of making money in our economic system inhibits many attempts to achieve social and environmental goals because of the costs involved. Some would argue that this division is entirely proper. We do not intend to embark on a discourse on a subject better left to political and economic theorists. And yet, as public utility regulatory commissions oversee the activities of service organizations with growing care and as environmental and financial agencies require increasing attention to the external effects of once independent actions, publicly held values have to be included in organizational goals. The incorporation of public values may range from grudging to enthusiastic, but inasmuch as major-facility decisions hinge on recognition of public values, it is essential. In fact, these questions will be given priority by the public over the considerations essential to an organization in pursuit of its distinct mission.

Another characteristic of goals, both internal and external, is that they are of course changeable, responding to shifts in society, the economy, scientific knowledge, and technology. The certainties of the 1950s were challenged by the growing social and environmental sensitivities of the 1960s. Current resource shortages and inflation, combined with continuing concern for the environment and growing distrust of aspects of technology, represent deeply conflicting and therefore even more complex demands. Other changes, such as affirmative-action policies, concern for women's rights, increasing labor demands for improved pay and working conditions, and the trend toward corporate diversification, are also affecting the goals and policies of many organizations.

The location planner, especially as an outside consultant, cannot resolve conflicts among internal organizational goals or inconsistencies between internal and external values. That is the responsibility of management. But the planner can help set a sound and commonly accepted framework for a site-selection study by requiring management, after thorough discussion between varying interests within the organization, to define financial, service, and environmental goals. In some cases, by participating in a site-selection study, the public at large can help reshape an agency's goals in terms of social and environmental responsibility. The work of committees with the Minnesota Department of Highways on Duluth's Interstate 35 is such a case, to which we will return later and again in a description of the project in Part Two.

DEFINING ORGANIZATIONAL OBJECTIVES

With an understanding of the organization's goals for consolidation or expansion, diversification, or redirection based on new technology, management is in a position to make plans for new facilities. Needed production or service capacity is strongly dependent on identification of current market demand or service requirements.

It was at one time possible to respond to pressing production needs and demands anticipated in the relatively short term. The much longer time that it now takes to get a facility approved and built means that planning must be based on a much less certain market. For a manufacturing company, considerable risk is involved since by the time the plant is approved, it may be too late to get into the marketplace with the product. This is less of a problem for those constructing the types of major facilities with which we are mainly concerned. But careful forecasting of demand for a product or service is essential. A state agency to which EDAW was recently under contract discovered an error in its forecasts which obviated the need for a very large facility after the site-selection study had been largely completed. Admittedly, projection of the need for facilities in the 1980s is significantly more difficult than it was in the more confident 1960s and early 1970s. How many people will be able to fly 10 years from now, for example, is a question requiring crystal gazing. Yet it must be asked, even if current demand appears to justify expanded airport capacity. Indeed, it must be asked if new major airport construction is even feasible today, given considerations of cost, land availability, and the viability of commercial aviation.

If it is determined that a new facility is the only way to carry out the organization's mission and further its goals, the next questions to be asked are:

· How much increased capacity is required?

· How many units of what type and size will provide this capacity?

· When will they be needed?

· How much should they cost?

· What general area will they serve?

· What relationships to complementary or competing facilities are desirable?

Mathey (March–April 1979) identifies the numerous considerations of operating costs, current organizational and industry capacity and demand, financing and investment strategies, and scheduling involved in answering such questions and identifying priority needs. Stafford (1979) lists the varying answers likely to be obtained from managers with different and specialized responsibilities. The answers may be arrived at by conventional manual methods of analysis. More often they may be derived from a computer program that can handle the intricately related considerations.

DEFINING THE PROJECT GOAL

The priority action selected from among the possible alternatives becomes the project goal. It may be quite simply stated:

· Provide a freeway link between points A and B.

· Build a petrochemical complex on the west coast to cut costs of shipping Pacific basin oil.

· Provide a new power source for anticipated growth in Region C.

· Construct a new university to serve current demand from Regions D, E, and F.

The goal has to be made considerably more definitive in terms of the population or market to be served, the permissible cost of the project, and the relative importance of environmental considerations before more specific objectives can be set. However, the analysis that goes into setting objectives may affect the specific project goals, so that it is often hard to separate the two.

DEFINING PROJECT OBJECTIVES

We are now getting closer to the operational aspects of site selection, setting objectives that can be measured by some standard or criterion of performance. Some of the key types of objectives for a major facility are suggested in Figure 4-1. Objectives and siting criteria for meeting them need to be as comprehensive and precise as possible, but they will of course vary with differing facility types and situations.

Figure 4-1 includes the words "options" and "select facility type." As we implied above, the nature of the facility is firmed up in the process of defining objectives. In the case of a manufacturing company, the desired geographic area to be served may be clear, but the exact facility (full processing, assembly, or distribution) may not be defined. Conversely, expansion into a new line of processing may be the project goal for which the general area of site search is still to be determined. Similarly, a utility company's project goal may be additional power generation capacity to serve a growing load center. Whether the need is best met by adding a unit to an existing facility or by a plant in a new location may not yet be clear. If a new plant is more desirable, what is the most appropriate energy source?

Several sets of objectives need to be listed and compared in order to reach the answers to such questions. It may be that the result of this step in the process is not a single answer but two or more equally acceptable options, but the scope of the inquiry is logically narrowed.

Approaches to refinement of project goals and development of project objectives vary widely among facility types, as do the groups who are normally involved. It has been stated that the sponsoring organization will have its own broad goals set by its governing body: the board of directors, regents, trustees, or commission. Objectives, on the other hand, tend to be set by a larger number of individuals or groups. There is no single right approach applicable to all situations. To illustrate the point, we will look at an industrial plant, a freeway, and a power plant.

A hypothetical corporation about to embark on a site search would need to develop:

· *Marketing objectives,* which include considerations relative to market locations, trends, and other characteristics

· *Objectives relative to time,* such as desired start-up time, growth phases, site-selection period, facility design period, and construction period

· *Profit objectives,* which include minimizing the costs of land, power and water utilities, waste disposal, labor, services, materials, transportation, distance from other support facilities, construction costs, taxes, and money costs

· *Objectives related to the social and economic environment,* which include minimizing adverse effects and maximizing beneficial effects on factors such as local economics, population, labor, cultural and educational facilities, other community facilities, local government structure and regulations, public attitudes, land-use patterns, aesthetic and visual character, noise, health facilities, security, and social organizations

· *Objectives related to the physical and biological environment,* minimizing adverse effects and maximizing beneficial effects on factors such as vegetation, wildlife, hydrology, water resources, soils, landforms, air quality, and water quality

While each group of objectives is essential to the site-selection process, the first three groups are most closely related to defining the facility itself and the general area of search. While the board of directors may establish some objectives, such as those involving scheduling, capital costs, and percentage of profit, the more operational objectives will in all likelihood be developed by management because of the intricacy of such factors as transportation, for example. Mathematical modeling techniques are often essential for balancing questions related to the critical link between points of supply and points of product distribution. Factors include transportation mode, transfer costs, the highly complex geography of freight rates, aggregate distance involved, volume of raw materials, and volume of products sold at the market.

Many more complex considerations are involved in broad industrial location studies to determine the types of objectives listed above. However, we are concerned here with the way in which goals and objectives are expressed to provide the necessary foundation for a comprehensive regional siting study process. The complexity of considerations that go into setting goals and standards

in any particular organization or type of activity is far beyond the scope of this book. Overall discussions will be found in *Principles of Industrial Location* by Stafford (1979), *Industrial Location* by Smith (1971), *Industrial Development* by Hunker (1974), and *Spatial Perspectives on Industrial Organization and Decision-Making* by Hamilton (1974), especially the chapter by Beyers and Krumme. Each contains an extensive bibliography of more specialized references.

In the past, the results of such strictly economic location analysis were almost all that were needed to begin identification and evaluation of sites. Managers with site-selection responsibility are now increasingly aware that environmental controls call for study of a broader range of concerns. Stafford points out that "manufacturers are, perforce, required to indulge in some regional systems analysis, as distinct from that all too common pattern of fragmented, local analysis" (1979:81). Our aim is to fill the need for a regional analysis method applied to and integrated into the more traditional regional location and site-selection techniques.

As we have suggested previously, some goals and objectives, such as those dealing with environmental and social conditions, are the particular concern of the public and special public-interest groups. These goals and objectives can be established in a number of ways: by management in consultation with others, by consultants, by citizens' advisory groups, or possibly, and perhaps most appropriately, by a combination of these methods. However they are developed, it is important that they be thoroughly discussed, understood, and generally agreed upon as to completeness and content.

In freeway planning, the primary concern for maintaining the integrity of neighborhoods may mean that a citizens' advisory committee is asked for assistance. In Duluth, where even the need for extension of Interstate 35 was in doubt, the fundamental project goal was stated as:

The determination of need for a traffic facility; and, if needed, the selection of the necessary alignment and facilities of maximum social and physical value and the least social and physical cost (Eckbo, Dean, Austin & Williams, 1972:32).

The state highway division initiated a major citywide community involvement program, recognizing the tremendously varying viewpoints of individual communities. The citizens' advisory committees developed five groups of objectives, shown in Table 4-1. It will be seen that some of these objectives are specific enough to be termed criteria and that no priorities are assigned to objectives at this stage.

TABLE 4-1   Objectives developed for a freeway siting study. Preliminary objectives should be developed by the project sponsor or, as in this case, by citizens' advisory committees at an early stage in the study.

Social Objectives

o   Increase access to existing facilities within the area.

o   Avoid division of compatible land uses.

o   Preserve viable land use areas:

Schools	Churches
Residences	Civic facilities
Recreational facilities	Commercial facilities
Institutional facilities	Visually pleasant areas and the view areas to them
Historic areas	Political areas
Industrial areas	

o   Separate incompatible land uses.

o   Link similar land-use areas.

o   Maximize accessibility of tourist destinations.

o   Locate facilities in areas of the greatest need of development.

o   Locate in areas requiring least relocation of employment and housing.

o   Improve access from housing to work.

Visual Objectives

o   Provide for the maximum clarity and understanding of the process of movement.

o   Maximize the driver's view and quality of visual experience.

o   Maximize potential for planting and urban beautification along facility routing.

Economic Objectives

o   Minimize absolute cost of facility construction.

o   Minimize absolute cost of general maintenance.

o   Increase potential for tourism.

o   Minimize disruption of existing businesses.

o   Provide for expansion of the business community by means of joint development.

o   Reveal the physical and cultural identity of the area surrounding the facility.

o   Create a pleasing visual element for all non-driving viewers.

Environmental Objectives

o   Avoid the destruction or alteration of all environmental (natural) resources.

o   Avoid increases in air, water, and noise pollution.

o   Link scenic and recreational resources.

o   Create greater access to those natural resources that can tolerate it and avoid those fragile areas that cannot.

o   Reveal the physical and cultural identity of the surroundings. Preserve important existing historical landmarks and artifacts.

o   Avoid areas of extreme fragility, such as erosion susceptibility, steepest gradient, insufficient soil, mechanical stability, and areas of endangered species.

o   Respect and consider elements of micro-climate.

o   Minimize cut and fill.

Land Use Objectives

o   Facilitate safe and convenient traffic movement.

o   Locate new and productive land uses.

o   Provide physical and visual access to presently unaccessible resources.

o   Link, for increased access, major recreational areas.

o   Conserve and enhance the existing urban form, scale, patterns, activities and textures.

o   Conserve and enhance unique physiographic elements.

o   Provide maximum physical access to the elements of the existing urban area.

o   Increase and strengthen public and private transportation capabilities--including bicycles and pedestrians.

o   Provide for urban expansion and growth potentials.

o   Consider potential uses as well as existing uses.

o   Preserve and utilize existing cultural and historic landmarks.

o   Maximize joint development.

o   Maximize use of the existing urban systems.

o   Create efficient access to and from the facility.

o   Strengthen existing business facilities by greater access and relieved congestion.

Objectives for some rather specialized public facilities, such as parks, airports, and some types of power-generating projects, will be set by the staff of public or quasi-public boards or commissions. Depending on the degree to which outside interests are represented on such single-purpose bodies, goals and objectives sensitive to public interests will be built into project goals and objectives. Staff may seek professionals in a variety of fields as consultants or advisers to assist in development of objectives as well as in actual site selection.

Project objectives for a power plant are usually set by the sponsoring utility company, although they may be set in the context of specific objectives for site-selection studies established by a regulatory agency. In Minnesota, for example, the Minnesota Environmental Quality Council has set statutory requirements for the power plant siting process, as has the California Energy Resources Conservation and Development Commission. Table 4-2 sets forth the Minnesota siting objectives.

To continue the discussion of how the sponsor, as opposed to a regulatory agency, establishes project goals and objectives, we will look at a recent study by the California Department of Water Resources (DWR).

DWR, whose mission is to keep California supplied with water, recently engaged in a power plant site search. A principal goal of the organization is to keep arid southern California supplied with water at an economic cost. In order to overcome potential problems of both shortages and increasing cost of power to maintain its ability to pump northern California's water south, DWR's objective was to develop alternative power sources of its own. It therefore studied alternative means of power generation, including geothermal power, hydropower, wind, biomass, and coal. Its organizational objectives were for additional power within a short period and "production of energy at a cost economically competitive with equivalent energy purchased from other sources" (California Department of Water Resources, 1978:2–1). A coal-fired power plant became the project goal, as the only realistic choice. Oil was ruled out owing to uncertain price and availability, as was nuclear power because of its cost and public attitudes even prior to the Three Mile Island incident. The limited number and controversial nature of potential hydropower sites and the undeveloped state of alternative energy sources left a clear choice.

TABLE 4-2   Statutory objectives for power plant siting.

SITE-SELECTION OBJECTIVES

The following objectives shall be applied in the selection of sites:

a   Preferred sites require the minimum population displacement and disruption of local communities and institutions.

b   Preferred sites minimize adverse health effects on human population.

c   Preferred sites do not require the destruction or major alteration of land forms, vegetative types, or wildlife habitats which are rare, unique, or of unusual importance to the surrounding area.

d   Preferred sites minimize the visual and audible impingement on waterways, parks, or other existing and proposed public recreation areas.

e   Preferred sites minimize the removal of valuable and productive land and water from other necessary uses and minimize conflicts among water users.

f   Preferred sites maximize reliability with respect to climate and geology.

g   Preferred sites permit significant conservation of energy or utilization of by-products.

h   Preferred sites are located near large load centers.

i   Preferred sites maximize the use of already existing operating sites and transportation systems.

j   Preferred sites allow for larger rather than smaller generating capacity.

Meeting in late 1978 with a team of consultants and its own staff representing a variety of specializations and interests, DWR examined available technology, fuel sources, costs, and typical environmental concerns and set the following project objectives. The coal-fired power plant would:

· Have a 1000-megawatt total capacity

· Generate 350 megawatts of power to satisfy the needs of DWR, with the first unit on-line in 1987

· Produce energy at a cost economically competitive with equivalent energy purchased from other sources

· Incorporate the best proven technological advances available in power plant design to control stack emissions and minimize other environmental impacts

· Utilize lesser-quality water (according to California Water Resources Control Board criteria) for cooling

· Obtain coal most probably from the western United States transported by rail, using the unit-train concept

· Be owned jointly by DWR, other public utilities, and private utilities

In addition to these objectives, which refined the nature of the proposed facility itself, DWR set the following environmental objectives for the site search:

· Candidate area identification should follow a line of environmental conservation.

· Sites should be technically and economically feasible, environmentally compatible, and socially acceptable within the constraints set by project goals and technical project objectives.

· Agricultural lands should be protected whenever possible, and the amount of productive land used by project facilities should be minimized.

· Displacement of permanent residents should be minimized, and areas of high population density should be avoided.

At this point, despite the lack of specificity of many of the project objectives, it may be possible to attach firm criteria to certain of them. These will often relate to areas which cannot be considered in the site search on technical or regulatory grounds. These are then included in the list of exclusion factors for use in the preliminary stage of the site-screening process. For example, areas to be exempt from site consideration for the DWR project included:

· Land with unfavorable topography (slopes of 10 percent or more)

· Portions of the coastal zone designated by the California Coastal Commission to exclude power plants

· Archaeological sites, historical monuments, and other unique cultural resources

· Local, state, and national parks and forests, wildlife sanctuaries, and other public lands where development is forbidden or restricted

· Class 1 air quality areas

The DWR project objectives also stated that areas such as active fault zones and major flood zones should be given low priority in site consideration and that landownership and failure to meet local air quality emissions standards should not be grounds for automatic exclusion of an area from consideration. These were all objectives that required refinement during the project definition and environmental analysis phases. Some of them also involved trade-offs with other considerations during the site-screening phase.

It is thus clear that at this stage in the process project objectives are not yet comprehensive, nor are they all translated into precise siting criteria. They generally express what is acceptable to the sponsor in terms of technical and regulatory feasibility and in terms of its broader social and environmental goals and objectives. But what is meant by such terms as *environmental conservation and compatibility* and *social acceptability?* Is it possible to set standards for effects on agriculture or displacement of population in absolute or only in relative terms? These are questions that we will explore more thoroughly in Chapter 6, looking at the relationships among project characteristics, regulatory standards, and generally or locally held values. In Chapter 5 we will describe how the nature of the project becomes progressively better defined so that additional siting objectives and criteria may be identified.

5 | PROJECT DEFINITION

THE PURPOSE OF DEFINING THE PROJECT

To the experienced site-selection manager the precise definition of a project may seem such a routine activity that it hardly warrants a chapter devoted to it. He or she will generally have a thorough understanding of all the elements of the proposed facility; will know the space requirements, the technologies involved, the number and type of workers needed, the utility requirements, the needs for transportation and proximity to other facilities, and a host of other characteristics. Such a manager also knows the impossibility of passing an appropriate judgment on a potential site without specifying the nature of the facility.

Project definition is thus a common operation in facility planning, although it may be called by other names such as *program development* or *schematic plan development*. In some cases the project definition may be so precise that the term *preliminary specifications* is used; others, when the project is as yet not well defined, may use the term *assumptions*.

The information that the site-selection manager calls for should meet the needs of whatever site-selection techniques are to be used, whether formal or informal. What we will examine here is the necessary degree of precision of information and whether it is set out understandably and systematically enough to meet the needs of a comprehensive, open site search.

Good project definition has two essential purposes. One is to permit refinement of the siting requirements that the siting study will aim to meet. The second is to facilitate an understanding of potential effects on the environment so that adverse effects can be minimized or avoided at the selected site.

The project definition serves the first purpose by providing information on the space needed to accommodate the facility; the kind of land which will permit the facility to be constructed economically and to function safely and efficiently; the desirable spatial relationship of the site to other land uses and facilities; and any special requirements for such conditions as air quality, water quality and quantity, power supply, labor supply and wage rates, and land and development costs.

The second purpose is also partially met by the description of siting requirements. The conversion of land and possible diversion of water, energy, labor, and other resources are in themselves effects which may or not be adverse depending upon the plant location. In addition, the project definition must describe other aspects of the facility that will alter the environment, including the dimensions and general appearance of the structure; construction phasing and any special construction activities; the number of workers to be housed during construction and operation of the facility; and the nature of the operation, function, or process, including traffic, noise, handling of any hazardous materials, and production of various wastes. Finally the schedule for review and permit application must be specified (EDAW Inc., February 1977).

In theory a voluminous amount of information could be generated to serve these two purposes. In practice the project definition should be limited to what is strictly relevant to site selection. For purposes of identifying candidate sites (described in Chapter 7), a relatively small number of key facility characteristics may be sufficient to screen out clearly unsuitable areas. At this stage the important items of project definition include certain fundamental siting requirements without which efficient, safe, or economic facility development would not be possible. They also include those unavoidable effects of the facility that would be unacceptable in areas with certain environmental characteristics.

As a site-selection study progresses from screening areas to identifying and then evaluating candidate sites, more detailed information on the project will become relevant. In addition, it may be necessary to make modifications to the proposed facility to fit the characteristics of the narrowing list of potential locations.

Project definition information therefore needs to be developed and presented in an orderly manner. It should permit the critical requirements or potentially impacting features to be distinguished from those which are either less important or relevant mainly to conceptual site plan development and local impact assessment in the site-evaluation stage.

The project definition should be presented in a manner that permits everyone participating in the study to have a clear understanding of what is proposed. All elements of the group involved in the decision should have an equal chance to grasp relevant technical processes. They should be equally aware of the reasons for requiring certain relationships with local or regional land uses and facilities.

The style of presentation is important because the general public will be involved at some point in the process. Even quite technically oriented professionals representing the public or government agencies may be unfa-

miliar with technology outside their own fields. Technical terms and processes therefore have to be explained, using straightforward language and graphic methods as much as possible.

WHEN IS THE PROJECT DEFINED?

Figure 4-1 indicated that selection of the facility type occurs as a result of considering goals and objectives for the project. Project definition, outlined in Figure 5-1, therefore overlaps the first step of establishing goals and objectives with considerable interaction between the two. It may be possible, as a result of setting agreed-upon goals and specific objectives for market, product, cost, profit, and other considerations, to be quite precise about the type of facility desired because only one will meet those goals. It will be recalled from the previous chapter that the California Department of Water Resources decision to develop a coal-fired power plant was felt to be Hobson's choice, given the agency's economic

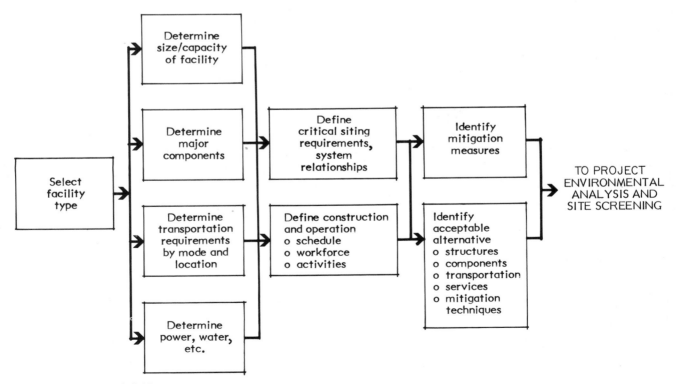

FIGURE 5-1 Project definition.

and timing objectives and constraints on other energy source availability (EDAW Inc., 1980). In other instances it is possible at this stage to identify the facility only in very general conceptual terms, which become more precise as site selection proceeds.

While the basic project type may be settled, component facilities may not be, and thus planning may have to proceed on the basis of alternatives. The fact that optional facilities or techniques often have to be identified because a final decision cannot be made until later suggests once again that the process phases we have identified are not completely clear-cut and linear. Some modifications may be made during the course of the siting study, as the sponsor's understanding of his or her needs is refined. Others may become desirable as findings are made relative either to potential environmental effects or to the opportunities for finding sites that satisfy both siting and environmental criteria.

Aspects of proposed facility design may be dependent on identification of established environmental standards and regulations as well as on less formal environmental performance standards independent of specific site location.

DEFINING THE PHYSICAL CHARACTERISTICS OF THE FACILITY

Even if its design is in very preliminary form, a proposed facility can be described adequately for purposes of screening areas. However, what needs to be known and can be precisely described prior to examination of actual sites differs from facility to facility.

There is a relatively limited list of characteristics that can be precisely defined for a freeway project until the process of selecting a possible alignment within a selected route begins. By comparison, the definition of a petrochemical plant or a power plant is extremely detailed and complex.

To begin with the freeway example, as the Duluth Freeway case study in Part Two illustrates, the only essentials in identifying potential corridors may be the general route origin and destination and the traffic volume to be served. As the study progresses to selection and comparative evaluation of alternative corridors, the following requirements also need definition:

· Needed interchanges with other routes

· Minimum right-of-way and number of lanes

· Minimum clearance over roads, railroads, and navigable waters

· Desired geologic, seismic, and hydrologic conditions

· Design speed, maximum grades, and minimum curve radii

· Construction activities, materials, and workforce

· Desirable maximum cost per mile

These components of the definition are thus relatively simple. Many are also somewhat flexible, allowing some trade-offs to be made between technical and cost criteria and socioeconomic, visual, and environmental criteria in the selection of alternative routes. A freeway project thus cannot be defined as precisely as many other major facilities until detailed alignments are prepared for final comparative evaluation. Problems of horizontal and vertical alignment, for example, may increase cost by requiring cuts or other modifications to the optimum alignment.

By comparison, definition of an underground power transmission system must be considerably more precise. Overhead transmission systems are relatively flexible in terms of technical routing requirements and construction activities. Underground systems and the activities involved in their construction are more complex, inflexible, and significant in their potential effects. Moreover, trench dimensions, construction activities, and, in some cases, tolerance of grades and curves vary among the several different cable systems available. In addition to cost and capacity requirements, the probable environmental conditions encountered will influence the type of cable selected, and this, in turn, will influence the effects of the system. To minimize adverse environmental consequences, selection of the most suitable route demands detailed knowledge of cable type, construction requirements, and operating characteristics (EDAW Inc., June–September 1976).

When we consider a major processing plant, a petrochemical plant, or a power plant, we are dealing with very detailed and complex information. First, the fixed physical components must be defined. These include site size and topographic requirements to accommodate the major structures, tanks and storage areas, roads and railroad sidings, parking areas, and loading platforms. Available fuel, raw materials, and utilities or, in some cases, the destinations of finished products establish general locational requirements relative to material sources, markets, and other facilities, as well as specific requirements with respect to transportation facilities and utilities.

There are also significant public concerns about innumerable potential effects on the natural, economic, social, and fiscal environments while the plant is being constructed and when it is in operation. These relate to the wastes generated, jobs created, strains imposed on local housing, schools, and infrastructure, and many other considerations addressed in Chapter 6.

WHAT IS AN APPROPRIATE FORMAT?

A method for organizing project definition data is needed. This organization must relate well both to the subsequent identification and to comparative evaluation of areas that satisfy siting requirements and the environmental standards set for the project.

Recommended basic categories are set forth below:

1 *Facility type and site requirements.* These requirements should be expressed as absolute requirements or in terms of desirable ranges:

· Facility type and capacity
· Type, area, and bulk of main structure or structures
· Total site acreage and topographic requirements
· Method of site acquisition

2 *Process description.* These items cover the essential operating characteristics of the facility wherever it is located:

· Raw-material requirements
· Fuel or power requirements
· Water quantity and quality requirements
· Solid, liquid, and gaseous waste products generated
· Technology of production or waste management
· End products

3 *Locational requirements.* The process description is next related to necessary or desirable locational characteristics:

· Market, load center, or population center
· Fuel or raw-material source or sources
· Transportation or transmission facilities for supply and distribution
· Water and power sources; waste disposal
· Other processing or support industries or facilities
· Labor force (size, skill, unionization)

4 *System relationships.* The numerous interrelationships among items in the first three categories need to be identified. (For example, a plant dependent on rail delivery of coal will have topographic requirements that may go beyond the site to provide for efficient construction of rail spurs.) This can be accomplished best by development of a network or flow diagram.

5 *Schedule.* The sponsor's scheduling requirements or preferences need to be included in siting criteria. Identification of the preferred schedule should be coordinated with and followed in design of the site-selection process.

· Phasing of construction
· Optimum dates for operation, first to final phase
· Time required for documentation and each permit application
· Total time to overall approval

6 *Activity identification.* It is valuable for evaluation of socioeconomic and environmental effects to identify in detail the probable activities that will occur during each of the following project phases:

· Preconstruction planning
· Construction
· Operation
· Maintenance

An example of activity identification can be found in Table 6-5 in the next chapter.

7 *Facility alternatives and options.* For each of the items listed above, it may be possible to identify an acceptable alternative or an optional approach to allow the project to be tailored to unavoidable suboptimum environmental or locational conditions. Options or alternatives may relate to the structure itself, fuel or materials sources, modes of transportation, waste or emission control technology, schedule, or other requirements.

8 *Absolute and optional siting requirements.* For purposes of progressively narrowing the geographic scope of inquiry it is essential to identify "must have" site requirements from the sponsor's viewpoint. These should be distinguished from optional requirements, which ideally are assigned an order of priority.

This general outline provides a structure that is applicable to virtually all types of major facilities. It can be expanded or otherwise adapted in various ways as appropriate to each type. The following examples illustrate, in summarized form, how the format can be adapted to the definition of three different types of facility.

The first example (Table 5-1) provides an outline of the first three items of project definition (facility type, process description, and locational requirements) as applied to a coal-fired power plant. Table 5-2 illustrates some of the details involved in component and process descriptions for a coal-fired power plant. System characteristics and requirements are presented in many cases as options, which allow for continuing refinement of the project and for varying conditions at the generally acceptable sites that may be selected.

While some narrative description and explanation of the project definition may be needed, a tabular format is usually desirable to organize project definition data. Table 5-3 provides a clear summary of the dimensions of a 1600-megawatt electric coal-fired power plant (Minnesota Environmental Quality Board, April 1978). Understanding of functions and potential impacts is also aided by graphic presentation methods. These will be discussed in the next section.

The following outline for a project definition appears

TABLE 5-1 Application of a project definition format to a coal-fired power plant. This table illustrates the type of information required to complete the first major items of project definition.

Facility Type, Size, and Site Requirements

1 Type, Area, and Bulk of Main Structures

Type - 1,000-MWe pulverized coal, direct-fired power plant.
Area - 2 sq. mi. without buffer
     5 sq. mi. with buffer.
Bulk of main structures
- Approximately 200 acres.
Components - see Table 5-2.

2 Topographic Requirements

Less than 10% slope
Outside flood area
Outside active fault zones
Outside volcanic areas
Outside liquefaction or subsidence zones
Outside active seismic zones

Process Description

1 Raw-Material Requirements

Cooling Water - (closed-cycle):
- Agricultural wastewater
- Municipal wastewater
- Brackish groundwater
Acre-feet per year or ±20,000 gallons per minute

Cooling Water (once-through):
- Ocean water
1 million acre-feet per year service (fresh) water

2 Waste Products

Bottom ash
Hopper ash
Fly ash
Sludge (SO_2)
Flue gases
Thermal wastes

Coal: 2.3 to 3.4 million tons per year

Fuel oil: Variable

Power: 10% of 1,000 MW (100 MW)

3 End Products

4 Technology

Locational Requirements

1 Market or Load Center

As close as possible.

2 Fuel or Raw-Materials Source

Must be accessible by rail or sea.
For rail access: Grades of less than 1%
For sea access: Must be coastal site.

3 Transportation Facilities

Road - Variable, depending on
     total project cost
Rail - Variable, depending on
     total project cost

4 Transmission Facilities

Supply: Link to transmission corridor of 115 kV or greater distribution.

5 Water Sources

Cooling Water
- Agricultural, municipal wastewater, or brackish groundwater
- Or ocean water
- Or fresh water

Fresh Water
- Any source of fresh water, i.e., city or county supply, well, etc.

Waste Disposal:
- Landfill and/or evaporation ponds
- Or ocean (for thermal waste) and above

6 Labor Force

Size
- 1,000 workers during peak construction phase
- 200 permanent workers

Skill

Unionization

TABLE 5-2 System and component option identification for a 1000-megawatt electric coal-fired power plant. In some cases, the facility type (the first major item in project definition) may require extensive description.

I **Type**
Pulverized coal direct-fired
A Fluidized Bed Combustion or
B Coal Gasification Combined Cycle or
C Coal Liquefaction or
D Cyclone Furnace-Fired

II **Handling and Storage System**   Area: 200 acres
A Terminal (unloading facilities)
   1 Unit train (20 cars) (1 per day)
      a gondola cars
      b hopper cars or
   2 Barge/ship and harbor or
   3 Truck or
   4 Slurry pipeline or
   5 Train/barge combination

B Coal Storage (pile)
   (Note: Base of pile may have to be lined with
          concrete or other material depending on
          soil conditions and to prevent contami-
          nation of groundwater.)
   1 Active storage (3-day supply) and
   2 Short-term reserve (30-day supply) and
   3 Long-term reserve (90-day supply)   Area: 20 acres
      a conical storage or
      b low-profile storage
      (Note: Coal is compacted to reduce amount
             of oxygen thus reducing fire hazard
             from spontaneous combustion.)

C Stockout and Reclaim System (coal feed)
   "stockout" - incoming coal to active pile
   "reclaim" - coal from storage and active piles
   to crusher
   1 Conveyors (most common) or
   2 Ground storage with gravity feed or
   3 Ground storage with mechanical feed or
   4 Vertical storage with gravity feed

D Coal Preparation
   1 Coal crusher (sized for 500-1000 tons/day
      depending on quality, i.e., Btu's, of coal) and
   2 Site (stores surge) and
   3 Pulverizer   Waste: pulverizer rejects

E Fuel Oil
   for starter fuel and back-up fuel

III Power Block (Steam generation)
1 Boiler (steam generator) and
2 Generator and
3 Condenser and
4 Heaters and
5 Deaerator and
6 Pumps

Area: 80 acres
Waste: bottom ash, hopper ash,
fly ash, sludge, flue gases,
thermal

IV Waste Handling System
1 Bottom and hopper ash
slurry removal iron boiler to evaporation pond
(water reused)
2 Particulate removal system (fly ash)
a electrostatic precipitators
b fabric filters
slurry removal to evaporation pond (same pond
as for bottom ash) or dry removal to landfill or
sale for use in some concrete mixes
3 SO_2 removal system (sludge)
a scrubber (limestone added to precipitate out
SO_2)
b various (other techniques exist but scrubber
is most common)
4 Stack (flue gases and thermal waste)

Area: 320 acres

V Cooling Water System
1 Cooling tower
a wet or
b dry or
c wet/dry or
2 Cooling lake or canal or
3 Ocean and
4 Make-up water (treated water)
(15,000 - 25,000 Ar/yr. for closed cycle)
(1,050,000 Ar/yr. for once-through cooling) and
5 Condenser and
6 Blow-down
a evaporation pond (reuse water) or
b ocean

Area: varies--see below
Area: 40 acres

Area: 600 acres
Area: ---------

Waste: dissolved solids (TDS)

VI Transmission System
1 Transformers
2 Switch yard
3 Transmission distribution

Area: 40 acres

TABLE 5-3   Tabular summary of project dimensions for a 1600-megawatt electric two-unit coal-fired power plant. Tables often offer the most appropriate format for communicating project definition information.

	HEIGHT ELEMENT	LENGTH IN FEET	BREADTH IN FEET	AREA IN IN FEET	ACRES	COMMENTS
1	Total site (including fuel and water storage and waste disposal)	-	8300'	8300'	1600-2400	Two-unit plant assumed, but 3-unit fuel plants of this capacity may be used.
2	Rail terminal facilities	20' max. to top of loaded car from road-bed	-	-	-	Typically a spur line with a loop at the plant site. Extensive railyards may be required.
3	Coal storage	40'	1700'	1700'	65 acres	-
4	Coal-handling equipment	60'	-	-	-	-
5	Coal preparation building	100'	70'	70'	-	A coal conveyor, a smaller version of element 6; rises at about 15 degrees to near the top of the building. One coal preparation building is assumed to serve the two units.
6	Coal conveyor	220'	600'	-	-	One conveyor is assumed to serve the 2 units; rises at about 15 degrees to near the top of the building. One coal preparation building is assumed to serve the two units.
7	Boiler building	250'	650'	150'	-	-
8	Turbine building	125'	850'	110'	-	-
9	Precipitators	65'	200'	-	-	Located between boiler building and base of stack, 1 or 2 per stack.
10	Stacks	650'	-	-	-	One stack per unit is assumed, but one stack may also serve 2 units. Assumed height in Minnesota. Taper from base at 2-3 degrees.
11	Stack plumes	450'-1500' from top of stack to centerline of plume	Widely variable	-	-	The slower the wind speed, the higher plume may rise within this range. Plumes may tend to be more noticeable in optimum recreation weather, i.e., with little overcast.
12	Cooling towers	50'	1800'	45'	-	Mechanical draft type with 64 cells assumed.
13	Cooling tower plume	To 200' above	Widely variable	-	-	Present mostly in winter, i.e., at ground level, time of low river recreational use.
14	Switchyard	80'	550'	550'	7 acres	-
15	Transmission system	80'-160' towers	-	-	-	Three or more sets of towers are probable, each carrying 1 or 2 circuits from 161 to 500 kV. Taller towers required at wide river crossings. See general notes or Transmission System sizes and area requirements.
16	Ash storage	40'	6000'	6000'	800 acres	Acreage covered over the 30-year life of the plant. Sulfur dioxide removal sludge ponds may also be necessary.

LEGEND - Not applicable or information not available.

	Voltage — kV			
	115-138	**161-230**	**345**	**500**
Spacing between cable terminations	6 ft.			25 ft.
Termination areas				
Single circuit terminations in existing substations	500 sq. ft.			8000 sq. ft.
Double circuit terminations in existing substations	1200 sq. ft.			18000 sq. ft.
Single circuit transition station	5000 sq. ft.			40000 sq. ft.
Double circuit transition station	10000 sq. ft.			80000 sq. ft.

FIGURE 5-2 Termination of a double-circuit 345-kilovolt gas dielectric system and typical spacing and area requirements relative to system voltage.

Reactor Station Area*	Voltage in kV		
	161-230	**345**	**500**
Single current reactors in existing substations or termination stations	1000-2000 sq. ft.		6000-8000 sq. ft.
Double circuit reactors in existing substations or termination stations	2000-4000 sq. ft.		12,000-16,000 sq. ft.
Single circuit reactor station	1 acre min.		2 acres min.
Double circuit reactor station	2 acres min.		4 acres min.

*Including cable terminations and other related high voltage equipment.

FIGURE 5-3 Reactors under construction for a 230-kilovolt single-circuit system and space requirements relative to system voltage.

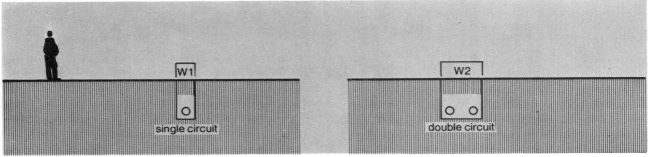

- HPOF pipe-type underground installations

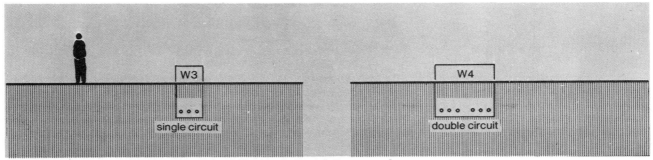

- Extruded dielectric and LPOF self-contained direct buried installations

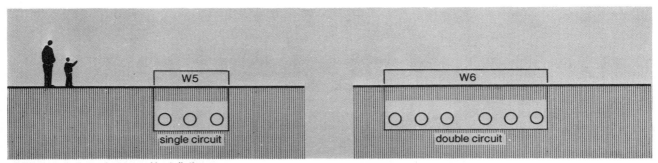

- Gas dielectric underground installations

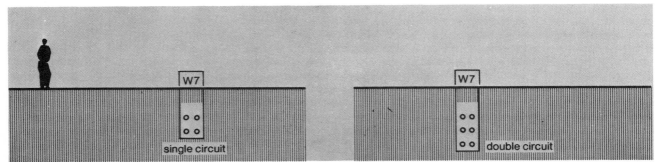

- Extruded dielectric and LPOF self-contained duct installations

FIGURE 5-4   Typical trench cross sections and dimensions of all cable systems, both single- and double-circuit.

52

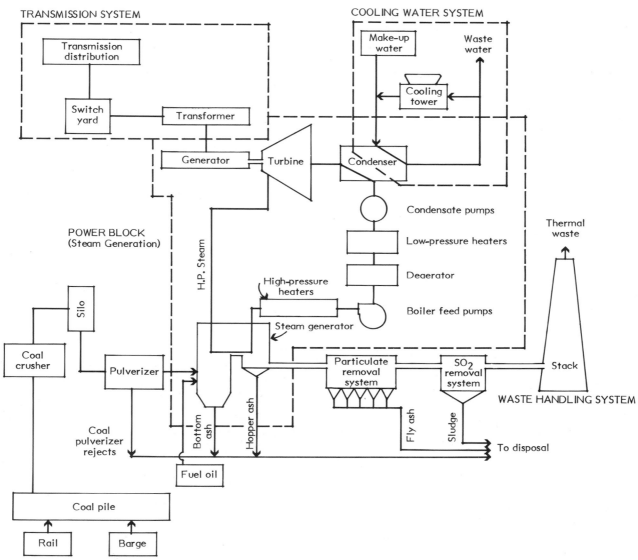

TRANSMISSION SYSTEM

COOLING WATER SYSTEM

POWER BLOCK
(Steam Generation)

WASTE HANDLING SYSTEM

FUEL & TRANSPORT HANDLING SYSTEM

FIGURE 5-5 Typical fossil-fuel plant system diagram.

to provide a contrasting format, and yet, when relevant, it covers the same basic subjects. It is included to emphasize the fact that each type of facility has unique kinds of components. In this case, the project definition was undertaken for the purpose of locating a state college. An extensive theoretical model that fitted into the statewide university system was developed with the following components:

1 *Area requirements.* Need for core area, housing, parking, athletics, research, expansion, open space, and reserve.

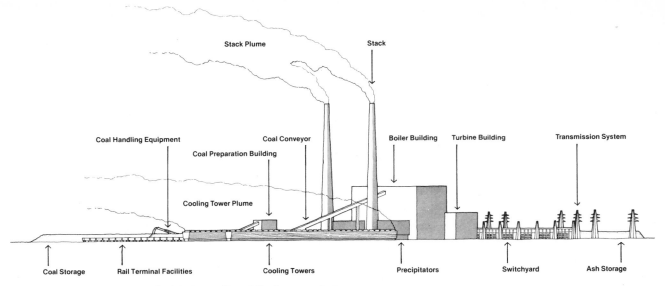

FIGURE 5-6   1600-megawatt electric two-unit coal-fired power plant.

.5 mile

1 mile

3 miles

4 miles

FIGURE 5-7   1360-megawatt electric two-unit coal-fired power plant: views from varying distances.

54

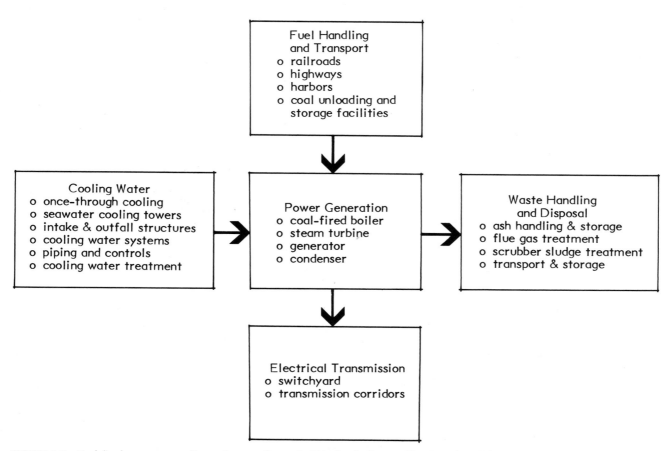

FIGURE 5-8 Coal-fired power generation system requirements. This simple diagram illustrates the relationships between power generation on-site and off-site requirements (water and fuel supply, waste disposal, and power transmission).

2 *Physical site characteristics.* Desirable slope, physiography, hydrology, soils, climate, and environmental quality.

3 *Population characteristics of students, faculty, and staff.* Current place of residence, marital status, and household size.

4 *Residential location.* On campus, off campus, within walking distance, and within commuting distance.

5 *Utilities and services.* Water, gas, electricity, sewage, storm water, fire protection, security services, and off-site and on-site costs.

6 *Accessibility.* Street and freeway access, traffic generation, public transportation, and population served.

A series of ten tables making projections in periods of years and/or by student population was developed. Some of these, such as the projections of student body and faculty size and facility requirements, were made for the

purpose of understanding the college itself. Others served the purpose of analyzing college-community relationships in such terms as housing needs, land use, and final impact.

GRAPHIC PRESENTATION METHODS

The project definition can be presented in a variety of forms. In addition to written statements, statistical tables, and lists of components, mathematical models, matrices, and diagrams or other graphic methods may be needed. Written and tabular information is essential, but graphic presentations can also explain systems, functions, and structures that otherwise can only be imagined.

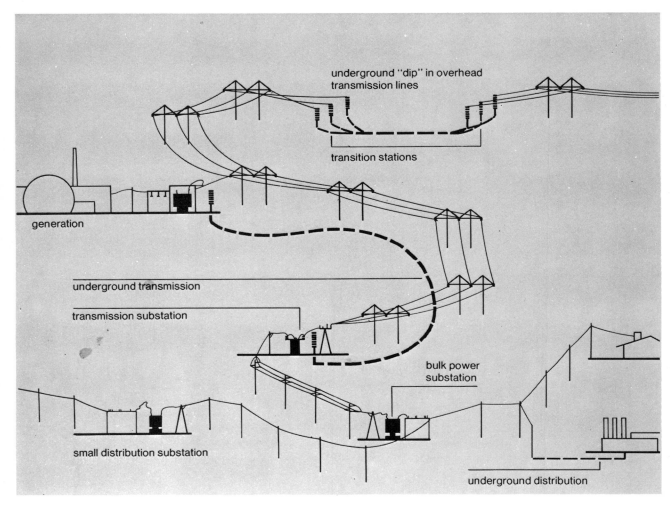

FIGURE 5-9 Typical applications of alternating-current underground transmission systems.

The basic components of a system can be illustrated by diagrams and perhaps by photographs of existing examples. Figures 5-2 and 5-3 show how much more understandable the space requirements of underground cable system components can be when presented in photographs as well as in tables. The implications of cable system choice for space requirements and certain construction impacts are made clear in Figure 5-4.

The relationships between system components can similarly be communicated effectively by diagrams. Figure 5-5 provides a flow diagram to accompany a coal-fired power plant process description. The diagram is made even more understandable by the drawing in Figure 5-6. Finally, a photograph of existing facilities (Figure 5-7) makes a proposal more tangible, particularly for lay participants in the siting process.

Graphic methods also help siting study participants understand the relationship of a project to off-site conditions. A diagram such as the very simple one in Figure 5-8 can enhance understanding of locational requirements by modeling the flow of supplies and products to and from a facility. The more graphic representation of electrical generating and transmission systems in Figure 5-9 shows how the relationship of the components of a linear system to its surroundings can be illustrated.

Once the site-evaluation phase of a siting study has been reached, idealized conceptual site plans and architectural models are useful for certain purposes. They can indicate the ideal building area, arrangement of structures and functions, buffer areas, and relationship to off-site facilities and communities. Models and plans or perspective drawings, even though in most cases they cannot be site-specific, assist in making judgments about relative visual impacts on candidate sites. We will have more to say on the use of drawings and models in Chapter 8.

In Chapter 6 we will look at how the components of the project definition are examined in light of the environmental conditions and standards that may be encountered.

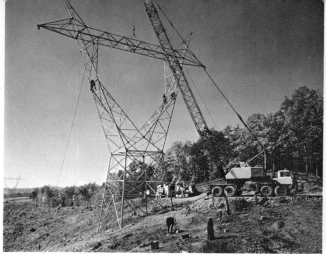

6 | PROJECT-ENVIRONMENTAL RELATIONSHIPS

PURPOSE

The fundamental objective of the site-selection process is to find a site that offers maximum environmental benefits and minimum adverse environmental impacts. This third phase of the process completes the framework for achieving this objective in the site-screening and site-evaluation phases.

Figure 3-1 showed that the identification of project-environmental relationships is based on the previously established project goals and preliminary objectives and begins as soon as the project has been sufficiently well defined to permit consideration of its demands and potential effects on the environment.

Although it is not possible to consider actual environmental conditions until candidate sites have been selected, this step moves beyond the hypothetical or idealized environment that was the context for the preliminary determination of project and environmental objectives. The examination of potential interactions between the project and the environment permits the important areas of concern to be identified. It is toward these areas of concern, which we term *factors,* that most of the work of data collection and analysis will be directed in the site-screening and site-evaluation phases.

Project-environmental relationships can be seen from two viewpoints. The first, which we have discussed in the two preceding chapters, is primarily that of the project sponsor. It covers the size, terrain, and amenities of the desired site, its location relative to needed materials and intended markets, and the physical and socioeconomic conditions required for efficient construction and operation. The second, with which the public is mainly concerned, covers the potential effects of the proposed facility on the environment of the site and its surroundings. These include the primary effects of the project on physical and biological conditions, such as air and water quality, and on vegetation and wildlife. They also include the secondary effects of fuel source or waste disposal site de-

velopment, haul and power transmission routes, and induced growth in site and market areas.

Both viewpoints need to be considered in order to identify an appropriate list of site-selection factors, anticipating the questions that will be asked about actual sites. For example, public interests will ask, "Will the facility diminish or degrade the water supply of the area surrounding the site?" Conversely, the project sponsor will ask, "Is the local water supply adequate to meet the requirements of the facility?"

Each type of question requires a response, but the answer will rarely be a clear yes or no. It may be necessary to accept compromises or trade-offs. The examination of project-environmental relationships therefore has two purposes. The first permits the sponsor and the study team to refine and expand the siting and environmental objectives and modify the project definition, if necessary. The second is to determine the standards or criteria to be used in conjunction with each area of concern and in measuring achievement of objectives. For certain factors only subjective, relative, or highly site-specific standards will apply. These cases may be identified as issues to be resolved, usually with some form of public input, before the relative importance of the factors and appropriate criteria can be established.

In the remainder of this chapter, we will examine various approaches to environmental analysis and recommend a structure to aid in identifying and organizing project-environmental relationships for site selection. We will also discuss various types and sources of environmental standards that may be used in the refinement of siting and environmental objectives.

APPROACHES TO ENVIRONMENTAL ANALYSIS

A variety of approaches to the identification and organization of project-environmental relationships can be found in a review of major-facility siting documents and environmental impact literature. We will consider three typical approaches before discussing our preferred organization. Each of the three has relevant aspects, but none is directly applicable to the needs of most site-selection studies.

An example of the first type is provided by a study of the environmental impacts of underground electric power transmission systems (EDAW Inc., 1975a). This study, prepared for the Energy Research and Development Administration and the Electric Power Research Institute (EPRI), was developed as a general handbook for utility planners. The emphasis here is on the nature of transmission systems and their generic effect on a variety of typical but hypothetical environmental conditions. The study offers valuable organizational tools, to which we will return in a later section.

However, such handbooks must deal with a broad rather than a specific facility type and be set in an undefined area of search. They tend to be unnecessarily comprehensive and, at the same time, insufficiently detailed to be applied directly in a specific facility-siting study.

The second approach is that of the *master environmental assessment,* providing the framework for site searches for various facility types within a region. This is a relatively new concept which has been developed and employed mainly at the federal level (although local comprehensive land-use plans are required to contain environmental documentation and analysis of their effects).

An areawide environmental assessment primarily directed to wastewater treatment facilities planning in a region of southern California is an example of this approach, the first such study for the federal Environmental Protection Agency (EDAW Inc., 1979b). While the siting handbook deals with the effects of a facility type in hypothetical settings, the master environmental assessment emphasizes documentation of actual environmental conditions. This type of document, if it were available for all regions within the area of study, could in theory save substantially on the data collection and analysis effort involved in many types of siting study. However, different types of major facilities place unique as well as common demands on a region. It is therefore unlikely that all such demands can be anticipated in a master environmental document.

The third and to date the commonest approach has been to follow a checklist of all possible effects of a proposed project in a specific (and usually confined) location. This all-encompassing review of conditions and effects is characteristic of, and its widespread use derives

from, the requirements of the 1969 National Environmental Policy Act (NEPA) and subsequent legislation in certain states. Impact statement guidelines call for a project description and a description of existing environmental conditions in terms of the following conditions:

1 Physical and biological conditions
   · Hydrology
   · Geology and soils
   · Vegetation
   · Wildlife
   · Air quality
   · Water quality and supply
   · Noise
2 Social and economic conditions
   · Population and growth
   · Land use and transportation
   · Income and employment
   · Fiscal conditions
   · Visual quality
   · Cultural features
   · Energy consumption

The project description and the environmental description are then related in order to identify adverse effects of the project on the environment. There are dangers in the compilation of environmental concerns and conditions without constant reference to project definition. The headings are clearly unspecific and require both thorough and imaginative interpretation to ensure that no minor but significant subcategory is overlooked. Moreover, this lack of specificity and application of the checklist description to the nature of a proposed project may lead to unnecessary effort in researching and describing aspects of the environment on which the proposal may have no significant effect at all.

The latter shortcoming of the legislative requirements for environmental assessment has, at least at the federal level and in the state of California, led to their amendment. It is now possible, in a preliminary review or initial study of a proposed action, to identify those environmental elements that are unlikely to be significantly affected. Research and evaluation may thus be focused on those impacts of probable real or perceived significance. Publication of an initial study and the public dialogue now required in deciding the scope of the environmental study can confirm that all the probable significant impacts have been identified.

Another problem with the exhaustive checklist approach is that it is usually employed for impact evaluation after the fact. It thus provides few built-in opportunities for resolving potential conflicts between project siting requirements and environmental conditions during a siting study.

Perhaps ideally in organizing environmental studies for a siting program, all the technical and economic requirements of the proposed facility would be arrayed against the economic, social, and environmental conditions in every area under consideration. However, the data gathering, preparation of display matrices, and analysis involved would be very time-consuming and impractical.

A focus is clearly required to limit the scope of a siting study, at least initially, to what is strictly necessary for selection of candidate areas and candidate sites. In most siting studies, a focus is given by the siting requirements which limit the area of search. But the geographic extent may range from relatively small areas (a metropolitan area in proximity to a deepwater port, for example, or a stretch of river with potential dam sites) to whole states or even larger regions. Further, as we have indicated, there are cases in which the facility itself may not be

tightly defined, so that a wide range of potential project-environmental relationships may require consideration.

THE PREFERRED ORGANIZATION OF THE ENVIRONMENTAL STUDY

To avoid the problems of environmental analysis associated with a wide-ranging siting study, the preferred approach (laid out in Figure 6-1) is, like the initial study, selective. In keeping with the spirit of the entire site-selection process that we recommend, the approach is designed to permit as much narrowing of the scope of the site-screening inquiry as possible, while ensuring that no relevant consideration is overlooked.

The environmental study begins with review and further study of the characteristics and siting requirements of the proposed facility in the context of environmental conditions typical of the probable area of search. The first step is to distinguish the more important siting re-

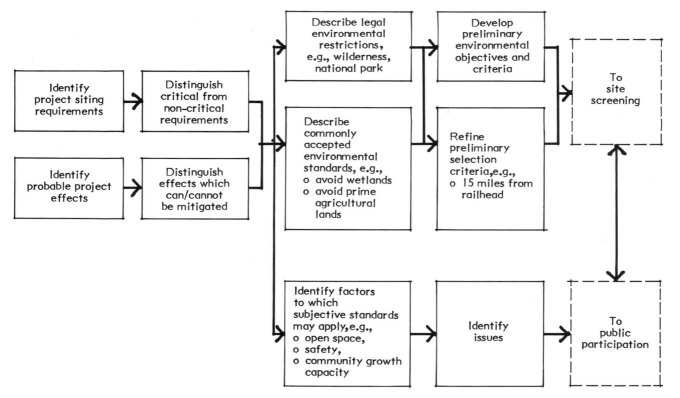

FIGURE 6-1 Project-environmental relationships.

quirements and potential environmental effects from those that are either less critical or relevant only in comparative evaluation of specific sites. The step involves consideration of measures that may be taken to mitigate undesirable effects and facility options that may allow some flexibility in siting requirements.

The next step is to identify all legal restrictions on siting the facility that may be encountered in the probable area of search and to research and describe commonly accepted standards for protecting environmental conditions from effects that cannot be mitigated.

These two steps result in a refinement of siting and environmental objectives, accompanied by standards or criteria by which to measure their achievement. They also allow a preliminary distinction to be made between environmental factors that are clearly unsuited to the facility and those whose intrinsic importance and local significance require further study. These so-called exclusion and evaluation factors are examined again, this time by citizen participants as well as by the study team, early in the site-screening phase (described in Chapter 7). Evaluation factors may be refined yet again in the site-evaluation phase (described in Chapter 8). However, the work of the site-screening and site-evaluation study participants in prioritizing, weighting, and using siting factors in data collection and analysis is greatly facilitated by careful and well-organized products of the project-environmental relationship study.

In addition to promoting selectivity among the myriad environmental conditions that could be studied, the approach we present has other valuable attributes. First, by identifying fixed project requirements and critical environmental restrictions, the approach ensures identification of an appropriate area of search and early exclusion of areas that are clearly unsuitable from the viewpoint of the public as well as the sponsor. Second, by examining the effect of project characteristics both in terms of their capacity for mitigation and in terms of relevant standards at the same time, the analysis results in a set of objectives and criteria that are as compatible and consistent as possible.

These attributes set the approach apart from many typical siting studies and impact analyses in which there is no early integration of project requirements and environmental considerations. In such cases, project proponents and analysts must frequently grapple with conflicting objectives from start to finish. At best, the conclusions are based on considerable subjective judgment as to whether a site offers the best possible fit between project and environmental objectives.

Application of the recommended approach requires a working understanding of several influential subjects related to environmental, economic, and technical features and effects of the facility. This is true despite the fact that we are dealing at this point with "typical" and "most critical" project-environmental relationships rather than with all of them. No list of siting factors needs to be, or is ever likely to be, complete. Nevertheless, it is desirable at the outset to consider potential areas of concern as comprehensively as possible. This lessens the likelihood of overlooking a critical factor.

The structure within which the analysis of project-environmental relationships and their potential significance is organized should offer:

· The ability to select and expand on critical relationships

· A clear link from a specific project characteristic or activity to the probable effects on conditions in typical or specific environmental settings, so that site or project modifications can be identified

· An identification of both direct impacts and the chain of indirect impacts of any aspect of the facility

· An identification of the probable area, duration, and magnitude of environmental impacts

· Any applicable standards for measurement of each impact

In the next two sections we will discuss the types and sources of information on siting requirements and environmental effects and formats for displaying relationships.

IDENTIFICATION OF SITING REQUIREMENTS

From the review of the project definition in the first task shown in Figure 6-1, typical siting requirements might include some or all of the following:

· Access to appropriate transportation facilities

· Availability of water of appropriate quality and quantity within a specified maximum distance of a selected market or load center

· Appropriate terrain and geology

· Available undeveloped land

· Access to power sources

· Availability of construction materials

· Freedom from seismic or flood hazard

· Location close to (or remote from) population centers

· Available waste disposal sites

· Availability of an appropriate construction and operating labor force

· Appropriate air quality for facility operation

An ideal siting process would identify sites that satisfy all these requirements and also avoid undesirable effects on the physical and biological environment and on the communities and individuals in the area of each site. This is rarely, if ever, possible. Selection of candidate sites that come close to the ideal demands some flexibility in the facility's design and siting requirements. It may be necessary to adapt the facility to fit the environmental conditions of sites that can provide the majority, but not all, of the requirements. Thus it is essential to identify the requirements that are critical to the functional and financial success of the facility.

Some of the critical siting requirements may be of sufficient importance to justify consideration or exclusion of certain areas regardless of environmental impact considerations. These should be distinguished from other more flexible requirements. For example, terrain with a slope of less than 10 percent and an access route with a grade of less than 1 percent along which to construct a spur to the railhead might be indispensable. A distance of less than 5 miles to the railhead might be desirable, but it could be extended if necessary and therefore would not be an absolute requirement. In this case, if access and other site-dependent costs were critical components of overall project costs, it would be appropriate to set an outside limit on distance to existing rail facilities.

Every effort should also be made to develop project options that can help to reduce potential impacts. The site-selection process can then focus on those effects of construction and operation which cannot be mitigated but which may be more severe in some environmental contexts than in others.

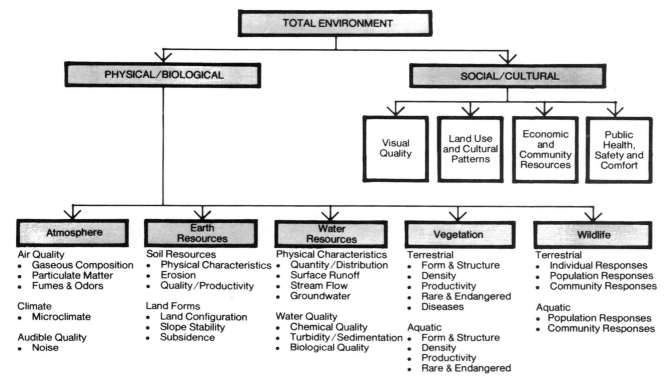

FIGURE 6-2 Physical-biological environmental structure. Environmental conditions required by or potentially affected by a major facility need to be structured to achieve comprehensive consideration of all relevant conditions and to avoid duplication.

IDENTIFICATION OF EFFECTS

Sources of Information

The sources of information for identifying probable effects of a proposed facility include:

· The project definition

· Examination of the history of similar facilities and documentation of siting studies

· The professional judgment and knowledge of the site-selection team

· Regulations and guidelines of agencies with jurisdiction over facility siting

· Regulations and guidelines of agencies with jurisdiction over environmental protection and planning

The project definition provides the framework for identifying the kinds of environmental factors to be considered. Potential impact relationships may be anticipated either from general and professional knowledge and experience or by examining the site-selection history of similar facility-siting projects. Other clear instructions are provided by the regulations, guidelines, and siting and operating objectives of agencies with jurisdiction over facility siting or over environmental protection and planning.

Such regulations may provide qualitative or quantitative standards by which the fit between project and environmental characteristics can be measured. In other cases, commonly accepted standards may be derived from literature or experience. In yet others, both the desirability of considering a factor and the standards by which its impacts should be evaluated may become issues to be resolved through broader and sometimes public examination. We will return to the subject of environmental standards in a later section.

Format for Identification and Analysis of Effects

To achieve the previously stated objectives of analysis, comprehensiveness, and selectivity, effects should be or-

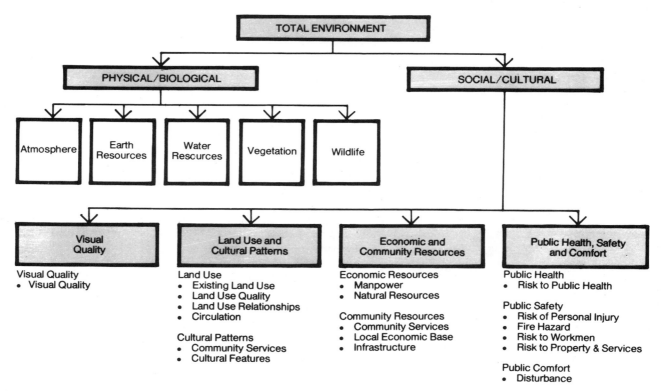

FIGURE 6-3 Social-cultural environment structure. This figure and Figure 6-2 illustrate a typical organization of environmental conditions. Each major category is capable of combination with others or of expansion through the addition of new categories or subcategories.

ganized under broad environmental condition categories. Figures 6-2 and 6-3 illustrate a typical array of environmental conditions developed for the EPRI study of environmental impacts of underground power transmission systems to which we referred earlier in this chapter.

Any category may be combined with others if it is believed to be of limited significance. Categories may also be expanded with subcategories as necessary during site screening or site evaluation.

It is helpful to list the components and activities iden-

Typical Construction Activities Required for Facilities	Urban-Suburban-Rural Street or Road				Suburban-Rural Off-Road				River Crossings	
	Transition, Reactor, Pressurizing and Cooling Stations	Manholes	Cable Systems	Access Roads	Transition, Reactor, Pressurizing and Cooling Stations	Manholes	Cable Systems (buried)	Cable Systems (surface)	Cable Systems (underwater)	Access Roads, Manholes and Stations
Site Preparation										
Survey	●	●	●	●	●	●	●	●	●	
Notification				●	●	●	●	●	●	
Relocation of Existing Improvements	○	○	○							
Field Office and Storage Yard	●	●	●		●	●	●	●	●	
General Activities										
Construction Equipment Operation	●	●	●	●	●	●	●	●	●	
Materials Delivery and Handling	●	●	●	●	●	●	●	●	●	
Labor Force	●	●	●	●	●	●	●	●	●	
Disposal of Wastes	●	●	●	●	●	●	●	●	●	
Clearing										
Structural Demolition	○									
Vegetation Removal	○			●	●	●	●	●	●	
Disposal of Vegetation	○			●	●	●	●	●	●	
Earth Work										
Pavement Breaking		●	●							
Surface Grading	○			●	●	●	●	●		
Excavation and Shoring		●	●			●	●			
Rock Fracturing	○	○	○	○	○	○	○		○	
Dewatering		○	○			○	○		○	
Excavation by Boring, Jacking or Tunneling			○				○		○	
Cut-and-Cover									○	
Jetting									○	
Installation	●	●	●	●	●	●	●	●	●	
Backfill and Restoration	●	●	●	●	●	●	●	●	●	

LEGEND
● Usually Required
○ Occasionally Required
☐ Seldom Required

Column "Access Roads, Manholes and Stations" (River Crossings): Same as off-road or streets depending on location of crossing

FIGURE 6-4 Example of a facilities construction activities matrix for underground power transmission systems.

tified in the project description and each environmental condition or attribute of a condition potentially affected. It is possible to construct matrices or tables on which to record the probability that the facility or aspects of it will have significant effects on given environmental conditions.

It will be recalled that in Chapter 5 we recommended use of the following project definition format, also taken from the EPRI underground transmission systems study, for purposes of identifying impacts:

· Physical description and presence of the facility and its components

· Preconstruction planning (including exploratory surveys and methods of acquiring rights-of-way and easements on sites)

· Construction (including site preparation, clearing, earthwork, installation, and site restoration)

· Operation and maintenance (including energy transmission, right-of-way maintenance, and system maintenance and repair)

At the time when the EPRI handbook was prepared, experience with underground electric power transmission was relatively limited. A variety of underground and aboveground energy facilities was studied in conjunction with the technical definition of each type of cable system to provide an indication of probable project-environmental relationships.

Figure 6-4 takes one category of activities, in this case construction, and indicates the frequency with which each activity occurs in the three typical environmental settings examined in the study. Various other settings could be substituted for or added to the street, off-road, and river-crossing situations. The relevant settings would depend upon the siting requirements and characteristics of the probable area of search for a given facility. This is the closest that one can come to determining the magnitude of an activity's effects until actual sites are considered.

Figure 6-5 takes the construction activities required for installation of a cable system across a river and identifies the conditions impacted and the type, duration, and area of impact.

It should be recognized that Figures 6-4 and 6-5 are included merely to suggest a process of thought and a format for organizing information. In terms of content, as we saw when we discussed the generic handbook approach to impact assessment, the figures cover a larger number of potential impacts in less detail than would be necessary in an actual siting study.

The next step in the thought process is to consider the chain of effects that each direct impact may have on other conditions. These are suggested in generic terms in Figure 6-6. Most environmental impact analyses include discussion of indirect or secondary impacts. Recognition of all but the most obvious is difficult without an orderly assessment structure. In Figure 6-7, the direct impacts of all activity categories on a single environmental condition, earth resources, are presented in an impact matrix. The matrix permits linkages with other environmental conditions in the form of indirect sources and indirect impacts to be recorded, as explained in Figure 6-8.

The impact matrix can be used in a simpler manner for initial identification of project-environmental relationships, as Figure 6-9 indicates. Here, the typical effects of the most significant features of a fossil-fueled power plant are related to ten broad environmental conditions (or impact variables). The matrix takes information from the project definition, generally following the organization described in Chapter 5. In many cases the potential impacts are expressed in ranges or are related to optional facility components. Both broad-scale and small-scale effects are apparent in the matrix, providing guidance to identification of factors for exclusion or evaluation. The matrix also provides an indication of the needed environmental data and relative degrees of detail. This level of analysis is generally adequate for site screening.

A similar approach has value in site evaluation. The categories need to become more detailed, using an organization that permits impact linkages to be displayed. However, several categories may be dropped at this point. For example, there is no need to deal with effects on aquatic wildlife if the candidate sites contain no rivers or lakes. From the opposite viewpoint, no consideration need be given to effects of a once-through cooling system on ocean water if closed-cycle cooling is selected.

As with the identification of siting requirements, it is essential in identifying potential effects of the facility to distinguish between those that are intrinsic to a given technical characteristic or component and those whose significance varies with environmental conditions. For example, varying levels of water consumption are associated with particular power plant capacities and cooling technologies.

Figure 6-10, taken from a site-screening manual prepared by EDAW for the California Energy Resources Conservation and Development Commission (1977), indicates that there is a 900 percent difference in annual water demand depending on whether the plant is nuclear or fossil-fueled, is in the 1000- or 4000-megawatt range, and has wet cooling towers or a cooling pond. The type

ACTIVITY		ENVIRONMENTAL CONCERNS				
PHASE	ACTIVITY	CONDITIONS POTENTIALLY IMPACTED	TYPE OF IMPACT	DURATION OF IMPACT SHORT TERM	LONG TERM	AREA OF INFLUENCE
4.5 CONSTRUCTION AT RIVER CROSSINGS						
4.5.1 General Activities	Refer to 4.3.1 General Activities of Construction in Streets					
4.5.2 Site Preparation	Refer to 4.3.2 Site Preparation of Construction in Streets					
4.5.3 Clearing	Refer to 4.4.3 Clearing of Construction in Off-Roads					
4.5.4 Earth Work	Cut-and-Cover	Water Resources	Changes in physical characteristics and quality	X		Immediate area and downstream
		Vegetation	Changes in aquatic vegetation		X	Immediate area and downstream
		Wildlife	Disturbance and loss of aquatic wildlife	X		Immediate area and downstream (larger when blasting)
		Public Health, Safety and Comfort	Risk of injury to workers working below grade	X		Immediate area
		Land Use	Change river's value as a recreational resource	X		Immediate area and downstream
		Atmosphere	Particulate matter	X		Immediate area and downwind
	Wading	Vegetation	Loss of aquatic vegetation	X		Immediate area and downstream
		Wildlife	Disruption of aquatic habitat	X		Immediate area and downstream
	Coffer Dams	Water Resources	Change in stream flow and turbidity	X		Immediate area and downstream
		Vegetation	Changes in aquatic vegetation	X		Immediate area and downstream
		Wildlife	Disturbance and loss of aquatic wildlife	X		Immediate area and downstream
		Visual Quality	Visibility of construction	X		Viewshed
	Barge or Shoreline	Water Resources	Water quality change by increased turbidity	X		Immediate area and downstream
		Vegetation	Changes in aquatic vegetation	X		Immediate area and downstream
		Wildlife	Disturbance and loss of aquatic wildlife	X		Immediate area and downstream
		Land Use	Change in land use quality as recreation resource	X		Immediate area and downstream
	Jetting	Water Resources	Changes in water quality and physical characteristics	X		Immediate area and downstream
		Land Use	Change river's value as a recreational resource	X		Immediate area and downstream
		Vegetation	Changes in aquatic vegetation	X		Immediate area and downstream
		Wildlife	Disturbance and loss of aquatic wildlife	X		Immediate area and downstream
	Boring and Tunneling	Public Health, Safety and Comfort	Risk to workers working below surface	X		Immediate area
		Water Resources	Alteration of groundwater	X		Immediate area
4.5.5 Installation	Refer to 4.3.5 Installation of Construction in Streets					
4.5.6 Restoration and Backfill	Refer to 4.3.6 Restoration and Backfill in Streets	Water Resources	Changes in water quality and physical characteristics	X		Immediate area and downstream
		Visual Quality	Benefits of clean up and landscaping		X	Viewshed
		Vegetation	Plants introduced during landscaping		X	Immediate area

FIGURE 6-5 Example of an activity–environmental concern matrix applied to typical underground electric power transmission system construction methods at river crossings.

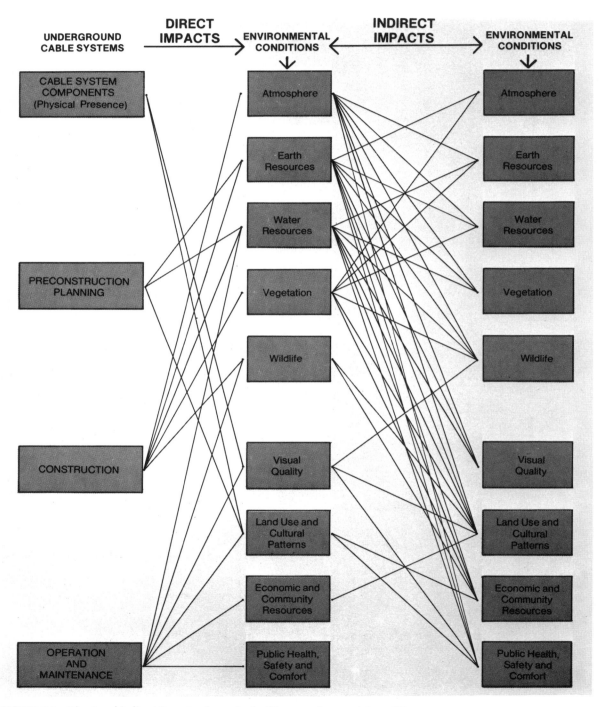

FIGURE 6-6 Direct and indirect impacts of a major facility on environmental conditions.

FIGURE 6-7 Sample impact matrix.

Direct Impacts

Impact Sources	TERRESTRIAL						AQUATIC			
	Form and structure	Species composition	Density	Productivity	Rare and endangered	Diseases	Structure and form	Density	Productivity	Rare and endangered
CABLE SYSTEM COMPONENTS (Physical Presence)										
Cables, buried or ducts			○	○						
Cables, surface		○	○							
Termination stations - new (HVAC)		○								
Manholes										
Reactor stations - new (HVAC)		○	○							
Terminal stations (HVDC)		○								
Grounding electrodes (HVDC)										
Access roads										
CONSTRUCTION										
Site preparation - field office and storage yard	●	●	●	●	△					
General construction - equipment operation	●	●	●	●	△					
Clearing - vegetation removal			△	●	△	●	●	●	●	△
Clearing - disposal of vegetation - piling and windrowing	●	●	●	●	●					
Clearing - disposal of vegetation - burning	●	●	●	●	△	●				
Clearing - disposal of vegetation - chipping	●	●	●	●						
Earth work - surface grading	●	●	●	△	△					
Earth work - cut-and-cover excavation and shoring	●	●								
Earth work - dewatering	●		●							
Earth work - river crossings - wading										
Earth work - river crossings - cofferdams							●	●	●	△
Earth work - river crossings - barge or shoreline							●	●	●	△
Earth work - river crossings - jetting							●	●	●	△
Backfill and restoration	●	●	●	●	△	△				
OPERATION AND MAINTENANCE										
Cable operation - thermal gradients (HVAC and HVDC)	●	●	●		△					
Off-road maintenance - vegetation control - herbicides					△	●				
Off-road maintenance - vegetation control - mechanical					△	●				
Off-road maintenance - natural	△	△	△	△	△					
Off-road maintenance - multiple uses of right-of-way	△	△	△	△	△	●				
Failure - consequences	●	●	●				●	●	●	●
Repair - correction of damage	△	△	△	△	△	△	●	●	●	△
CHANGES IN OTHER ENVIRONMENTAL CONDITIONS (Indirect Sources)										
Atmosphere - air quality - gaseous composition					△✱	△✱				
Atmosphere - climate - microclimate	△✱		△✱	△✱	△					
Earth resources - soils - physical characteristics	△		△	△	△	△				
Earth resources - soils - erosion			△	△	△					
Earth resources - soils - quality/productivity	△	△	△	△						
Earth resources - land form - slope stability	△✱									
Earth resources - land form - subsidence	△✱									
Water resources - physical characteristics - quality/distribution	△	△								
Water resources - physical characteristics - surface runoff	△	△								
Water resources - physical characteristics - groundwater	△	△·								
Water resources - water quality - chemical quality							△	△		
Water resources - water quality - turbidity/sedimentation							△	△		
Water resources - water quality - biological quality							△	△		
Wildlife - terrestrial - population dynamics			△✱							
Wildlife - terrestrial - community dynamics			△✱							

Impact Legend

- ● Short-Term
- ○ Long-Term
- △ Either Short or Long or Both
- ◆ Accidental cause
- ✱ Low probability of occurrence

Indirect Impacts

		△✱				Gaseous composition	Air quality	ATMOSPHERE
		△				Microclimate	Climate	
△		△				Physical characteristics		
△		△				Erosion	Soils	EARTH RESOURCES
△		△				Quality - productivity		
		△✱	△✱			Quality - distribution	Physical characteristics	WATER RESOURCES
△	△	△				Surface runoff		
△	△	△				Population dynamics	Terrestrial	WILDLIFE
●	●	●				Community dynamics		
△	△	△	△	△	△	Visual quality		VISUAL QUALITY
		△✱				Community identity	Cultural	LAND USE AND
		△✱				Cultural features	patterns	CULTURAL PATTERNS

and size set for a proposed plant are thus critical factors in areas where water is a concern. The potential effect on water supply may be mitigated by use of optional cooling technology or reduction in plant size. However, even if the project can be scaled to meet such concerns, the vol-ume of water, as we saw in Tables 5-1 and 5-2 in the preceding chapter, will still show significant variations depending on the quality of water available in different locations.

The task of distinguishing effects that are capable of

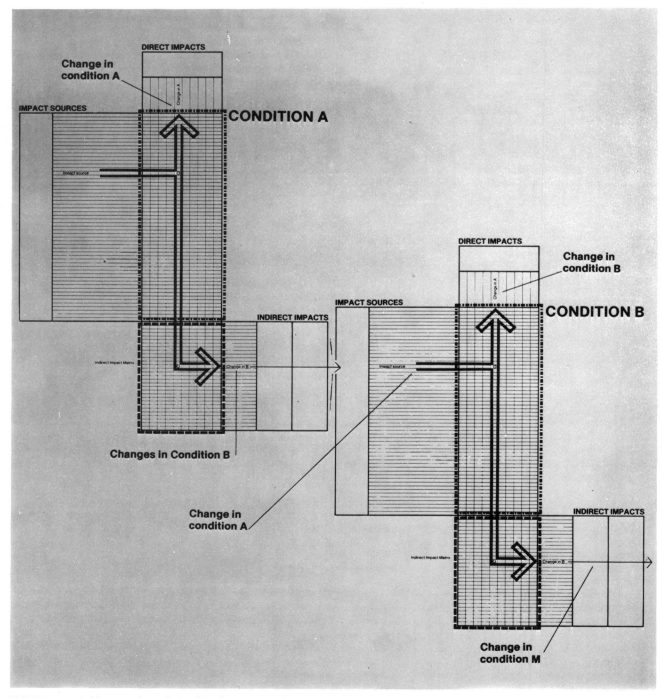

FIGURE 6-8   Guide to tracing relationships between condition-impact matrices.

mitigation clearly involves close coordination with the task of project definition and identification of siting requirements. In addition to facility modification, reduction of typical impact levels may be achieved through application of advanced (and often more costly) techniques of site preparation, construction, emission control or treatment, waste disposal, or noise reduction. To some extent, however, potential impacts may be mitigated or avoided entirely through the siting process itself. This may occur at the site-screening level through application of exclusion factors. Alternatively, in the case of features of smaller scale or lesser importance, it may be accomplished in the process of identifying candidate sites or actually laying out a site or precise route alignment.

REFINEMENT OF OBJECTIVES AND ENVIRONMENTAL CRITERIA

The examination of potential environmental effects and siting requirements may allow an expanded and refined list of objectives to be drawn up. Table 6-1, for example, is more thorough than the preliminary objectives of the same sponsor that were listed in Chapter 4 (Table 4-2). However, the objectives still lack qualitative and quantitative specificity.

The ability of candidate sites to meet technical siting objectives can be determined in most cases only by applying quantitative measures, such as degree of slope, miles to rail access, or water availability expressed in gallons per minute. These measures, which we have discussed in Chapter 5 and earlier in this chapter, are incorporated in the list of site-selection criteria and are restated as data factors, as shown in Table 7-1.

Similarly, the identification of environmental effects and the statement of environmental objectives are of little use in the siting process unless they are accompanied by more specific criteria. However, the determination of appropriate environmental criteria is often more complex than the quantification of siting requirements.

Environmental effects imply changes in environmental conditions either in kind or in degree. Conditions for which identification or measurement of change is not difficult and on which there is general agreement concerning the acceptability of various degrees of change allow clear-cut criteria to be developed.

The sources used in developing environmental criteria naturally include the project definition and the already identified project-environmental relationships. They also include various legal regulations and restrictions, govern-

ment policies for environmental protection, and a variety of values placed less officially on environmental conditions.

Legal regulations include the siting, impact prevention, or impact mitigation requirements of a number of federal, state, and sometimes regional agencies with which a facility must comply. These often result in absolute criteria for exclusion. For example, the regulations governing many types of public domain lands preclude construction of major facilities. To increase the acceptability of a proposed project, however, it may be thought advisable to establish around certain public lands a buffer zone of specified width which should also be avoided. Thus even clear-cut regulations may be subject to interpretation or more stringent expression in siting criteria.

There are other types of legal regulations that are considerably more difficult to apply to siting objectives. To qualify and quantify an objective stated as "Satisfy federal air quality regulations" requires familiarity with the complexities and frequent amendments of the Clean Air Act. Some criteria for avoidance may be identified first on the basis of well-defined standards. Certain areas are designated as *attainment or prevention of significant deterioration areas,* where ambient-air standards are attained and must not be allowed to "significantly deteriorate." These preclude additional stationary sources of air pollution.

Currently in the case of various types of nonattainment areas, reasonably available control measures are required for lowest achievable emissions, and emissions from a proposed project are permissible only if offset by extra controls or by shutdown of an existing source of the same pollutants. The project definition identifies the type, volume, and duration of gaseous and particulate emissions to be expected. But the data cannot be related to ambient-air quality in particular areas because candidate areas and sites have not yet been selected.

In this case, if we assume that the project definition already incorporates the best proven technology for emissions control, the criteria may allow for selection of areas which have achieved attainment for pollutants produced by the project in insignificant amounts but which offer offset potentials for others.

Before we proceed further, we should note that the term *standards* has been used earlier in the section and will be used again in the following sections. To avoid confusion, since the words *standards* and *criteria* are virtually synonymous in most contexts, we should define the manner in which they are used here. *Standards,* legal or otherwise, apply to protection of environmental quality in general or in particular locations but not to specific

Environmental Impact Variables

IMPACT SOURCES	VIEW	NOISE	HEALTH/SAFETY	SOCIOECONOMICS
Boiler stack, turbine/generator and other plant structures, including switchyards.	Stack 500-700 feet high; boiler 200+ feet high; buildings partially suitable for architectural treatment.	Stack fans may produce noticeable noise at site boundary.	Health hazards of stack emissions; monitored & controlled (see Air Quality).	Permanent staff of 60-120/1000MW.
Coal handling, coal storage, ash storage, scrubber, sludge storage.	Large areas.	2 unit trains/day/ 1000MW (1 full & 1 empty) create noise from mine to plant.	At-grade highway crossings hazards between mine & plant.	
Land acquisition & plant construction.				Tax base changes; possible long-term community changes.
Cooling water systems (alternatives).				
o Wet cooling towers (with storage reservoir if required).	o Mechanical draft 50-80 feet wide and several hundred feet long.	o Mechanical tower fan noise may carry beyond site boundary.	o Fogging and icing may affect nearby roads, airports, etc.	
	o Storage reservoir may be sizeable.		o Fogging and icing may affect nearby roads, airports, etc.	
o Cooling ponds (ponds serve as storage reservoir also).				
o Dry cooling towers.	o Roughly 50% larger cooling area required than for wet towers.	o Mechanical tower fan noise may carry beyond site boundary.		Capital and operating costs greater than wet cooling towers.
Transmission system.	o 1 or more transmission lines/1000MW.	o Higher voltages produce audible noise-especially during fog.	Some hazard to aircraft near airports or agricultural areas where aerial spraying is used.	Capital cost: $100,000 to $150,000 per mile of line.
	o Each transmission line has 4 to 6 towers per mile. Each tower 90 to 150 feet or more in height.	o Higher voltages produce radio and TV interference, especially in rural areas of low signal strength.		
	o Cleared rights-of-way visible.			
Pipeline (if required for supply of make-up water).	Pipeline underground but cleared right-of-way visible.			Capital cost: $500,000 to $1,000,000 per mile of pipeline.
Railroad (new) (if required for coal delivery or plant construction).	Excavated grade and cleared vegetation visible.	High noise levels from train operation.	At-grade highway crossings hazardous.	Capital cost: $200,000 to $300,000/mile.

FIGURE 6-9 Environmental impact matrix: physical presence and operation of impacts of coal power plants.

LAND USE	VEGETATION	WILDLIFE	WATER QUALITY	WATER QUANTITY	AIR QUALITY/CLIMATE
100-200 acres occupied/1000MW.	Clearing of areas occupied plus construction laydown. Vegetation effects in environs from stack emissions- some species particularly sensitive to SO_2.	Habitat loss in cleared areas. Physical presence may disturb some species in environs.	Make-up water required for plant systems (minor relative to cooling system requirements).	Treated sewage effluent.	12,000 lb/hr/1000MW SO_2; 720 lb/hr/1000MW particulates, also NO_x, CO, trace elements, water vapor.
o 20 to 50 acres/ 1000MW for handling & storage; storage 40 feet deep. o 50 to 100 acres/ 1000MW for ash & sludge storage.	Clearing of areas occupied.	Habitat loss in cleared areas. Physical presence may disturb some species in environs.		Surface drainage must be controlled to protect quality of surface and ground-water supply.	Based on NSP Sherco-Sibco Application November 1, 1974.
Change to power generation; some lease-back of exclusion areas for other uses.	Removal of all vegetation in area of plant structures.	Displacement or loss of all species in area of plant structures.			
o 10 to 50 acres occupied/1000MW plus storage reservoir which may be up to several thousand acres. o 1500 to 2000 acres (nuclear) occupied/1000MW. o 1000 to 1500 acres (fossil) occupied/ 1000MW.	Reservoir must be cleared. Aquatic species may populate reservoir.	Reservoir may provide new habitat. Intake of make-up water will entrain & destroy drifting organisms of intake screens.	Make-up water of 25,000 (nuclear)& 15,000 (fossil)acre-feet per year/ 1000MW consumed by evaporation.	Blowdown contains concentrated (3-10 times) substances originally in make-up water plus chemicals (chlorine & others added by plant).	Fogging and minor increases in temperature and humidity.
	Ponds must be cleared. Aquatic species may populate ponds.	Ponds may provide new habitat. Intake of make-up water will entrain & destroy drifting organisms of intake screens.	Make-up water of 15,000+ (nuclear) & 9,000 (fossil) acre-feet per year/ 1000MW consumed by evaporation.	Blowdown same as wet towers except may also contain entrained drifting, or swimming organisms from pond.	Fogging and minor increases in temperature and humidity.
20-100 acres/ 1000MW occupied.					Minor increase in temperature.
Rights-of-way 150 to 250 feet or more wide.	Rights-of-way in wooded areas must be cleared of trees.	Vegetation clearing may be + or -. Some hazards to flying birds.			Minor amounts of ozone may be produced by higher voltage lines.
Less than 1 acre/mile actually occupied by towers.					
Right-of-way 50 feet or less wide.	Right-of-way in wooded area must be cleared of trees.	Vegetation clearing may be + or -.			
Right-of-way 50 to 100 feet or more.	Right-of-way must be cleared and maintained.	Vegetation clearing may be + or -. Train hazards to larger mammals.			

TABLE 6-1 Objectives developed for a statewide power plant siting study. These objectives, refined as a result of examining project-environmental relationships, should be compared with the preliminary objectives in Table 4-2.

A TECHNICAL AND REGULATORY OBJECTIVES

1 System energy supply and reliability requirements.

2 Provide adequate acreage, water, and fuel.

3 Provide suitable foundation conditions, reasonably level terrain, and no flooding hazard.

4 Provide accessibility by rail and highway with adequate transmission outlets.

5 Satisfy safety and federal air, water, and other regulations.

B ENVIRONMENTAL OBJECTIVES

1 Avoid or minimize impacts on:
   o highly productive agricultural areas
   o designated scenic and recreation areas
   o historical and archaeological sites
   o productive vegetation and wildlife areas, particularly those used by rare or endangered species, designated as preserves, used as scientific study areas, and those of commercial or recreational importance
   o natural landmarks and mineral resources
   o designated land uses such as airports and military reservations
   o surface and groundwater supplies

2 Avoid disruption of centers of population density, including urban centers, rural communities, and cross-road settlements.

3 Avoid disruption of areas of special cultural or ethnic character.

4 Avoid conflicts with existing and proposed land uses.

5 Minimize the number of individual landowners adversely affected by site and rights-of-way acquisition.

C ECONOMIC OBJECTIVES

1 Minimize total site-dependent construction costs, including:
   o transmission lines and substations
   o railroad access spur
   o highway access
   o site preparation, including earthwork and foundations
   o water conveyance and storage reservoir
   o exhaust gas treatment
   o cooling system components (ponds vs. towers)
   o seismic design

2 Minimize total site-dependent operating costs, including:
   o energy losses in transmission
   o fuel delivery and handling
   o water supply losses and pumping costs
   o waste treatment and disposal
   o outages due to meteorological/climatological conditions

D OPPORTUNITY OBJECTIVES

1 Maximize use of existing facilities for transmission, access, etc.

2 Locate near load centers.

3 Maximize multiple-users of project by considering the following:
   o beneficial uses of waste heat for warming irrigation water, heating green-houses, etc.
   o use of domestic or agricultural waste waters for cooling water make-up
   o use of solid wastes as boiler fuel
   o beneficial uses of fly ash and other wastes

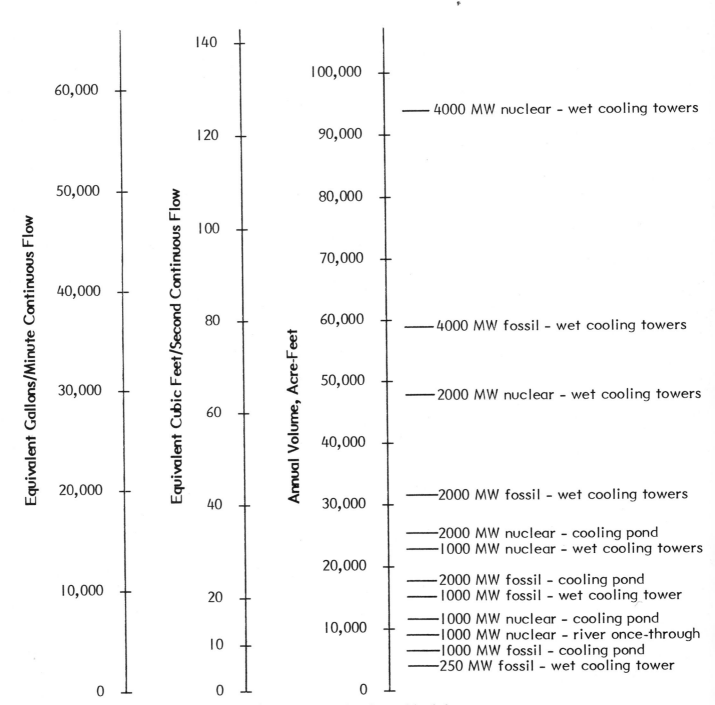

FIGURE 6-10 Typical range of consumptive water use for base-load nuclear and fossil plants.

facilities. *Criteria* are standards developed to measure and guide achievement of the site-selection objectives of an actual project.

Numerous government agencies set standards for environmental change that are nonmandatory and therefore negotiable. Nevertheless, the greater the extent to which a proposed project complies with such standards or offers acceptable trade-offs, the less controversial it is likely to be. For example, federal and state fish and wildlife agencies are charged with protection of wetlands. If a project is located in wetlands, the sponsor may be required to purchase and donate existing wetlands for permanent protection to compensate for the loss. Alternatively, restoration of damaged wetlands in the vicinity may be required. Thus a nonmandatory standard can have all the force of a legal one. The sponsor may choose either to avoid wetlands or to accept the trade-off. Once citizen participants review the siting objectives and criteria, they may, applying their own values, require avoidance.

Some criteria may be derived from general standards commonly accepted by environmental organizations and other segments of the general public or expressed in the planning literature. These standards are unenforceable but are nevertheless influential. One example relates to the socioeconomic effects of a project. The project objectives and definition express locational requirements in terms of land proximity to materials or markets and the size and skills of the labor force for both construction and operation. However, the disruptive effects of the influx of a large labor force on smaller communities is well documented in environmental impact literature. Criteria regarding the appropriate minimum community size might be developed in such a case. Standards for protecting visual quality provide another example. Numerous handbooks for siting responsively and unobtrusively are available. However, prior to site selection only a general commitment to visual quality preservation is possible.

In the two preceding paragraphs we touched on two areas that further complicate the determination of criteria: public values and site-specific standards. Both deserve further examination.

Commonly accepted standards are frequently local in nature and require special criteria to be established for use in candidate site identification and evaluation. Examples include general objectives for managing the rate of population growth in a city or region, policies for the type and scale of industrial development, and policies for the conservation of open space and agricultural land. All may be expressed in available planning documents but in practice require further examination with local officials and residents.

The way in which some legal and commonly accepted standards are viewed tends to be colored by vested interests and by the economic circumstances and residential, recreational, and working environment of different population groups. While generally accepted standards may exist relative to individual environmental conditions, they probably do not exist in a way that indicates their importance relative to meeting standards set for another condition. Similarly, the value placed by people on the visual quality of the rural environment in the abstract may differ from the value that would be assigned it in relation to avoidance of urban air pollution. Values change according to the context of choice available both in space and in time. Air quality, visual quality, and open space, for example, are viewed differently when energy is costly or jobs are needed.

IDENTIFICATION OF ISSUES

In addition to the complex questions of public values related to individual impacts, conflicts are often encountered in attempting to mesh project and environmental requirements and characteristics in a siting study. A region meeting project siting objectives and criteria in terms of location, topography, water supply, and access may not meet regulations and environmental criteria or policies for nondegradation of air quality, maintenance of scenic, recreational, or cultural amenity areas, preservation of important terrestrial or aquatic habitats, or avoidance of development pressures associated with a major facility.

All these conflicts and varying public values can be defined as issues. To the experienced facility planner with prior general knowledge of facility requirements, environmental conditions, and regulatory policies, issue identification may be almost a matter of instinct. Examination of the site-selection history of similar facilities may also aid in issue identification.

For example, the requirement that no residents be allowed in the area surrounding a nuclear power plant will clearly become a public issue. It is difficult to find regions offering unpopulated sites that also satisfy other siting criteria. While most people do not wish to live near a nuclear plant, it is probable that even fewer wish to be relocated from their homes. The need for relocation is therefore an issue on which no broadly accepted standard exists. It must be thought through in the context of the needs of affected residents (interest groups) and of other issues. In other words, the value placed on relocation relative to other values must be established. This process (called *weighting*) is addressed in Chapters 7 and 8.

Issues may surface very early in the study in relation to appropriate criteria for exclusion or selection of regions or areas for further study. Alternatively and probably more frequently, they surround the selection and design of criteria for comparing candidate areas. In either case, it is important to identify potential issues as early and as thoroughly as possible. If they can be anticipated and resolved at each step in the siting process, project delay can be minimized and the probability of success increased. The methods for conflict resolution will be described in Chapters 7, 8, and 10 on site screening, site evaluation, and public participation.

7 | THE SCREENING PROCESS

INTRODUCTION

In discussing the importance of defining project goals and objectives in Chapter 4, we related that step in site selection to the more common experience of looking for a new house. Perhaps the easiest way to introduce the screening process is to continue the analogy. The criteria by which to assess the relative ability of houses to meet the buyer's needs and wants are applied to houses on the market. Those that do not meet the criteria are screened out. The prospective buyer screens out houses that cost too much, houses that have too few rooms, and houses in neighborhoods that do not meet his or her needs for convenience to shopping, schools, and work.

Houses that pass the first test have to be compared carefully, one against the others. Many factors have to be weighed because each house that is seen has desirable and undesirable attributes and the buyer wants to find the house that meets his or her most important criteria or comes closest to meeting all the criteria in a balanced way. If it becomes apparent that no houses meeting the price and location criteria also meet the size criterion, a compromise may have to be made. If size is most important, locational preference may have to be sacrificed. If location is critical, two bedrooms and a den, rather than three bedrooms, may become acceptable.

Having gone through this process several times and in many different situations, most people are quite familiar with the basic steps and considerations involved. What may not be so clear are some of the techniques, nuances, and problems that arise in using the screening method in a conscious and accountable way for siting major facilities and routing linear systems.

Screening produces a limited list of sites suitable for further consideration. The comparative evaluation of each site on the list is the subject of Chapter 8. In house hunting, screening is a system for selecting potential choices by using predetermined criteria to eliminate clearly unsuitable houses. In major-facility site selection, the list is arrived at in a sequence of steps that reduces the geographic area of study with each step taken. Figure 7-1 illustrates the concept as applied to the state of California and to a region in Colorado.

The two diagrams express in more specific form the principle discussed in Chapter 3 and illustrated by Figure 3-1. As the geographic area of study is progressively reduced, the data required and the criteria by which the data are measured increase in number and level of detail. Because detailed evaluation and comparison of specific sites is expensive and time-consuming, a major objective of the screening process is to reveal the few best possible sites in the shortest time with the least expenditure of resources. As we shall see, application of the appropriate criteria at each stage of screening is what makes it possible to achieve that objective.

Before discussing the screening phase in detail, it is essential to understand both the intended product and the step-by-step process. Figure 7-2 sets out the entire process, which can be applied either in whole or in part to the siting of virtually any major facility. The methodology presented here is of necessity an idealized version of the process. Adaptations are necessary according to the characteristics of a particular project. Further adjustments of the methodology will also be called for in the future by new technologies, changing regulations and social values, and evolving perceptions of environmental quality.

DESIGN OF THE SCREENING PROCESS

A precise program of study is of course essential to any planning effort. The time taken to lay out the steps in the site-screening phase of a siting study is indispensable to a reliable and cost-efficient product. For internal purposes the idealized structure of the process in Figure 7-1 needs

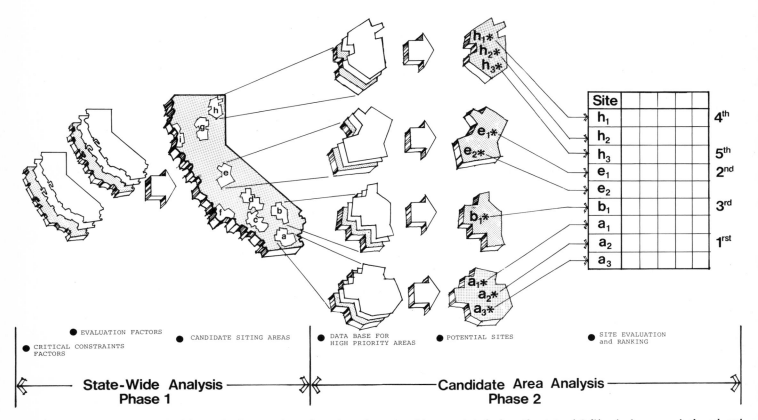

FIGURE 7-1 Site-screening methodology. The diagram above shows how the geographic area of study, here the state of California, is progressively reduced to a smaller number of candidate sites. The diagram on the opposite page illustrates the basic analytical steps in the selection of candidate areas and candidate sites. The inventory of candidate sites is then subjected to comparative evaluation as discussed in Chapter 8.

to be adapted and refined to identify responsibilities, critical information requirements, timing, and products for each task in a detailed diagram or network. A simplified version may be desirable for purposes of public participation. It should indicate the general task relationships and specify key review and decision points involving the project team, the decision-making group, and the reviewing agencies.

Two key decisions to be made at the start of the screening process involve the makeup of the group to be involved in the process and the geographic extent of the study. The two decisions are somewhat interrelated, and both depend on a careful review of the objectives of the program.

The Decision-Making Group

The group involved in making decisions at key points in the site-screening process varies from study to study. In many cases the sponsoring industry or agency itself,

PLATTE RIVER
POWER PLANT SITING PROCESS
EDAW inc.

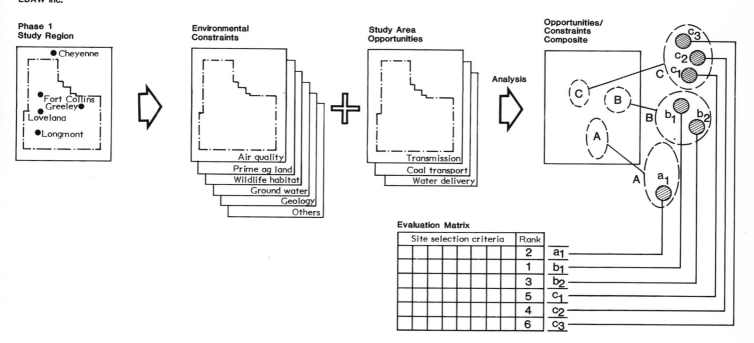

Phase 1
Study Region

Environmental
Constraints

Study Area
Opportunities

Opportunities/
Constraints
Composite

Analysis

Air quality
Prime ag land
Wildlife habitat
Ground water
Geology
Others

Transmission
Coal transport
Water delivery

Evaluation Matrix

Site selection criteria								Rank	
								2	a_1
								1	b_1
								3	b_2
								5	c_1
								4	c_2
								6	c_3

using either in-house or outside technical assistance, conducts the screening phase, involving the public in the later site-evaluation phase. In other cases the industry involves an outside technical advisory committee or a citizens' advisory committee as a participant throughout the process. In still other cases, especially when a review or regulatory agency is deeply involved, the decision-making group may include the applicant, the regulatory agency, and members of the general public at various stages in the process. As we have seen in previous chapters, the latter is generally the preferable approach.

Since a number of individuals are involved, the rules for participation have to be clearly established as an integral part of the design of the process and understood by all involved. To return once more to our analogy, selection of a new house may involve only one decision maker—yourself. If a couple is jointly making the decision, differing values may emerge to complicate the process. Clearly, when it is desirable to make a group decision, techniques for arriving at a balanced and representative expression of values are necessary. The participants and the points in the process at which they will be asked for a

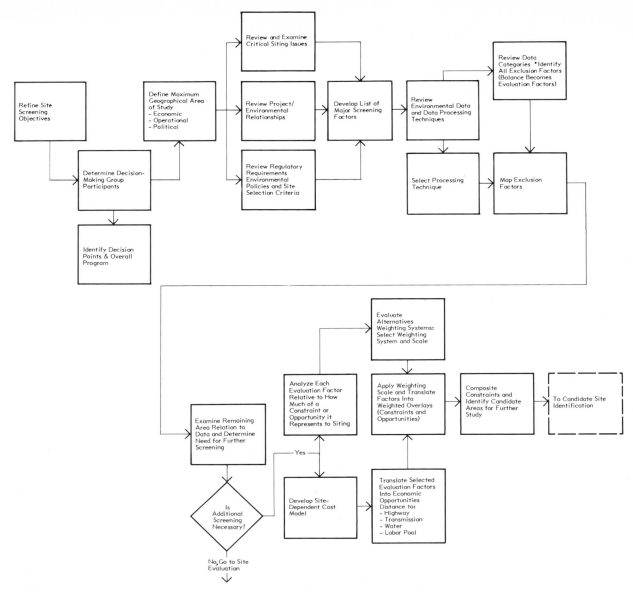

FIGURE 7-2a The site-screening phase of site selection, showing the steps to candidate area identification.

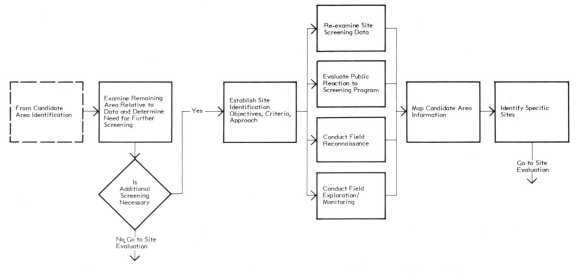

FIGURE 7-2b The site-screening phase, showing steps to identify candidate sites within candidate areas.

decision need to be clearly identified at this early stage. The makeup of the decision-making groups and techniques for eliciting their participation are discussed at length in Chapter 10.

Defining the Study Area

The other key decision to be made at this stage is the definition of the maximum geographical area of study. Any early limitation of the extent of the study should be based on defensible economic, operational, jurisdictional, or other factors. The goals, objectives, and preliminary criteria discussed in Chapters 4 and 6 provide the basis for discussion and documentation of this decision, which may be made either before or after defining the decision-making group and schedule.

Many government and private siting programs have included extensive investigations to find an optimum site within a study area which itself was chosen quite arbitrarily. Stafford, in analyzing case studies, interviews, and gaming experiments, finds that in private industry

[d]ecision-makers rapidly and drastically transform the infinite complexities of the optimal location into a relatively simple, intellectually manageable, situation. . . . Selection of an area of search, at the subnational, or, more commonly, the regional scale . . . involves the rather imprecise, and usually arbitrary or impressionistic delimitation of the specific area of search. . . . The vast majority of the possible locations are never explicitly considered (Stafford, 1979:11).

While Stafford admits that his evidence spans a 20-year period, only relatively few major companies today approach study area delimitation more rationally. What is true of private industry frequently is also true in government. Project Seafarer, which we have previously discussed, provides a case in point.

The consequences of ignoring the importance of the first major screening decision can be critical, especially if a high degree of flexibility does in fact exist from region to region or even from state to state. A well-conducted and well-documented screening from nation to state or from state to region can be an important step toward local project acceptance.

In addition to aiding final project approval, careful determination of the area of search may have important economic or operational benefits. As we have seen in Chapters 4 and 6, project goals and objectives may be firmly established but not all criteria are absolute. Premature limitation of project scope may preclude later identification of desirable trade-offs between criteria or altera-

tion of criteria. This caveat having been expressed, the study area boundaries, as a practical matter, should be selected to eliminate as much area from unnecessary consideration as is consistent with the gross level of data appropriate at the first stage.

Perhaps the clearest factor limiting the geographic scope of a study is that of jurisdiction. A state university, government agency, or regional utility company will generally be restricted to the area in which it intends to provide service. However, for a one-of-a-kind federal facility, such as Project Seafarer, or a state-run facility, such as the proposed California Department of Water Resources power plant, the scope is much broader.

The same broad geographic scope confronts many large industrial firms. For a distribution company the focus will be restricted to a known or anticipated market area. Other industries may be technically dependent on sizable port facilities or raw-material production sites. But for those for which delicate economic trade-offs exist between proximity to raw-material sources, power and water sources, availability of appropriate labor, and alternative transportation modes and markets, the scope may have to remain broad. A large number of factors may have to be used to select several regions for preliminary analysis in terms of comparative costs.

The planners of linear facilities such as roads, pipelines, and transmission lines, for which origins and destinations are known, will first define the practical lateral limits of their study areas. These limits may be defined by political, jurisdictional, economic, service area, or natural physical boundaries, but in any case they will allow sufficient lateral space to preclude the possibility of missing a suitable route outside the area.

Once the overall geographic limits of the study have been established, the first phase of the study directed toward identifying candidate areas can begin. *Candidate areas* are areas that possess no attributes which would be absolutely incompatible with project objectives and characteristics.

IDENTIFICATION OF SITE-SCREENING FACTORS

The first step in candidate area identification is to develop a list of major screening factors. These are the significant environmental, economic, social, and engineering characteristics or resources of an area that will impact on or be impacted by the construction and operation of a major facility. The factors will permit some parts of the area of study to be excluded from examination and others, the candidate areas, to be evaluated relative to each other.

Selection of the factors to be used is critical to successful and efficient candidate area identification. It is obvious that if any major factor is not properly addressed, all future decisions about potential sites will be unbalanced. However, development of a single complete list of factors is not always possible. The difficulty lies in the fact that frequently each candidate region may possess a number of unusual or unique aspects that require the addition of special screening factors. The initial screening-factor list, while being as comprehensive as possible, should allow additions to be made within the same framework as the screening progressively narrows.

The selection of factors is based on numerous sources which should be reviewed by all study participants. The primary basis for the list will be provided by the site-selection objectives and criteria discussed in Chapters 4, 5, and 6, but participants will also need to consider the information upon which those objectives and criteria are based. The review should include:

· Project definition and siting requirements

· Project-environmental analysis

· Regulatory requirements and environmental policies

· Critical siting issues

Two additional sources that need to be considered in developing the factor list include:

· The quality and comprehensiveness of existing information

· Examples from other relevant screening studies

The review of sources provides the opportunity to ensure that all participants in the process are familiar with the products of the goals and objectives, project definition, and environmental relationship tasks. The reexamination of these task products and of options and opportunities for project modification and impact mitigation is also a prerequisite to making any compromises required by site-screening findings. Thus regular feedback between the site-screening process and the earlier tasks can occur.

Structuring the Factor List

The listing of screening factors should be structured to allow study participants to categorize all factors and subfactors appropriately. A useful structure is shown in Figure 7-3. It avoids duplication, permits a consistent hierar-

chy of details to be developed in each category, and ensures comprehensiveness. Most important, it is also readily adaptable to the weighting procedures described later in this chapter and in Chapter 8, "The Site-Evaluation Process." This typical list of factors, of course, may require expansion or refinement for a particular project. Table 7-1 shows a list developed for a statewide screening study for a 1000-megawatt electric coal-fired power plant in California. The categories used show both similarities and dissimilarities with the general list in Figure 7-3.

The data factor structure in Table 7-1 should be compared with the list of objectives found in Table 6-1 in the preceding chapter. It will be evident that it represents the logical reordering of the stated siting and environmental objectives and the incorporation of criteria identified during the project-environmental analysis. In response to an objective stated as "Minimize disruption of agricultural activities," agricultural lands become a data factor in the land-use category. If the desirability of avoiding only prime agricultural land has been specified in the siting criteria, Class I and Class II soils and irrigated and irrigable soils, which are measures of agricultural productivity, are listed as subfactors. Some objectives require interpretation in developing the factor list. Table 7-1 shows, for example, that at least in the candidate area selection phase of this study it was found neither relevant nor possible to consider disruption of visual quality per se. The objective is addressed, however, in connection with restricted land-use categories such as scenic road buffers.

An example of the way in which factors may be altered as the screening progresses is seen in Figure 7-4. In this project, the Duluth Freeway Routing Study, five successive levels of "screens" were used.

Figure 7-4 also illustrates some other important points. First, the process of screening can occur even when the nature of the facility itself is not clear or when considerable design flexibility exists. Second, the factors used to identify candidate areas or routes can be quite limited indeed, especially when relatively few alternatives exist. In this study, which is discussed in depth in Part Two, Case Study 6, the goal of Screens I to III was the selection of a corridor from among alternatives. Use of multiple factors was reserved until economic and technical feasibility factors had eliminated unsuitable alternatives. Screen IV used fewer but more refined factors to select a facility type. Screen V used the multiple-factor list to evaluate and select from specific designs in a step equivalent to site evaluation. A final point illustrated by Figure 7-4 is that although the goals and objectives, project definition,

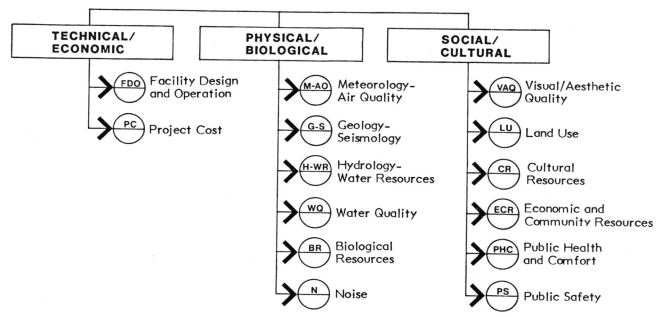

FIGURE 7-3 Screening data categories which may be reused in site evaluation. Logical factor categories are critical to efficient data collection and analysis. They ensure comprehensiveness, avoid duplication, and permit a consistent hierarchy of details to be developed within each category.

project-environmental relationships, and site-screening steps are usually sequential, they are not necessarily so.

Site-Screening Factors and Data Needs

The first purpose of ordering screening factors is to ensure the timely collection and storage of data for the study area while avoiding premature and perhaps unnecessary effort. The second is to guide the manipulation and interpretation of the data.

Once the screening factors have been identified and classified, it is possible to design the data collection effort and to determine the most appropriate and cost-effective method of data processing and spatial or other types of display. The two other principal determinants of the choice, the geographic area of study and the makeup of the study group participants, have already been established. Chapter 9 contains a discussion of the way in which these considerations, together with others relating to data base adequacy, graphic design principles, and future uses of the study, affect the data collection and processing effort.

THE CLASSIFICATION OF FACTORS

To return to Table 7-1, it can be seen on close examination that most factors represent varying degrees of constraint on the siting of the facility while some represent opportunities. If each factor in any list of screening factors were placed on a continuous scale by the decision-making group, it would be possible to isolate all those factors at the extreme end of the constraint scale and label them *exclusion factors* (see Figure 7-5). In other words, siting the facility is undesirable in, and sometimes adjacent to, an area where one of these factors is present. One or more of the constraining factors may be so extreme that areas where they occur should be excluded from consideration.

By identifying exclusion areas first, the need to gather further information on them is eliminated. The screening effort can then be focused quickly on those areas where potential sites can be found.

Figure 7-6 illustrates how the screening factors were organized for the statewide study in Minnesota to identify candidate areas for nuclear and fossil-fueled power plants (EDAW Inc., 1975b).

TABLE 7-1 Data factor structure for a statewide power plant siting study.

CATEGORY	DATA FACTOR	SUBFACTOR	CATEGORY	DATA FACTOR	SUBFACTOR
LAND USE	Forests	o National forests o State forests	NATURAL HAZARDS (cont.)	Volcanoes	o Areas of potential volcanic hazard
	Parks and recreation areas	o National parks, monuments, and recreation areas o Areas 0-5 miles from above areas o State park lands o Areas 0-5 miles from state park lands o Federal wilderness areas		Seismicity	
			ELECTRICAL ENERGY AND DWR SYSTEM	Transmission	o Existing transmission right-of-way of 115 kV or more o Existing fossil-fuel power plants
	Wilderness	o Areas 0-5 miles from federal wilderness areas o USFS and BLM roadless areas		Power plants	o Existing fossil-fuel power plants; mile buffer zone o Existing non-fossil-fuel power plants o Proposed power plant sites
	Military reservations				
	Airports	o Commercial o Military o Areas 0-5 miles from airports		DWR facilities	o DWR water conveyance facilities o DWR water service area o DWR electrical energy demand area
	Urban areas				
	Scenic roads	o State scenic highways o 0-5 mile buffer for scenic roads	ECONOMICS	Site-dependent costs	
	Indian reservations		SOCIO-ECONOMICS	Labor supply	o Distance to labor pools o Labor supply regions
	Agricultural lands	o Prime agricultural soils o Irrigable lands o Irrigated lands		Community compatibility	o Resort/recreation areas o Areas of unique cultural character
CRITICAL ENVIRON-MENTAL RESOURCES	Areas of special significance, critical habitats, and protected areas	o Important marshland habitat for waterfowl and water-associated wildlife o Migratory-duck winter range o Bighorn sheep range (areas of high concentration) o Critical salmon and steelhead spawning and nursery habitat o Federal and state wildlife refuges o Areas 0-5 miles from federal and state wildlife refuges	AIR QUALITY	Prevention of significant deterioration (PSD)	o Federal Class I area o Federal Class I area buffer o Proposed state Class A areas o Proposed state Class A areas buffer
				Terrain impingement	o Areas 0-10 miles from 1000-foot elevation change o Areas 10-20 miles from 1000-foot elevation change
	Coastal zone	o Areas of coastal zone excluded from power plant siting		Ambient-air quality	o Nonattainment areas for SO_2 o Nonattainment areas for NO_2 o Nonattainment areas for particulates o Nonattainment areas for oxidant
WATER SUPPLY	Ocean-water sources Groundwater basins with poor-quality waters Municipal/industrial wastewater sources Agricultural drainage sources			Emission offset potentials	o Counties with NO_2 emissions less than proposed plant o Counties with NO_2 emissions greater than proposed plant o Counties with SO_2 emissions less than proposed plant o Counties with SO_2 emissions greater than proposed plants
COAL SUPPLY	Railroad delivery	o Areas 0-15 miles from capable railroad o Areas over 15 miles from capable railroad			
NATURAL HAZARDS AND TERRAIN CONSTRAINTS	Terrain	o Areas of more than 500 feet of elevation change per mile		Emission regulations	o Areas where 1000-MW coal-fired power plant would not meet local emission regulations
	Faults	o Faults with historic displacement o Major Quaternary fault o Minor Quaternary fault			

SCREEN I   Evaluate transportation alternatives to ascertain whether the route could generate enough traffic to justify construction of more than a 2-lane city street.

SCREEN II   Compare traffic assignment and 1995 projections of facility improvement alternatives.

SCREEN III   Evaluate the surviving alternatives individually and comparatively on the basis of the total impact on the environs, according to the following factors:

A Natural Features
   Vegetation   Wildlife
   Topography   drainage/hydrology
   Rock outcrops   soils
B Air/Noise/Water Pollution
   Traffic volume   Traffic type
   Emission controls
   Vehicle speed
   Highway vertical configuration
   Observer distance from highway
   Erosion during construction
   Runoff-pollution of lake, stream,
     and groundwater
C Land Use
   Compatibility of land uses
   Linkage between uses
   Definition and transition
D Historical/Cultural
   Building preservation
   Building enhancement
E Visual Impact
   Integration with environment
   Views from/of facility
   Series of visual elements
   Visual continuity of elements

F Social Impact
   Land acquisition effects
   Neighborhood cohesion/division
   Safety
G Economic Impact
   Commercial activity expansion
     and development
   Minimize disruption and relocation
     of businesses
   Increased employment/construction
     and post-construction
   Increased revenues from tourism
H Road Traffic Movement
   Improve access to CBD
   Reduce congestion in city
   Separation of commercial and
     private traffic
   Minimize peak seasonal demand
   Feasibility of public and non-
     automobile transportation
I Facility Cost and Financing
   Right-of-way acquisition
   Resale value
   Net acquisition cost

SCREEN IV   Determine facility type, specifying requirements for:

Landform criteria   Route continuity
Traffic quality   Traffic demand
Safety   Phasing

SCREEN V   Evaluate separate design variations within the remaining corridor by using the Screen III factors. Divide variations into study areas relating to major design issues.

FIGURE 7-4 Screening methodology and factors developed for a freeway-routing study. Varying factor categories and levels of detail may be employed as the screening process progresses.

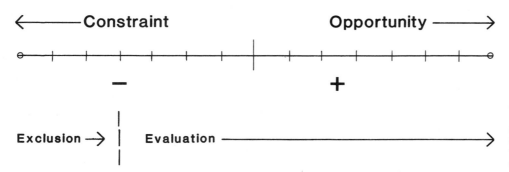

FIGURE 7-5 Scale of relative constraints or opportunities represented by data factors. One or more of the constraining factors may be so extreme that areas where they occur should be excluded from consideration.

Exclusion Factors

Exclusion factors may be specified by legislation or regulations, or they may be identified by the decision-making group. In the Minnesota case, the factors requiring exclusion had been specified in the state's enabling legislation for power plant siting and included:

· *National*. Parks, historic sites, historic landmarks, historic districts, monuments, wilderness areas, wildlife refuges, and wild, scenic, or recreational rivers.

· *State*. Wild, scenic, or recreational rivers and their land-use districts, parks, scientific and natural areas, and wilderness areas.

· *Other*. Nature conservancy preserves and areas where a power plant's water needs would result in groundwater "mining."

In addition, all appropriate state, federal, and local agencies were contacted and asked to identify other exclusion factors. These included:

· *Federal*. Areas with populations of 25,000 or more now or within 50 years (nuclear plants only).

· *State*. Areas surrounding major airports, all lake surfaces, and areas exceeding ambient-air quality standards.

The resulting map displaying all exclusion areas is shown in Figure 7-7. As can be seen, only approximately 10 percent of the state was removed from further consideration.

The coal-fired power plant siting study for the California Department of Water Resources offers a strong contrast with the Minnesota study. Figure 7-8 shows that roughly 75 percent of the state was eliminated from further consideration on the basis of exclusion factors alone. While geographically the two states are very different, it is clear that the selection of exclusion factors can have a major influence on the scope and outcome of a siting study.

In the California study a type of Delphi decision-making procedure was used to arrive at those factors felt to merit exclusion. The Delphi technique is characterized by an iterative methodology that begins with autonomous assessments or value assignments by each participant. These value assignments are then statistically summarized, providing a group-based measure to which each participant can respond. A group discussion is then conducted, completing one iteration. The next iteration is initiated with the reassignment of values based on feedback gained through the discussion process. Since in California 11 individuals were included in the voting, it was agreed that a vote of 11 to 0 or 10 to 1 was needed to place a factor in the exclusion category. If the vote on any factor was more evenly split, the factor was discussed and a second ballot was taken. The results can be seen in Table 7-2.

While the process thus far appears quite clear-cut, we should add a note of caution regarding the danger in overgeneralizing about what might constitute exclusion. For example, an early decision to avoid certain airsheds because of stringent air quality requirements may result in excluding areas that could in fact be considered given the most recent advances in air cleanup technology. Therefore, if any possibility exists for mitigating impacts on certain sensitive areas, it is often wise to consider the factor as an evaluation factor rather than as an exclusion factor.

The recommendation that we have made in earlier chapters to retain areas or factors for further study when in doubt also applies to those affected by changing or potentially changing public values. For example, had the California power plant siting study been performed a year later, urban areas might have been treated as an evaluation factor rather than as an exclusion factor as identified in Table 7-2. We have alluded to the substantial consequences of this emerging change in values earlier

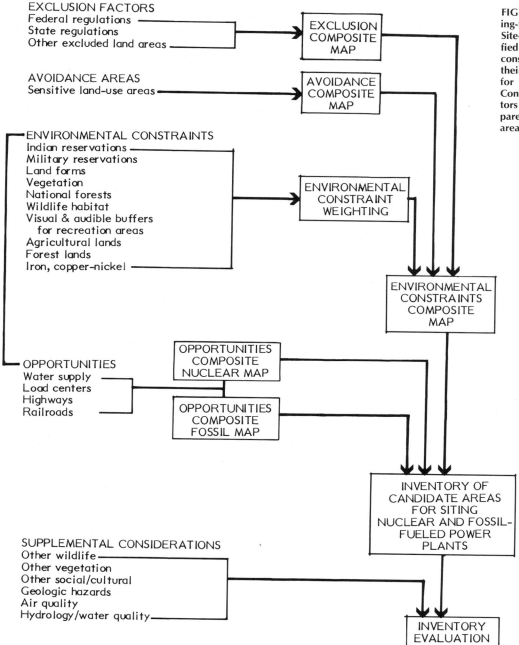

EXCLUSION FACTORS
Federal regulations
State regulations
Other excluded land areas

EXCLUSION COMPOSITE MAP

AVOIDANCE AREAS
Sensitive land-use areas

AVOIDANCE COMPOSITE MAP

ENVIRONMENTAL CONSTRAINTS
Indian reservations
Military reservations
Land forms
Vegetation
National forests
Wildlife habitat
Visual & audible buffers
  for recreation areas
Agricultural lands
Forest lands
Iron, copper-nickel

ENVIRONMENTAL CONSTRAINT WEIGHTING

ENVIRONMENTAL CONSTRAINTS COMPOSITE MAP

OPPORTUNITIES
Water supply
Load centers
Highways
Railroads

OPPORTUNITIES COMPOSITE NUCLEAR MAP

OPPORTUNITIES COMPOSITE FOSSIL MAP

INVENTORY OF CANDIDATE AREAS FOR SITING NUCLEAR AND FOSSIL-FUELED POWER PLANTS

SUPPLEMENTAL CONSIDERATIONS
Other wildlife
Other vegetation
Other social/cultural
Geologic hazards
Air quality
Hydrology/water quality

INVENTORY EVALUATION

FIGURE 7-6 Sample screening-factor processing diagram. Site-screening factors are classified according to the degree of constraint or opportunity that their presence would represent for siting the proposed facility. Constraint and opportunity factors are then mapped and compared to arrive at candidate areas for further evaluation.

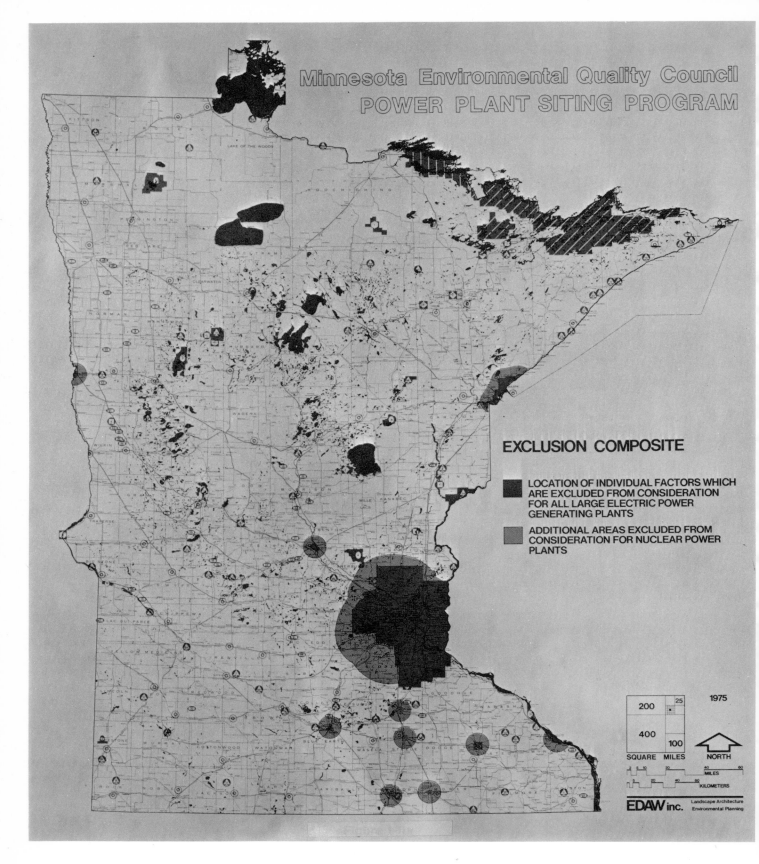

Minnesota Environmental Quality Council
POWER PLANT SITING PROGRAM

EXCLUSION COMPOSITE

LOCATION OF INDIVIDUAL FACTORS WHICH ARE EXCLUDED FROM CONSIDERATION FOR ALL LARGE ELECTRIC POWER GENERATING PLANTS

ADDITIONAL AREAS EXCLUDED FROM CONSIDERATION FOR NUCLEAR POWER PLANTS

1975

200 | 25
400 | 100
SQUARE MILES

NORTH

MILES
KILOMETERS

EDAW inc. Landscape Architecture
Environmental Planning

FIGURE 7-7 Exclusion composite map resulting in limited exclusion areas. Identification and application of exclusion factors limit the area for which further information must be gathered and analyzed.

90

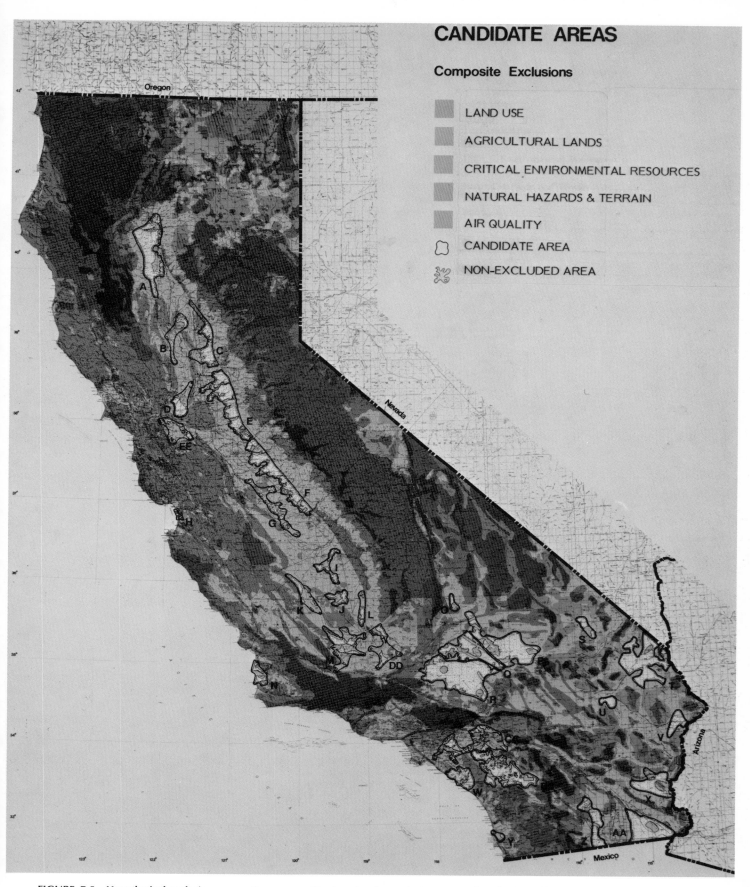

FIGURE 7-8   Hypothetical exclusion composite map resulting in extensive exclusion areas. The selection of factors deemed to require exclusion can have a major bearing on the scope and outcome of a siting study.

TABLE 7-2 Representative classification of screening factors by ballot. Study participants may be asked to categorize factors for exclusion or evaluation by vote. A second ballot may be taken, after further discussion, on factors not clearly ruled exclusionary by the first ballot.

Category	Data factor	Sub-factor	Recommendation of discipline specialist	First ballot Exclusion	First ballot Evaluation	Second ballot Exclusion	Second ballot Evaluation	Results
Land use	Forests	o National forests	Exclusion	11	0			Excluded
		o State forests	Exclusion	11	0			Excluded
	Recreation areas and parks	o National parks, monuments, and recreation areas	Exclusion	11	0			Excluded
		o Areas 0–5 miles from national parks, monuments, and recreation areas	Exclusion	6	5	3	7	Evaluation
		o State park lands	Exclusion	11	0			Excluded
		o Areas 0–5 miles from state park lands	Exclusion	6	5	2	8	Evaluation
	Wilderness	o Federal wilderness areas	Exclusion	11	0			Excluded
		o Areas 0–5 miles from federal wilderness areas	Exclusion	6	5	3	6	Evaluation
		o USFS and BLM roadless areas	Exclusion	7	4	8	1	Excluded
	Military reservations		Evaluation	2	9	2	9	Evaluation
	Airports	o Commercial	Exclusion	11	0			Excluded
		o Military	Exclusion	10	1			Excluded
		o Areas 0–3 miles from airports	Exclusion	10	1			Excluded
	Urban areas		Exclusion	8	3	9	0	Excluded
	Scenic roads	o State scenic highways	Exclusion	10	1			Excluded
		o 0–5 mile buffer for scenic roads	Exclusion	9	2	6	3	Evaluation
	Indian reservations		Exclusion	9	2	8	1	Excluded
	Agricultural lands	o Prime agricultural soils	Exclusion	11	0			Excluded
		o Irrigated lands	Exclusion	11	0			Excluded
		o Irrigable lands	Evaluation	1	10			Evaluation
Environmental resources	Areas of special biological significance, critical habitats, and protected areas	o Important marshland habitat for waterfowl and water-associated wildlife	Exclusion	10	1			Excluded
		o Migratory deer winter range	Exclusion	7	4	9	0	Excluded
		o Bighorn sheep range (areas of high concentration)	Exclusion	10	0			Excluded
		o Critical salmon and steelhead spawning and nursery habitat	Exclusion	10	1			Excluded
		o Federal and state wildlife refuges	Exclusion	11	0			Excluded
		o Areas 0–5 miles from federal and state wildlife refuges	Evaluation	8	3	2	8	Evaluation
	Coastal zone	o Areas of coastal zone excluded from power plant siting	Exclusion	10	0			Excluded
	Rivers	o Federal wild and scenic rivers	Exclusion	10	0			Excluded
		o State wild and scenic rivers	Exclusion	10	0			Excluded
		o State-protected waterways	Exclusion	6	4	9	2	Excluded
	Rare and endangered wildlife habitat		Evaluation	0	9			Evaluation
Site-dependent costs	Coal supply	o Areas 0–15 miles from 'capable' railroad	Evaluation	0	11			Evaluation
		o Areas over 15 miles from 'capable' railroad	Exclusion	9	2	1	9	Evaluation
Socioeconomics	Labor supply	o Distance to labor pools	Evaluation	0	11			Evaluation
		o Labor supply regions	Evaluation	0	11			Evaluation
	Community compatibility	o Resort recreation areas	Evaluation	0	11			Evaluation
		o Areas of unique cultural character	Evaluation	0	11			Evaluation

in this book. Had urban areas remained potential siting areas, an additional and extensive array of social, economic, environmental, and engineering factors would have been required. As it happened, this concern surfaced late in the study, requiring a rapid reiteration of previous steps to find an urban candidate site and satisfy the changed political values.

The scale of the study is another important consideration in assigning factors to the exclusion group. For example, at the statewide level it is usually not possible to exclude all rare and endangered wildlife habitats because the range of some species may be very wide. However, identification only of critical habitat areas is difficult at a coarse map scale because these areas may extend no more than a few square miles. This factor, therefore, can be dealt with satisfactorily only at the candidate area level.

Classification of factors for exclusion or evaluation may also vary according to the objectives of the study. For example, a regulatory agency such as a state energy commission, which needs a map identifying all areas potentially suitable for power plant siting, may treat a screening factor differently from a utility searching for the three best plant sites in the shortest possible time.

Evaluation Factors

The screening factors remaining after all exclusion factors have been identified and mapped are termed *evaluation factors*. Each factor represents a level of constraint or opportunity for finding an acceptable site. The underlying premise is that all geographic areas can be said to have physical, biological, economic, and social characteristics which either constrain or provide opportunities for development. In some cases, they may offer both. It is the analysts' task to understand and interpret these characteristics in terms of the requirements of the proposed development.

A large volume of information and value judgment is involved in handling evaluation factors. There is thus a practical requirement for a relatively simple, straightforward way of presenting both the information and the judgments which brings them clearly into focus when they are summarized. Techniques for doing this are called *factor mapping* and *compositing*. Factor mapping is the mapping of individual categories of information important to the project. Compositing, or the superimposition of several factor maps on a base map, is discussed later in the chapter.

Ground slope and foundation geology are two very common examples of factors of importance to major facilities because they directly relate to engineering feasibility and construction costs. Steep slopes and poor foundation material will result in excessive and costly grading and foundation structures and thus represent constraints. Slope and foundation geology maps will identify acceptable and unacceptable conditions for combining with other important factors.

CONSTRAINT FACTORS   The determination of a constraint involves a judgment related to either the potentially harmful modification of some existing factor by a particular action or the inability of the particular factor to support the proposed facility. The basis for the judgment must therefore be made clear on the factor map or in an accompanying report, or both. Similarly, the criteria for acceptable modification of the facility or other measures for mitigation of harmful effects should be made explicit.

Whenever possible it is desirable to rate each factor in terms of its relative suitability for the proposed development. Most readers will be familiar with *slope maps*, on which the percentage of slope of the land is classified according to a predetermined formula, such as 0 to 10, 11 to 20, 21 or more. The purpose in such a case is to identify areas of least constraint, moderate constraint, and severe constraint to development. The importance of moderate or severe slope constraints can then be examined relative to other constraint factors, as discussed later in the section "Weighting Systems."

In some cases, it may not be possible with generalized information for a given factor to rate the suitability of areas for the development of all major project features. This point is illustrated by Table 7-3, which displays the way in which geologic structure types may be analyzed and grouped for screening purposes. The geologic conditions in Class A areas generally represent constraints, while those in B and C areas involve both constraints and opportunities. On balance, the chances of finding easily developable sites for structures appear greater in B areas. However, C areas may contain some equally suitable but less easily developable sites for structures, should consideration of other screening factors preclude focusing on B areas.

Constraints to development are likely to occur to some degree in all the general factor categories, depending on the specific facility type and size. So data have to be collected, interpreted, and directly recorded or summarized in map form for each relevant category. These may include landforms, visual conditions, noise conditions, health and safety conditions, community so-

TABLE 7-3 Example of geologic unit constraint and opportunity interpretation. The rating of constraint factors often involves detailed interpretation and judgment. In this example, Class A areas generally represent constraints. On balance, Class B areas appear to offer more opportunities for developable sites than Class C areas.

MAP UNIT	GENERAL DESCRIPTION	LIGHT STRUCTURES	HEAVY STRUCTURES
A	Unconsolidated sand, gravel, silt, and clay at 5 to 10 feet thick. Average thickness 30-50 feet. Most areas have poorly developed soil profiles. Generally moderate permeability. Non-expansive.	Generally suitable but may be subject to possible flood hazard from storm runoff.	Moderate settlement potential could require special foundations. Possible flood hazard from storm runoff. Excessive well pumping could cause subsidence.
B	Primarily older alluvium consisting of gravels, sand, silt, and clay. Average thickness 20-30 feet. Moderate to well-developed soil profile. Also includes some sandstone and sandy shales. Generally moderate permeability but locally low to very high. Low to moderate shrink swell potential may be high locally.	Generally suitable with few restrictions.	Generally suitable. Locally expansive soils or rock could necessitate special foundation design. Blasting may be required in areas of exposed rock.
C	Exposed or near-surface clay shale bedrock. Shallow to deep soil cover. Low to moderate permeability. Moderate to high expansive clay content.	Slab-on-grade or shallow foundations may crack and buckle where expansive soil or rock is present.	Generally suitable but special foundation design may be necessary for structures with low tolerance to differential settlement. Blasting may be required in areas of exposed hard rock.

ON-SITE WASTE DISPOSAL

Generally questionable for disposal of sanitary wastes due to moderately high to high permeability. Local and down-gradient water quality would have to be protected.

Some areas are suitable but conditions are variable. On-site studies required to determine suitability of a given location. Local and down-gradient water quality would have to be protected.

Generally suitable. Soils and weathered rock may be useful for lining ponds or reservoirs.

HOLDING RESERVOIRS

Possible excessive seepage losses. Storm runoff could cause rapid sedimentation and could require additional storage capacity.

Condition generally suitable but some areas may require lining to avoid excessive seepage.

Sealing generally unnecessary as seepage losses are generally low.

cioeconomics, land use, access, vegetation, wildlife, hydrology, water quality, air quality, climate, and geology.

The most useful product at this stage is a series of maps prepared at a convenient common scale which clearly depict each factor constraining siting of the proposed development. If they are done on clear film overlays, these maps can be readily compared, composited, printed, photographed, and displayed. Overlays and common-scale mapping are not necessary, however, if it has been decided to computerize the mapping and compositing of information. We should explain at this point that compositing is a graphic method of summing up and displaying all factor information for the purpose of identifying areas of least constraint and greatest opportunity for facility siting. A discussion of the considerations involved in selecting the precise method to be used will be found in Chapter 9, "Data Needs and Analysis." Examples of constraint maps, manual and computer-drawn, can be seen in Figure 7-9, pages 97–102 and 104–109.

Examination of Table 7-3 raises another subject related to constraint analysis. That is the ability of mitigating actions to overcome part or all of the undesirable effects of another action. Some common mitigating actions include landscaping, revegetation, erosion control, sound deadening, emission control, cooling ponds, and light baffling. However, the additional cost of mitigation may also be an important offsetting consideration. In the case of the project for which Table 7-3 was developed, for example, the additional expense of sealing holding reservoirs would generally be required to avoid seepage from some sites in Class B areas.

Mitigation possibilities generally work hand in hand with the rating of each factor's suitability for the proposed development. It is thus essential to understand how each constraint factor operates and what, if anything, can be done to mitigate the effects under various sets of circumstances. In general, the more suitable an area is for the particular use, the less the mitigation required. Conversely, the greater the amount of mitigation that is necessary, the lower the suitability. But in some cases the greatest potential for locating suitable sites may exist in a constrained area where successful mitigation can be undertaken. All screening processes must be capable of handling this situation. Constraint factors should therefore be kept identifiable and separable so that they can be reevaluated if necessary after the screening composite has been assembled.

OPPORTUNITY FACTORS   Opportunities emerge, like constraint factors, from the identification of project-en-

vironmental relationships. In Figure 7-6, the principal opportunities related to power plant location were listed as water supply and access to power-use load centers, highways, and railroads. Some of these opportunities are common to many other kinds of industrial development in addition to those peculiar to particular industries.

Other common opportunity factors include power supply availability and access to labor force, markets, and raw-material supplies. Increasingly frequently, other factors being reasonably equal, an industry will also consider advantageous local tax policies, favorable government attitudes, and low land costs as prime opportunities.

Historically, many industries and public agencies have designed their site searches around the identification of opportunity areas. As we have emphasized previously, this approach has serious shortcomings in its lack of comprehensiveness. When little or no organized attention is given to the less obvious constraints, it is impossible to apply an overall measure or accounting system for balancing and making trade-offs between opportunities and constraints and among differing kinds of constraints. In fact, the one-sided, opportunity-oriented search has had much to do with the "environmental" problems facing certain industries and such public agencies as highway departments. This is not to say that opportunities should be played down in the site search but to emphasize the need for perspective and balance.

As in the case of constraints, overgeneralization should be avoided. While an area normally will not be eliminated solely because no clear opportunities exist, the presence of opportunities must be carefully weighed against constraints existing in the same area. However, sufficient importance needs to be given to opportunities to ensure that they are not overshadowed by constraints, especially when the constraints may be mitigated.

Opportunities are also relative to a degree and are therefore subject to weighting. Some opportunity factors can be translated into direct site-dependent dollar costs and mapped, thus permitting direct comparison with mapped constraints and other types of opportunities. Examples of manual and computer-drawn opportunity maps are given in Figures 7-10, 7-11, and 7-12.

Information for opportunity factors is usually available from existing sources, but in some cases, such as water supply opportunities, extensive technical, legal, and political analysis may be necessary before a realistic opportunity map can be prepared.

While the opportunity factor maps illustrate the location of potential opportunities, they usually do not illus-

Seafarer Corridor Analysis
Upper Michigan Region

by EDAW inc.
San Francisco, California

under contract to
GTE Sylvania
Communication Systems Division
Needham Heights, Massachusetts

for
U.S. Navy
Naval Electronic Systems Command
Washington, D.C.

VEGETATION I
Wetlands Dominant

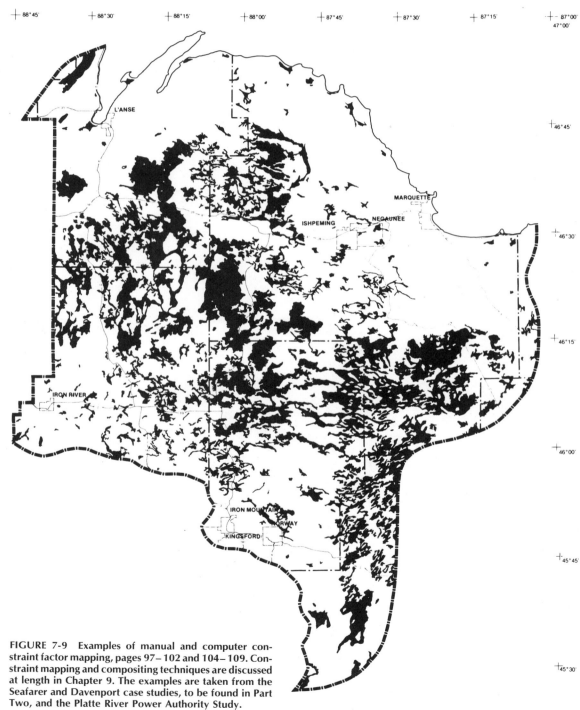

FIGURE 7-9 Examples of manual and computer constraint factor mapping, pages 97–102 and 104–109. Constraint mapping and compositing techniques are discussed at length in Chapter 9. The examples are taken from the Seafarer and Davenport case studies, to be found in Part Two, and the Platte River Power Authority Study.

Seafarer Corridor Analysis
Upper Michigan Region

LAND OWNERSHIP
Private Land

by EDAW inc.
San Francisco, California

under contract to
GTE Sylvania
Communication Systems Division
Needham Heights, Massachusetts

for
U.S. Navy
Naval Electronic Systems Command
Washington, D.C.

Seafarer Corridor Analysis
Upper Michigan Region

by EDAW inc.
San Francisco, California

under contract to
GTE Sylvania
Communication Systems Division
Needham Heights, Massachusetts

for
U.S. Navy
Naval Electronic Systems Command
Washington, D.C.

WILDLIFE I

Baraga Plains Waterfowl Management Area
Craig Lake State Park, Primitive Area
Sharp Tail Grouse Management Areas

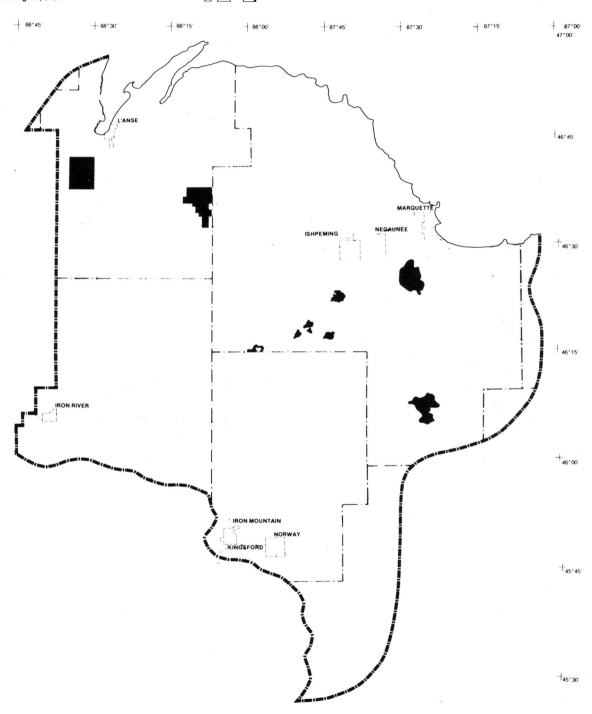

99

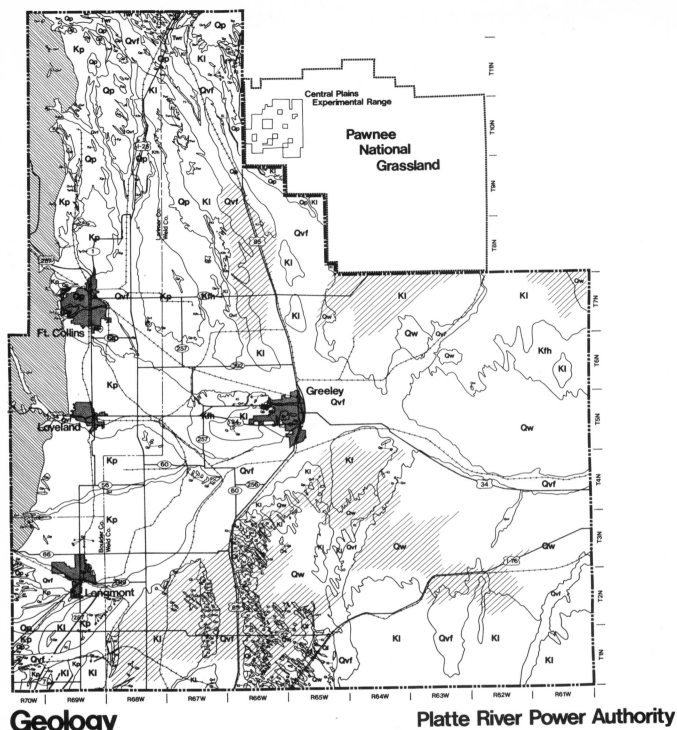

Geology

Qw	Windblown Sand & Silt	
Qvf	Quaternary Valley Fill, Alluvial, and Terrace Deposit	
Ql	Loess Deposits (partial mapping)	
Qp	Pediment & Alluvial Fan Deposits	
Tar	Arikaree Formation	
Twr	White River Formation	
Kl	Laramie Formation	
Kfh	Fox Hills Sandstone	
Kp	Pierre Shale	

Strippable Coal Deposits

Undifferentiated Rocks Older Than Pierre Shale

Faults

Platte River Power Authority

POWER PLANT FEASIBILITY STUDY

EDAW inc.
Environmental Planning

STUDY AREA LIMITS

1000 A.

10,000 Acres

0 1 2   8 Miles

N

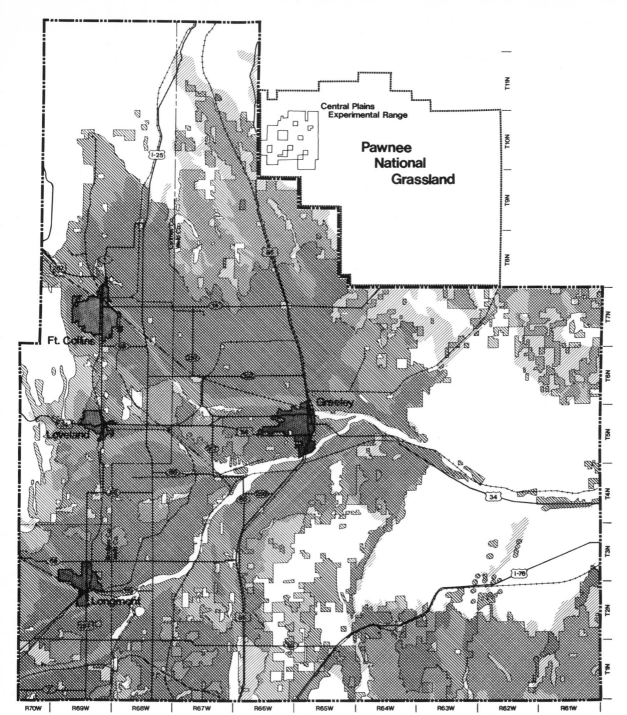

Prime Agricultural Lands

Generally Prime Irrigated Cropland

Dry Cropland

Generally Class I & II Soils

Range and Other Land Uses

Platte River Power Authority

POWER PLANT FEASIBILITY STUDY

EDAW inc.
Environmental Planning

101

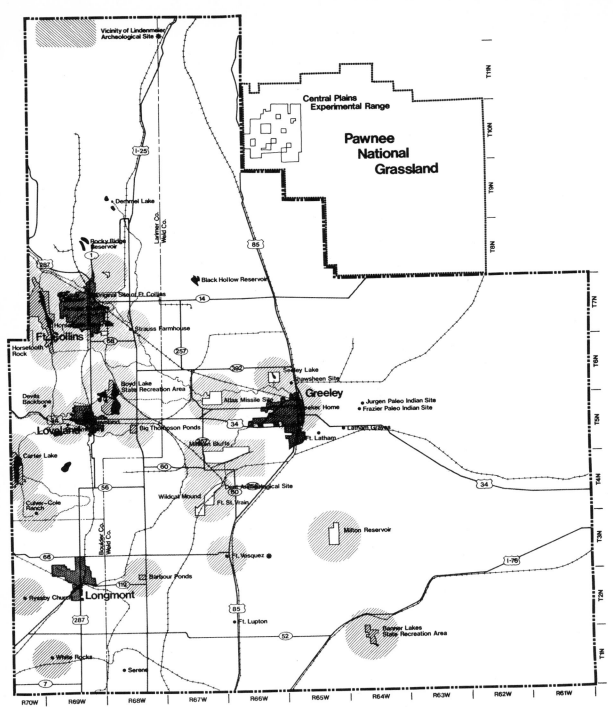

Cultural Resources

Platte River Power Authority

POWER PLANT FEASIBILITY STUDY

EDAW inc.
Environmental Planning

Legend:

 Existing Recreation Area

 Proposed Recreation Area

● Historic/Archaeological Site & Scenic Landmark

Buffer Zone

✴ Site Listed in National Register of Historic Places

Open Space Trail Proposals

 Reservoirs Leased for Recreation

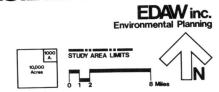

trate the technical, environmental, and economic diffi-culties in extending new pipelines, rail spurs, roads, or transmission lines to all parts of the region. These diffi-culties can be handled in several ways. The simplest method is to assume that all candidate areas must be within a given distance of existing opportunities. Figure 7-10, in which areas more than 30 miles from water sources were classified as undesirable, illustrates this ap-proach. A second method of extending opportunities to all parts of a region is shown in Figure 7-11, in which site-dependent cost penalties were computed manually for a number of locations in the region and cost contours were then drawn for all areas. This particular example shows the capital cost of new rail spurs and the present worth of fuel delivery charges for the life of a two-unit coal-fired power plant.

If computer mapping of screening factors is used, a third method of considering opportunities emerges. This method uses the computer to route new facilities to all parts of the study area and to compute the resultant site-dependent cost penalties as well as the resultant environ-mental consequences (in terms of miles of new corridor, land use traversed, vegetative clearing required, and other effects). An example of the model for this type of computer analysis is shown in Figure 7-13 along with an example of the resulting computer maps.

WEIGHTING SYSTEMS

Comprehensive screening studies usually result in site-selection factor lists containing fifty or more factors. Combining these factors into one or a few composite maps suitable for identification of candidate areas usually requires some form of weighting system because not all constraints preclude facility siting to the same degree. The weighting system provides a means of making trade-off decisions among screening factors. These trade-offs are based on both the relative **importance** of each screen-ing factor and the **magnitude** to which it might be im-pacted by or impact on the proposed facility type.

Public values are a desirable input to any weighting system and are most appropriate for establishing relative-importance values for the screening factors. Public values are particularly significant when establishing the importance of local concerns such as land use, aesthet-ics, socioeconomic factors, public health, and public safety.

Weighting should be restricted to the smallest possi-ble number of factors. Overly complex data systems and weighting schemes should be avoided, particularly for the benefit of the nonprofessional public who will be re-viewing and in some cases ratifying study results.

One of the simplest ways to reduce the number of fac-tors to be weighted is to handle economic factors sepa-rately. By reducing a factor's magnitude of potential im-pact to a site-dependent dollar penalty, it is easily combined with the dollar penalties of other economic factors. Its importance relative to the other constraint and opportunity factors can be clearly identified by exam-ining the extent to which it affects total site-dependent costs. Another way to reduce the number of factors to be weighted is to handle opportunity factors separately. Be-cause opportunities involve factors which influence the basic feasibility of facility construction or operation, they are closely related to site-dependent costs and therefore can be mapped in dollar terms as shown in Figures 7-11 and 7-12.

The weighting system is greatly simplified by separat-ing out economic opportunity factors since only environ-mental screening factors remain. Two basic weighting schemes are recommended, depending on the complex-ity of the environmental factor list. One is a factor overlay scheme that can be used if the number of factors is small. The other is a numerical system which is more appropri-ate for a large number of factors.

Factor Overlay Weighting

In the ideal regional screening case, it would be possible to find candidate siting areas that avoided all environ-mental constraint factors. In this case, all factors could have the same weight. The candidate areas would be de-termined by combining all factors on one candidate con-straint map and outlining the blank areas. No trade-offs would be necessary, and the decision presumably would be acceptable to everyone.

Unfortunately, composite maps of environmental constraint factors seldom have any blank areas. Candi-date areas must usually be located where some environ-mental constraint is also present, so that a trade-off is re-quired.

A modification of the ideal case, using only the more important factors, can produce useful results when the factor list is not extensive. The overlay of important fac-tors in effect gives each factor the **same** weight. Figure 7-13 is an example of this approach. In this example, however, buffer zones were used for some screening factors. This offers a means of giving a factor greater

PHYSICAL CONSTRAINTS TO LANDSCAPE MODIFICATION

PHYSICAL CONSTRAINTS TO LANDSCAPE MODIFICATION

General:

The map of physical restrictions to landscape modification was derived from the slope, slope instability and physiography maps. The map indicates zones of the degree of physical restrictions to landscape modification.

Definitions:

Extensive - Slopes over 50% or landslide areas, or course lines.

Major - Slopes of 21%-50% or areas of high risk of slope instability.

Moderate - Slopes of 11%-20% or areas of moderate risk of slope instability.

Minor - Slopes under 10% and areas of low risk of slope instability.

Use:

The physical restrictions to landscape modification map when related to transmission line development implies the following actions for each zone of constraints.

Extensive - The necessity for extensive grading operations, the very high risk of further landsliding, or the high risk of stream siltation within this zone makes it a consideration for transmission line development only when no other opportunities exist and when detailed designs assure that the problems related to the zone can be overcome.

Major - Cuts and fills should be engineered and planted to insure slope stability, fills should be compacted, and access roads should be designed to minimize the concentration of runoff.

Moderate - Access roads should be designed to minimize the concentration of runoff.

Minor - No special actions.

Source:

1. Slope Map.

2. Slope Instability Map.

3. Physiography Map.

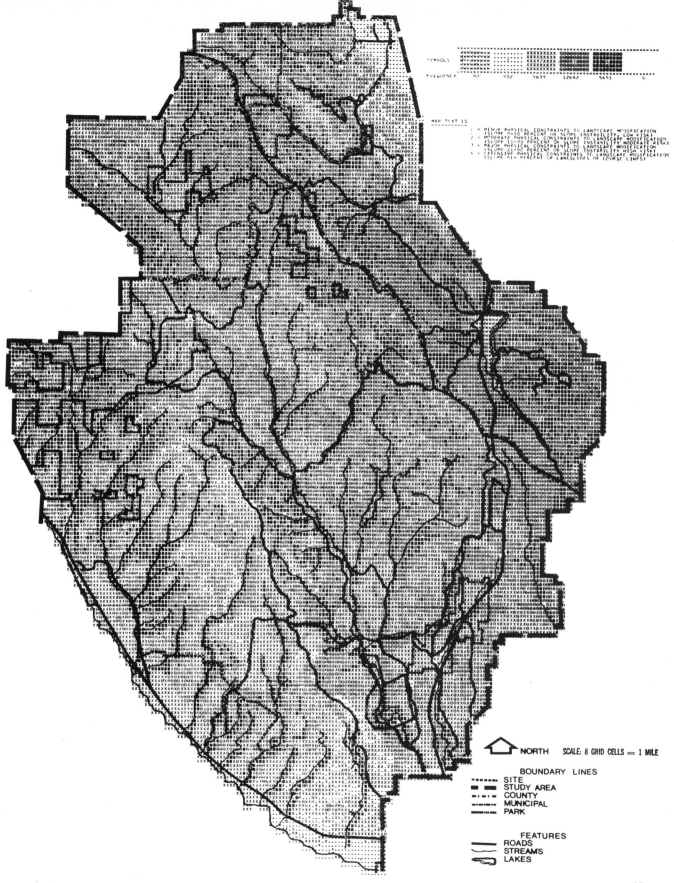

SYMBOLS

FREQUENCY   92   402   5639   12642   5451   0

MAP TEXT IS

1 = MINOR PHYSICAL CONSTRAINTS TO LANDSCAPE MODIFICATION
    (SLOPE 0-10 PERCENT OR SLOPE INSTABILITY, LOW RISK)
2 = MODERATE PHYSICAL CONSTRAINTS TO LANDSCAPE MODIFICATION
    (SLOPE 11-20 PERCENT OR SLOPE INSTABILITY MODERATE RISK)
3 = MAJOR PHYSICAL CONSTRAINTS TO LANDSCAPE MODIFICATION
    (SLOPE 21-50 PERCENT OR SLOPE INSTABILITY HIGH RISK)
4 = EXTENSIVE PHYSICAL CONSTRAINTS TO LANDSCAPE MODIFICATION
    (SLOPE 51+ PERCENT OR LANDSLIDES OF COURSE LINES)

NORTH   SCALE: 8 GRID CELLS = 1 MILE

BOUNDARY LINES
SITE
STUDY AREA
COUNTY
MUNICIPAL
PARK

FEATURES
ROADS
STREAMS
LAKES

105

SOCIAL–CULTURAL CONSTRAINTS TO LANDSCAPE MODIFICATION

SOCIAL-CULTURAL CONSTRAINTS TO LANDSCAPE
MODIFICATION

General:

The map of social-cultural constraints to landscape modification
was derived from the existing and anticipated development and
recreation map and the maps of historical and archaeological sites.
The constraints map depicts the areas where the greatest and least
potential social and cultural disruptions would occur if the existing
landscape were to be changed.

Definitions:

Extensive - Built-up areas of densities greater than one dwelling
unit per acre, historical or archaeological sites.

Major - Built-up areas of densities of one dwelling unit per
2-5 acres or anticipated built-up areas of greater than one
dwelling unit per acre.

Moderate - Anticipated built-up areas of densities of one dwelling
unit per 2-5 acres.

Minor - Areas not included in the above.

Use:

The social-cultural constraints to landscape modification map when
related to transmission line development implies the following actions
for each zone of constraints.

Extensive - The necessity to relocate individuals, businesses,
industries or institutions within this zone makes it a consideration
for transmission line development only when no other opportunities exist. When there are no other opportunities, development
in this zone should follow the path of least social disruption and
plans for making the right of way useful to the community should
be implemented. Historical or archaeological sites should be
avoided. When the sites are difficult to avoid, special detailed
designs should be developed to insure that excavation, the
potential for improved public access, or the appearance of towers,
rights of way or access roads do not degrade the value of the
sites.

Major - This zone should be avoided. When better opportunities
are unavailable rights of way and access roads should be designed
to minimize interference with the existing or anticipated use of
the landscape.

Moderate - Rights of way and access roads should be developed to
minimize conflicts and provide opportunities for the anticipated
land use.

Minor - No special actions.

Source:

1.   Existing and Anticipated Development and Recreation Map.

2.   Historical Sites Map.

3.   Archaeological Sites Map.

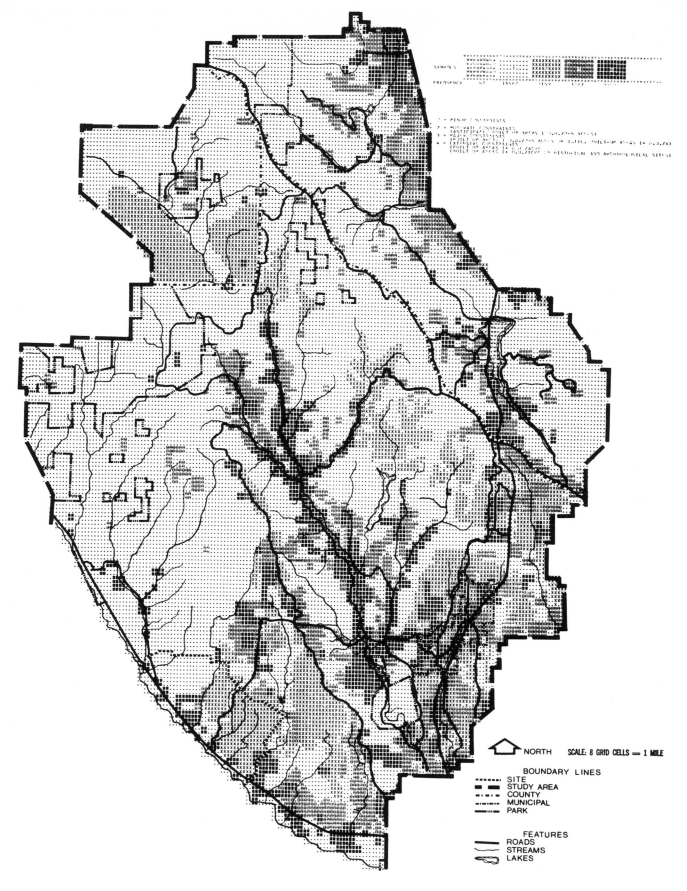

VISUAL CONSTRAINTS TO LANDSCAPE MODIFICATION

VISUAL CONSTRAINTS TO LANDSCAPE MODIFICATION

General:

The map of visual constraints to landscape modification was derived from the maps of existing and anticipated development, recreation, visibility, slope instability, timber trees, discontinuous canopy and physiography. The constraints map depicts the areas where visual quality is of greatest and least importance to the general public.

Definitions:

Extensive - Scenic areas within 4 miles from the viewpoint, or existing and proposed parks, or existing and proposed scenic highways, or existing and potential reservoir sites, or built-up areas of densities greater than one dwelling unit per acre.

Major - Private recreation areas or potential recreation areas, or built-up areas of densities of one dwelling unit per 2-5 acres, or anticipated built-up areas of densities greater than one dwelling unit per acre.

Moderate - Scenic areas beyond 4 miles from the viewpoint, or visually accessible areas, or anticipated built-up areas of densities of one dwelling unit per 2-5 acres, or soil vegetation contrast areas, or areas of a high risk of slope instability in discontinuous canopy, or ridges, or course lines, or slopes over 50% in areas of discontinuous canopy areas, or timber tree areas.

Minor - Visually degraded and other areas not included in the above.

Use:

The visual constraints to landscape modification map when related to transmission line development implies the following restrictions for each zone of constraints.

Extensive - The visual quality of this zone is an irreplaceable resource of great importance to the public and must be preserved. From significant points of viewing, transmission line development within this zone should not appear to have cleared rights of way, continuous alignments of over 3 towers, or ground modification incompatible with the surrounding landscape. Towers and conductors should be designed and treated to blend with or enhance the existing landscape. There should be no highly visible towers within 1000 feet of significant view or activity points.

Major - The visual quality of this zone is of special importance to many people. From significant viewpoints, transmission line development should not appear to have cleared rights of way.

Moderate - The visual quality of this zone is of general importance and/or highly susceptible to visual degradation. Within scenic areas beyond 4 miles from the viewpoint, transmission line development should not appear to have continuous cleared rights of way for more than 2 tower spans. In the areas of soil-vegetation contrast, steep slopes and high risk of slope instability in discontinuous canopy, the impact of access road construction should be minimized by special treatments of cuts, fills, and road beds. In timber tree areas, cleared right of way should be designed not to appear continuous. Within visually accessible areas and anticipated built-up areas of densities of one dwelling unit per 2-5 acres, towers should be screened from view. Background should be used to prevent silhouetting of towers on ridges. Course lines should be spanned to prevent clearing of vegetation.

Minor - No special actions.

Source:

1. Existing and Anticipated Development and Recreation Map.
2. Visibility Map.
3. Slope Instability Map.
4. Timber Tree Map.
5. Discontinuous Canopy Map.
6. Physiography Map.

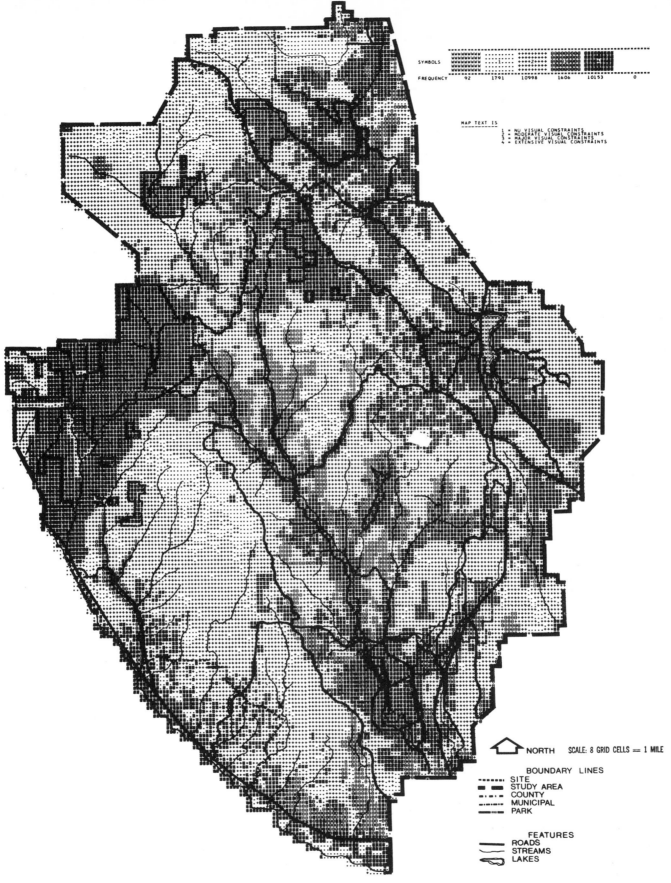

SYMBOLS	WWWWWWWWW WWWWWWWWW	1			
FREQUENCY	92	1791	10998	1606	10153	0

MAP TEXT IS

1 = NU VISUAL CONSTRAINTS
2 = MODERATE VISUAL CONSTRAINTS
3 = MAJOR VISUAL CONSTRAINTS
4 = EXTENSIVE VISUAL CONSTRAINTS

NORTH   SCALE: 8 GRID CELLS = 1 MILE

BOUNDARY LINES

SITE
STUDY AREA
COUNTY
MUNICIPAL
PARK

FEATURES

ROADS
STREAMS
LAKES

109

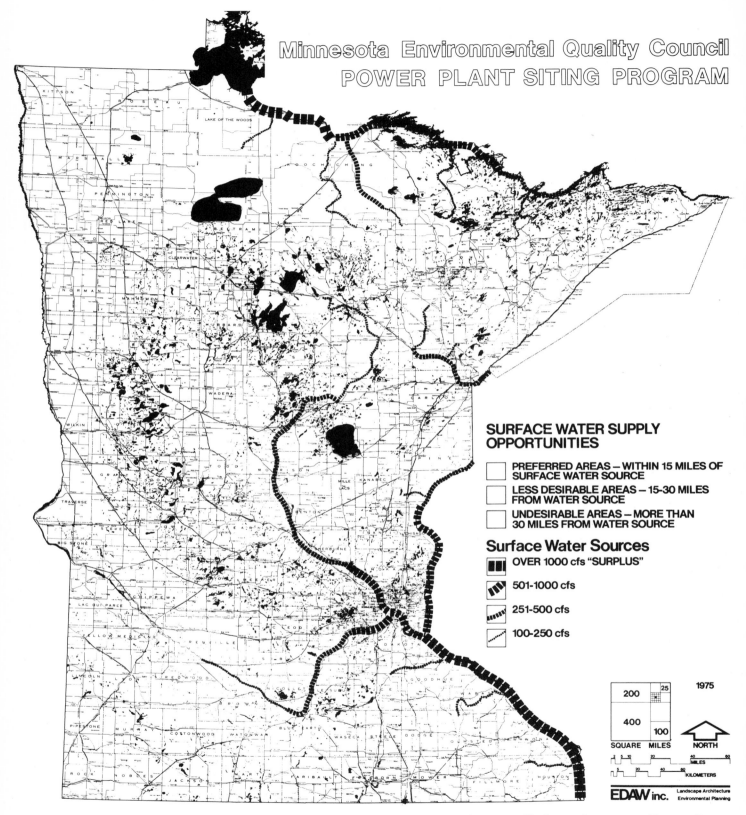

FIGURE 7-10   Example of a manually drawn opportunity factor map. Assumptions regarding acceptable distance from opportunities permit the opportunity factor map to be composited directly with constraint overlays.

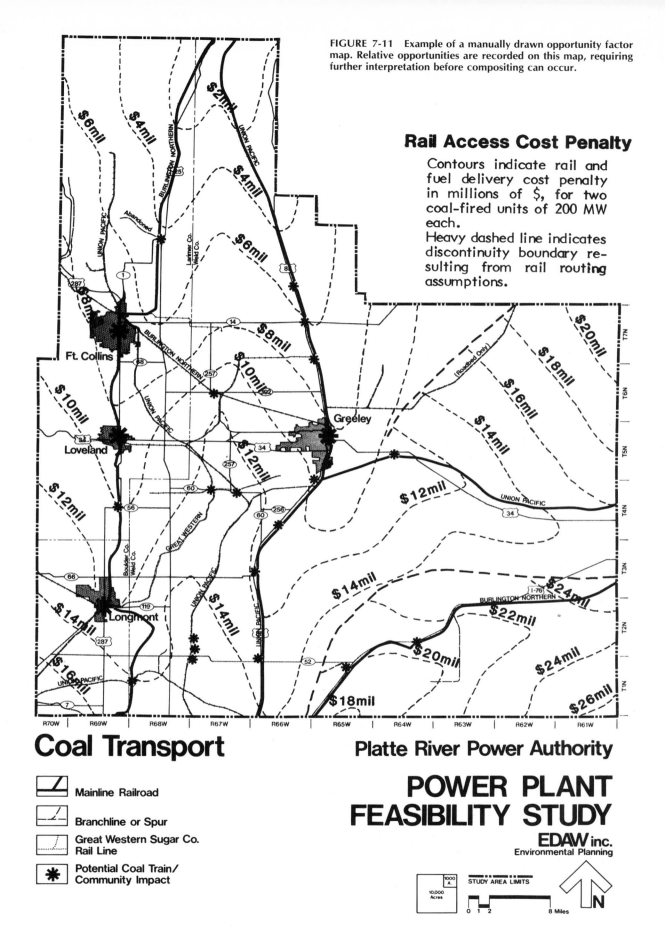

FIGURE 7-11 Example of a manually drawn opportunity factor map. Relative opportunities are recorded on this map, requiring further interpretation before compositing can occur.

Rail Access Cost Penalty

Contours indicate rail and fuel delivery cost penalty in millions of $, for two coal-fired units of 200 MW each.

Heavy dashed line indicates discontinuity boundary resulting from rail routing assumptions.

Coal Transport

Platte River Power Authority

POWER PLANT FEASIBILITY STUDY

EDAW inc.
Environmental Planning

Mainline Railroad

Branchline or Spur

Great Western Sugar Co. Rail Line

Potential Coal Train/ Community Impact

STUDY AREA LIMITS

1000 A

10,000 Acres

0 1 2   8 Miles

N

FIGURE 7-12 Examples of transmission access cost modeling and map output. Mapping based on assumptions as to relative opportunity levels and subsequent compositing may be entirely computerized.

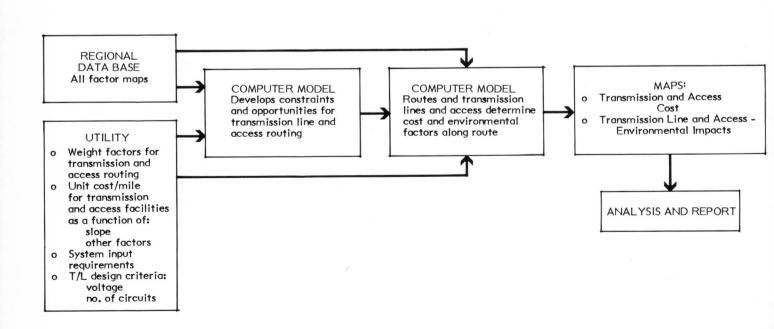

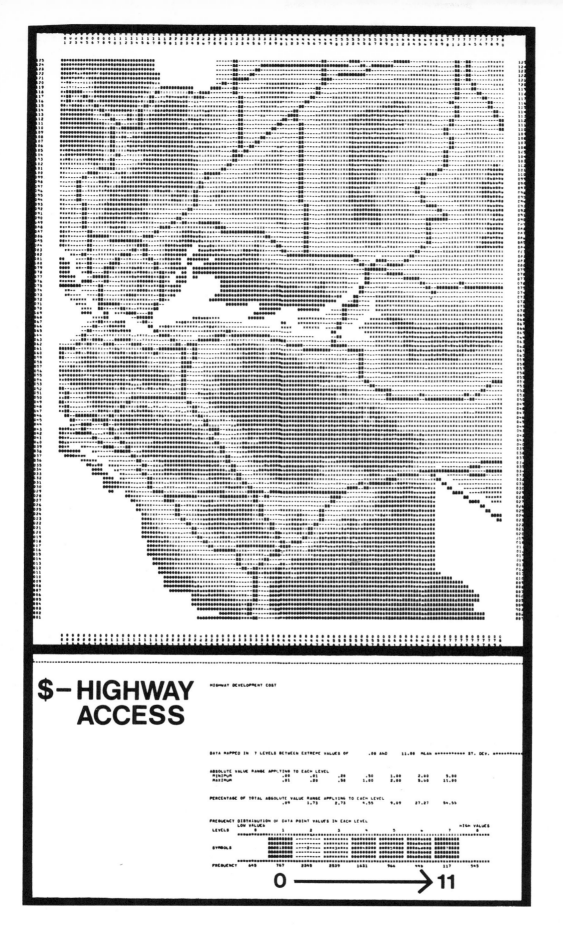

$−HIGHWAY ACCESS

HIGHWAY DEVELOPMENT COST

DATA MAPPED IN 7 LEVELS BETWEEN EXTREME VALUES OF .00 AND 11.00 MEAN ＝＝＝＝＝＝＝＝＝ ST. DEV. ＝＝＝＝＝＝＝＝＝＝

ABSOLUTE VALUE RANGE APPLYING TO EACH LEVEL
MINIMUM   .00   .01   .20   .50   1.00   2.00   5.00
MAXIMUM   .01   .20   .50   1.00   2.00   5.00   11.00

PERCENTAGE OF TOTAL ABSOLUTE VALUE RANGE APPLYING TO EACH LEVEL
               .09   1.73   2.73   4.55   9.09   27.27 54.55

FREQUENCY DISTRIBUTION OF DATA POINT VALUES IN EACH LEVEL
LOW VALUES   HIGH VALUES
LEVELS   0   1   2   3   4   5   6   7   8

SYMBOLS

FREQUENCY   645   767   2340   2539   1631   966   449   117   545

0 ⟶ 11

113

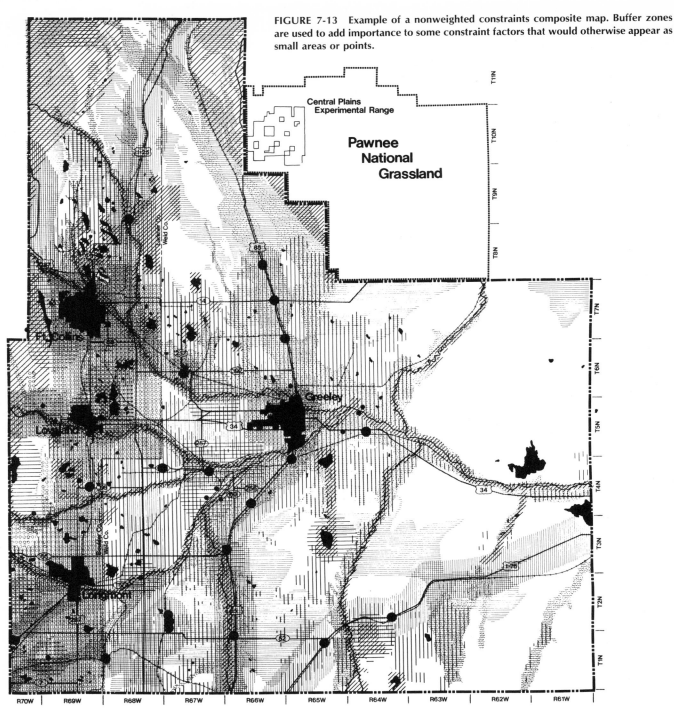

FIGURE 7-13 Example of a nonweighted constraints composite map. Buffer zones are used to add importance to some constraint factors that would otherwise appear as small areas or points.

Central Plains
Experimental Range

Pawnee
National
Grassland

Constraints Composite

Platte River Power Authority

Irrigated Cropland		Mineral Deposits & Geologic Restrictions
View Quality Buffer Zones		Primary Groundwater Resources
Wildlife Habitat Buffer Zones		Major Perennial Watercourses & 100 Yr. Floodplains
Cultural Resources Buffer Zones		Reservoirs
Zoning Restrictions & Population Centers		Cities & Surrounding Urban Areas

POWER PLANT
FEASIBILITY STUDY

EDAW inc.
Environmental Planning

114

Repeat for each planning region
(should be independent of fuel type)

Step 1 Decide relative importance of the three broad categories of factors (refer to Figure 7-3):

o Technical/Economic $\underline{\quad x \quad}$
o Physical/Biological $\underline{\quad y \quad}$
o Social/Cultural $\underline{\quad z \quad}$ $X + Y + Z = 1000$ points (example)

Step 2 Within Physical/Biological and Social/Cultural categories, decide the relative importance of each technical area:

Physical/Biological
(Y points total)

o Meteorology/Air Quality Y_1
o Geology/Seismology Y_2
o Hydrology-Water Resources Y_3
o Water Quality Y_4

o Biological Resources Y_5
o Noise Y_6

$\overline{=Y}$

Social/Cultural
(Z points total)

o Visual/Aesthetic Quality Z_1
o Land Use Z_2
o Cultural Resources Z_3
o Economic & Community
  Resources Z_4
o Public Health & Comfort Z_5
o Public Safety Z_6

$\overline{=Z}$

Step 3 Within each technical area, decide the <u>importance</u> of each individual screening factor.

▲ Public and Staff

- -

▼ Staff

Repeat for each fuel type and planning region

Step 4 Decide magnitude of potential impact on each screening factor.

Step 5 Compute screening factor weight = (importance of factor) x (magnitude of factor) and normalize the factor weight to the technical areas of importance.

Step 6 Compute composite weight for all locations in region = summation of screening factor weights at each location.

FIGURE 7-14 Numerical weighting system for regional screening.

Relative Importance

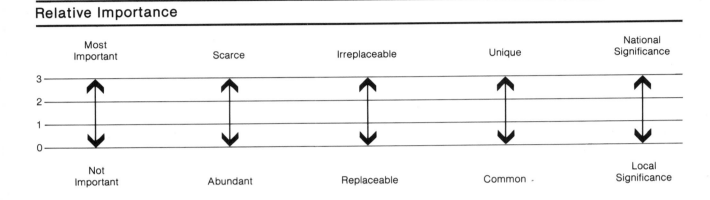

Magnitude of Impact

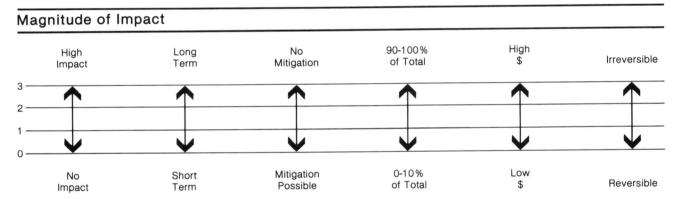

FIGURE 7-15 Example of the importance and magnitude of impact weighting scales. Each constraint factor may be weighted relative to others (in this case on a scale of 0 to 3) according to various measures of importance and magnitude of impact.

importance in the screening without resorting to a numerical weighting system.

Some thirty constraint factors were mapped for the Platte River Power Authority Study (EDAW Inc., June–September, 1976). In the constraints composite map only ten of the most important screening factors have been included, but since they overlap each other in many areas, they define a wide range of constraints to siting.

It should also be noted that with careful preparation of the composite each screening factor can still be identified. The white and lightly hatched areas in Figure 7-13 show clearly how the candidate siting areas were identified in this particular study.

Numerical Weighting

When a large number of screening factors must be combined into an environmental constraint map, some form of numerical weighting system is necessary. One system suggested to the California Energy Resources Conservation and Development Commission is laid out in Figure 7-14.

This system closely parallels a system used in Minnesota in the statewide power plant siting study. In the Minnesota case, site-selection criteria had been established by the legislation that set up the study. A representative advisory committee of thirty people was given the re-

Seafarer Corridor Analysis
Upper Michigan Region

by EDAW inc.
San Francisco, California

under contract to
GTE Sylvania
Communication Systems Division
Needham Heights, Massachusetts

for
U.S. Navy
Naval Electronic Systems Command
Washington, D.C.

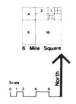

6 Mile Square

Scale
0 1 2   4   6

North

COMPOSITE CONSTRAINTS

DATA CATEGORIES

Right-of-Way Opportunities
Avoidance Features
Vegetation I
Land Use
Land Ownership
Cultural & Recreational
Wildlife I
Surface Water

Utility Buffers
Vegetation II
Mineral Extraction
Governmental
Wildlife II
Surficial Geology
Slope

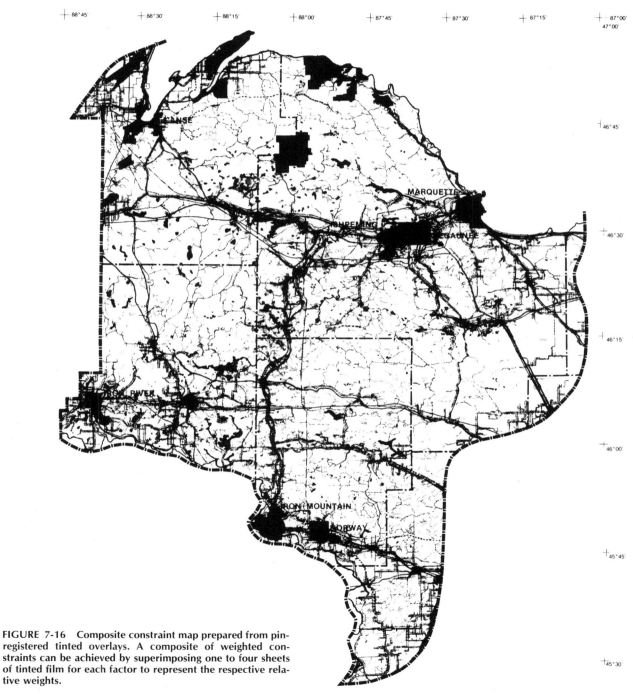

FIGURE 7-16 Composite constraint map prepared from pin-registered tinted overlays. A composite of weighted constraints can be achieved by superimposing one to four sheets of tinted film for each factor to represent the respective relative weights.

117

TABLE 7-4 Worksheets recording factor weightings. Study participants may be asked to determine factor weights by vote, using importance and magnitude-of-importance weighting scales.

PLANT TYPE: NUCLEAR
MAGNITUDE OF IMPACT

map number	weightable data categories	area / acres	magnitude of impact on ssc
7	EXCLUSION AREAS COMPOSITE (Areas not Feasible by Existing Siting Regulations)		
13	AVOIDANCE AREAS COMPOSITE		
14	SITE SELECTION CRITERIA (aa) Local Communities and Institutions		
	- Indian Reservations	2,220,721	
	- Military Reservations	53,000	
16	SITE SELECTION CRITERIA (cc) Unusual land form, vegetation & wildlife		
	RARE, UNIQUE OR UNUSUAL LAND FORMS		
	- Areas of Greatest Local Relief (100 feet or more/square mile)	X	
	- Glacial Features; Kame Fields, Eskers, Drumlins; Karst Topography	335,872	
17a	RARE, UNIQUE OR UNUSUAL VEGETATION		
	- Prairie Remnant (Proj. 80)	25,000	
	- Scenic Timber (Proj. 80)	225,280	
	- Rare Flora (Proj. 80)	507,904	
	- Other Scientific and Natural Areas (Proj. 80)	1,710,270	
	- National Forests	4,905,411	
	- State Forests	3,000,000	
18a	RARE, UNIQUE OR UNUSUAL WILDLIFE HABITAT		
	- Exceptional Game Habitat (Proj. 80)	2,045,542	
	- Federal Waterfowl Production Areas	103,000	
	- Trout Streams (Map 8)	X	
	- Drainage Areas Tributary to Trout Streams		
	- Prairie Chicken Range	294,912	
	- Peregrine Falcon Range	1/6 of state	
	- Bald Eagle Nesting Range	540,672	
	- Timber Wolf Range	1/3 of state	
	- Whooping Crane Range	1/2 of state	
19	SITE SELECTION CRITERIA (dd) Visual & Audible Impingement on Recreation Areas*		
	- Buffer Zones for Visual and Audible Impingement on Recreation Areas - Areas within 2 miles of Recreation Resources classified as Exclusion or avoidance.		
	- Areas within 2.1 to 5 miles of Recreation Resources classified as Exclusion or Avoidance.		

PLANT TYPE: NUCLEAR
MAGNITUDE OF IMPACT

map number	weightable data categories	area / acres	magnitude of impact on ssc
	SITE SELECTION CRITERIA (ee) Valuable & Productive Land & Water VALUABLE AND PRODUCTIVE LAND		

20a	- Agricultural Lands Suitable for Irrigation.
	- Agricultural Productivity -
	    - Soil of High Productivity (TDN)
	    - Soil of Medium Productivity		

20b	- Forest Productivity
	    - Soil of High Productivity
	    - Soil of Medium Productivity		

20c	- Iron Deposits	X	
	- Copper - Nickel Deposits	X	
	- Urban Areas (MLMIS 1969 MAP)	X	
	- Existing Marsh (MLMIS 1969 MAP) - Prairie Marshes	NA	
	- Wild Rice Marshes	30,000	
	VALUABLE AND PRODUCTIVE SURFACE WATER SUPPLIES		
20e	- Areas Tributary to National or State Wild, Scenic & Recreational Rivers	2,301,952	
	- Areas Tributary to BWCA or Voyageurs National Park	2,739,814	
20f	- Lakes	3,411,200	
	STATE OF MINNESOTA	51,205,760	
*	EXCLUSION & AVOIDANCE AREAS WITH RECREATION POTENTIAL		

1	EXCLUSION AREAS - NATIONAL
	    - Wilderness Areas (BWCA)
	    - Voyageurs National Park
	    - Historic Sites and Landmarks
	    - Natural Landmarks
	    - Wildlife Refuges
	    - Monuments
	    - Wild, Scenic, and Recreational Riverways		

2	EXCLUSION AREAS - STATE
	    - State Parks
	    - Scientific and Natural Areas
	    - Wild, Scenic and Recreational Riverways		

8	AVOIDANCE AREAS - STATE - Trout Streams		

9	AVOIDANCE AREAS - STATE
	    - Registered Historic Site
	    - Historic District		

10	AVOIDANCE AREAS - STATE AND NATIONAL
	    - State Recreational Rivers
	    - State Recreational Trails
	    - National Recreational Trail		

11	AVOIDANCE AREAS
	    - County Parks
	    - Metropolitan Parks		

TABLE 7-5 Example of constraint factor weights. These weights were derived by combining magnitude-of-impact and relative-importance weights assigned by ballot, using the worksheet in Table 7-4.

Weights

6.1	–	Buffer zones for visual and audible impingement on recreation areas – 2 miles
6.0	–	Scenic timber
5.2	–	Agricultural lands of high productivity
5.1	–	Exceptional game habitat
4.8	–	Prairie remnant
4.4	–	Iron deposits
4.2	–	Copper-nickel deposits
4.1	–	Indian reservations
3.6	–	Buffer zones for visual and audible impingement on recreation areas – 2.1-5 miles
3.4	–	Forest lands of high productivity
3.3	–	Other scientific and natural areas
3.1	–	Glacial features
2.9	–	National forests
2.8	–	Agricultural lands of medium productivity
1.6	–	Forest lands of medium productivity
1.2	–	Military reservations

TABLE 7-6 Data factor suitability worksheet. By considering potential impacts in terms of costs, data factors may be placed in avoidance (exclusio straint, or opportunity catogories before numerical weights are assigned, as shown in this example from the Seafarer, Michigan, study.

DATA FACTOR	AVOIDANCE	CONSTRAINT HIGH	MODERATE	LOW	COMMENTS*	QUALIFICATIONS
Corporate boundaries	X		X (buffer)		2, 3, 5	One-mile buffer from corporate limit.
Urban settlements (U-1, U-2, U-3 on land use data map)	X		X (buffer)		2, 3, 5	One-mile buffer from settlement limit.
Rural settlements (R-1, R-2 on land use data map)	X		X (buffer)		2, 3, 5	One-half-mile buffer from settlement limit.
Planned developments	X				2, 3, 5	
Special preserves	X				4, 5	WUPPAD Land Use Plan
Cemeteries			X		2, 5	
Prison facilities	X				5	
Building clusters			X		2, 3, 5	
K. I. Sawyer A.F.B.			X		2, 5	

*Comments (cost):   1-Construction; 2-Mitigation; 3-Operation & maintenance; 4-Biological; 5-Social.

TABLE 7-7 Constraint-weighting worksheet. Constraints previously assigned simple high, medium, or low ratings may be weighted numerically for compositing.

CONSTRAINT CATEGORY	DATA VARIABLE	WEIGHTING INDEX
VEGETATION I	Wetlands dominant	4
LAND USE	One-mile buffer around urban settlements	3
	One-half-mile buffer around rural settlements	
	Building clusters	
	K. I. Sawyer Air Force Base	
LAND OWNERSHIP	Private Land	3
CULTURAL AND RECREATIONAL	Upper Peninsula Experimental Forest	3
	State Parks lands	
WILDLIFE I	Baraga Plains Waterfowl Management Area	2
	Craig Lake State Park -- primitive area	
	Sharp-tail grouse management areas	
SURFACE WATER	3, 4, 5, 6, and 6+ order perennial streams	2
UTILITY BUFFERS	One-mile buffers around o electrical substations o electrical switching stations o electrical generating stations o telephone central exchanges	2

TABLE 7-8 Relative importance of evaluation categories: tabulations. Importance rankings may be derived by asking each study participant to arrange evaluation factors from least critical to most critical and to assign numerical values reflecting the relative difference in importance between the factors.

Evaluation Category	Participant											Group Ranking	Group Average	Standard Deviation
	1	2	3	4	5	6	7	8	9	10	11			
Air quality/ meteorology	2.04	2.04	1.50	1.20	1.53	1.50	2.29	1.90	2.03	3.55	1.72	1	1.93	.58
Environmental resources	1.84	1.03	1.00	1.28	1.35	.86	1.14	.95	2.11	1.99	1.55	3	1.28	.40
Natural hazards & terrain	1.63	1.03	1.00	.64	.90	1.26	1.71	.95	.82	.76	1.06	5	1.07	.33
Land use	1.84	.78	1.00	1.28	1.53	1.18	.86	.95	1.21	1.00	1.29	4	1.17	.30
Load center/ DWR system	.82	2.04	1.50	.85	1.09	1.42	.86	.95	.82	.59	.86	5	1.07	.41
Site-dependent costs	.60	1.03	1.50	1.28	1.35	1.42	.86	2.38	.98	.59	.86	4	1.17	.51
Socio-economics	.41	.51	.50	.42	.90	.79	.57	.48	.82	.74	1.20	6	.67	.24
Water supply	.82	1.54	2.00	2.55	1.35	1.57	1.71	1.44	1.21	1.77	1.46	2	1.58	.44

sponsibility for familiarizing itself with the needs and intricacies of the power industry and making the final recommendations. The committee members soon found that they not only needed to resolve several basic policy issues by discussion and vote but also had to assign relative values to the site-screening factors. In this case, it was determined that areas where opportunity factors existed could be considered favorable. Opportunity factors did not therefore require weighting. What was needed was a way of determining the degree to which the environmental constraints of one area limited its suitability relative to the constraints of other areas. As a result, a voting procedure was devised to arrive at weights reflecting the consensus of the committee.

Two different elements were determined to enter into the total weight. The first was the *relative importance* of the factors to be weighted in relation to all other factors. The second was the *magnitude of the impact* that a power plant would have on the particular factor. Two ballots were used to elicit the value placed by each committee member on these subjects. Relative importance and magnitude of impact scales were rated from 0 (not important and no impact) to 3 (most important and high im-

pact). Figure 7-15 displays the considerations that entered into these ratings.

As in the California method (Figure 7-14), the final weight for each environmental constraint factor was found by multiplying the importance rating by the magnitude-of-impact rating for each constraint and for each member's vote. The forms used in the weighting exercise are shown in Table 7-4.

Application of the method produced a list of weights for each of the constraint factors, which of course contained surprises for some members of the committee. A repeat of the voting and calculations produced little significant difference from the first balloting. The results are shown in Table 7-5.

The total numerical scores for each area within the state were tabulated and displayed in color on the composite constraint map. The darker the color, the greater the constraint and the higher the point value. The product can be found in Figure 9-9 in Chapter 9.

Another method that deserves discussion and has proved to be extremely versatile combines numerical weighting with a manual overlay technique using pin-registered tinted acetate film. In this method, a single tint is

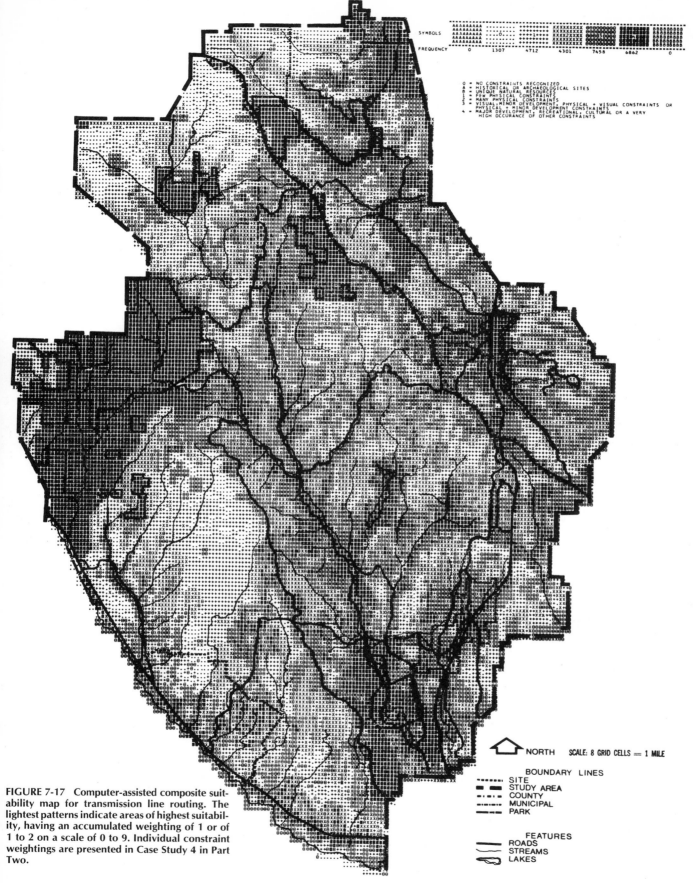

0 = NO CONSTRAINTS RECOGNIZED
A = HISTORICAL OR ARCHAEOLOGICAL SITES
B = UNIQUE NATURAL RESOURCES
1 = FEW PHYSICAL CONSTRAINTS
2 = MANY PHYSICAL CONSTRAINTS
3 = VISUAL-MINOR DEVELOPMENT, PHYSICAL + VISUAL CONSTRAINTS OR
    PHYSICAL-MINOR DEVELOPMENT CONSTRAINTS
4 = MAJOR DEVELOPMENT, RECREATIONAL, CULTURAL OR A VERY
    HIGH OCCURANCE OF OTHER CONSTRAINTS

NORTH   SCALE: 8 GRID CELLS = 1 MILE

BOUNDARY LINES

SITE
STUDY AREA
COUNTY
MUNICIPAL
PARK

FEATURES

ROADS
STREAMS
LAKES

FIGURE 7-17 Computer-assisted composite suitability map for transmission line routing. The lightest patterns indicate areas of highest suitability, having an accumulated weighting of 1 or of 1 to 2 on a scale of 0 to 9. Individual constraint weightings are presented in Case Study 4 in Part Two.

123

	General	Specific	Numerical Scale
High impacts, major technical problems, or high costs	High	H+	9
		H	8
		H-	7
		M+	6
	Medium	M	5
		M-	4
		L+	3
Low impacts, minor technical problems, or low costs	Low	L	2
		L-	1

FIGURE 7-18 Common rating scale for all evaluation categories.

TABLE 7-9 Sample evaluation matrix. Individual ratings in each evaluation category are combined with the weighted rating of its category to produce a weighted total score for each candidate area.

Evaluation Category		A	B	C	D	E	F	G	...	X	Y	Z	AA	BB	CC	DD	EE	Relative Value
Air quality/ meteorology	Rating/	H	H	H	L	H-	H+	H		L+	H+	H+	M	M	M	M-	M+	
	Weighted Rating	15.44	15.44	15.44	3.86	3.51	15.44	15.44		5.79	17.34	17.37	9.65	9.65	9.65	7.72	7.72	1.93
Water supply	Rating/	M	L	L	L-	L	L-	L-		M+	L-	L-	L-	L+	L	L+	L	
	Weighted Rating	7.90	3.16	3.16	1.58	3.16	1.58	1.58		9.48	1.58	1.58	1.58	4.74	3.16	4.74	3.16	1.58
Environmental resources	Rating/	L	H	L+	M	L	L	H		M	L-	L+	M-	L+	L+	L-	M-	
	Weighted Rating	2.56	10.24	3.84	6.4	2.56	2.56	10.24		6.4	1.28	3.84	5.12	3.84	3.84	1.28	5.12	1.28
Land use	Rating/	M	M-	M	M-	M-	M-	M-		L	H	M	L+	M-	H	M-	M+	
	Weighted Rating	5.85	4.68	5.85	4.68	4.68	4.68	4.68		2.34	8.19	5.85	3.51	4.68	9.36	4.68	7.02	1.17
Site- dependent Costs	Rating/	L	L	L	M	L	L	L		L	M	H	H	H	H	H	H	
	Weighted Rating	2.34	2.34	2.34	5.85	2.34	2.34	2.34		2.34	5.85	9.36	9.36	9.36	9.36	9.36	9.36	1.17
Natural hazards & terrain	Rating/	L	L+	L	M-	L	L	L+		L-	M	H-	M	M+	M+	M+	M	
	Weighted Rating	2.14	3.21	2.14	4.28	2.14	2.14	3.21		1.07	5.35	7.49	5.35	6.42	6.42	6.42	5.35	1.07
Load center/ DWR system	Rating/	M	M-	M-	L+	L+	L+	L+		L+	L+	L+	M-	L	L	L-	L+	
	Weighted Rating	5.35	4.28	4.28	3.21	3.21	3.21	3.21		3.21	3.21	3.21	4.28	2.14	2.14	1.07	3.21	1.07
Socio- economics	Rating/	M-	L-	L-	L	M-	M-	M		L+	M-	L	L	L	L	L	L+	
	Weighted Rating	2.68	.67	.67	1.34	2.68	2.68	3.36		2.01	2.68	1.34	1.34	1.34	1.34	1.34	2.01	.67
Weighted Total		44.26	44.02	37.72	31.20	34.28	34.63	44.06		32.64	45.57	50.04	38.26	42.17	45.27	36.61	42.95	

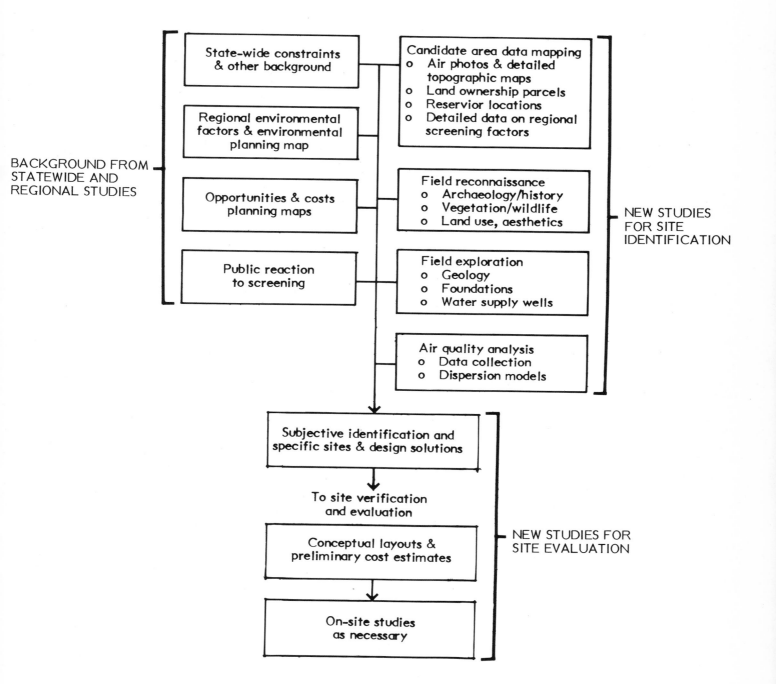

FIGURE 7-19 Site-identification information flow diagram. Further examination of regional screening data together with new, more detailed candidate area studies must occur before candidate sites can be identified.

FIGURE 7-20   Example of a candidate site map. One or several candidate sites may be found in each candidate area. This 250-square-mile area produced three potentially suitable sites.

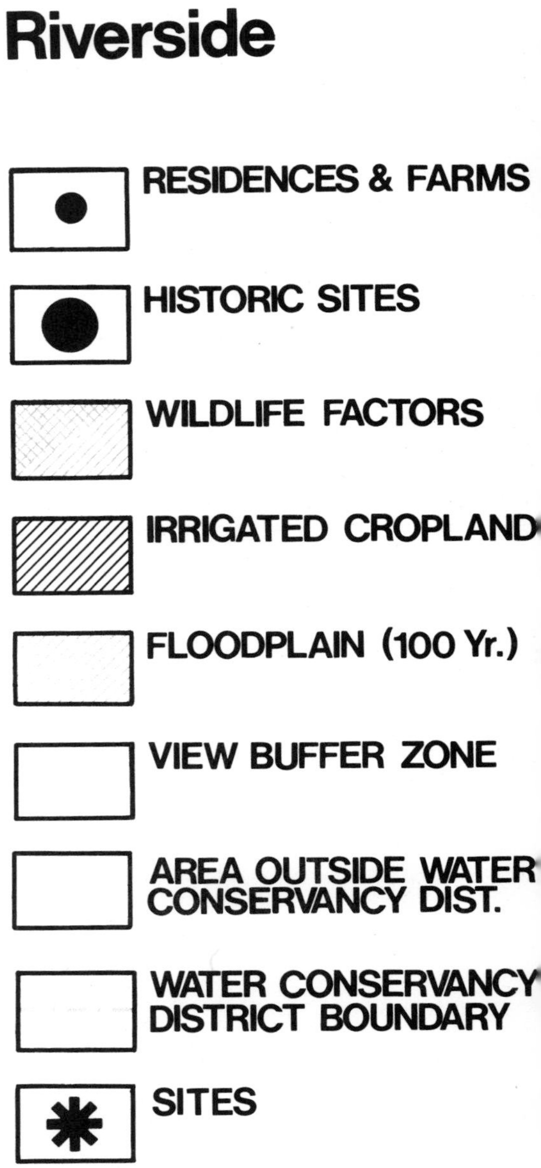

Riverside

RESIDENCES & FARMS

HISTORIC SITES

WILDLIFE FACTORS

IRRIGATED CROPLAND

FLOODPLAIN (100 Yr.)

VIEW BUFFER ZONE

AREA OUTSIDE WATER CONSERVANCY DIST.

WATER CONSERVANCY DISTRICT BOUNDARY

SITES

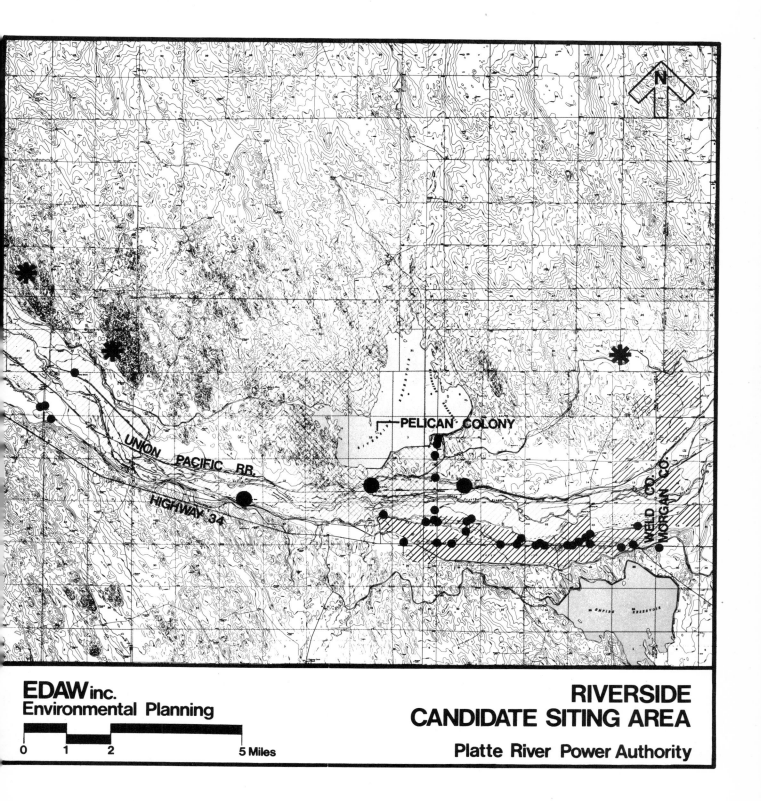

PELICAN COLONY

UNION PACIFIC R.R.

HIGHWAY 34

WELD CO.
MORGAN CO.

EDAW inc.
Environmental Planning

0   1   2   5 Miles

RIVERSIDE
CANDIDATE SITING AREA

Platte River Power Authority

used throughout the series of overlays. One or more map overlays are prepared for each factor, the number representing the relative weight assigned in each case. The intensity of the tone built up when all overlays are composited and viewed on a light table is an accurate representation of the total weight at any point on the base map. The number of total sheets inserted equals the highest possible numerical weight. Figure 7-16 illustrates an application of this method to the site search for the Seafarer communications system in the northern Michigan region. In this case a pale-yellow tint was used. Wherever the tint appeared on all constraint overlays (which numbered thirty-six), superimposition produced a dark orange, representing most severely constrained areas. This system allows for total flexibility in changing weights and instantly illustrates the effect on the overall composite. The system is easily adapted to viewgraphs for overhead projection for meetings and, of course, to color slides and photographic reproduction.

Assignments of weights in the Seafarer case were made by a multidisciplinary team including representatives from the federal government, the design engineers, and the environmental consultants. Voting was tabulated on the forms shown in Tables 7-6 and 7-7.

Weighting systems are also valuable for compositing environmental data for the selection of optimum routes for linear features such as transmission lines, highways, pipelines, and railroads. In the transmission line routing study for a California utility from which we drew previously for an example of opportunity factor mapping, a computer-assisted process was used to generate both individual data maps and weighted composite maps. A weighting scale of 1 to 9 was applied to key constraints from each data map to derive the composite suitability map shown in Figure 7-17.

Further examples and discussion of the considerations involved in selecting an appropriate compositing method will be found in Chapter 9.

As part of the statewide siting study for the California Department of Water Resources, the Delphi process, which was used to distinguish exclusion from evaluation factors, was also used to examine and weigh evaluation factors. The eight major categories of evaluation factors were discussed and arranged by each of eleven participants from least critical to most critical. Each participant was then asked to assign numerical values reflecting the difference in importance between the least and the most critical categories (i.e., twice, four times, ten times, or more times as important). Next, values were assigned to the six intervening categories. All eleven ballots were

normalized, and standard deviations were calculated (see Table 7-8).

In this study, numerical weights were also used in candidate area evaluation, the final step in site screening, which we will cover later. Once the **relative importance** of the categories had been set, the thirty-one candidate areas were rated relative to how well they satisfied each data category. Ratings were based on such considerations as low cost, minimal adverse environmental impact, and high mitigation potential. A rating scale of 1 to 9 was used as shown in Figure 7-18.

Scores for all candidate areas were tabulated and then multiplied by the weight assigned to each data category to arrive at an overall ranking or ordering of areas (see Table 7-9). From this display, it was fairly easy to select those candidate areas that had the highest probability of containing acceptable sites in order to concentrate further investigations in these areas.

Weighting will be discussed again in Chapter 8 as it applies to site evaluation. Before leaving the subject in this chapter, it is well to point out that there are many ways of determining weights that have not been discussed here. It is a subject in which there is much interest and in which there will be continuing experimentation. The Bibliography indicates source material for other systems, but as will be seen, most sources involve mathematical models and calculations that are not understandable to the general public and therefore are not described here.

IDENTIFICATION OF CANDIDATE AREA

After completion of constraint and opportunity composite maps and any site-dependent cost maps, identification of candidate areas is a relatively simple task. The constraint and opportunity maps are overlaid and examined to find areas relatively free of constraint where opportunities are available. These are then defined as *candidate areas*. Areas of moderate or even greater constraint may also be identified for further study if the overlay of opportunities and site-dependent costs indicates an economic advantage sufficient to produce a favorable constraint-cost ratio.

IDENTIFICATION OF CANDIDATE SITE

Following the identification of candidate areas, field reconnaissance studies should be conducted to verify their adequacy. The characteristics and potential advantages and disadvantages of the areas should then be summarized for review and comments. If the number of candidate areas is very large, a further rating procedure (or a ranking procedure such as was used in the California Department of Water Resources Power Plant Siting Study) may be necessary to select those suitable for further study.

Identification of specific sites within selected candidate areas requires extensive investigations. First, the candidate areas should be reviewed again to determine those with the characteristics necessary for the proposed facility. Then the background information from previous studies as well as information from new, more detailed studies and field explorations must be evaluated to define potential sites. Figure 7-19 illustrates the general flow of information in this decision-making process. The ultimate product of the site-identification phase will be the confirmation of a series of specific sites and an analysis of detailed impacts covering the full range of technical, socioeconomic, and environmental questions.

If the candidate area produced by previous screens is small enough or of such a character that only one or a very limited number of alternative sites can be identified, another screening phase may not be necessary. In such a case, field inspections by technical staff, design solutions, and management analysis may identify the best site in the area. However, if the candidate area is large and still contains many potential site areas, another screening phase will be required. In this case the data requirements will be of a finer grain to match the reduced scale of the area being inspected. Similarly, different or more limited criteria may be used since the area has already passed at least one previous screen.

Figure 7-20 illustrates a candidate area of such size that a number of alternative candidate sites exist within it. This 250-square-mile area had been identified as the result of a regional screen covering a 3000-square-mile area. As will be seen from the illustration, the second screening, which used eight constraint factors, revealed three suitable sites. The result is a reasonably limited number of sites ready for the detailed analysis, evaluation, and final site-selection process to be discussed in Chapter 8.

8 | THE SITE-EVALUATION PROCESS

INTRODUCTION

The inventory of several specific and broadly acceptable sites achieved through the site-screening process now has to be evaluated in greater detail so that the most suitable site can be identified. As with the process of screening, it is possible to begin and end a site-evaluation study at key decision points within the entire process, depending on the requirements of the facility, the site characteristics, and the procedures of the body responsible for the final decision.

The sequence of steps in site evaluation, laid out in Figure 8-1, is conceptually similar to that of site screening. The process differs mainly in terms of detailed content, requiring the facility to be related more closely to specific sites. It permits the sites to be ranked in terms of relative suitability rather than merely screening out those that do not meet the objectives and criteria being applied.

SITE VERIFICATION

The sites to be evaluated will have been identified by a process that depended primarily on information from secondary sources. While every attempt will have been made to ensure the validity of the information, conditions are constantly changing, particularly in terms of how land is used.

The first task is to inspect and study each alternative site to determine its general character and the appropriate location for the facility within the site. This investigation will not be as detailed as that required prior to final site planning but must be sufficient to confirm the overall feasibility of the site for the proposed facility. Primary considerations will include those related to the physical safety and efficient operation of the facility, such as soils and geology, water supply, labor supply, and access—

the original siting requirements. In addition, each environmental condition, physical-biological and social-economic, must be reported in sufficient detail to confirm that the already identified site-screening objectives and criteria have been met.

Even if aerial or remote photography has been used in site selection, it is often valuable to fly over the sites as well as to conduct a field inspection on the ground. Low-level aerial views can quickly furnish the necessary update of information and can provide insights not always readily acquired on the ground. Some surprises may be in store since even county planning agencies are not always aware of current developments throughout their jurisdictions and in incorporated communities. Areas thought to be vacant or in dry farming may be found to be newly planted with irrigated crops such as fruit trees or grapevines. Alternatively, land eliminated from consideration because it was shown on land-use maps in agriculture may show indications, in the form of "For sale" signs or unkempt orchards, of imminent conversion to urban use.

The site-verification study may result in slight adjustments to the actual site area located previously. The adjustment can range up to a few miles in order to retain beneficial site attributes while minimizing undesirable ones.

PREPARATION OF CONCEPTUAL LAYOUTS AND COST ESTIMATES

Detailed questions of site suitability, such as cost of construction and operation, visual impact, and water and power availability to meet precise requirements, cannot be answered in the rather abstract terms used in site screening. The facility must be laid out within each site. The layout is conceptual only, but it may range from rudimentary sketches to quite highly developed schemes.

131

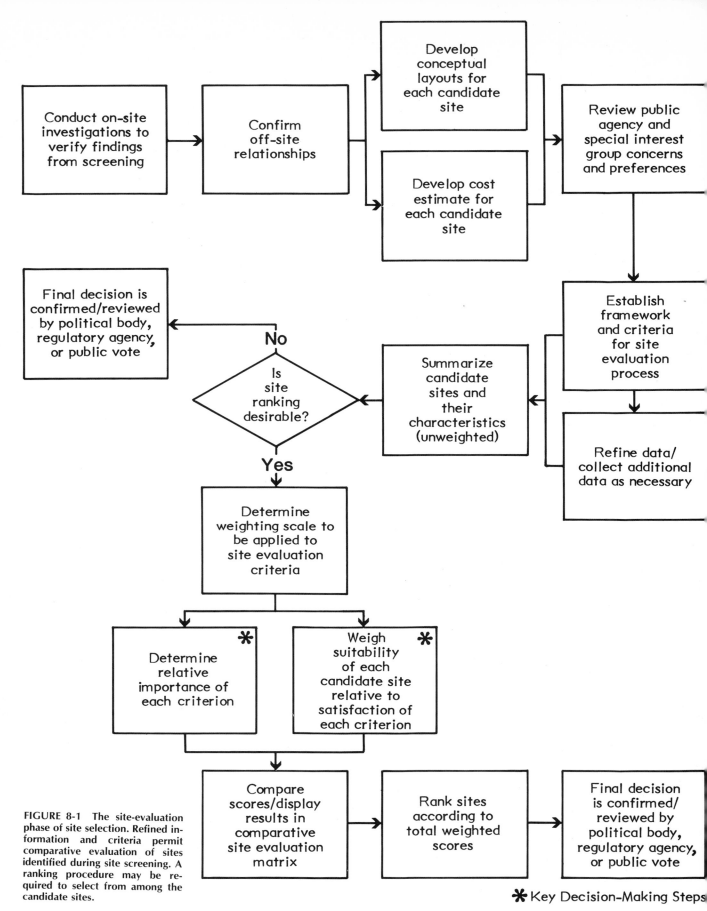

FIGURE 8-1 The site-evaluation phase of site selection. Refined information and criteria permit comparative evaluation of sites identified during site screening. A ranking procedure may be required to select from among the candidate sites.

Simple sketches, accompanied by conceptual engineering solutions to such problems as confined space or long distance to transportation facilities, are typically all that are required when a large number of alternative sites is available for evaluation. More detailed design work is required to distinguish between a smaller set of alternatives of widely varying characteristics.

Examples of simple conceptual site plans can be found in Exhibits 4-7 through 4-9 in Part Two. They were prepared for a power plant site-evaluation study at Davenport, California.

REVIEW OF AGENCY AND PUBLIC CONCERNS

The objective of this step is to define the questions to be addressed in evaluating the conceptual plans for each site. In some cases, many of the questions may have been identified already in legislative guidelines for the review process. For example, any power plant proposal in California must be prepared according to prescribed procedures established by law and contain specific items of information. A notification of intention (NOI) must be submitted for three alternative sites. Review of this document leads to selection of a preferred site and preparation of an application for certification, emphasizing engineering aspects of the project, and an environmental impact document, covering socioeconomic and ecological impacts. The NOI is the primary documentary forum for discussion of the advantages of alternatives in terms of engineering (including any choice of plant type), impact levels, and impact mitigation. A similar review proposed at the federal level is compared with the California NOI procedure in Table 8-1.

Despite the prior involvement of review agencies and citizen representatives in the screening process, attitudes and concerns usually change as the planning of a major facility comes closer to reality. Therefore, the type and level of the review agency or agencies and the interests that need to be involved at the site-evaluation stage may also change or expand.

The citizens' advisory committee may be broadened to represent each potentially affected community. Alternatively, it may be appropriate to establish new local committees or to conduct local attitude surveys. Several techniques for broadening public participation at this point are covered in Chapter 10.

Local agencies will now be in a better position to express their concerns and preferences than they were during the more general screening phase. While local general plans, if they are thorough and up to date, will make provision for anticipated or desired demand for land and services to support new industry, they are rarely able to anticipate a major facility of the type we are discussing. So planners, public works directors, utility company planners, and other officials need the chance to make at least a preliminary assessment of their ability to handle the facility. Discussions with state agencies need to be continued. Issues related to the direct and indirect or growth-inducing effects of the facility need to be reviewed with regional water pollution, air pollution, planning, transportation, and other agencies. Finally, local citizens and special-interest or watchdog groups active in the area of each candidate site may have unanticipated concerns that need to be incorporated in the criteria by which the sites are evaluated.

ESTABLISHING THE FRAMEWORK FOR SITE EVALUATION

When the questions to be resolved during the site-evaluation process have been defined, the criteria for evaluating responses to these questions can be established. Then the analytical methods and data factors to be used in making the findings relative to the criteria can in turn be identified. This procedure is identical to that used in site screening. Working backward in the manner shown diagrammatically in Figure 8-2 will permit the refinement of data needs that are closely related to their use.

Site-Evaluation Criteria

Many of the original site-screening criteria also can be directly applied in site evaluation. Some may no longer have any relevance since the sites will have been selected to avoid certain features or conditions. For example, objectives of avoidance of highly productive agricultural areas, designated scenic and recreation areas, historic and archaeological sites, and areas of significant vegetation and wildlife may have been met by every site. More commonly, however, some compromises will have been necessary, requiring each site to be evaluated anew according to the degree to which such criteria are met.

New or revised criteria may be required to measure the attainment of some objectives. It may be found, for example, as it was in certain sites identified in the California power plant siting study, that in avoiding prime irrigated agricultural lands the sites have been located in dry-farmed lands that appear to be more productive.

TABLE 8-1 Site acceptability review: a comparison of the steps currently required by the state of California and those proposed by federal agencies for review and approval of proposed power plants.

Notification of Intention California	Early Site Review Application (ESR)* Federal (Proposed)

o Filing of NOI
One document covering safety and other environmental areas
Reviewed by:
1 Commission staff
2 Federal, state, regional, and local agencies including the Public Utilities Commission
3 Coastal Zone Conservation Commission
 	
o Public Hearing
 	
o Staff Review/Preliminary Report
1 Conformity with:
  a forecasts
  b applicable laws
2 Relative merit of each site
3 Safety & reliability
 	
o Final Report
1 Acceptability or unacceptability <u>with</u> any conditions imposed on the acceptability
 	
o Public Hearings
 	
o Decision on NOI
	o Filing of Early Site Review (ESR) Application
	Two separate reports:
	- ESR - Site Safety Report
	Reviewed by:
	1 Nuclear Regulatory Commission
	2 Advisory Committee on Reactor Safeguard (ACRS)
	- ESR - Environmental Report
	Reviewed by:
	1 Nuclear Regulatory Commission
	2 NEPA - Commenting Agencies
	
	o Staff Review/Findings
	1 Site Safety Evaluation Report (SSER)
	2 ACRS Letter Report
	3 Draft Site Environmental Statement (DSES)
	4 Final Site Environmental Statement (FSES)
	
	o Staff Site Position (SSP)
	1 Acceptability or unacceptability <u>with</u> any conditions imposed on the acceptability
	2 5-year tenure
	
	o Public Hearings
	
	o Atomic Safety and Licensing Board Decision (ASLB)
	
	o NRC Site Approval
	
	* Early site review can precede <u>or</u> be concurrent with the construction permit application.

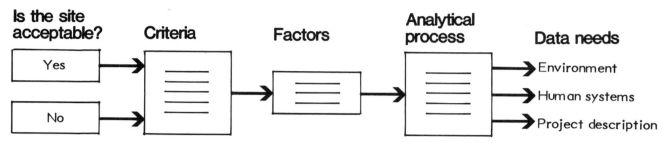

FIGURE 8-2 The process of identifying site-evaluation data needs.

Thus a new criterion based on the actual productive value of land rather than the value interpreted from less direct indicators such as soils and irrigation may be established. New data to measure conformance with such a criterion will be required from local agricultural advisers. This is the most difficult kind of criterion to define because it requires judgment about current relative values and anticipation of future conditions.

With respect to most socioeconomic factors two interrelated criteria, *absorption capability* and *suitability,* will be used. Neither one can be established in terms that are equally applicable to each community under consideration. Absorption capability is a measure of the capacity of the housing market, transportation facilities, and public services to meet the needs of construction, operations, and related service workers. Absorption capability and the fiscal resources to expand capacity vary widely among communities. Once they have been determined, suitability will depend on the community's goals and objectives as expressed in the general plan and other documents, by elected officials, and by the public through public meetings, news media, and other forms of communication. The suitability of change is often a subjective judgment and will vary among communities and interest groups and over time. In the future, however, increasing attention to questions of jobs-housing imbalance and growth and travel patterns can be anticipated at the regional level. Steps to avoid or minimize problems such as excessive commuting may eventually place limitations on community autonomy.

Visual impact is another factor for which criteria have tended to be subjective and site-specific. In this case, it is possible to develop consistent criteria for the facility and sites in question. The approach to visual impact criteria and assessment in general is becoming more systematic and objective.

In addition to the criteria that require a good deal of interpretation, there are many that will be set by the regulations and guidelines of review agencies, as was discussed in Chapter 6. Examples include the various criteria for noise relative to land use which are set by the U.S. Departments of Transportation and Housing and Urban Development and by the U.S. Environmental Protection Agency. With the proposed facility tied closely to specific sites, it is now possible to determine more accurately whether such firmly established standards will be met.

Whenever possible, just as in site screening, the problem of determining criteria for site evaluation can be simplified by converting as many factors as possible to dollar penalties. These dollar penalties can be added to other site-dependent costs which have to be expressed in monetary terms.

Establishment of the criteria to be used is normally the responsibility of the project sponsor and the site-selection planners, but the completeness and adequacy of the criteria should be reviewed by the original decision-making group or an expanded group. In site evaluation as in site screening, considerable subjective judgment is exercised by those performing the evaluation, so the criteria and the rating system to be used must be spelled out clearly. This is particularly true when those who are performing the evaluation are not responsible for making the final selection. A site-evaluation study designed to permit others to make the final decision is provided by the West Oahu College case study in Part Two.

Data Base Refinement

In practice, to speed the process of site evaluation, many of the data required for each site may have to be assembled in advance of, or at least concurrently with, defining the criteria and analytical methods to be applied. The placement of these tasks in Figure 8-1 suggests the close links between them and the fact that in refining and adding to the data base, both criteria and analytical processes must be anticipated. Guidance will have been provided by the review of agency requirements and interest-group concerns, however, and other data needs will have emerged during site investigation and conceptual layout preparation.

It is important to remember in designing the data collection and analysis effort for site evaluation that a more detailed documentation of the project and its effects will be required after the preferred site has been selected. The depth, if not the scope, of the effort can therefore be limited to what is strictly required to select a site. This is particularly true if there is a legal requirement to select alternative choices. The guiding principle should be to provide adequate information to permit the project planners and participants to reach appropriate conclusions. The study should not be so detailed that a commitment is built into one or more of the candidate sites. If any finding or other change during the course of the evaluation suggests the need to look at other sites, it should be possible to do so.

The basic factor categories used for organizing site-screening data will also be applicable to site evaluation. (Figure 7-3 provides a reminder of how these categories may have been set up.) State and regional screening data for each site can thus be reused. Naturally the site-specific concerns and information requirements are more extensive. Table 8-2, which lists some typical concerns under one of the fourteen categories in Figure 7-3, illustrates the manner in which the scope of inquiry is broadened as the geographic scope is narrowed. A number of highly site-specific local concerns may be added as a result of the project planners' observations or public review.

Table 8-3 provides an example of how the data analysis may be organized to evaluate the relative ability of sites to meet suitability criteria. (See Figure 7-3 for an explanation of the symbols used.)

Analytical Procedures

In addition to detailed data collection for each site, several special studies may be required to develop information in a form appropriate for the application of criteria. These environmental studies will proceed in close coordination with the preparation of conceptual engineering, design, and site plans.

This study procedure for the evaluation of alternative power plant studies and preparation of a California NOI

was developed to satisfy the well-developed legislative requirements for evaluating alternative sites for a complex facility. The logical sequence and feedback points among the studies are generally applicable to a wide variety of facilities. It should be noted that the procedure offers opportunities for continued project modification and impact mitigation.

Space does not permit an extensive discussion of the analytical procedures that may be necessary at the site-evaluation stage. Nor could we expect to identify every procedure required for a variety of facility types. We will therefore select and describe two environmental studies, socioeconomic and visual, to indicate the level of consideration that may be required at this stage.

SOCIOECONOMIC STUDIES Though other socioeconomic studies may be required, we will describe only those needed to determine absorption capability and suitability. Project definition information on construction and operational labor requirements, probable income levels, and project phasing provide the basic input to these studies.

1 *Demographic and employment analysis.* The first task requires determination of the regional and local labor market, potential employment sources, unemployment patterns, available skills, and propensity to commute or relocate. The project labor force is then allocated by residential location. Family size, age distribution, and school-age children of employees are determined to arrive at the projected total direct population increase. By using an employment multiplier estimated by observation, economic-base research, or survey techniques, the support population is then calculated.

2 *Community service capacity analysis.* The net addition of population, service requirements, traffic, and expendable income will have measurable effects on local and regional environmental and fiscal conditions.

A general examination should be made of the housing market, existing and already planned transportation, utility, and public service infrastructure capacity, and fiscal conditions. Each element should be assessed in light of:

· New service demands imposed by the proposed facility at each phase
· New property or in-lieu tax revenues generated by the project during and after construction; other revenues generated by growth in population, employment, sales, and property value
· Ability of new revenues to support additional service demands

In some cases the officially expressed goals, objectives, and plans for the communities under study may provide clear answers to the question of capacity and the suitability of growth. Extensive planning may be required in other cases, particularly when a facility of the nature proposed has not

TABLE 8-2 Typical issues and data needs for a single data category, hydrology–water resources.

 Will the site and associated facilities be subject to flooding from:
- o storm runoff or stream flooding
- o failure of upstream dams or other impoundments
- o river blockage or diversion?

 Would project-related impoundment failures pose a flooding hazard to downstream areas?

 Does the project have access to an adequate water supply considering:
- o water rights
- o long-term water use priorities (local, state, international)
- o long-term drought conditions?

 Will the project affect groundwater by:
- o basin over-draft or mining
- o disturbance of aquifer recharge areas
- o salt water intrusion?

 Has the project considered:
- o use of wastewaters for cooling system make-up
- o beneficial uses of waste heat or other waste discharges?

been anticipated or when the facility is likely to set a growth trend. Major growth in direct, support, and induced employment will be associated with a college or university, an airport, or a large light industrial plant. Without adequate planning in advance, the potential exists for problems of housing, traffic congestion, and related air quality to develop and service provision to become unmanageable.

VISUAL ANALYSIS These studies call for photographic simulation, using a simple model of the proposed facility in addition to conceptual site plans. The model should represent the height, bulk, and general conformation of the facility but need not be detailed.

The objective of the visual impact analysis is to determine the significant visual effects of the plant at each site, considering opportunities for use of existing screening or landscaping and the potential for plant design or site plan modification. Each site can then be compared on the basis of the best possible design solutions.

The study should emphasize the project's impact as perceived from local roads, freeways, centers of population, residences, and recreational sites, using the following steps:

· Determine the visual characteristics of the proposed project.

· Determine the characteristics and quality of existing landscape at each alternative location.

· Select representative view locations in the region of each site.

· Photographically simulate the appearance of the proposed project in the landscape from selected viewpoints.

· Determine the degree of visual change resulting from the project by analyzing the difference between the existing and proposed landscape character.

· Recommend measures to mitigate significant adverse impacts.

Figure 8-3 shows the conceptual layout for an alterna-

TABLE 8-3 Example of data factor analysis for site evaluation. Evaluation of the suitability of a candidate site according to each data factor and subfactor (detailed as shown in Table 8-2) requires input from and provides output to a number of other factor categories.

(LU) Land-Use Evaluation

Concern (Abbreviated Listing)	Suitability Criteria	Input from:
LU 1 Conformance with public goals and land-use plans	Plans and criteria of involved agencies	(ECR 2) (N 1) (N 2) (N 3) (CR 1) (VAQ 1) (VAQ 2) (LU 2) (LU 4) (LU 5)
LU 2 Protection of designated land uses	Plans of responsible agencies	(N 1) (N 2) (N 3) (VAQ 1) (VAQ 2) (BR 1)
LU 3 Avoid hazardous land uses	NRC	
LU 4 Protection of valuable or productive lands	Fed., state, and local agency guidelines	(G-S 3) (CR 2) (BR 3) (CR 1)
LU 5 Adequate control of long-term development in site environs.	NRC	

Other Agency Reviews	Staff Analysis & Recommendations	Output to:
Numerous agencies	Compile public goals and plans; resolve differences through public participation; assess conformance.	
Numerous agencies	Verify applicant's identification and analysis of designated uses.	(LU/1)
Federal NRC, FAA, DPT	Verify applicant's analysis, field, field person.	(PS/5) (FDO/1)
Numerous agencies	Aerial photo and field reconnaissance to verify applicant's identification and analysis of valuable lands; consider: barriers to use, ownership or management of parcels, physical taking, growth inducement near site.	(LU/1)
NRC, regional, and local land	Coordinate with appropriate agencies to verify applicant's plans.	(PS/3) (LU/1)

FIGURE 8-3 Site layout for a visual impact analysis. The conceptual site plan, laying out plant components on a topographic map, is a prerequisite to determining visibility from surrounding viewpoints as well as technical feasibility, cost, and other environmental impacts.

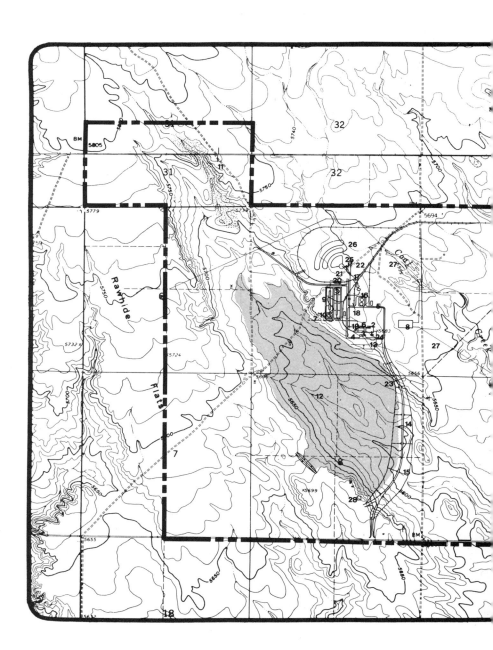

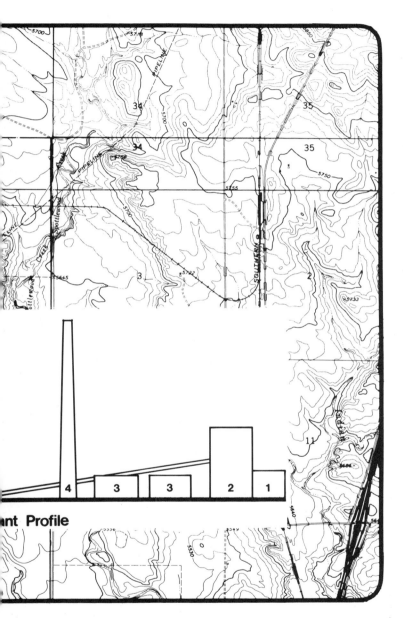

nt Profile

Facilities

1. Turbine–generator building
2. Steam–generator building
3. Air quality control
4. Chimney
5. Warehouse
6. Cooling water discharge line
7. Cooling water discharge structure
8. Substation
9. Bottom ash storage ponds
10. Recycle basin
11. Ash/scrubber waste disposal area
12. Cooling pond
13. Cooling water intake structure
14. Main access road
15. Cooling pond dam
16. Fuel oil tanks
17. Coal transfer building
18. Coal transfer building 2
19. Coal transfer building 3
20. Coal unloading structure
21. Coal stockout
22. Active coal storage
23. Cooling pond discharge structure
24. Administration building
25. Coal reclaim structure
26. Reserve coal storage
27. Transmission lines
28. Cooling pond water treatment building

Site Layout

Rawhide Energy Project

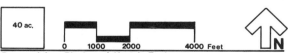

40 ac.

0   1000   2000   4000 Feet

N

Prepared by: Black and Veatch Engineers

tive power plant site. Figure 8-4 shows how the plant may be photographically simulated by using a model. Important views of the plant at each site may then be classified and mapped as shown in Figure 8-5. Figure 8-6 illustrates one method for assigning numerical visual intrusion ratings.

THE SITE-EVALUATION SUMMARY

Once the data required for each evaluation factor have been collected, a number of directions may be taken. First, the list of acceptable sites and their documented qualities may be presented without ranking to those who will make the final decision. Second, the sites may be compared and ranked by staff, with or without public input, and submitted to decision makers. Third, those who make the final decision may rank the sites themselves after receiving assistance from staff and ascertaining the opinions of the public and of regulatory and other affected agencies. Any of these courses is appropriate, depending upon the specific circumstances in each case.

Regardless of the manner in which the final selection is made, the first step is an essential one. It requires information on the manner in which the sites satisfy each criterion to be arranged in the form of nonweighted matrices. Table 8-4 gives an example of a project cost matrix. Table 8-5 is an example of an unranked summary of evaluations in which the candidate sites are rated by using mainly nonquantitative measures. In the latter, no attempt is made to distinguish the importance level of each factor or to give an overall rating to each site. It is left to the reader to form his or her own judgment as to overall relative suitability. Again, the assumptions underlying these ratings can be found in the case history of the West Oahu College site selection studies in Part Two.

A key decision must be made at this point. It may be possible from the simple summary of evaluations to discern one site that is clearly superior in its ability to meet most or all site-evaluation criteria. This judgment may be based on an overall impression or on a single factor, such as the potential impact on a critical habitat, to which most project participants and reviewers assign a high level of importance. If such a judgment cannot easily be made, the process of evaluation is continued by applying a weighted scale to site-evaluation criteria so that the sites can be ranked according to total weighted scores.

SITE RANKING

Let us assume that it is found desirable to rank each site in a formal manner. The procedure laid out in the second part of Figure 8-1 requires the participants in the evaluation process to determine the relative importance of each criterion. This is undoubtedly one of the most controversial steps in the evaluation process, as it is in site screening. Many attempts have been made to assess and compare the importance of impacts on conditions in such diverse areas as biology, health and safety, visual quality, and community economics. Each method strives to place the variety of factors relating to engineering, economics, and environmental and social values on a common scale. In its way, the task may be as difficult as assigning weights to screening factors.

As we have seen in Chapter 7, the difficulty of weighting screening factors lies in achieving a consensus among individuals representing varying values. The difficulty is compounded by the need to give adequate distinction to several factors which group themselves at one end of a scale when a single factor, such as air quality, is considered of overriding importance. An additional problem encountered in the site-evaluation phase is that the factors and the criteria by which they are measured are no longer being considered in relatively abstract terms. Because the decision-making group now has specific sites in mind, it may also have knowledge of certain anomalous situations that complicate the assignment of consistent weights.

It is extremely important in using a weighting process that its limitations are clearly understood. There are no universal formulas. The importance of many factors is often a matter of subjective judgment that changes with time and with the individual or group making the judgment. Because no system of weights or values is final, flexibility and simplicity are the keys to success. The advantage of a weighting process is that it can serve as an effective tool in reaching a decision and in subsequently communicating the decision rationale to others. The process can also eliminate arbitrary decisions and offer a means of ensuring some consistency from decision to decision.

One of the simplest ranking methods involves a concern-by-concern comparison of the alternative sites. Concerns that are similar for all sites are simply eliminated from the analysis. Attention is then focused on the concerns that have significant differences between sites. In many instances this approach may greatly reduce the

1 Dominant

2 Dominant

3 Codominant

4 Codominant

5 Subordinant

6 Subordinant

FIGURE 8-4 Photographic simulation for visual impact analysis. Superimposition of plant model photographs on photographs from selected viewpoints is essential to visualizing the type and magnitude of the impact of a major facility on the landscape.

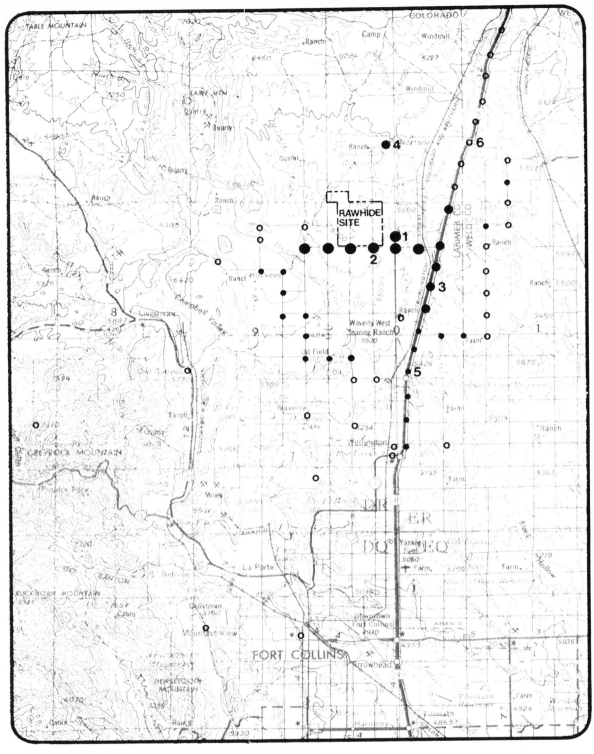

Legend

- ● **Dominant**
- ● **Codominant**
- · **Subordinant**
- ○ **Little or Not Seen**

Visual Impact
Rawhide Energy Project

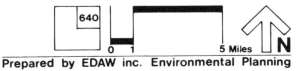

FIGURE 8-5 Assessment of visual impact magnitude from selected viewpoints. Impacts may be rated qualitatively or, as illustrated by Figure 8-6, quantitatively.

Prepared by EDAW inc. Environmental Planning

TABLE 8-4   Calculation of site-dependent costs. The comparative evaluation of candidate sites may be simplified in part by the conversion of as many factors as possible to dollar costs.

	Candidate		
Evaluation Factor	Site 1	Site 2	Site 3
Railroad			
Miles	12.0	12.0	1.5
Cost x 10^3 ($200/ft)	$ 12,672.00	$ 1,584.00	$ 3,168.00
Coal delivery			
Miles	915.0	900.0	899.0
Cost x 10^3 ($300,000/mi) (excess over 500 mi)	$124,500.00	$120,000.00	$119,700.00
Transmission			
Miles to 500-KV Substation	70.0	60.0	62.0
500-KV Substation to midway	220.0	220.0	220.0
Total Cost x 10^3 ($500,000/mi)	$ 73,500.00	$ 68,500.00	$ 69,500.00
Road			
Miles	0.5	1.0	2.0
Cost x 10^3 ($300,000/mi)	$ 150.00	$ 300.00	$ 600.00
Water supply			
Pipe size	36"	36"	36"
Pipe miles	59	57	57
Pipe cost	$ 28,037.00	$ 27,086.00	$ 27,086.00
Elevation Diff. (ft)	500	200	200
Intake pump ($50,000/100 ft)	$ 250.00	$ 100.00	$ 100.00
Reservoir cost	---	---	---
Well cost	---	---	---
Tunnel cost	---	---	---
Common costs	$ 21,600.00	$ 21,600.00	$ 21,600.00
Total Water Costs	$ 49,887.00	$ 48,786.00	$ 48,786.00
Seismic			
Zone	Good – 0.1g	Good	Good
Cost	Base	Base	Base
Sum total (in millions)	$ 260.7	$ 239.2	$ 241.8
Amount over base	$ 67.7	$ 46.2	$ 48.8
Rating	M–	L+	L+

Visual Intrusion Values Relative to Distance, Screening and Backdrop
800 MW Single Unit Coal Fired Power Plant

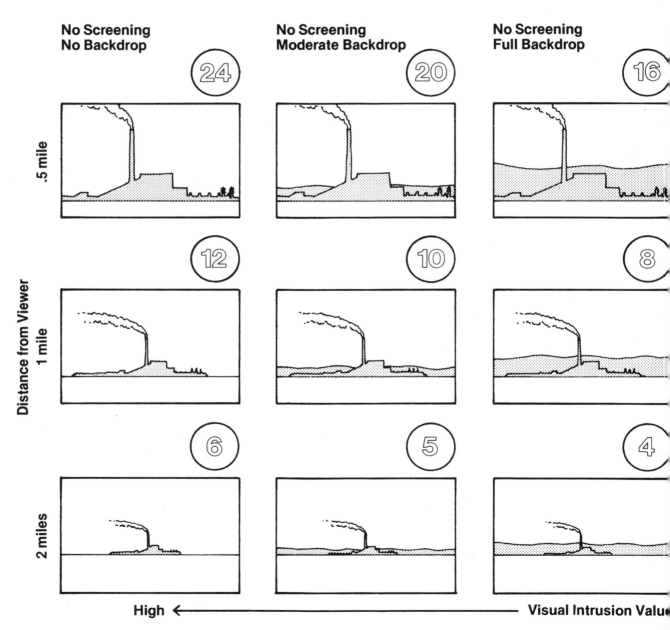

Notes:

 Illustrative Visual Intrusion Value. 1 is Lowest, 24 is Highest.

All Screening is Solid.

The Frame of Each Illustration Represents the Full Field of View.

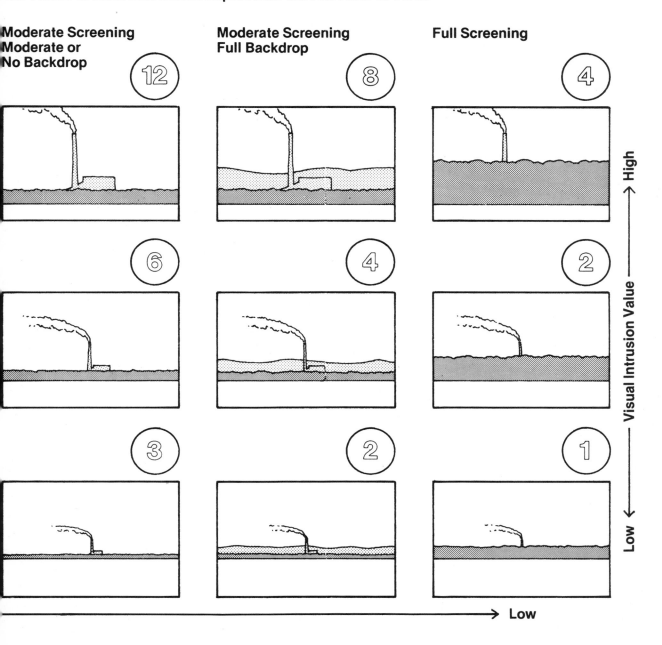

TABLE 8-5 **Unranked summary of evaluations. The results of the comparative evaluation of candidate sites may lend themselves to selection without the use of a ranking procedure, as in the case of West Oahu College.**

	MAKAKILO	EWA	HONOULIULI
A EFFECT ON THE WELL-BEING OF THE USERS			
1 User convenience			
a Access to campus by students, faculty and staff	Poor	Fair	Good
b Access from campus to existing or proposed community	Negligible	Limited	Fair
2 User comfort			
a Suitable climate	*	*	*
b Freedom from nuisance	Good	Smoke & Dust	Smoke & Dust
c Design potential	Excellent	Fair	Good
3 User safety			
a Freedom from flooding (no sites are in Tsunami or Blast Zones)	Acceptable	Acceptable	Borderline
b Freedom from traffic hazards	Acceptable	Acceptable	Borderline
B EFFECT ON THE RESIDENTS OF THE NEIGHBORING COMMUNITIES			
1 Community-campus relationship			
a Community access to campus	Good	Fair	Good
b Campus "spill-over" at acceptable level	Questionable	Acceptable	Acceptable
c Campus as community resource (impact on community)	Moderate	Moderate	Significant
2 Shared development of community			
a Any necessary expansion jointly managed or controlled	*	*	*
b Complementarity of campus facilities proposed	Medium	Low	High
c Economic contribution to an existing community	Negligible	Marginal	Significant
3 Impact on quality of community life			
a Aesthetic benefits (visual appropriateness)	Appropriate	Questionable	Appropriate
b Environmental effects	Moderate	Slight	Slight
c Freedom from over-crowding (traffic congestion)	Light	Average	Average
C EFFECT ON THE RESIDENTS OF THE REGIONAL COMMUNITY			
1 Avoid excess regional urbanization			
a Utilization of existing development capacity	Yes*	No	Yes*
b Protection against uncontrolled development	Protected	Unprotected	Somewhat
2 Regional environmental impact			
a Minimize air pollution	*	*	*
b Minimize decrease in ground water recharge	Moderate	None	None
c Minimize intrusion of campus buildings and grounds	*	*	*
3 Effect on distribution of regional services			
a Compatible with water and sewer networks	Yes & Unknown	Yes & Yes	Yes & Yes
b Compatible with road network	Yes	Questionable	Yes
c Compatible with public transportation and rapid transit*	Very poor	Poor	Good
D EFFECT ON ALL THE RESIDENTS OF THE COUNTY AND STATE			
1 Effect on economic development			
a Preserve agricultural potential*	Yes	No	No
b Employment created or lost	*	*	*
2 Effect on open space			
a Preserve natural environmental potential	Good Effect	Negative Effect	Moderate Effect
b Conserve unspoiled areas (no sites are "natural areas")	*	*	*
3 Effect on land use policy			
a Respect state land use laws and procedures	Yes	No	No
b Respect county general plan and zoning laws and procedures	Yes	No	No
c Preserve future public policy options	Yes	No	No
E EFFECT ON ACADEMIC OBJECTIVES			
1 Appropriate size and shape			
a Accommodates primary activities	Good	Excellent	Good
b Accommodates support activities such as housing, parking	Excellent	Excellent	Excellent
c Accommodates future expansion (to planned "upper limit")	Excellent	Excellent	Excellent
2 "Fit" with UH system			
a Relationship with existing and planned campuses	Satisfactory	Satisfactory	Satisfactory
b Relationship to centralized UH facilities and services	Satisfactory	Satisfactory	Satisfactory
3 Contributions to student learning			
a Campus ambience and variety	Medium	Low	Medium
b Setting appropriate to educational style	Excellent	Fair	Good
F EFFECT ON TOTAL COSTS			
1 Capital costs			
a Site acquisition and improvement	High & Significant	Low & Moderate	Low & Moderate
b Facility construction differential	Severe & Moderate	Normal & Moderate	Normal & Slight
2 Extra operating and service costs			
a On campus	Negligible	Negligible	Negligible
b Off campus	Negligible	Negligible	Negligible
3 Tax revenues foregone (or gained)			
a Campus - per 100 acres	$13,447	$54,386	$54,386
b Surrounding extra development	Neutral	Neutral	Neutral

* Certain criteria do not lend themselves to this rating system.

number of decisions necessary to identify the preferred sites. Examples of concerns similar to all sites might include water sources, volume of water consumed, public exposure to accidents, local fiscal effects, and effects of construction on the community.

The ranking of sites is also made easier if a number of factors have been reduced to dollar penalties. The dollar penalties can then be added to other site-dependent costs. Differences between sites in terms of the costs of an access road, rail spur, transmission line, or pipeline, for example, may be partially reduced or virtually eliminated by this technique. The cost of mitigation measures necessary to eliminate differences between sites may also be handled in this way. Ranking can then proceed on the basis of a limited number of factors.

Even with the use of these techniques for simplifying decisions, a number of unrelated factors will have to be weighted to reach a final site ranking in most cases. Some form of comprehensive weighting process is necessary, therefore, to guide the decisions.

Recommended Weighting Procedure

The recommended weighting process is a simple numerical system which has been used frequently and is closely related to the weighting system described for screening candidate areas in Chapter 7. This system was devised for ranking power plant sites but is easily adapted to other kinds of facilities for which the major categories of concern are somewhat different. For the purpose of power plant site selection, as shown in Figure 7-3, there are fourteen groups of factors categorized under three major headings: technical-economic, physical-biological, and social-cultural.

Like the system shown in Figure 7-14, the site-evaluation weighting process has two major steps:

· Determine the *relative importance* of each major category (technical-economic, physical-biological, social-cultural) and each factor to be considered (e.g., meteorology–air quality, geology-seismology, etc.)

· Determine the magnitude of impact (how well the site satisfies each factor or minimizes adverse impact).

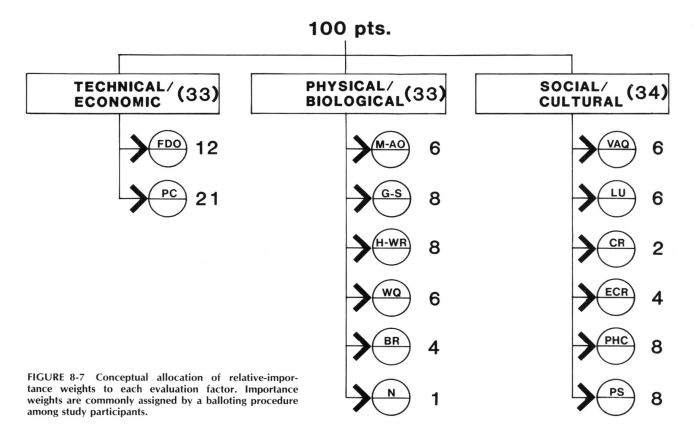

FIGURE 8-7 Conceptual allocation of relative-importance weights to each evaluation factor. Importance weights are commonly assigned by a balloting procedure among study participants.

For each factor, the weighted importance rating is multiplied by the impact rating, and the sum of the products (or scores) results in a composite value for each site.

1 *Relative importance.* It is recommended that a simple numerical scale be used to establish relative importance. If 100 points are used, to be distributed among the fourteen factor groups in Figure 7-3, the relative importance of each can be displayed. It may be advantageous in the initial application of such a system to assume that each of the three broad categories will receive equal weight in the determination of site acceptability. An example is shown in Figure 8-7.

2 *Magnitude of impact.* It is suggested that a scale of 0 to 10 be used to indicate the degree to which each site avoids adverse impacts within each area of consideration. The ratings should normally be made by the technical project team and committee members as a result of their review and analysis. If the ability to satisfy criteria in a particular factor category is

such that the site is clearly unacceptable in terms of that factor, a rating of 0 is assigned. A rating of 10 is assigned if the site clearly meets a criterion or, alternatively, if the factor under consideration has no reference to the site. If the concerns within a factor category can be properly resolved by a specific set of mitigation measures, a notation is made and a condition (or set of conditions) is established.

3 *Site ranking.* A site-evaluation matrix (see Figure 8-8) is used to enter the factors (here termed *areas of consideration*), their weights, and the sites for comparison. For each factor and each site, the importance weight of the factor is multiplied by the previously determined degree of acceptability of the site (0–10), and the product is entered in the appropriate place. The total of all products per site will provide the composite value of each site for comparison and ranking with the others. The weighting methodology allows a visible comparison of two or more sites in terms of each factor considered. The system also offers a means of focusing on those

Areas of Consideration		**Sites**					
		1	2	3	4	5	6
Symbol	**Weight**						
	12	x					
	21						
	6						
	8						
	8						
	6						
	4						
	1						
	6						
	6						
	2						
	4						
	8						
	8						
Total of Products							

x Enter product for each site for each area of consideration by multiplying weight by degree of satisfaction (on a scale of 0 to 10) previously determined.

FIGURE 8-8 Simplified example of a weighting worksheet for site evaluation. The relative-importance weights assigned in the previous task (Figure 8-7) are combined with values on a numerical scale indicating the degree to which each candidate site satisfies each evaluation factor.

issues that are critical to the overall site decision. Most important, the weighting methodology provides a mechanism for reflecting the decision maker's position on key siting issues such as cost versus social, environmental, or other locational considerations.

Alternative Weighting Procedures

A variation on the recommended system of weighting, scoring, and ranking alternatives in terms of multiple factors and criteria is the so-called partial-pair comparison. This approach was used during the Duluth Freeway Routing Study and is described in Case Study 6 in Part Two.

As in the recommended process, the first step is to use expert judgment as well as factual estimates to rank the alternatives separately according to each of the factors. Each alternative is then compared with another according to a subjective evaluation that involves all the elements of a particular data factor and a subjective decision as to whether the alternative is "better" or "worse" than another, according to the relevant criteria. A third alternative is compared first with the worse of the previous two and, if deemed subjectively to be "better," is then compared with the "better" of the previous two. After completion of this comparative ranking, panel consensus places the alternatives on a numerical scale on which relative distance between alternatives is felt to be a subjectively valid measure of relative ability to satisfy the factor-related criteria.

This procedure is repeated for each factor. Finally, policy or importance weights are applied to the factors so that a composite ranking of each alternative can be determined.

During the partial-pair comparison, it may be possible to reject any alternative with a score on one factor that is far below the scores of the others. By permitting alternatives to be dropped prior to weighting, this system falls midway between a simple summary and a complete ranking method, which may be an advantage in some siting situations.

CONCLUSION

With the application of either rating or ranking to the alternative sites, one site will, after the results are subjected to a test of intuitive plausibility, emerge as the most suitable.

The next steps of detailed engineering, site planning, environmental impact statement preparation, and final license applications are not in the scope of this text. As a result of the comprehensive but selective and directed work that has preceded the final selection, those steps should run smoothly.

Although we have concluded our discussion of the site-selection process, there are two fundamental components of the process, data needs and analysis and citizen participation, that warrant further examination. We will review our coverage of these components and expand upon some basic principles in the two final chapters of Part One.

9 | DATA NEEDS AND ANALYSIS

THE NEED FOR A DATA PLAN

There is virtually no limit to environmental data. Every day new and better data become available. Data are thus dynamic, and to use them one must either pretend that time has stopped or make allowance for changes. Sometimes data are also incomplete, in the sense that what we need to know may not be available without extensive original work or because our understanding of certain environmental processes is limited. So the user must make do with what is known and respond conservatively to what is not.

Failure to accept the fact that data change and are never current for more than an instant has caused decisions to be obsolete as soon as they are made. Failure to comprehend the fact that data are at once limited and limitless has led to "analysis paralysis," the common malady of immature planners whose decisions are postponed indefinitely because the data are not complete or current. "Completeness" must therefore be considered in terms of probable adequacy.

While scientific investigation seeks to identify fact and establish certainty regardless of time parameters, a siting study must realistically make the best possible choices with the data available by a required commitment time. On the other hand, data must be collected selectively, in keeping with the phases and iterations of the decision-making process. It is not uncommon for projects to be delayed again and again because of inadequate information. Often this is the reason given for developing excessive volumes of data. What this practice really demonstrates is an inability to distinguish the relevant issues and relevant coverage or details. Information which is unnecessary to a key decision must be weeded out. It is distracting and confusing, and it inhibits making sound decisions.

Obviously a data plan is needed to avoid the common pitfalls of data collection. A data plan specifies the data that are to be collected, how they will be recorded, and how they will be used in the siting process. The plan should reflect and support the needs and phases of the study. In addition to improving the efficiency and rationality with which decisions are made, a good data plan is politically advisable. If the manner in which the data base has been compiled can be questioned, the conclusions based upon it will come under attack regardless of their apparent validity. A comprehensively organized and well-presented data base will be hard to criticize. It will also allow all interested parties to examine the logic of each conclusion. If issues of conflicting values arise, each party can refer to the data to arrive at its own conclusions.

CONSIDERATIONS IN IDENTIFYING DATA NEEDS

The flow of decisions needed to collect and manipulate siting data appropriately is laid out in Figure 9-1. The foundation for building the data plan is provided by the siting criteria and the factors associated with them, the definition of the project, and the project phase (site screening or site evaluation).

It will be recalled from Chapter 7 that siting objectives and criteria provide the basis for defining generic data needs. For example, the following nine objectives established for the Rawhide Transmission Line Siting Study in Colorado (EDAW Inc., 1978) determined the siting factors:

· Minimize disruption of agricultural operations and potential agricultural uses.

· Minimize disruption to and relocation of residential and business property.

· Minimize disturbance to public lands, public facilities, and cultural resources.

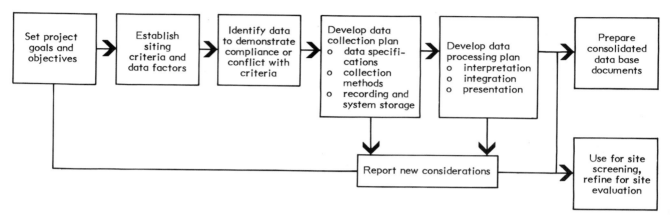

FIGURE 9-1 Data management process. The steps in the data management process run concurrently with the steps in the site-selection process described previously and diagrammed in Figures 4-1, 5-1, 7-2, and 8-1. Data findings and availability may produce feedback to early steps in the site-selection process.

· Minimize disturbance to wooded and marshland wildlife habitats.

· Minimize length of line in the waterfowl flight zone.

· Minimize prominent views of the line from roads.

· Minimize prominent views of the line from houses.

· Avoid conflicts with existing electrical distribution lines.

· Minimize conflicting visual relationships with other structures or disorderly variations in the transmission line itself.

The types of data that should be collected become readily apparent from these objectives. They include agricultural lands (location, quality, configuration, operations), residential properties (location of structures), public lands (location, configuration, status), and views (distance, visibility, quality, viewers).

Detailed subfactors will be determined by the criteria used to measure achievement of objectives. For example, the first objective above, "Minimize disruption of agricultural operations," establishes agricultural land as a siting factor. Prime (Class I and Class II) soils and irrigability which reflect potential soil productivity may be established as criteria for guiding and measuring achievement of the objective. Agricultural data must therefore be collected for these subfactors.

In the later site-evaluation process, more detailed criteria may be established to measure the actual agricultrual use and relative productivity of each site. Application of these criteria will probably require collection and analysis of local land-value data and crop reports as well as discussion of trends with local agricultural advisers to

assist in data interpretation. Thus, criteria must be refined and analytical methods specified before any new site-specific data needs can be identified. Table 9-1 traces the steps to identification of needed data for one data factor, air quality.

Critical issues arising from the importance and complexity of a factor, ambiguous objectives, or clearly differing values or professional opinions require very careful interpretation and judgment in refining appropriate criteria and determining data needs. For each factor, data needs and analysis methods should be defined by specialists in the appropriate professional discipline. These specialists will also direct data collection and analysis.

The data collected are then presented in a manner that readily permits alternative sites or routes to be developed and evaluated. Figures 9-2 and 9-3 present examples of data presentation for the Rawhide Transmission Line Siting Study.

Project Definition

The details and areal coverage of the data depend on the level of siting precision required at each phase, as discussed below. They also depend on the nature and size of the facility. For example, many of the objectives listed above are applicable not only to transmission lines of varying size but also to other types of major facilities. The manner in which the data needs are interpreted requires reference to the narrative and graphic project definition. The discussion of project-environmental relationships in

TABLE 9-1   Example of the determination of data needs. Taking one data factor (air quality) as an example, this table displays the steps taken to determine data needs. Note that not all topic-specific data will be required before the site-evaluation phase of the site-selection process.

Objective

Comply with present and proposed air quality standards and other applicable regulations.

Criteria

The specific existing and proposed regulations regarding the various pollutants and their applicable levels, as well as those on critical air basins, non-degradation, etc.

Required Findings

Will plant emissions violate or contribute to violation of any air quality standards or regulations at candidate sites? Which, and how often?

Analytical Process

Cursory air quality modeling to determine any limiting standard or regulation, assuming "worst case" meteorological conditions including plume trajectory analysis.

Data Needs

Base unit data: General description of topography; plant location.
Form: Map of air basin and map of projection vicinity.

Topic-specific data

Setting: Meteorological parameters, e.g., wind speed, direction, stability frequencies, height of mixing layer.

Existing air quality and location of nearest monitoring station or three months of monitoring results (SO_x, NO_x, particulates, CO, HC, O_x).

Map of area classification with regard to significant deterioration.

Project definition: Emission rates of all pollutants (full load and yearly average), stack height, control devices, and degree of efficiency.

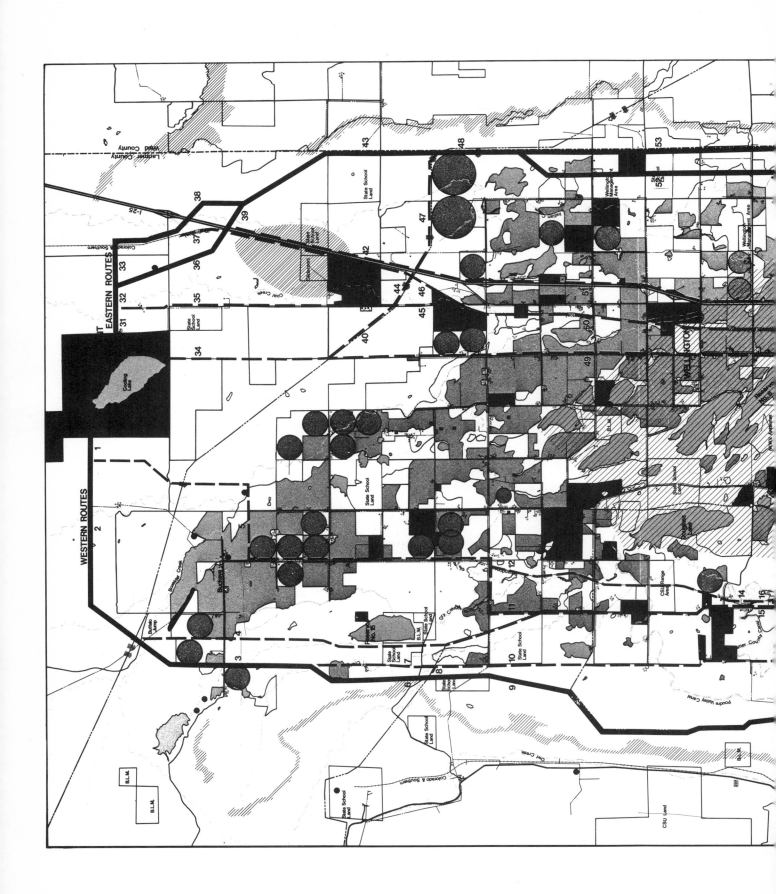

Planning Factors and Alternative Routes

RAWHIDE ENERGY PROJECT
Transmission Routing Study

EDAW inc.
Environmental Planning

Date: January 31, 1978

N

0   2000   6000 Feet

Map 3

Proximity of buildings to possible transmission line along roads:
- Homes within right-of-way
- Homes within 50-100'
- Homes beyond 100'
- Auxiliary Buildings
- Commercial Building
- Institutions
- Oil Wells
- State Highways
- County Roads
- Railroads
- Streams
- P.V.R.E.A. Distribution Lines
- P.S.C. Distribution Lines
- Transmission Lines
- Substations

- Desirable Line Crossings
- Public and Reserved Lands
- Open Space Trails
- Cultural Resources
- Airspace Zones
- Subdivisions
- Communities
- Rangeland
- Center Pivot Irrigation
- Non-irrigated Cropland
- Irrigated Cropland
- Waterfowl Flight Area
- Seasonal Lakes
- Lakes &/or Reservoirs
- Ridgelines
- Routes Having Greatest Compliance with Evaluation Criteria
- Alternative Routes Evaluated

50 Acres

500 Acres

FIGURE 9-2 Example of data factors used in facility routing. It is taken from a relatively site-specific selection study, and factors are accordingly quite detailed.

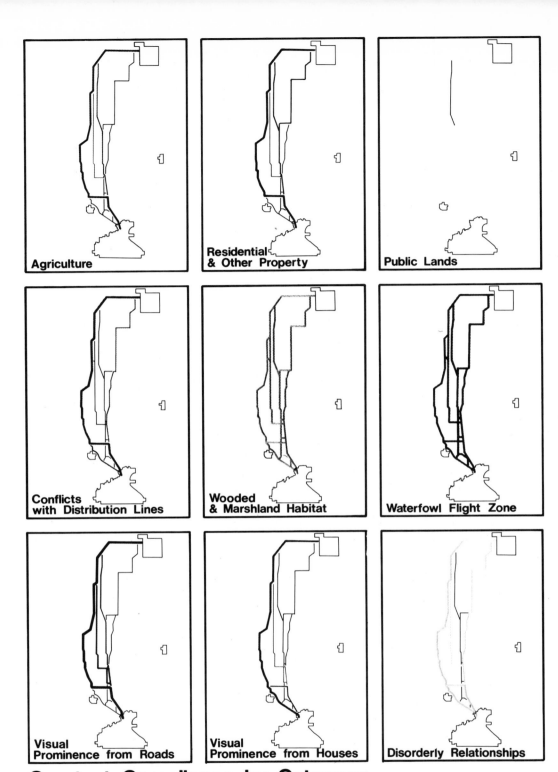

Greatest Compliance by Category

Western Route Evaluations

——— **Best**
———— **2ND Best**
———— **3RD Best**

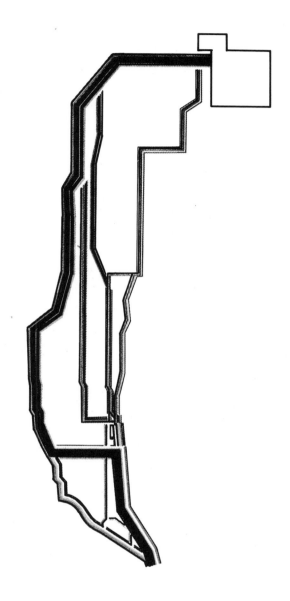

Greatest Compliance Composite

FIGURE 9-3   Alternative route evaluation by individual data factors and composite evaluation.

Chapter 6 provided examples of the way in which the area of potential impact varies with scale and technical differences within the same facility type.

We may refer again to the Rawhide Study for an example. There a broad-corridor-scale analysis for transmission lines would have been meaningless since the location of the lines in the particular landscape was clearly limited to road rights-of-way and landownership–land-use boundaries. To assess residential conflicts, it was necessary to know whether structures would fall within 50 feet (plus or minus 5 feet) of the alignment. The locational tolerance of this information was so fine that it had to be collected by a combination of aerial photography and field measurement with an optical range finder. The data were symbolized and recorded on 1:24,000-scale U.S. Geological Survey (USGS) base maps, which can show finely detailed data.

Project Phase

The data plan must match the narrowing geographic scope and increasing detail required as the study progresses through each stage. It will be recalled, for example, that relatively few data items need to be collected for the entire region of study in order to identify exclusion areas unsuitable for a fossil-fueled power plant. If large areas can be excluded, the coverage needed for site-screening data can be substantially reduced. If exclusion of much of the region is not possible, relative suitability can still be established on the basis of rather coarse data. For site evaluation very detailed information need be gathered for only a few small areas.

To be overly detailed is as bad as being overly general. The details displayed should be consistent with the tolerance of the analysis at each phase. To take an extreme example, the problem with showing such details as individual trees in a routing study is that every tree must be then taken into account even if it is not necessary to the analysis. This level of detail also suggests a level of accuracy which may not be possible, necessary, or even desirable.

When there are gross differences between alternatives, only approximate values need be determined. But when differences are small, the quality of the data must receive

TABLE 9-2 Example of a data worksheet format. The data plan should include specific instructions for the collection and display of data under each factor, using a uniform format.

Demographic Data Unit

Purpose

This data unit is to describe the population of the region around the site in terms of number, composition, trends, employment, income, and other parameters. Its objective is to provide a base unit of direct social and economic effects and ability of the community to accommodate growth.

Population characteristics				
Data Element	Unit	Scope	Source	Presentation format
Number	Person	50-mi. radius; 1900–1970 by census years & 1975 interim	U.S. Census — State & local agencies	Maps: 50-mi. & 10-mi. radius. Table
Age structure	Total persons by 10-year increment	Same	Same	Table

particular consideration in order to determine whether or not the value differences are meaningful.

THE DATA PLAN

The scope, scale, and type of data to be collected and analyzed depend on a balancing of the three considerations of site-selection factors, facility type, and phase with several other practical and often constraining factors. The latter include the availability of appropriate base maps, the quality of the data base itself, the project schedule and budget, the need for comparative studies of other facilities, graphic considerations, and the groups that will require access to raw data and analysis. The data plan that emerges should specify at a minimum the spatial extent, frequency, duration, and method of data collection; scale and format of data presentation; and method of data recording and analysis. An example of the way in which the plan may be structured uniformly for each factor is shown in Table 9-2. This table may be compared with Table 9-1, which demonstrated how data needs are determined, and goes several steps further in specifying unit, scope, source, and format. While these examples relate to site evaluation, a similar but simpler approach applies to the site-screening data.

Large sets of information at various scales and levels of detail must be developed and used in site screening and evaluation. The organization of this information into a structured system is perhaps the most critical task in any siting program. Without it, important information can be mislaid, overlooked, or duplicated. A data base that is simple and easy to use offers repeated opportunities for efficient multiple use by the various team members and other project participants and for referencing, revision, and updating of geographic-based and tabular information.

Table 9-3 provides a checklist of what needs to be taken into account in designing a data system. The checklist was drawn up to aid planning agencies in compiling data systems but is equally applicable to sponsors of many major facilities. Before turning to techniques for handling data, it may be helpful to examine some of the points on the list more thoroughly.

Purpose and Objectives

Many siting studies are once-only efforts. If another project is contemplated in the future within the same area of study, it may be worth considering methods of

data storage that are easily retrievable, permitting updating rather than duplication. Since the early site-screening steps in a large-scale siting study must rely on often very outdated USGS maps, retaining the updated information plotted from field or aerial observation can help provide a focus to the next study. If new transmission systems will be needed after the siting of a power plant, it is probably worth the extra effort to extend the coverage and type of data collected. Even if repeated use for other projects is not contemplated, repeated use during the siting study at hand can be expected and should be anticipated. It should also be remembered that much effort involved in preparation of the impact assessment can be saved if the siting data base is available for reuse.

System Characteristics

One way to anticipate needs for reuse is to ensure that basic data which are mapped are retained separately from interpretations, composite factor maps, and weights. This builds in flexibility, a desirable characteristic of virtually any data system.

As we have indicated, requirements for coverage and accuracy vary with the project phase. It is desirable, however, to design data terminologies, coordinates, tabular formats, and other properties that are consistent from one planning level to another. This means that statewide information should be a logical generalization of regional information, which in its turn was logically derived from local data. Figure 9-4 graphically demonstrates this funneling process.

The process must be documented to convey a clear understanding of the basis for each decision in the generalization process. Whether data system functions are best accomplished by manual or computerized means is not a matter of sophistication but a rational response to considerations of complexity, accuracy, time, budget, and availability of information.

METHODS AND SOURCES OF DATA COLLECTION

Who Should Collect the Data?

Data collection activities provide significant opportunities to meet with individuals and agencies with an interest in or authority over various aspects of the project. Early contacts with these individuals are generally appreciated and establish a basis for trust and cooperation

TABLE 9-3   Organization of a regional environmental data system. Organization follows a logical sequence of steps designed to ensure compatibility between the system and its intended use.

I   Define purpose & objectives of system

A   Single use vs. repeated use
B   Resource planning tool
C   Environmental assessment tool
D   Tailored to specific project type(s)

II   Identify desirable system characteristics

A   Flexibility
B   Accuracy
C   Coverage
D   Sophistication

III   Identify system constraints

A   Time
B   Budget/Manpower
C   Level of existing information

IV   Evaluate alternatives & select most suitable system

V   Design program

A   Environmental data collection
   1   Factors to be included
   2   Level of detail
   3   Sources of information (existing mapping, aerial photo interpretation, field survey, etc.)

B   Data interpretation & mapping
   1   Mapping procedures
   2   Correlation of factors
   3   Identification of opportunities & constraints

C   Weighting
   1   Technique
   2   Participants

D   Compositing
   1   Method of display
   2   Subsequent use

VI   Program implementation

VII   Evaluation & updating

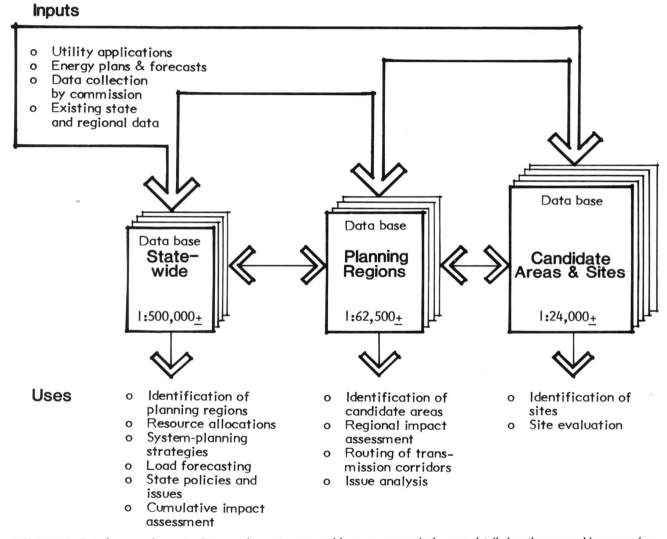

FIGURE 9-4 Data base requirements. Data requirements grow and become progressively more detailed as the geographic scope of an inquiry is narrowed.

throughout other phases of the study. In general, personnel making these contacts should be qualified in their fields, peers with the individuals contacted, and briefed on the project sufficiently well to serve as ambassadors for the adequacy and objectivity of the study. They should be neither advocates nor adversaries of the project.

Visits for the purpose of data collection, especially

early in the study, should be coordinated among members of the project team. Large multidisciplinary agencies, such as the U.S. Forest Service, will often insist on an initial high-management-level meeting to establish the objectives and ground rules of the data effort before directing the team to various departments. This approach reduces interruptions of agency personnel and efficiently directs the team to the most knowledgeable sources. It also allows immediate cross-referencing of data resources by the various disciplines.

Letters and telephone communications should precede visits to allow assembly of materials in advance and ensure that any required authority has been granted. When more junior staff members are used in the collection effort, they should be introduced by managing experts in their field, who should also follow up to ensure maintenance of professional standards.

Data Records

All information gathered should be annotated with the collector's name and comments on the source, date, derivation, probable validity for the intended purposes, and notes on other related materials that may prove useful. All source information should be filed along with the collector's annotations and indexed for easy retrieval. This procedure can help to avoid the problems that often later arise over interpretation of data. It is also important because siting studies should be regarded as legal processes. The annotations may be the critical proof of an otherwise questionable interpretation.

A useful tool in planning and managing the collection effort is a data-source matrix which lists data requirements along the side and all potential sources along the top. Various symbols can be used at the intersections to indicate responsibility, appropriate phase, and availability. The matrix developed for the Tyrone Energy Park Transmission Line Study (Figure 9-5) provides an example.

Preliminary integration of the results may occur in workshops attended by project team management and discipline specialists. Such sessions provide an opportunity to exchange and verify data and assumptions and aid in identifying important relationships and remaining conflicts between disciplines.

Data Sources

The political unit having the broadest jurisdiction over a siting study area is usually the best starting place for identifying data sources. This is also logically the first place to go for the broad-scale data required for site screening. At the state level, there is the governor's office; at the multicounty level, there are councils of governments (COGs); then there are county offices, city offices, and district offices. Virtually all agencies, at whatever level of government, operate independently and require separate contacts, although knowledgeable individuals are usually able to direct the investigator to helpful counterparts elsewhere. Additional help is available in the rosters or fact books published by many states, which provide phone numbers, addresses, and functions of all agencies and departments. Information on federal agencies can be found in *The United States Government Manual*.

A number of state and other agencies maintain data files and inventories either generated by them or assembled from other sources. It is essential to recognize, however, that single points of access to data required for major siting studies, even at a coarse site-screening scale, rarely exist. For example, in California relevant statewide data files and inventories are maintained by at least eleven agencies or offices. Each is directed toward different user groups, few are integrated for mutual accessibility, and several are not current or are incomplete for their purposes. Thus, depending on the site-screening factors being used, each one may have to be consulted but be approached with caution.

Table 9-4 indicates the type of data which some statewide agencies in California have to offer. These sources were inventoried and evaluated by EDAW as consultants to the state's newly created Energy Resources Conservation and Development Commission.

Information source guides may also be available from nongovernment organizations. The availability, quality, and ease of retrieval of data banks vary widely from state to state and change frequently over time. It is therefore wise to supplement guides with personal inquiries.

Despite the existence of the various California data files, it was necessary to contact or consult documents published by five federal agencies and two state agencies in compiling the map of land-use evaluation factors for the California Department of Water Resources Power Plant Siting Study.

Universities in the area of study are particularly valuable sources of reports, studies, research papers, and locally knowledgeable individuals. Banks, utilities, and telephone companies have research departments which should not be overlooked as sources of demographic and economic information. Several large utility companies, for example, are developing computerized data banks.

Site screening can normally be accomplished entirely through the use of published and unpublished reports, mapped data, interpretation of existing aerial photographs, and personal or telephone interviews. Site verification and site evaluation must also involve field studies on the ground and, very usefully, from the air.

Scheduling the Data Collection Effort

Data priorities should be established so that the information most likely to affect siting decisions can be evaluated early for sufficiency and supplemented as necessary in the process of narrowing the number of alternatives.

The timing of field studies can often be critical in areas where seasons are marked, and problems should be anticipated in good time so as to avoid critical delays. Rain, snow, poor visibility, cold weather, and heavy summer foliage can prevent the gathering of some data or obtaining useful aerial photographic coverage. In many areas,

TABLE 9-4 Existing statewide data bases in California. Most states offer a similar range of statewide data. Completeness, recency, and ease of retrieval vary widely among states and agencies.

---

o   The Office of Planning and Research Environment Data System - Computer readout of scenic, scientific, recreational, and educational resource areas; production areas; and hazardous areas. Keyed to USGS 7-1/2-minute quad maps and agency contact. Incomplete.

o   CALTRANS Transportation Support Information System (TPSIS) - Socioeconomic profiles of small areas, census data files, transportation, computerized facility and trip survey data, and socioeconomic projections.

o   CALTRANS California Transportation Plan EIR Statewide Environmental Data Maps Small-scale, but uniform, maps for thirteen environmental, economic, and cultural topics.

o   The Office of Planning and Research Development Guidelines for Areas of Statewide Critical Concern.

o   The State Department of Parks and Recreation Landscape Province Studies.

o   the California Natural Areas Coordinating Council's Inventory of Natural Areas - Inventory and description of unique or represenative landscapes and habitats.

o   The State Department of Parks and Recreation Information Inventory and System - Recreation facilities and visits (automated).

o   The State Department of Finance Population Research Unit (periodic estimates and projections by City and County).

o   The State Department of Water Resources - Water quality and quantity (automated).

o   The State Board of Equalization - Retail sales data for businesses and areas (automated).

o   The State Department of Fish and Game - Endangered and rare species; areas of special biological significance; critical habitat and protected areas.

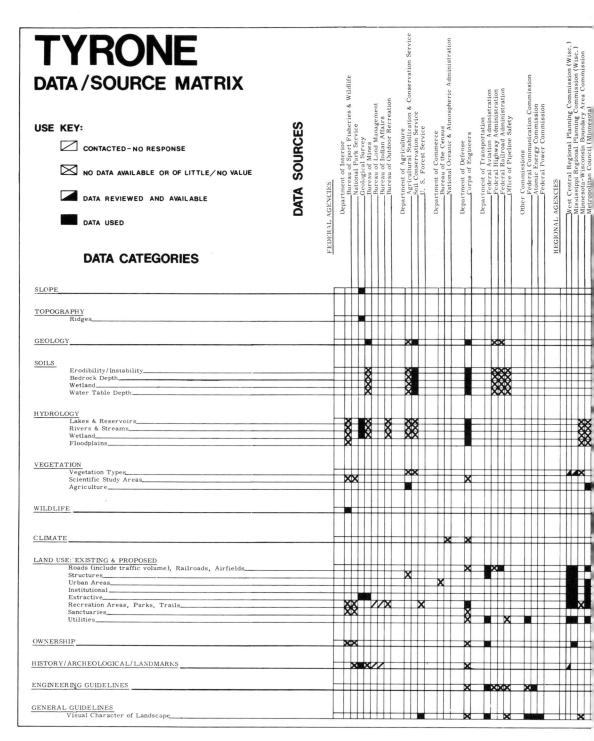

FIGURE 9-5 Sample format for recording and managing data collection. Careful recording and annotation of data are essential because siting studies should be regarded as legal processes. A data-source matrix is a valuable method of coordinating and summarizing all data collection efforts.

WISCONSIN STATE AGENCIES
- Department of Agriculture
- Department of Industry, Labor and Human Relations
- Department of Local Affairs & Development
- Department of Natural Resources
  - Bureau of Environmental Impact
  - Bureau of Planning
  - Division of Environmental Protection
  - Division of Forestry, Wildlife, and Recreation
  - Division of Tourism and Information
- Natural Beauty Council
- Natural Resources Committee
- Scientific Areas Preservation Council
- Water Resources Council
- Department of Transportation
  - Division of Aeronautics
  - Division of Highways
  - Division of Planning
- State Historical Society
- Public Service Commission
- Wisconsin Statistical Reporting Service

MINNESOTA STATE AGENCIES
- Department of Aeronautics
- Department of Highways
- Minnesota Historical Society
- Indian Affairs Commission
- Department of Natural Resources
  - Bureau of Engineering
  - Bureau of Planning
  - Game and Fish Division
  - Lands and Forestry Division
  - Parks and Recreation Division
  - Waters, Soils, and Minerals Division
- State Soil and Water Conservation Commission

COUNTY AGENCIES
- Wisconsin (county - county seat)
  - Barron - Barron
  - Buffalo - Alma
  - Chippewa - Chippewa Falls
  - Dunn - Menomonie
  - Eau Claire - Eau Claire
  - Pepin - Durand
  - Pierce - Ellsworth
  - St. Croix - Hudson
- Minnesota
  - Goodhue - Red Wing
  - Dakota - Hastings
  - Washington - Stillwater

CITY AGENCIES
- Red Wing - City Council Planning Commission

CLIENT RESOURCES
- Northern States Power
- Mark Hurd - Air Photos

MISC. REFERENCE SOURCES
- University of Wisconsin
  - Madison
  - River Falls
  - University Extension
  - Geological & Natural History Survey
- University of Minnesota
- Minnesota Geological Survey
- Wisconsin Society for Ornithology, Inc.
- Wisconsin Indian Head Country
- Public Telephone Companies
- Clarkson Map Company
- Williams Bros. Pipeline Company
- Great Northern Oil Terminal Company
- Wisconsin Gas Company
- Northern Natural Gas
- Midwestern Gas
- St. Croix Valley Natural Gas Co., Inc.
- International Union for Conservation of Nature and Natural Resources
- Severn Wildfowl Trust
- American Geographical Society
- Harvard University, Dept. of Landscape Arch.
- University of Penn., Dept. of Environmental Design
- Iowa Academy of Science

adverse weather conditions will make access and operations extremely difficult. Holidays, hunting seasons, and summer vacations also may frustrate the scheduling of meetings with officials, and extra time allowances need to be made during these periods.

DATA ANALYSIS AND ORGANIZATION

The reporting of findings, statistical data, and analysis with clarity demands a format that is as nearly uniform as possible from factor to factor.

For example, for purposes of classifying siting factors it may be advisable, if complex issues are likely to arise, to request the representatives of each discipline to report their data findings and recommendations for classification within a set format. An appropriate format would be:

1 *Summary.* An overview of the statewide siting factors considered and the conclusions reached.

2 *Approach.* An explanation of the approach used to analyze the siting category as well as a brief discussion, when appropriate, of alternative approaches not used; also, an explanation of procedures used in processing data.

3 *Assumptions.* A list of premises and assumptions made in the analysis of data.

4 *Results.* Results of the analysis in tabular and/or map form with an explanatory text.

5 *Siting interpretation.* Evaluation of factors, designation of buffer zones, and recommendations as to whether the factors be considered exclusion or evaluation factors.

6 *Validity.* A qualifying statement on any limitations of the data which may exist.

METHODS OF ORGANIZING MAPPED DATA

In addition to normal requirements for presentation and interpretation of tabular and narrative data, whenever possible data should be transferred to map form at a common scale. Because of the geographic nature of the comprehensive siting process, map graphics are central to both the study process and the presentation of conclusions. This places particular demands on careful handling of mapped data.

The manner in which information is interpreted, rectified, transferred, and depicted on maps should result from an understanding of its ultimate role in the siting decision. This understanding will indicate the relationship of each category of data to other categories and the need for locational accuracy. Factors affecting mapping decisions include the area of coverage, the budget and time available for the study, the user groups, the degree of detail of data types, the method of weighting to be used, and the likelihood that weights may be altered during the process. There are also a number of cartographic design principles to be considered in setting up the mapping component of a siting study.

Map Scale

If factor maps are to be drafted and composited in final form by hand, they must be prepared at a common scale. The choice of scale for site screening, candidate area evaluation, and site evaluation depends on the size of the study area at each stage in the process, the areal extent of the facility, the data detail required, and the base maps that are available. Table 9-5 provides a summary of appropriate scales for each use.

Some other practical considerations affect the choice among acceptable options. First, the drafting time can be reduced by avoiding the judgment often involved in translating existing data sources to another scale. If alteration of scale is essential, photographic reduction or enlargement should be considered. Second, drafting time can be saved by working at a smaller scale rather than on large sheets, which can be unwieldy. Finally, limitations of press size and readability should be kept in mind if the sheets are to be reduced and printed.

Interpretation and Transfer of Data

Sometimes more than one basic data map will derive from the same source. This commonly occurs with soil and vegetation maps. The boundaries between soil types and between vegetation types may be interpreted under slightly different rules according to the siting and environmental factors important to a particular project. Boundaries are not precise, but they can often be considered coincident. However, the transition zones between types may be so broad as to allow wide differences in the placement of the boundary by separate individuals. When correlation of the data maps is attempted later, "sliver zones" develop and complicate the study unnecessarily. The problem needs to be resolved early by establishing clear and coordinated ground rules for each component of the mapped data base.

Graphic Techniques

Making useful maps is a sophisticated graphic design problem requiring judgments in the selection of line weights, textures, colors, values, and symbols as they relate to emphasis, order, orientation, and readability. Poor maps contain data but tell no story and make interpretation and analysis difficult. Key factors should jump out at the observer. In the Calaveras Water Master Plan, which involved selection of a site for a proposed hydropower project, high erosion hazard was a major factor influencing the decision. It was depicted in the strongest color relative to other rock types. Figure 9-6 shows the effectiveness of the strong color.

Important relationships between overlapping data should be apparent. In most siting studies, it is desirable to avoid good agricultural lands. All high-class soils represent a constraint even if they are not in agricultural use. Existing dry cropland on nonprime soils may be represented as equally constraining. When dry cropland coincides with prime soils, the constraint level is generally higher. The combination of irrigated cropland with prime soils provides the highest constraint. The Platte River Power Authority Study Map (Figure 9-7) illustrates how the gradation can be achieved with one color hatching. Range and other land uses stand out clearly as potential opportunity areas.

Symbolism should be so obvious that it is grasped immediately and is easily remembered. Reference points should be recessive but sufficient for orienting to the true ground locations. For example, in the Platte River view relations map, Figure 9-8, it is possible to imagine views from the major roads in the region despite the highly symbolic technique employed.

Graphic design must also be responsive to drafting and reproduction limitations; upon reduction, lines too close to one another merge, letters may become unreadable, and superimposed halftone patterns will create moiré effects. The smallest readable area in which a shape or tone is shown is $1/10$ inch square at the final reduced size. Areas smaller than that should be shown as points. A four-times reduction is usually the maximum for retention of graphic quality.

For cost-effective mapping, sheet sizes should be selected to conform to efficient press modules at the final printed size. Use of color is not necessarily more effective than black and white or than use of a single color with black and white. The map scale, the number of data categories on a single map, and budget constraints usually determine the decision to use color. There are times when color is the only appropriate choice, as will be readily apparent by examining the Rawhide Transmission Line Siting Study maps in Figure 9-3. These were originally produced in nine contrasting colors.

Map graphics are central to both the siting study process and the presentation of conclusions. With careful planning, the same graphics can be used for both purposes and can be the source material for a variety of products, including large hand-colored wall maps, interim large-scale black-and-white planning maps, reduced full-color report maps, transparent overlays, and 35-millimeter slides.

Large-scale mapping programs for statewide or large regional studies usually require a specially drawn outline base map to avoid distracting the user with too much information. An alternative is a simple map showing county boundaries and major places and roads. The base map for the Minnesota Power Plant Siting Program (seen in Figures 9-9 and 9-10) is an example. For smaller areas or detailed site-evaluation sites, a USGS base is usually appropriate. An unscreened positive film provides an easily read base for drafting overlay data maps. Screened, it provides adequate but unobtrusive orientation.

Basic data are usually drafted on prints of the base map and later on film overlays in register with the base. This permits easy compositing of overlays for purposes of both study and printing.

Compositing Graphics

The graphics program should be designed with the objective of revealing paths or islands where the best siting opportunities exist. Sometimes it is best to show unfavorable siting factors (constraints) on one map, as in Figure 9-9, and favorable conditions (opportunities) on another, as in Figure 9-10. It may be desirable to combine the two for a cost-benefit analysis.

Compositing maps on a single map shows the distribution and overlap of all influencing factors. There are several ways in which this can be done either manually or by computer. Both methods have advantages and disadvantages, some of which are summarized in Table 9-6.

GRAPHIC WEIGHTING AND MANUAL COMPOSITING
The simplest and most economical method of compositing factor maps involves the use of separate but coordinated textures in individual data maps which can be overlaid to form a composite. Priorities or significance can be communicated by the graphic impact that one texture has over another. Comparison of the Platte River composite constraint map which was shown in Figure 7-13 with the agriculture and viewshed data maps, Figures 9-7 and 9-8, shows that the individual data factors can be easily identified in the composite. However, comparison of the composite map with the factor maps shows that the capacity for producing a weighted composite is ex-

TABLE 9-5   Mapping scales: limitations and recommendations. The choice of map scale to be used at each phase of the site-selection process depends upon the study area size, facility size, level of detail required, and available base maps.

Mapping Scale		Minimum Area of Resolution (1/10" x 1/10")	Map Size for State within 50 miles of Adjacent Area
Ratio	Distance/Inch		
1:4,000,000	1"=64±mi.	40± sq. mi.	9' x 12'
1:2,000,000	1"=32±mi.	10± sq. mi.	19" x 24"
1:1,000,000	1"=16 mi. 1640± acres	2.6±sq. mi.	37" x 47"
1:750,000	1"=12 mi. 920± acres	1.4± sq. mi.	50" x 62"
1:500,000	1"=8 mi.	410± acres	75" x 94"
1:250,000	1"=4 mi.	102± acres	13' x 16'
1:125,000	1"=2 mi.	25± acres	N/A
1:62,500 USGS 15-minute	1"=1 mi.	6± acres	N/A
1:24,000 USGS 7.5-minute	1'=2,000'	1± acre	N/A
1:12,000	1"=1,000'	0.2± acre	N/A
1:2,400	1"=200'	0.01± acre	N/A

Typical facility sizes (excluding cooling ponds, reservoirs, off-site facilities)

o   Nuclear or fossil (coal) site for several 1,000-MW units

o   Structures for 1,000-MW unit (turbine/generator, boiler or reactor and adjacent structures, excluding switchyard, waste disposal, etc.)

o   Combined cycle plant sites

o   Combined turbine sites

Map Size for Typical Study Region of 00 mi. x 200 mi.	Map Size for Typical Candidate Siting Area of 10 mi. x 10 mi.	Recommendations
/A	N/A	
/A	N/A	
" x 12"	N/A	
" x 16"	N/A	for state-wide screening
2" x 25"	N/A	
5" x 50"	2.5" x 2.5"	for planning region screening of major facilities
0" x 100"	5" x 5"	
* x 16'	10" x 10"	
/A	27" x 27"	for site identification
/A	54" x 54"	
/A	22' x 22'	

,000 – 2,000 acres

00' x 400'±
r 3.6± acres

0 – 50 (?) acres

– 10 (?) acres

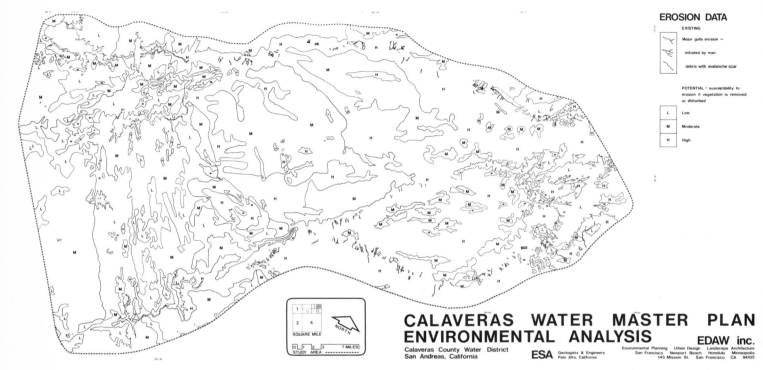

EROSION DATA

EXISTING

Major gully erosion — initiated by man

debris with avalanche scar

POTENTIAL — susceptibility to erosion if vegetation is removed or disturbed

L   Low

M   Moderate

H   High

CALAVERAS WATER MASTER PLAN
ENVIRONMENTAL ANALYSIS
Calaveras County Water District
San Andreas, California

ESA Geologists & Engineers
Palo Alto, California

EDAW inc.
Environmental Planning   Urban Design   Landscape Architecture
San Francisco   Newport Beach   Honolulu   Minneapolis
145 Mission St.   San Francisco   CA   94105

FIGURE 9-6 Sample data map using a range of values to aid interpretation and analysis. Key factors should be immediately apparent. In this example, high erosion hazard is the key factor and receives the strongest tone.

tremely limited. A new map must be drafted if weights are changed or data are updated.

A more flexible graphic weighting and compositing technique involves the use of one-color film overlays for each constraint type. A product of this process, the Project Seafarer composite constraint map (which was presented in Figure 7-16) illustrates its graphic and easily readable quality. The cost of producing film overlays is relatively high, but the data maps can be manipulated easily and inexpensively. The system offers the advantage of easily altering graphic weights through the insertion of additional colored film in any category during the study process. Some thirty film overlays were used to arrive at the Seafarer composite, and Figure 7-17 shows that the base and composite opportunities maps were clearly visible beneath the overlays.

NUMERICAL WEIGHTING   When numerical weights are assigned to constraint factors, as we described in Chapter 7, each part of the study region will receive a numerical score, the sum of all the weighted constraints pres-

ent. A new map can then be made. This may be done manually, using graduated values or colors, as was seen in the example from the Minnesota project (Figure 9-9).

This method offers unlimited flexibility in handling weighted scores and results in a very graphic product. However, it is difficult to manipulate, and updating data or altering weights assigned to constraints requires the map to be reworked. The method is comparatively economical if no manipulation of the composite is required.

When values are placed on the data and multiple correlations, the ability to recomposite with altered values, or statistical analysis is contemplated, the use of a computer should be considered. Although a computer is capable of all manual mapping and analytical functions, it is generally not time- or cost-effective unless it is to be used iteratively. Computer mapping and compositing do, however, offer unlimited flexibility in weighting constraints, very rapid compositing, and the lowest cost for manipulating and updating data once the system has been set up.

Offsetting these advantages are the high initial cost of

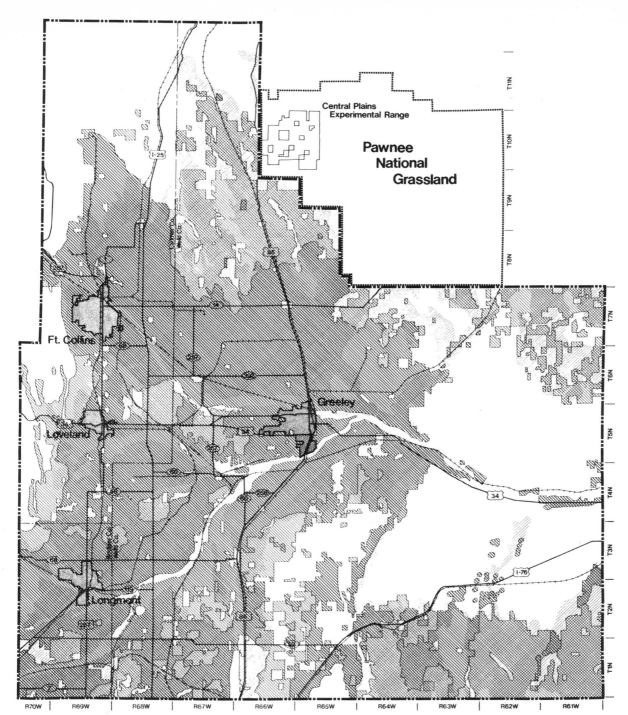

Prime Agricultural Lands

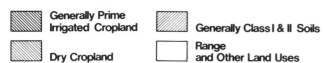

Generally Prime
Irrigated Cropland

Dry Cropland

Generally Class I & II Soils

Range
and Other Land Uses

Platte River Power Authority

POWER PLANT
FEASIBILITY STUDY

EDAW inc.
Environmental Planning

FIGURE 9-7 Sample data map using hatching to aid interpretation and analysis. Clear gradation may be achieved by simply using a single color or black and white.

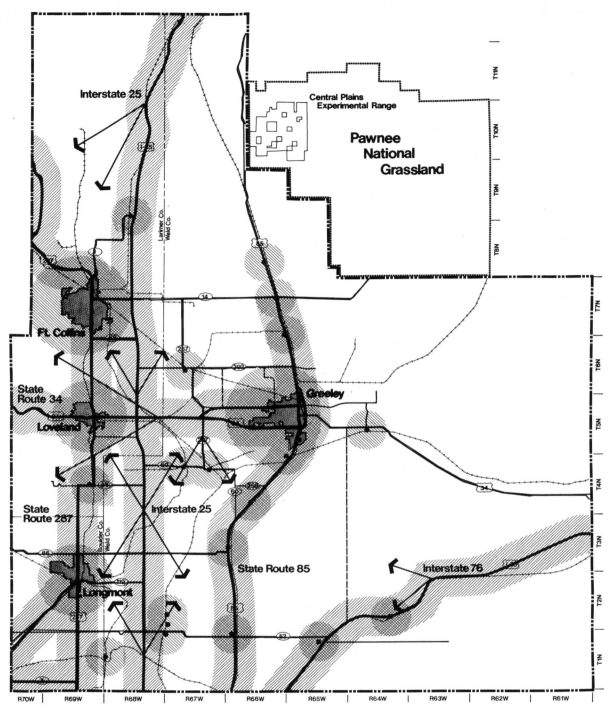

View Relations

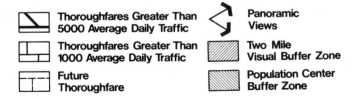

	Thoroughfares Greater Than 5000 Average Daily Traffic		Panoramic Views
Thoroughfares Greater Than 1000 Average Daily Traffic			Two Mile Visual Buffer Zone
Future Thoroughfare			Population Center Buffer Zone

Platte River Power Authority

POWER PLANT FEASIBILITY STUDY

EDAW inc.
Environmental Planning

FIGURE 9-8 Sample data map using symbolism. Symbolism should be so obvious that it is grasped immediately.

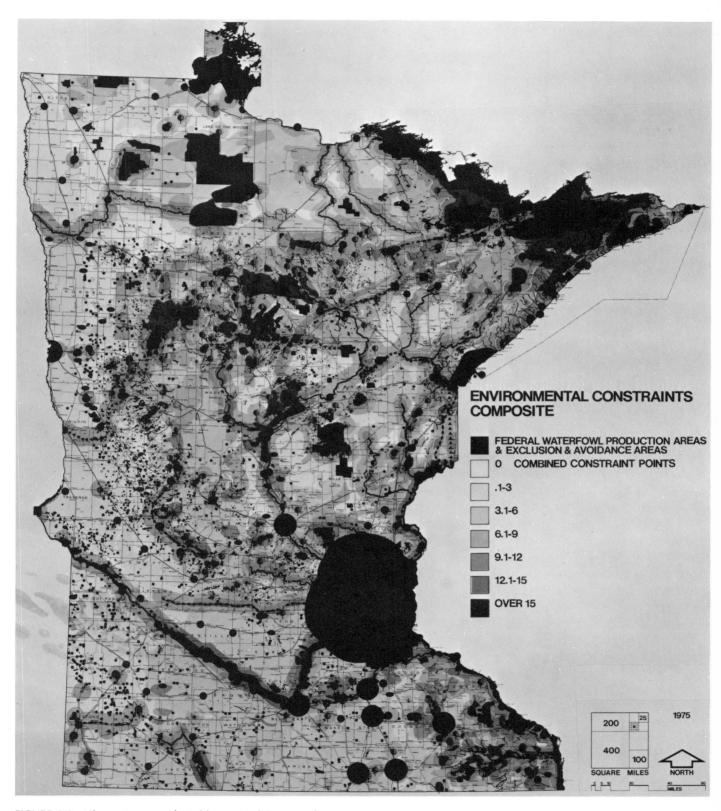

ENVIRONMENTAL CONSTRAINTS
COMPOSITE

FEDERAL WATERFOWL PRODUCTION AREAS
& EXCLUSION & AVOIDANCE AREAS

0   COMBINED CONSTRAINT POINTS

.1-3

3.1-6

6.1-9

9.1-12

12.1-15

OVER 15

FIGURE 9-9   Minnesota power plant siting constraints composite.

TABLE 9-6 Comparison of environmental data base systems.

Example	Area of Coverage	Used for Locating	Characteristics
Minnesota Power Plant Siting Program	Statewide	Power plants	Numeric weighting/ manual compositing
Davenport Transmission Routing Study	500 sq. mi.	Transmission line	Numeric weighting/ computer compositing
Platte River Power Plant Siting Program	3,000 sq. mi.	Power plant	Graphic weighting patterns/manual compositing
Project Seafarer Environmental Siting Studies	5,000 sq. mi.	Navy communications system	Graphic weighting tones/ manual compositing

Advantages	Disadvantages
1 Weighting—unlimited flexibility 2 Very graphic product 3 Economical if composite manipulation not required	1 Difficult to manipulate composite 2 Updating data requires map rework
1 Weighting—unlimited flexibility 2 Quick turn-around time for compositing 3 Lowest cost in manipulating data and updating once set up	1 Computer not always trusted 2 If cell compositing, mapping less readable and understood 3 Higher initial cost in establishing data base
1 Most economical method 2 Individual data factors identifiable in composite	1 Weighting extremely limited 2 Updating data requires map rework
1 Quick turn-around time for compositing 2 Low cost in manipulating data 3 Very graphic product 4 Best understood by general public	1 Weighting flexible but limited 2 Updating data requires map rework

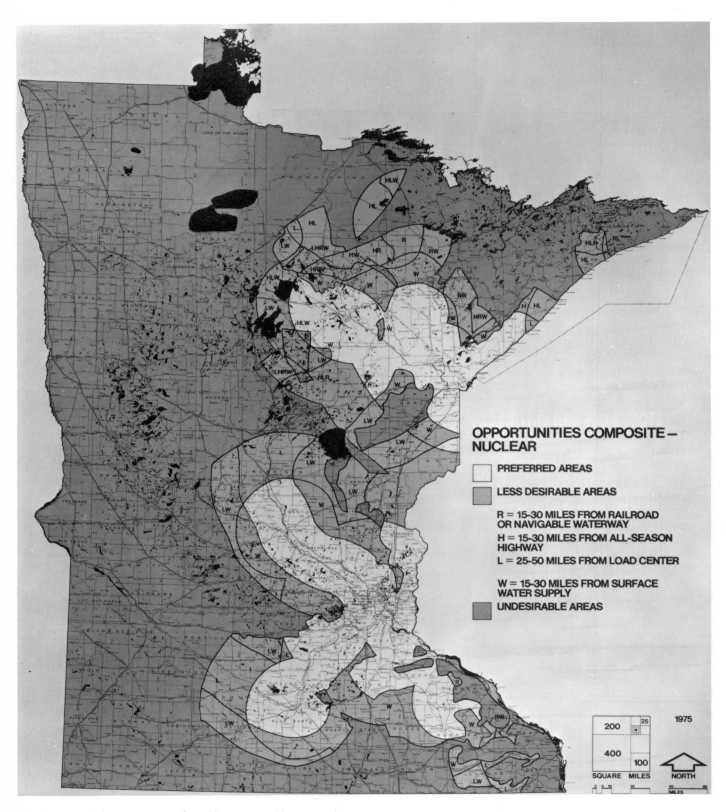

OPPORTUNITIES COMPOSITE —
NUCLEAR

PREFERRED AREAS

LESS DESIRABLE AREAS

R = 15-30 MILES FROM RAILROAD
OR NAVIGABLE WATERWAY

H = 15-30 MILES FROM ALL-SEASON
HIGHWAY

L = 25-50 MILES FROM LOAD CENTER

W = 15-30 MILES FROM SURFACE
WATER SUPPLY

UNDESIRABLE AREAS

1975

FIGURE 9-10   Minnesota power plant siting opportunities composite.

establishing the data base, less easily readable and understandable mapping if individual cells are composited, and the fact that programming or input errors are not easily caught. Theoretically, computer-drawn maps can be as well presented as manually prepared maps. In reality, they often require some manual assistance to make them understandable. Line-printer maps are the hardest to deal with because of the horizontal sheet limitations and the lack of geographic orientation points. The printed characters usually obliterate reference information such as contours, roads, rivers, and towns, as illustrated by the Davenport Transmission Routing Study composite constraint map in Figure 7-18.

Many of these difficulties are already being overcome by the software capabilities and hardware of new systems coming into general use. Grid cells are now small enough to permit considerable digitizing flexibility, previously attainable only with coordinate string (polygon) systems, which are less desirable for mapping spatial information. Larger storage capacity and higher-speed data manipulation capability linked with large-screen color video display units are already close to feasibility. This process will permit rapid checks for accuracy, almost instant display of altered factor combinations and weighting, and more graphic communication with study participants.

There are no set rules governing the choice of method. The needs of any project generally exist in a unique combination. As previously emphasized, it is important not to assume that the more sophisticated the method, the better the results. While the rapid development in data processing and computer graphics need to be watched and carefully assessed, there is no point in using the computer for unnecessary processing of data. Much can be said for consistency, but running information through the computer for the sole purpose of producing a map in the computer's style is wasteful and often results in unnecessary errors, generalities, and diminution of clarity.

CONCLUSION

Much of what we have said on the subject of data is based on experience in assembling and handling data in the absence of relevant, consistent, up-to-date, and comprehensive data banks. Many states and industries (mainly utility companies) are attempting to remedy this situation. Some years in the future, perhaps, basic data for site selection may become more easily obtainable. In addition, technological developments such as low-level LANDSAT imagery will simplify the updating of some types of information, such as land use. Recent developments in computer storage and programming already aid in rapid interpretation: for example, the interpretation of computerized topographic data available from USGS.

Whatever the nature of change in the rapidly expanding fields of data banks and computer mapping, the principles and processes we have set forth will remain relevant. Indeed, the principles regarding selectivity, organization, verification, and the need to make do with incomplete data may become even more relevant.

10 | CITIZEN PARTICIPATION

Previous chapters have presented a focused but comprehensive process for major-facility siting. The objective of this process is to achieve solutions that satisfy the concerns of sponsors and other affected interests as closely as possible and avoid adversarial conflict. Citizen participation has been mentioned frequently as an integral part of the process. In this chapter, it may be helpful to provide a more detailed examination of the purpose and structuring of participation programs.

THE PURPOSE OF CITIZEN PARTICIPATION

First, we will give further consideration to the reasons for public participation. Many agencies and industries are committed to public participation in their siting decisions, but their commitment may spring from widely varying motives. For this reason programs of participation may take different forms. Often the potential value of public participation is not achieved because neither its benefits nor its pitfalls are fully understood.

At one end of the scale are project sponsors motivated mainly by sensitivity to public relations. Their concern is to find locations that offer good potential for local acceptance and even welcome as well as technical and economic feasibility. Such sponsors may conduct discreet public opinion surveys to find out where their facility would be well received.

A survey published by *Fortune* in 1977 showed heavy reliance on behind-the-scenes investigations and polling (Belknap Data Solutions Ltd., 1977). However, exclusive emphasis on the public relations approach can have drawbacks. First, resistance may be encountered when the proposal is finally made public. Secrecy itself tends to generate suspicion. Moreover, perceptions of a project change once the reality of an abstract site begins to affect people directly. Second, some communities may be so anxious to obtain new jobs, tax revenues, and income sources that the broad range of environmental issues is given insufficient examination. Finally, the sponsor may be tempted to subjugate some siting criteria to the apparent ease of project approval or the offer of financial incentives.

Early publicity is often avoided because land values tend to rise with the prospect of a potential major-facility development. Some firms have attempted to minimize this problem by acquiring land anonymously in anticipation of project approval. The experience of Dow Chemical Company at Montezuma Hills, which we described in Chapter 1, suggests the wisdom of merely acquiring options.

Discreet polling of local attitudes to a proposed project has value but only if it accompanies the comprehensive process of screening presented in earlier chapters. If siting and environmental factors can be shown to be potentially suitable at a given candidate site, then the fact that the facility is locally desirable provides a good basis for obtaining an option on the site and seeking project approval through negotiation.

At the other end of the scale from the public relations approach to "participation" lie various forms of real public involvement in the siting decision. Participation does not mean mere consultation or review for the sake of appearance, nor does it mean token compliance with legal requirements. The state of California, for example, requires full public participation in energy planning and site and facility certification. The Council on Environmental Quality (CEQ) now requires broad public representation in all projects for which a federal environmental impact statement must be prepared. All affected and interested agencies and citizens are to be involved in defining the issues to be studied, an activity which the CEQ terms *scoping*.

The purpose of public involvement should be the

transfer of real knowledge. It should rest on the recognition that in most cases open discussion has benefits which outweigh any problems of premature disclosure. Citizens or their representatives need objective and accurate information about the proposed facility and its potential impacts. Unless the gap between real and perceived consequences is narrowed, participants can neither protect public interests nor aid the sponsor through informed contributions to the siting process. Without such contributions, the sponsor cannot be forewarned of potential opposition. Nor can the sponsor understand the latitude for negotiation and recognize all appropriate project modifications.

Recent siting and environmental studies for a major mining operation within an Indian reservation in the state of Washington illustrate the value and necessity of an open exchange of information. Native Americans involved in scoping the environmental impact statement noted the need to address the project's effects on the quality of life and the availability of housing on the reservation. Although these were not mandated items of inquiry, the information allowed the project sponsor to approach these potentially volatile issues constructively.

DESIGN OF THE PROGRAM

Achievement of full public participation, whether in response to a legal requirement or as a matter of choice or prudence, requires planning. Effective participation results from a carefully designed approach to the characteristics of a given project and the interests potentially affected by it. It takes effort to counter any one of a series of problems associated with citizen participation. These include distrust, apathy, or disinterest, unfamiliarity with the technology and potential effects of a project, poor past experiences, dominating special interests, and the sacrifices necessary for individuals to spend considerable time in workshops or meetings.

The design of a full-participation program requires consideration not only of why participation is desirable but also of which persons should participate, when their participation is appropriate, and how their participation can be made effective.

Program design must be accomplished at the outset of the study. It is extremely difficult to insert a participatory component efficiently and credibly into an established siting process unless the process itself is altered. If the structure is altered to permit community participation, earlier decisions have to be reexamined to confirm or

change them. It is obviously desirable to avoid such duplication of time and effort. Further, if citizens' expectations of influencing decisions are raised, they cannot be satisfied merely by participation in a program of education and issue definition (Arthus D. Little, Inc., 1976).

In a sense, in previous chapters we have described the role of the site selectors and planners as attorneys, responsible for the type of evidence gathered and its presentation in a clearly organized manner. Selection of a participation process and its participants is akin to jury selection. The aim is to work with a group that overall is fair and impartial, in that it at least represents a balance of interests even if it is not composed solely of fair and impartial individuals. The site selectors and the planners provide the evidence in a clearly organized manner for the jury to weigh. The two big differences from the jury system are that we hope not to be dealing with an adversary situation and that the jury makes a series of step-by-step decisions before reaching the final verdict.

Designers of a participation program should also consider who should run the program. In many cases, a program can be conducted more effectively by independent individuals who are experienced in citizen participation than by the project sponsors and planners. Participation experts are not proponents. They understand their audience, and they can help the designers to present what is proposed in understandable terms.

One additional point needs to be made before we look further at the mechanics of a formal program of participation. Effective participation demands good listening on the part of the sponsor. Good listening is as important in informal settings as in formal ones. Much can be learned by frequenting the places where people talk and do business, whether in city halls or coffee shops and bars.

SELECTION OF PARTICIPANTS AND TIMING OF PARTICIPATION

Answers to questions regarding the breadth and timing of participation are closely related. The major influencing factors are the geographic extent of the inquiry and the degree to which a broad policy framework already exists to guide the inquiry.

The larger the geographic scope of the study, the less easy it is to involve a broad segment of the lay public directly. This means that statewide siting studies, for example, should be guided by a group that is representative of the interests of the public at large. This group may be specially selected from a range of technical, governmental, academic, and lay interests, as is the case in Minnesota, where such a structure is mandated by state law to examine power installations. In the statewide power plant siting study for Minnesota, the group was asked to interpret and expand on some very general existing criteria.

Alternatively, the group may be composed exclusively of government agency staff, at least in the early stages. The rationale for such an approach is that fundamental philosophical positions on the part of the public have been stated through the democratic process and the issues to be resolved in site screening are largely matters of technical interpretation of policy. For example, in the case of the California statewide power plant siting study, guidelines and suitability maps existed for the coastal zone, originally established through public initiative. Most of the coastal zone was therefore already excluded from consideration. The staff of the sponsoring agency and its consultants felt confident that such broad-scale concerns had been publicly and adequately expressed, which permitted them to examine and weigh the relative value of each factor on more strictly technical grounds, drawing on the expertise of specialized state staff members and consultants. This was a case of public participation through responsible staff interpretation.

When the focus of a siting study is initially on a relatively small study area or becomes narrowed through the site-screening process, a broader segment of the public can be involved. In fact, it becomes less a matter of choice. It may not be imperative if local participatory planning has already adequately established policies and plans for accommodating the facility. But if questions of community growth and economic development are raised by the proposed siting of a major facility, decision making rather than mere reactive participation becomes especially important. It may be necessary to structure a dialogue on regional goals and priorities in order to understand the implications of a facility and to provide the appropriate framework to accommodate them if they are acceptable. The reaction to the perceived growth-inducing potential of the proposed Rawhide energy project in Colorado provides an example of the need to go back to basic regional planning considerations and policies.

In some cases, as we saw in Chapter 1 in discussing the successful Duluth Freeway extension in contrast to examples of freeway-planning failures, there can be no substitute for close involvement of the variety of local interests directly affected by a proposed facility.

It must be emphasized that there are no rigid formulas for designing participation programs. It is a matter of doing what will work in specific circumstances. If the fa-

cility type per se is not controversial (although admittedly it is difficult to imagine such a type), participation efforts can be concentrated on local site-evaluation issues. This may also be the appropriate or necessary approach when dealing with a facility type which already is governed by specific location regulations or with one whose need is dictated by national policy. However, in such a case it is essential to be able to demonstrate a rational and defensible procedure for arriving at the sites to be evaluated locally.

In designing the participation schedule, it may be desirable to undertake initial studies in-house. A representative group of participants may be brought in once ground rules have been established and issues have been identified. Participation may be expanded even further when candidate sites have been selected.

In summary, we recommend that separate (but coordinated) public participation plans be designed for site-screening and site-evaluation studies as follows:

· Define the screening and site-evaluation methodology as a series of detailed steps.

· Identify the objectives of public participation in the process.

· Identify the information or input required of the public.

· Identify the source of needed information (state agencies, special-interest groups, utilities, etc.).

· Identify the points in the process where public input would be most valuable.

· Evaluate methods or tools for involving the public.

· Select those tools which most effectively meet the needs.

· Develop a plan tied to the various steps in the methodology.

· Begin implementation of the plan.

· Monitor and refine the plan on a continuing basis.

Figure 10-1 shows a recommended public participation plan for a statewide site-screening study and illustrates the relationship between each step and the sequence of site-screening tasks. Table 10-1 shows a comparison of screening and site-evaluation objectives. It also suggests various tools available to major-facility planners. These will be discussed in the next section.

SITE-SCREENING AND SITE-EVALUATION PARTICIPATION TECHNIQUES

The literature on effective citizen participation techniques may be consulted for more detailed and extensive discussion of participation programs. We do not propose to duplicate such discussions unnecessarily; however, it

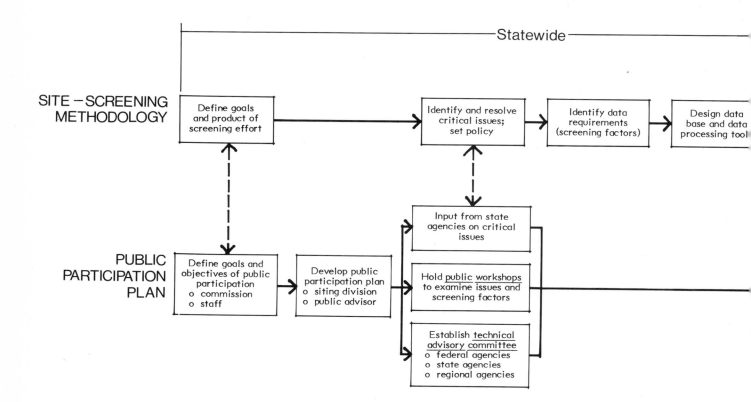

FIGURE 10-1 Public participation in site screening. Citizen participation programs may be carried on concurrently with the later phases or in some cases with all phases of the siting process. This diagram should be read in conjunction with the site-screening process diagram, Figure 7-2.

is valuable to examine the available techniques briefly in relation to the major-facility site-screening and site-evaluation process.

The approaches which have been used in siting studies conducted by EDAW include:

· Communication, via direct mail, notices, or mass media

· Citizens' advisory committees and/or technical advisory committees

· Public opinion surveys

· Workshops

· Public meetings

· Public hearings

Each approach will be described at the most appropriate point in the following discussion. Frequently, most or all of these approaches will be appropriate at some point during the site-selection process. The committee approach is typically most heavily relied upon, particularly in cases such as statewide siting studies which are least geographically specific.

Another approach, which we have not applied to the site-selection process to date, is the workbook, a presentation of background information and related questions prepared for wide public dissemination in which space is provided for respondents to record their preferences regarding suggested alternative solutions. A good example is that prepared by the National Park Service to assist it in developing plans for the future of Yosemite National Park (U.S. Department of the Interior, 1975). Workbooks are expensive to prepare and are most effective in relation to single-area plans and local planning issues which are capable of relatively simple explanation. However, the ap-

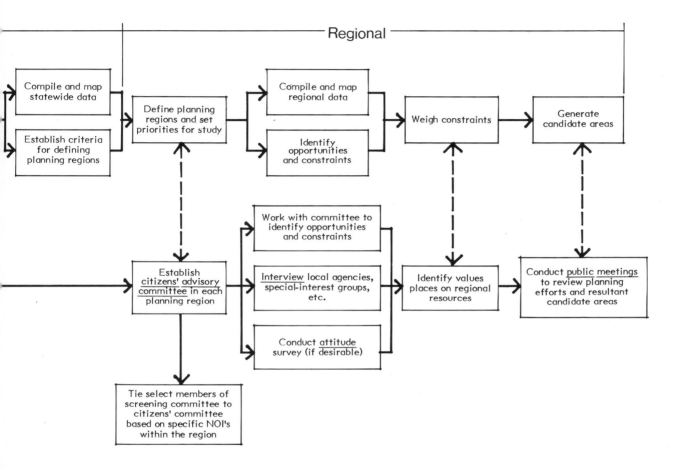

proach has been adopted on a smaller scale in the form of worksheets for identification of issues and weighting of evaluation factors by direct participants in siting studies.

Project Publicity

In a study involving very broad participation from its initiation, publicity is desirable. The options range from news releases and radio and television spots to mass mailing of information or questionnaires. All these have been used successfully in public planning programs. For example, the National Park Service Yosemite workbook represents what might be called a wide-scale saturation approach, in which several thousand copies of the workbook were mailed.

The value of mass communications as a tool in major-facility siting studies may be quite limited because of the technical complexity of the issues and the expense involved in analyzing any responses requested. Nevertheless, site selectors should be alert to such possibilities. Increased public awareness of opportunities to participate can be achieved through publicity and can enhance the credibility of a siting program.

Advisory Committees

Since advisory committees, both technical and lay citizens' committees, represent the most often used form of participation in both site-screening and site-evaluation studies, we shall have most to say about how they are put together and how they function.

TABLE 10-1 Objectives and methods of public participation in site screening and site evaluation. It is usually desirable to design separate participation programs for each phase of the siting study.

	SCREENING	SITE EVALUATION
CHARACTERISTICS	o Statewide or regional o Long term, on-going process	o Site-specific o Short-term process commences after selection of candidate sites
OBJECTIVES OF PUBLIC PARTICIPA-TION PROGRAM	o Identify the various "publics" concerned with power plant siting o Identify key siting issues o Identify opinions on issues and attitudes toward power plant siting o Determine values placed on statewide & regional resources o Differentiate among regional attitudes & values in various parts of the state o Develop mechanism for incorporating public values & attitudes into a continuous site planning process	o Identify the various "publics" concerned with a specific project proposal o Identify key siting issues o Identify opinions on issues o Determine values & priorities placed on local & regional resources o Determine values placed in areas generally recognized to require subjective evaluation (visual impact, desired life style, community character, etc.) o Develop mechanism for directly applying public attitudes & values to the site decision
TOOLS	o Public workshops & meetings o Citizens' advisory committee (broad representation & interests) o Informational programs (mass media) o Attitude survey & opinion polls o Interviews with state & regional special interest groups, etc.	o Public hearings (informational & adjudicatory) o Public workshops & meetings o Citizens' committee (local representation) o Informational programs o Attitude surveys & opinion polls o Interview with county & city agencies, special-interest groups, key individuals, etc.

THE PUBLIC SEGMENT INVOLVED A full citizens' advisory committee (as opposed to an initial screening committee consisting solely of government agency representatives) usually must be rather large to be properly representative. The size of the group that can function effectively and provide all members with the opportunity to participate varies widely, but it will generally range from 25 to 100 members. Larger groups tend to require structuring in several smaller committees to permit adequate participation by each member. In some cases, it may be necessary to restrict subcommittee size to a maximum of 10 members.

The qualifications required of committee members depend on the nature of the siting project. Often committees dealing with relatively localized siting studies are made up of community leaders who may be chosen on the basis of their representation of an interest group. In the case of less geographically specific studies, involving weighting of site-selection factors in a more abstract sense, members are selected more often for their professional and technical knowledge and skills. It is also desirable to include representatives of a balanced range of interest groups and government agencies, especially if they have special knowledge and expertise to offer.

There are instances in which participants in committees or workshops must be experts because of the highly technical nature of the decisions to be made. Again, a balanced and comprehensive set of viewpoints must be striven for. However, the participants may act as individuals as well as representatives. The work with the California Energy Resources Conservation and Development Commission in developing thermal power plant siting procedures, the California Department of Water Resources fossil-fueled power plant siting studies, and the Department of the Navy's Project Seafarer are cases in which technical decision making preceded public involvement (EDAW Inc., 1977; 1980; April 1976). In these studies, each committee member represented both his own agency's interests and responsibilities and his personal concerns.

The participants in the National Coal Policy Project mentioned in the Introduction were selected in part because of their leadership roles in environmental and industrial organizations. They did not purport to speak either for their organizations or for the environmental and industrial communities at large, as these issues were felt to be too complex and controversial for either side to speak with a single voice.

Choice of membership is most often by appointment of the sponsoring agency or, in the case of a private sponsor, of the sponsor and the reviewing agency. In some instances interest groups have been asked to appoint members, while in other instances popular elections have been held. The system used in power plant siting in Minnesota is probably the most common. In that state the power plant siting staff of the state government requests nominations from county and local governments, regional development commissions, and environmental and other interest groups and individuals. When recommendations are received, the staff selects a committee with balanced representation of professional skills and background, geographic areas, and interest groups. The makeup of the committee for the statewide study is indicated in the following list:

· Representatives of utility, municipality, and state interests (20)
· Active committee staff members (4)
· Consulting staff (5)
· Consultant—geology-seismology (1)
· Consultant—nuclear licensing (1)
· Minnesota Department of National Resources—explanation and interpretation of current policies (1)
· Consultant—meteorology–air quality (1)
· Consultant—engineering (1)
· Minnesota Geology Survey (2)
· U.S. Geological Survey (1)
· University of Minnesota—vegetation and wildlife; agricultural productivity (1)
· Hamline University (1)

Participants also included eleven members of an ad hoc water appropriations committee, comprising representatives of the geological survey agencies, universities, the Minnesota Department of Natural Resources, and the Upper Mississippi River Basin Commission.

A similar procedure, involving nominations by a variety of groups and selection by local planning staff, generally is used in small-area studies.

HOW THE COMMITTEE FUNCTIONS Initially, the agency concerned must provide organizational and administrative assistance to the committee in order to develop a working structure and to define the objectives to be accomplished. Chairperson, schedule, and agenda must be chosen, and subcommittees may need to be established to deal with specific issues.

The first task is to orient the committee to its tasks. Education on the technical aspects of the project as defined, the preliminary site-selection objectives and criteria, and possible environmental relationships is carried out by the sponsoring or reviewing agency. Consultants may assist in this process and also with the identification of issues with regard to specific decisions to be made by the committee.

The principal functions of the committee are to examine the importance of siting factors, to place relative weights upon them, and especially to assist in making decisions on questions in which serious conflicts or other issues must be resolved. It will be remembered that the subject of weighting siting factors has been discussed in Chapters 7 and 8.

Finally, the committee participates in the application of weighted factors to the candidate area selection process and makes recommendations regarding preferred and alternative sites during the site-evaluation process. The committee's recommendations are then included in a report of findings, which may also include a minority opinion.

To assist the committee in achieving consensus and arriving at decisions, there are several available group process techniques. We will return to these later.

RELIABILITY AND UTILITY OF THE COMMITTEE APPROACH The citizens' advisory committee tends to have a broadly defined purpose which assumes acceptance of the sponsoring or reviewing agency's goals. It has limited power and authority to question those goals. Thus, the possibility exists for the committee to lose respect for the agency, should the agency's decisions be contrary to the committee's recommendations.

Another potential problem is that use of an unchanging committee structure may block participation of groups not represented on the committee and thus introduce bias. We have emphasized the need for representative participation as a means of eliminating bias in the selection process. A solution may be to establish review points during a long siting study at which further appointments can be made; however, a latecomer will be at a disadvantage by not having been a party to earlier discussions and decisions. Another possible solution is to open citizens' advisory committee meetings to the public. This requires particularly well-designed techniques both to provide opportunities for all members of a larger group to participate and also to bring newcomers up to date. Open committee meetings are often attended by disruptive community lobbyists who may believe that their interests are being misrepresented or ignored if they have not been a party to previous discussions.

The principal value of the committee is that representatives of public interests and professional or scientific disciplines can move through a mass of evidence and opinion in an orderly way. The effort to eliminate bias and to give representation to all types of interests is clearly critical to the success of this approach.

The problems associated with committees and the need for broad but balanced representation are equally important in the case of site-evaluation committees. As we will note again in discussion of opinion polling, as the selection process draws nearer to the reality of specific sites, interest is heightened and expressed attitudes can change.

GROUP PROCESS TECHNIQUES Carefully designed techniques to ensure balanced participation must be applied in committees and workshops. Even in relatively small committees established to set objectives or participate in factor weighting where a large percentage of participants are technically knowledgeable professionals, there is a danger that the interests of dominant personalities can assume undue importance. This is even more true with the more predominantly lay groups involved at the site-evaluation stage.

First, the logistics of each meeting demand care to ensure that all members are able to attend. Necessary materials must be available in sufficient time before the meeting to be reviewed. These materials should include a report on actions or discussion at the preceding meeting.

Second, at each meeting, after initial presentation of the substance and objectives of the session it is valuable to record, on newsprint or on a blackboard, each member's reactions and ideas before they are discussed. After discussion members should have an opportunity to rank the complete list of issues or ideas in order of importance. The votes are then counted so that the list can be discussed again and reordered.

This is a simple modification of the Delphi process. More sophisticated versions, involving weighting to account for variations in technical knowledge and individual relative-importance assignments as well as numbers of votes received, may also be appropriate. A separate ballot may be required to develop sufficient differentiation between factors assigned lower importance values if a single issue, such as air quality, is considered so important that its weighting on the importance scale causes bunching at the lower end.

In workshop situations there is always a danger of domination by one or a few individuals. For this reason it is valuable to consider single items, allow time for silent recording of reactions, and proceed, by round robin, to have each individual describe a single idea or concern in turn. In this way everyone has an equal opportunity and obligation to be heard. Balloting, after all items and reactions have been recorded, may also be accomplished in secret.

These techniques have the advantage of not only permitting but also encouraging equal participation by committee or workshop members. More representative decisions tend to occur when individual participation levels are high. The techniques are generally preferable to the more traditional approaches, which include deference to or consultation with an "expert" or authority, majority rule, minority control, or discussions aimed at consensus. Such approaches tend to produce confusing results, lead to dissatisfaction or alienation of some members, or be excessively time-consuming.

TIME AND COST CONSIDERATIONS   The structure of the committee is tied to the life of the site-selection program. Typically, meetings are held twice monthly over a period of months. In Minnesota, for example, a committee on a single power plant siting study will usually be active for 4 to 6 months. Meetings are usually held in the evening since many members are employed. Site-selection committee members, unlike citizen participants in most other types of planning projects, are usually reimbursed for travel and subsistence expenses. The committee generally needs the support of one staff member over its active life. In addition, consultant assistance with committee briefing must be added to the cost, depending upon the time period and degree of support involved. In the Minnesota case, costs were found in 1975 to run between $10,000 and $15,000 for a committee active for 4 to 6 months.

Public Opinion Surveys

Sample surveys may be designed to solicit several kinds of information. They may measure the degree of public awareness and knowledge of an issue and its importance relative to other issues or provide more detailed information on public attitudes toward each issue. Surveys take time, averaging 3 to 4 months to plan and design, pretest, conduct, and analyze. They are also relatively costly, particularly if the personal-interview technique is used. Telephone interviews are lower in cost and generally are the

most appropriate approach. While the cost can be reduced substantially by mail questionnaires, the response rate is often very low and can skew results.

Surveys may be worth the effort involved in siting studies when there is a lack of intuitive feeling for public reaction. They are versatile in that they may be carried out on a statewide, regional, or local basis and be designed to assess response to any issue. However, timing is extremely important because public opinions are subject to quite rapid change. A survey held when the public does not have a good grasp of the issues will have very different results from one conducted after the public has begun to identify with the positions of various interest groups.

Public attitudes toward siting a facility can be assessed during the candidate site evaluation process in a way which is usually not possible during the site-screening process. Part of the candidate site evaluation process involves assessment of whether communities near one site support or oppose the siting to a greater or lesser degree than communities near the other sites.

The clearest expression of public opinion prior to identification of actual alternative sites will tend to be somewhat abstract. Statewide or countywide referenda may have been taken in support of or in opposition to the particular type of facility in question. However, there would need to be similar referenda in other states or counties to make an early determination of relative desirability of the facility. Moreover, such an abstract expression of opinion is frequently made without possession of all the pertinent factors and is also highly subject to political and other pressures. Third, even in the event of support expressed in abstract geographic terms, the more localized subsequent reaction to a specific site could differ significantly.

It is for these reasons that public opinion polls at the site-evaluation stage are not the most effective feasible way to assess opinion. The manner in which a question is phrased too often determines its outcome. Further, polls often elicit respondents' stated, rather than true, attitudes. True attitudes, known as *revealed preferences*, are indicative of individual or community values. For example, the members of a community may say in a survey that they value open space very highly, but upon examination the community is found to contain little open space and is developing the remainder of it. The revealed preference is shown in the fact that the community is unwilling to devote many resources to maintenance of open space.

A more appropriate and revealing approach to determining the relative desirability of a facility includes the following steps:

1 *Review existing public attitude studies and surveys for local communities.* The purpose of this step is to become familiar with the community's stated preferences on issues of concern.

2 *Review environmental reports on file for each area and comments received.* This step will indicate how community public agencies and citizens have responded in the past to projects that have affected the environment.

3 *Interview key persons.* Interview individuals who represent and shape public opinion, including leaders of various interest groups and public agencies such as elected officials, union leaders, environmental groups, business leaders, and other influential citizens.

4 *Survey community values.* This step provides general impressions of the character and values of the community on subjects of environmental concern: air quality, open-space preservation, zoning, community aesthetics, etc.

5 *Analyze constraints.* Examine factors which might affect community values and ability to allocate resources toward environmental protection, including social factors such as level of income and political structure and natural factors such as topography and climate.

This approach was used in a socioeconomic analysis for the Rawhide energy project in Wellington, Colorado. (The key-person interview form used in that assessment appears in Table 10-2.)

The output of such an analysis is a summary of stated attitudes and revealed preferences toward the construction and operation of a major facility and to the potential environmental impacts on communities near each site. Differences in community attitudes and preferences and differences in constraints between study areas should be emphasized. The final product may be a matrix which summarizes for each site stated preferences, revealed preferences, and constraints concerning topics relevant to the major-facility type proposed.

Workshops

As an alternative to polling public opinion, either the site-identification or the site-evaluation stage is an appropriate point at which to hold a workshop in each candidate area, thus opening the process to broadened participation. Again, participants should be nominated by representative groups and selected on the basis of balancing interests. Displays of descriptive and explanatory material, also provided prior to the workshop, can be accompanied by a brief discussion of the factors used to select the alternative sites. However, emphasis should be on explaining the probable effects of the facility and their

mitigation. This is not a universally necessary or applicable approach at this stage, but it can help to refine siting objectives and criteria and provide a good feel for local attitudes.

Full Public Review and Site Approval

Regardless of the extent and type of prior public participation, once a tentative site has been selected, there probably will be an adjudicatory public hearing. This hearing may be preceded by an informational hearing or hearings to review the proposal. Public hearings have long been a requirement of governmental planning at all levels. They are intended to provide the public with an opportunity to question and challenge the proposed actions of a public agency either in proposing or in approving a project. Many hearings proceed smoothly and provide helpful insight into the way in which a project can be improved, in addition to aiding the decision to approve or disapprove it. But everyone with experience in public- or private-sector planning can probably recall a stormy hearing at which a proposal was shouted down. If the appropriate comprehensive process of site selection has been followed, overwhelming protest should be avoidable. Nevertheless, it is useful to review the nature of the hearing process and some ways to avoid its pitfalls.

There are no qualifications for participation in public hearings. This suggests that broad representation is possible. However, participants are seldom a representative group. Hearings tend to attract individuals or interest groups that feel they have something at stake in the outcome of the hearing. This is especially true when there has been no previous commitment to public involvement so that the hearing itself must be used to carry out an external or legal requirement for citizen participation.

The frequent structure of a public hearing is a formal one in which an agency hears a proposal or presents its own plan to the public, soliciting "for the record" the testimony of interested groups and individuals. There may or may not be response to questions and comments, depending upon the style of the agency. Hearings are usually treated as legal proceedings and may be recorded either on tape or by a court reporter, or both, so that a transcript may be prepared. It is also possible to submit written material for the record.

Because of the formal nature of the hearing and the fact that it is generally held toward the end of the planning process, there is usually little opportunity for citizens to interact with public officials or for their views to be incorporated in the plan ahead of time. Generally, testimony presented consists of statements for or against

TABLE 10-2   Example of a key-person interview schedule. This simple survey instrument was prepared for a power plant siting study in Colorado.

I   **Background characteristics of respondent**

   1   What is your occupation?

   2   How long have you lived in the Wellington area?

   3   (If moved here recently)...What made you decide to move to the Wellington area?

II   **Perceptions of conditions in Wellington**

   1   What do you perceive to be the major advantages of living in the Wellington area?

   2   What are some of the disadvantages?

   3   How do you view the economic status of the Wellington community?

   4   What do you view as significant issues currently existing in Wellington?

   5   How do you view the prospects for growth in the Wellington area?

   6   What are likely to be advantages associated with growth in Wellington over the next 10 years? What may be some of the disadvantages?

   7   How do you view the relationship between Wellington and the Fort Collins area?

   8   What could/should be done to make Wellington a better place in which to live?

III   **Perceptions of the power plant...how will it affect life in Wellington?**

   1   What do you know about the power plant proposed to be located outside of Wellington?

   2   What is your opinion concerning the development and location of the proposed plant?

   3   What do you perceive to be the potential adverse effects of the proposed plant?

   4   What may be some of the advantages of the plant?

   5   Do you feel that there are likely to be disproportionate costs or benefits of the plant upon particular segments of the community? More specifically, which groups do you feel will be likely to benefit and which may be adversely affected?

   6   What is your overall opinion as to the necessity of developing additional electric power capacity in the area?

the proposed program or project, so the session takes on the nature of closing arguments rather than input to the development of a plan. The emotionalism often associated with hearings can lead public officials to discount the validity of testimony presented.

Constructive responses at the public hearing can be encouraged by recognizing the proper role of the hearing in the planning and participation process. Distribution of descriptive material prior to and during the hearing and the chance to be heard at the hearing cannot dispel the resentment of citizens who feel that decisions have already been made behind closed doors. Reliance on hearings for input to decisions has led to lawsuits and abandonment of plans.

If public hearings are used only to publicize a decision to which citizen representatives have consistently contributed, then much value can be derived from the hearing process. This can range from confirmation of the acceptability of the decision to recommendations for modifications which would increase the level of acceptability.

There are several ways in which to enhance the value of public hearings through good attendance and thorough understanding of the process which led to the decision. First, hearing notices need to be displayed prominently. A very small notice in a newspaper can easily be missed. The mailing of notices to people living in the immediate vicinity of the proposed site is usually a legal requirement. It may be worth the extra expense of expanding mailings to community groups and neighborhood associations or perhaps seeking community service time on radio and television.

Second, every effort should be made to include with the notice mailing a summary of the proposal and the process that led to it, so that participants in the hearing come well informed.

Third, in addition to wide publication of the hearing and distribution of materials, it is generally most valuable to schedule public review meetings at key decision points prior to the public hearing. In addition to structured committee and workshop participation by citizen representatives, if the broader public is invited to open information meetings, the potential buildup of opposition can often be avoided. Relatively informal public hearings enhance the feeling of openness, increase understanding, and provide insights into those factors which are particular concerns and require the most careful treatment. Without trying to suggest that one or more public meetings in addition to continuing committee participation can guarantee smooth sailing for the most controversial project, we note that in many cases a final public hearing has proceeded uneventfully because questions from the general public had been received and answered earlier in the process.

A final point to be made is that the traditional physical arrangement of the room in both meetings and hearings, typically modeled after courtrooms, tends to be one of hierarchy and authority. This tends to allow only limited, impersonal, and rigid communications, placing both public officials and citizens in defensive, adversary relationships. This one-way communication flow provides inadequate opportunity for an honest, in-depth exchange of information, intimidates some participants, and encourages hostility.

An alternative to the customary arrangement has been successfully used in Oregon for a series of workshops around the state to formulate land-use planning guidelines. Here, large halls rather than council chambers were arranged informally with display and information areas, a corner screen and presentation area, and round tables for workshop discussions with resource people in each major area of interest. The workshops were conducted at daylong sessions or on several consecutive evenings. While setting these up involves considerable effort, the resulting increase in involvement and understanding may be worth the expenditure. The approach could usefully be adapted to informational public meetings and hearings (Appleby, 1978).

In terms of the overall budget for the citizen participation program, the expenses connected with the public hearing can generally be expected to amount to about 10 to 20 percent. They include the time of a hearing officer and court reporter and the cost of tape recordings, transcript, and mailings.

CONCLUSION

This chapter brings this part of the book to an end. What we have endeavored to show here and elsewhere is that thorough research, openness, and good listening can pay off in the majority of cases.

The general public, in the broadest sense, may not be directly involved until late in the program. Nevertheless, democratic representation on advisory committees and awareness of general and local public attitudes in the early stages of projects are essential to minimizing later controversy.

The case studies in Part Two are representative of a wide range of participation levels. They can be read for their information on participation as well as for illustrations of site-selection problems and technical approaches.

TWO

Case Study 1 | THE WEST OAHU COLLEGE SITE EVALUATION

History and Scope of This Study

In Chapter 1, we discussed the rather extensive history of efforts by the Board of Regents of the University of Hawaii to locate a new college. That discussion emphasized the importance of clearly defining basic organizational objectives and policies before identifying a project goal. This case study deals with the study undertaken by EDAW in 1973 and illustrates an approach to site evaluation.

By the time EDAW began work, the university's goals and objectives had been redefined and a campus profile (presented in Chapter 5) had been developed, providing site requirements and information on the number and location of staff and students.

Site-screening criteria had been developed by a special twelve-member Site-Selection Advisory Committee under the direction of the board of regents. The committee represented the west Oahu communities, state agencies, the city and county, and the university. Thirty-five sites had been selected for analysis and preliminary and secondary screening. Those sites which survived the first and second screens were then evaluated in detail by EDAW, using the committee's criteria (see Exhibit 1-1).

As we mentioned in Chapter 1, one of the most sensitive aspects of the West Oahu College site selection was its relation to state land-use policy in the central Oahu area, where intense conflict exists over preservation of agricultural lands in the face of severe urban pressure.

Realizing that policy guidance was needed in the area, the Hawaii Department of Planning and Economic Development undertook studies on the impacts of alternative growth policies. A progress report in February 1972 demonstrated that benefits could accrue under certain conditions of compact growth, job development at Ewa, and concern for environmental protection and preservation of prime agricultural lands.

When the new campus was originally discussed in terms of a major university of 25,000 students, it was thought by some that it would have an urbanizing influence of three to four times the student enrollment. The decision to provide a 4-year "commuter" college of 7500 students had the effect of reducing the potential urbanizing influence dramatically to a maximum of about 50 percent of the student body. Even this relatively small influence could be greatly reduced by providing for student housing, commercial, and recreational needs on campus.

If it were felt desirable that the campus be related closely to a community, two alternatives appeared possible: first, the college could be located adjacent to an existing community; second, a new community could be permitted to develop in relation to the college. One possible site (Makakilo) was in an existing urban district where such development was permissible.

All other sites being considered were in the agriculture district and would require rezoning by the Hawaii Land Use Commission and an amendment to the City and County General Plan. Two sites (Ewa-Honouliuli and Waiawa Ridge) had been offered free by the owners, who were desirous of building new communities in the respective areas. One site (Mililani) lay in an area where Oceanic Properties expected to build an extension of its new community, Mililani Town. The last site (Puu Kapuai) had no accompanying urban development proposal.

Three of the sites (Ewa, Puu Kapuai, and Waiawa) would be quite isolated if community development proposals did not materialize. The Mililani site would be separated from its existing community by a freeway if a closely related addition to Mililani Town were not built. The Honouliuli site, being adjacent to Waipahu, would not necessarily require new community development.

The two maps shown as Exhibits 1-2 and 1-3 depict the relationship of the sites to some of the land-use and natu-

EXHIBIT 1-1   Sites considered.

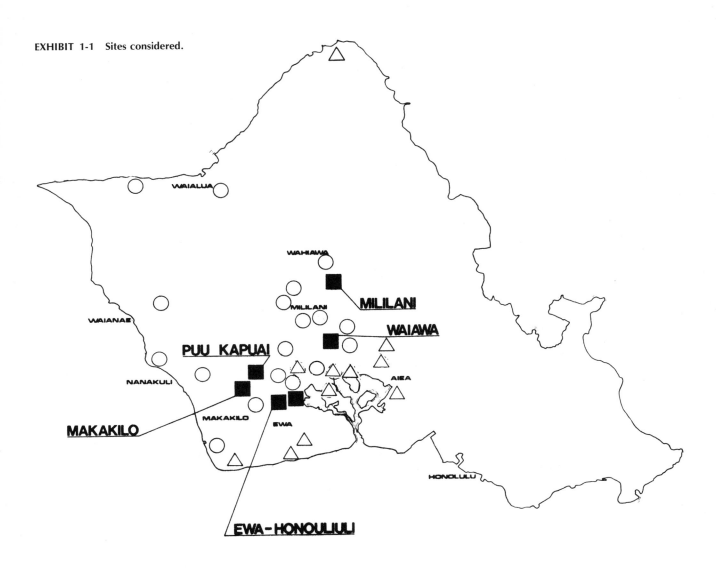

MILILANI

WAIAWA

PUU KAPUAI

MAKAKILO

EWA-HONOULIULI

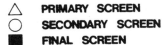

LEGEND

△ PRIMARY SCREEN
○ SECONDARY SCREEN
■ FINAL SCREEN

N

0 1 2 3
MILES

SITES CONSIDERED
WEST OAHU COLLEGE - SITE SELECTION STUDIES

ECKBO, DEAN, AUSTIN & WILLIAMS·PLANNING
PARK ENGINEERING, INC. CIVIL ENGINEERING
ALAN M. VOORHEES & ASSOCIATES   TRAFFIC

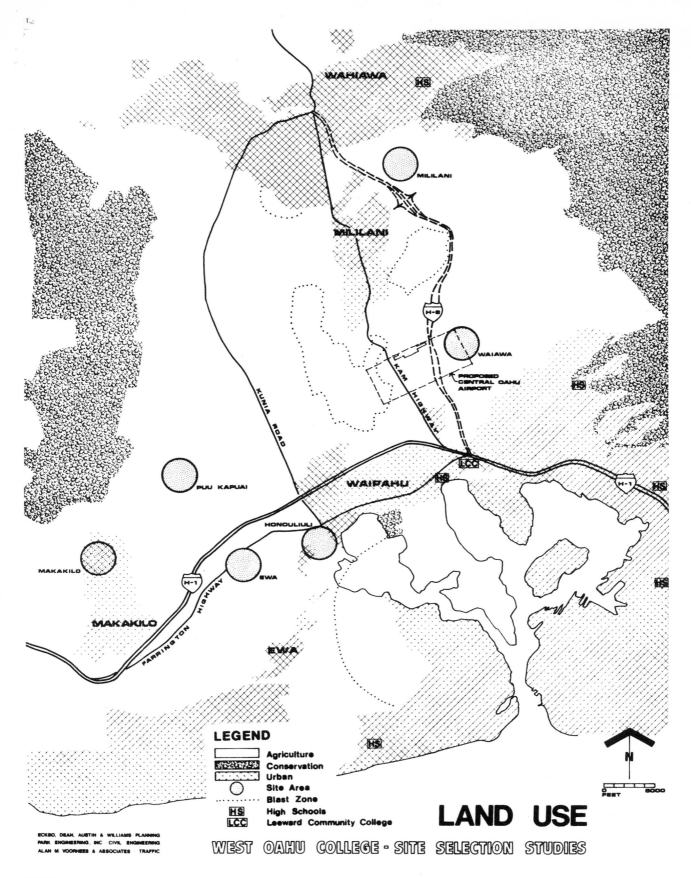

LEGEND

	Agriculture
	Conservation
	Urban
◯	Site Area
....	Blast Zone
HS	High Schools
LCC	Leeward Community College

LAND USE

WEST OAHU COLLEGE - SITE SELECTION STUDIES

ECKBO, DEAN, AUSTIN & WILLIAMS PLANNING
PARK ENGINEERING, INC. CIVIL ENGINEERING
ALAN M. VOORHEES & ASSOCIATES TRAFFIC

EXHIBIT 1-2 Land use.

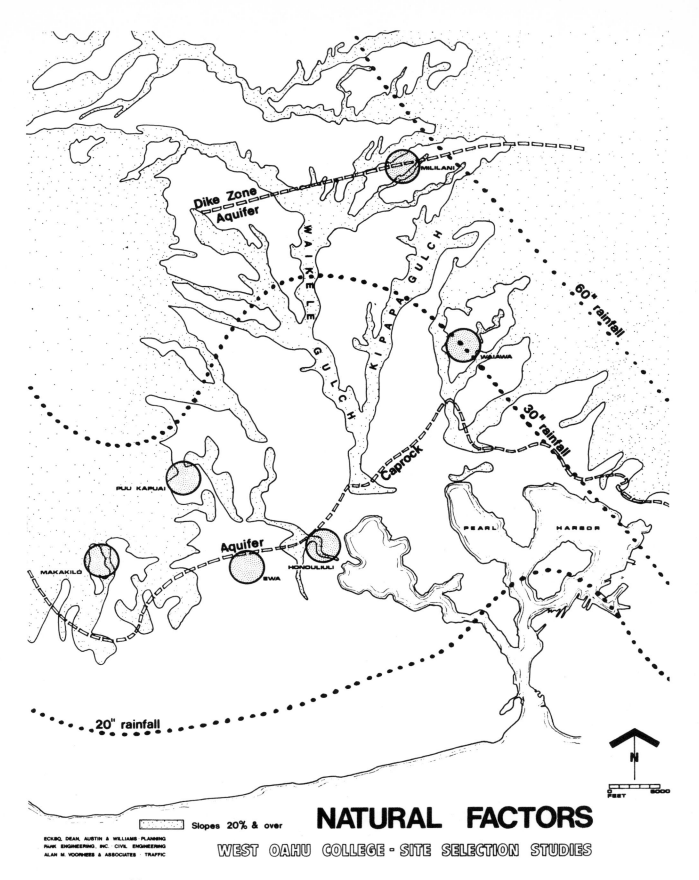

Dike Zone Aquifer

WAIKELE GULCH

KIPAPA GULCH

60" rainfall

30" rainfall

Caprock

Aquifer

PUU KAPUAI

MILILANI

WAIAWA

PEARL HARBOR

MAKAKILO

EWA

HONOULIULI

20" rainfall

N

0   5000
FEET

⬚⬚⬚⬚ Slopes 20% & over

NATURAL FACTORS

WEST OAHU COLLEGE · SITE SELECTION STUDIES

ECKBO, DEAN, AUSTIN & WILLIAMS · PLANNING
R.M.K ENGINEERING, INC. CIVIL ENGINEERING
ALAN M. VOORHEES & ASSOCIATES · TRAFFIC

EXHIBIT 1-3 Natural factors.

198

ral features of central Oahu. These show some of the considerations that had been taken into account in reaching a decision.

Process

The site-screening process necessarily differed from the process which we have been describing in Part One, in that it began with a rather large universe of potential sites which were then screened to six for detailed evaluation. This approach, as opposed to screening out large areas first and then selecting candidate sites within each candidate area, may be appropriate or even dictated in relatively small geographic study areas.

Specifically in this case the site-evaluation process was not required to select a site through ranking each one. Therefore the study stopped short at the first key decision-making point we showed in Figure 7-1, leaving the decision to the board of regents on the strength of the unranked evaluations. This case study thus provides an illustration of the application of unweighted criteria. The criteria developed by the Site-Selection Advisory Committee, upon which the following evaluations are based, required testing each site area in terms of the impacts of the campus on the users, the neighboring communities, the regional community, the county and state as a whole, academic objectives, and total costs. This wide range of factors went into policy areas far beyond the physical, social, and cost criteria usually employed in site evaluation.

To evaluate each potential campus site the consultants prepared a theoretical model or program depicting ideal site conditions for West Oahu College. As we emphasized in Chapter 5, in which the model was previously discussed, there is an important advantage to this method in that it establishes basic guidelines and makes possible meaningful comparisons among sites. It was recognized that the "policy" criteria in particular would necessarily call for subjective judgments rather than highly quantified analysis during the evaluation of alternatives; thus, it was mandatory that the model be specific enough to permit comparison of the alternatives.

The campus population, the activity assumptions, the physical character of the campus, and the area requirements were all firmly established in the model. The model also identified siting characteristics which would be considered ideal if achieved. These included slope (not more than 20 percent and preferably 5 percent), physiography, hydrology, soils, climate, and accessibility. To determine relative travel times to the various sites, the distribution of the population in central leeward Oahu

was determined for the year 1984, when the college was to reach its maximum enrollment (see Exhibit 1-4).

The assumptions and siting requirements became the factors and criteria to be used in evaluating each site's ability to meet the idealized campus program. The summarized evaluation of three of the sites can be found in Table 8-5. A very simple system of ratings was used as appropriate to each evaluation factor:

· Poor, fair, good, excellent

· Yes, no

· Good, moderate, or negative effect

· Low, medium, high

· Appropriate, questionable, inappropriate

· Light, average, heavy

How were these summary evaluations arrived at? It will be recalled from examination of Table 8-5 that the committee placed heaviest emphasis on the impact of a site on general affected "publics": campus users, immediate neighbors, regional neighbors, and residents of the county and state as a whole. In the following pages we will describe the process of evaluation leading to the factor rating that was displayed in Table 8-5 in highly summarized form. We will take one category, environmental effects (B.6.b in the table), as an example and discuss both the subfactors that entered into the summary rating and the manner in which each factor was individually evaluated and rated.

Environmental Factors

The environmental effects summary rating is a composite of the effects of college construction on flood control, drainage and runoff, erosion hazard, and water supply. The summary ratings were adjusted to take further account of effect on vegetation and open space (factors which were also used to arrive at visual appropriateness ratings in B.6.a).

FLOOD CONTROL, DRAINAGE AND RUNOFF (EXHIBIT 1-5) These factors are interdependent. The ratings shown in Exhibit 1-5 and used in the environmental effects summary rating are the composite of the ratings in Exhibit 1-6, "Drainage," shown later.

The "drainage" impact of the campus was measured in terms of (1) the variation in annual rainfall, (2) the differences in soil permeability, (3) the differences in ground slopes, and (4) the degree of difficulty in constructing detention ponds.

EXHIBIT 1-4 Projected population for 1984.

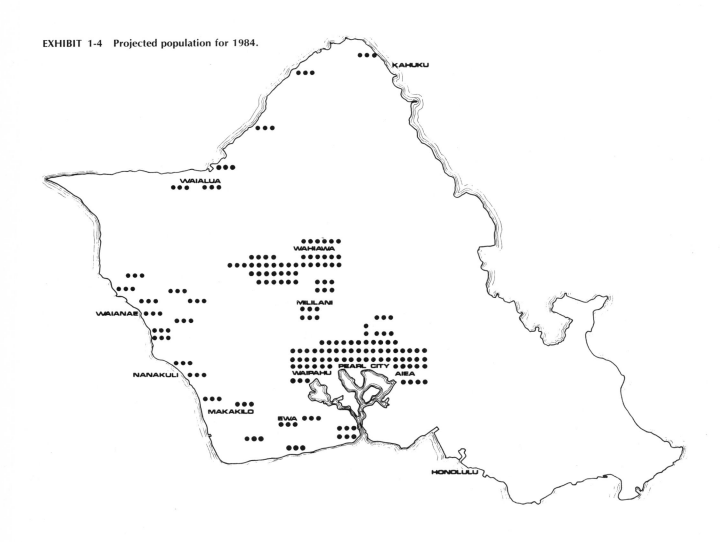

LEGEND:
EACH DOT ● = 1000 PEOPLE
WITHIN SERVICE AREA

STRAIGHT LINE INTERPOLATION · 1984
BASED ON 1970 CENSUS
1995 ATPO·DPED

0 1 2 3
MILES

1984
PROJECTED POPULATION
WEST OAHU COLLEGE · SITE SELECTION STUDIES

ECKBO, DEAN, AUSTIN & WILLIAMS · PLANNING
PARK ENGINEERING, INC. · CIVIL ENGINEERING
ALAN M. VOORHEES & ASSOCIATES · TRAFFIC

Site area	Slight	Slight to moderate	Moderate	Significant
Makakilo	· · ·	· · ·	· · ·	X
Ewa	X	· · ·	· · ·	· · ·
Honouliuli	· · ·	X	· · ·	· · ·
Puu Kapuai	· · ·	· · ·	X	· · ·
Waiawa	· · ·	· · ·	X	· · ·
Mililani	· · ·	X	· · ·	· · ·

EXHIBIT 1-5   Flood control, drainage, and runoff effect.

The criteria used to rate Item 1 are given under another objective: "Minimize decrease in groundwater recharge." The following criteria were used to measure the effect that soil permeability (Item 2) would have on the drainage impact:

· *Slight effect.* Site with soil permeability greater than 2.0 inches per hour.

· *Moderate effect.* Site with soil permeability between 0.63 and 2.0 inches per hour.

· *Significant effect.* Site with soil permeability less than 0.63 inch per hour.

The criteria used to measure the effect that the slope of the land (Item 3) would have on the drainage impact are shown below:

· *Slight effect.* Two or more of the four drainage factors of rainfall, permeability, slopes, and detention ponds are rated "slight effect."

· *Moderate effect.* Site with slopes between 4 and 10 percent.

· *Significant effect.* Site with slopes greater than 10 percent.

The criteria used to rate Item 4, the degree of difficulty in constructing detention ponds, cannot be explicitly defined, but they were based on analysis of the topography of the site.

The composite rating of the four factors was arrived at as follows:

· *Slight effect.* Two or more of the four drainage factors of rainfall, permeability, slopes, and detention ponds are rated "slight effect."

· *Moderate effect.* Two or more of the four drainage factors are rated "moderate effect."

· *Significant effect.* Two or more of the four drainage factors are rated "significant effect."

EROSION IMPACT (EXHIBIT 1-7) The erosion hazard ratings of the U.S. Soil Conservation Service were used to measure the erosion impact of the campus. The results were modified with supplementary "judgment" considerations of the relative difficulties involved in constructing desilting ponds. These judgment considerations were based on analysis of the topography of the site.

· *Slight effect.* Site which has a "none to slight" erosion hazard rating as determined by the Soil Conservation Service and which has no degree of difficulty in constructing desilting basins.

· *Moderate effect.* Site which has a "moderate" erosion hazard rating and no degree of difficulty in constructing desilting basins or a site which has a "moderate" erosion hazard and a significant degree of difficulty in constructing desilting basins.

· *Significant effect.* Site which has a "severe" erosion hazard rating or a site which has a "moderate" erosion hazard rating and a significant degree of difficulty in constructing desilting basins.

Sites	Rainfall	Permeability	Slope	Detention pond	Composite
Ewa	Slight	Moderate	Slight	Slight	Slight
Honouliuli	Slight	Moderate	Slight	Moderate	Slight to moderate
Mililani	Significant	Moderate	Slight	Slight	Slight to moderate
Waiawa	Moderate	Moderate	Moderate	Moderate	Moderate
Puu Kapuai	Moderate	Slight to moderate	Moderate to significant	Moderate to significant	Moderate
Makakilo	Moderate	Slight	Significant	Significant	Significant

EXHIBIT 1-6   Drainage.

Site area	Slight	Moderate	Significant
Makakilo	. . .	. . .	X
Ewa	X	. . .	. . .
Honouliuli	X	. . .	. . .
Puu Kapuai	. . .	. . .	X
Waiawa	. . .	X	. . .
Mililani	X	. . .	. . .

EXHIBIT 1-7 Erosion hazard.

WATER SUPPLY IMPACT The following criteria were used to arrive at the summary ratings shown in Table 8-5:

· *Slight effect.* Water supply may be provided to the campus without developing additional sources.

· *Moderate effect.* Water supply can be developed on or near the site with a moderate effect on the existing water supply.

· *Significant effect.* Water supply may have to be imported from a remote source to minimize the effect on the existing water supply.

A SUMMARY RATING (EXHIBIT 1-8) The ratings given each site in terms of drainage, erosion hazard, and water supply were combined to achieve the summary environmental effects rating shown in Exhibit 1-8. The basis for the summary rating was as follows.

· *Excellent.* All the factors of drainage, erosion, and water supply are slightly affected by the campus.

· *Good.* Two of the factors are slightly affected by the campus. The remaining factor is moderately affected.

· *Poor.* One or more of the factors is significantly affected by the campus.

Sites	Drainage	Erosion hazard	Water supply	Rating of sites
Ewa	Slight	None to slight	Slight	Excellent
Honouliuli	Slight to moderate	None to slight	Slight	Excellent
Mililani	Slight to moderate	Slight	Moderate	Good
Waiawa	Moderate	Moderate	Significant	Poor
Makakilo	Significant	Significant	Moderate	Poor
Puu Kapuai	Moderate	Significant	Moderate	Poor

EXHIBIT 1-8 Summary environmental effects rating.

EFFECT ON VEGETATION AND OPEN SPACE One further subfactor, rating the effect of each site on open space, was used to complete the environmental effects factor. Though all sites were still in open land and, technically speaking, use of any of them would destroy vegetation and open space, realistically the effect of development on the open space of the central Oahu area would vary from site to site. This effect was closely related to the "visual appropriateness" factor shown in Table 8-6. Waiawa and Ewa would, in the consultant's judgment, have a poor effect, and the other sites would have a slight effect.

The final summary evaluation based on all environmental effects subfactors is shown in Exhibit 1-9. The adjustment for open-space effects dropped the rating for Makakilo shown in Exhibit 1-8 from significant to moderate. The rating for Waiawa was raised from moderate to significant.

Each of the ratings we saw in the evaluation summary in Table 8-5 was built up in a similar manner from ratings for detailed subfactors. In addition to the summary and detailed ratings and accompanying explanation, a narrative evaluation was provided for each site, accompanied by a map showing generalized land-use and natural features. We quote below the narrative summary for the area containing two of the six sites, Ewa and Honouliuli, in the shortened form prepared for public information.

Ewa-Honouliuli Area

This large area west of Waipahu and north of Ewa contains the present urban area of Honouliuli (see Exhibit 1-10). Owned by the Campbell Estate and presently planted to sugarcane, it has many potential college sites available. The Campbell Estate has been studying the

Site area	Slight	Slight to moderate	Moderate	Significant
Makakilo	. . .	. . .	X	. . .
Ewa	X	. . .	. . .	. . .
Honouliuli	X	. . .	. . .	. . .
Puu Kapuai	. . .	. . .	. . .	. . .
Waiawa	. . .	. . .	. . .	X
Mililani	. . .	X	. . .	. . .

EXHIBIT 1-9 Summary of environmental effects.

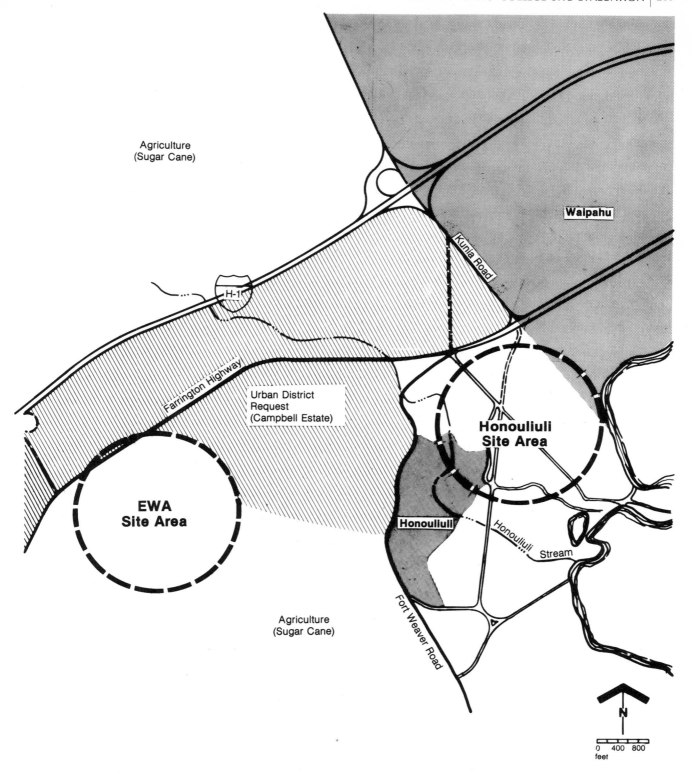

Agriculture
(Sugar Cane)

Waipahu

Kunia Road

H-1

Farrington Highway

Urban District
Request
(Campbell Estate)

Honouliuli
Site Area

EWA
Site Area

Honoulliuli

Honouliuli Stream

Fort Weaver Road

Agriculture
(Sugar Cane)

N

0   400 800
feet

EWA-Honouliuli
West Oahu College - Site Selection Studies

EXHIBIT 1-10   Ewa-Honouliuli.

possibilities of developing a new town in the area for many years, and part of its planning has included a college campus.

A number of potential site configurations are possible in the area north of Ewa. One favorable configuration adjacent to the Farrington Highway has been utilized for the analysis required by this study. It is called the Ewa site area. Considerable flexibility is possible in the final selection of a site in this area if the decision is made to do so.

Another favorable site area overlooking West Loch is also available in the general area; it is called the Honouliuli site area. Because the two site areas are quite different, they are dealt with separately.

EWA AREA This site area on the Farrington Highway about 3 miles west of the center of Waipahu has been offered by the Campbell Estate. It is relatively flat land at an average elevation of 140 feet and is presently in sugarcane. The following is a summary of evaluations:

1 *Effect on the well-being of the users.* Access to this site from the service area is fair; access to the existing services of Waipahu is limited because of distance; there are smoke and dust from cane operations; the site is acceptable from the standpoint of traffic hazards.

2 *Effect on the residents of the neighboring communities.* Community access to the site area is only fair because of distance; campus spillover effect would be acceptable; distance would moderate the impact that the college might have on Waipahu; visually, a campus here would be questionable; it would have slight environmental effect, however, and would be average from the standpoint of traffic congestion.

3 *Effect on the residents of the regional community.* Aside from an existing water line and highway, there is no excess development capacity to be utilized. The site would be unprotected from uncontrolled development; it would have no effect on groundwater recharge; it is compatible with regional water and sewer networks; compatibility with the regional road network is questionable, and relationship to presently planned public transportation is currently poor but potentially good.

4 *Effect on all residents of county and state.* Use of this area would remove prime land from production, would have a negative effect on preservation of open space, would require rezoning under the State Land Use Law and an amendment to the City and County General Plan, and would not preserve future public policy options in this area.

5 *Effect on academic objectives.* The site is excellent from the standpoint of available size and shape, would fit satisfactorily with the University of Hawaii system, but is only low to fair with respect to ambience and as an educational setting.

6 *Effect on total cost.* A site in this area has been offered free; on-site and off-site improvement costs are both moderate.

HONOULIULI AREA This site is adjacent to Waipahu on the Farrington Highway and is bordered on three sides by West Loch and the Honouliuli Stream floodplain. It has been offered by the Campbell Estate. It lies at an elevation of about 50 feet and is presently in sugarcane. The following is a summary of evaluations.

1 *Effect on the well-being of the users.* Access to this site from the service area is among those evaluated best; access from the site to Waipahu facilities is fair because of closeness; realignment of Fort Weaver Road may conflict with the best configuration of the site; smoke or dust from cane operations could be a nuisance; design potential is good; there is a flood hazard which should be considered in the campus design; the site is borderline with respect to traffic hazards, probably requiring a pedestrian overcrossing.

2 *Effect on the residents of the neighboring communities.* Community access to the site area is good; campus spillover effect would be acceptable; a campus at this site would have a good impact on the Waipahu community; complementarity of its facilities would be very high, and it would make a significant economic contribution to the community; a campus would be visually appropriate in this location; it would have slight environmental effect and would be average from the standpoint of traffic congestion.

3 *Effect on the residents of the regional community.* Existing development capacity in terms of commercial services, roads, water, and sewers exist; the site is somewhat protected from uncontrolled development by topography; it would have no effect on the groundwater recharge; it is compatible with regional water, sewer, and road networks and has a good relation to planned public transportation facilities.

4 *Effect on all residents of county and state.* Use of this area would remove prime land from production; it would have a moderate effect on the preservation of open space; it would require rezoning under the State Land Use Law and an amendment to the City and County General Plan; it would not preserve public policy options in this area; because of its adjacent position to the urban district of Waipahu, however, its total effect on these issues would be somewhat less than if the areas were not contiguous.

5 *Effect on academic objectives.* The site area is good from the standpoint of available size and shape though limited because of topography; it would fit satisfactorily with the University of Hawaii system and is a good setting for student learning.

6 *Effect on total cost.* A site in this area has been offered free; on-site and off-site improvement costs are slight and moderate, respectively.

Conclusion

As a result of the unranked summary evaluations and supporting material presented to the board of regents, the Honouliuli site was chosen. However, for reasons discussed in Chapter 1, the site has not been developed.

Case Study 2 | THE TYRONE ENERGY PARK TRANSMISSION LINE STUDY

Scope of This Study

The scope of this study, like that of the West Oahu College example, was limited to the latter part of the site-screening process in a relatively confined area. Northern States Power Company required two 345-kilovolt single-circuit lines from its proposed Tyrone power plant near Eau Claire, Wisconsin, to the switchyard at its existing power plant at Prairie Island, southwest of Minneapolis–St. Paul, Minnesota. It also required one 345-kilovolt single-circuit line to each of three other Wisconsin destinations, Eau Claire, Afton, and King (see Exhibit 2-1). The study's objective was to provide environmental analysis, definition of a number of possible corridors within the four predefined general routes, comparison of these corridors, and selection of one corridor in each route on the basis of environmental and financial cost. Each selected corridor would have a width of 1 mile to permit location of the best specific alignment by the subsequent detailed evaluation.

The limits of the study area were quite narrow, being determined by the given origin and destination points and by a reasonable maximum deviation from the straight line between origin and destination. This study area was then refined by defining a number of natural barriers which might be encountered.

Corridor-Selection Process

Exhibit 2-2 presents the process developed for corridor selection in diagrammatic and summarized form. The first step in the process was to define potential corridors. The following data factor maps were produced at a working scale of 1:62,500, or approximately 1 inch = 1 mile.

Geology and climate were excluded, the scale being inappropriate. Geologic data were used, however, in developing three soil maps: erosion and slope instability, water table depth, and bedrock depth.

Each data factor was evaluated to determine the de-

gree of constraint that it would represent in the location, design, and operation of the system. The degree of constraint was based on two factors: the potential adverse changes in environmental conditions that could occur and the potential beneficial or adverse economic effects that could occur.

The significant environmental conditions which could be adversely affected by the above actions were determined to be:

· Water quality

· Soil resources

· Unique natural and cultural resources: archaeological sites, historical sites, natural landmarks, wildlife, and vegetation

· Wildlife habitat

· Visual quality

· Forest resources

· Agricultural resources

· Recreation resources

· Other existing or potential land uses

· Public safety and comfort

· Continued use or occupancy

· Extractive activities

Significant economic effects could occur from:

· Cost of mitigation measures in design or construction required to limit adverse changes in environmental conditions

· Difficulty in right-of-way acquisition

· Route location in areas of difficult construction

· Route location along existing utility corridors or other linkages

The major actions in the establishment and maintenance of the transmission line system that might cause changes in the environment were identified as:

· Route configuration

· Structure location and style

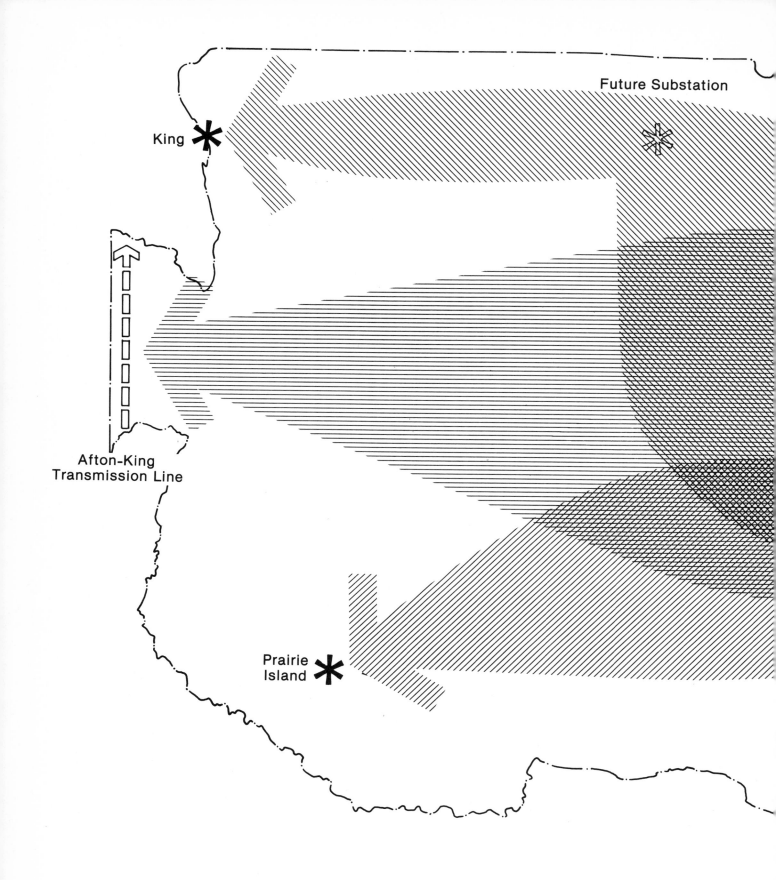

King

Future Substation

Afton-King
Transmission Line

Prairie
Island

EXHIBIT 2-1   General transmission line destinations from Tyrone Energy Park.

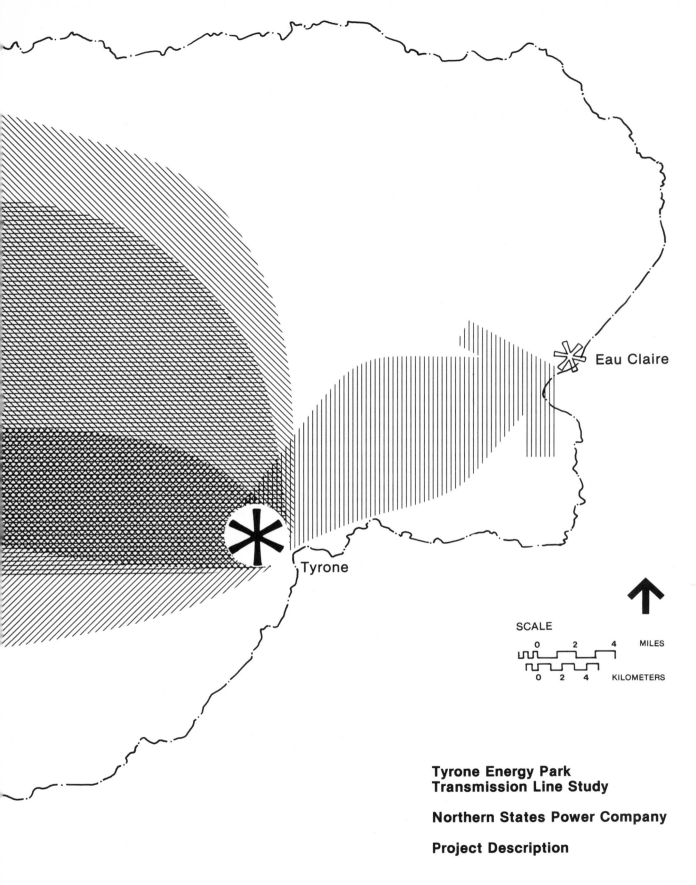

Tyrone

Eau Claire

SCALE

| 0 | 2 | 4 | MILES |

| 0 | 2 | 4 | KILOMETERS |

Tyrone Energy Park
Transmission Line Study

Northern States Power Company

Project Description

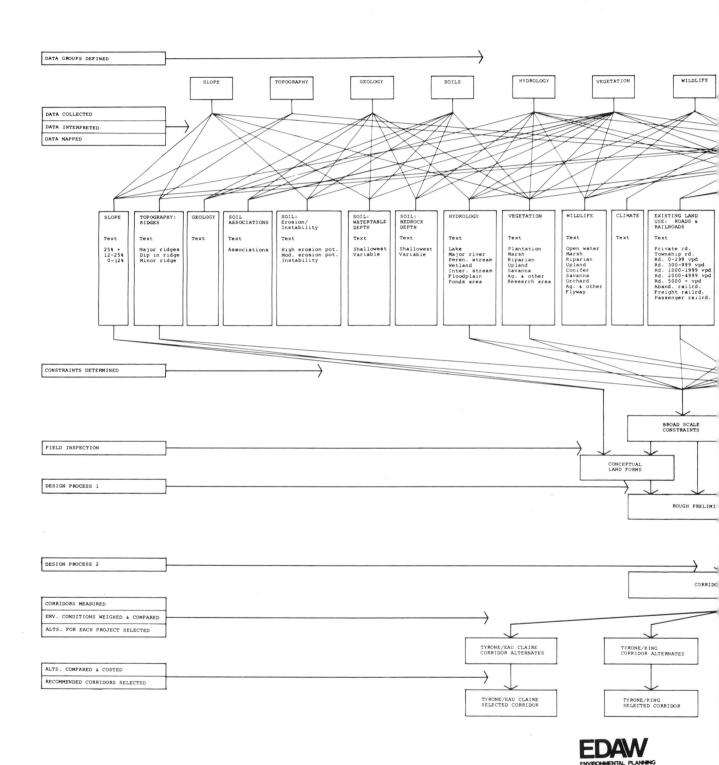

EXHIBIT 2-2   Diagram of the corridor-selection process.

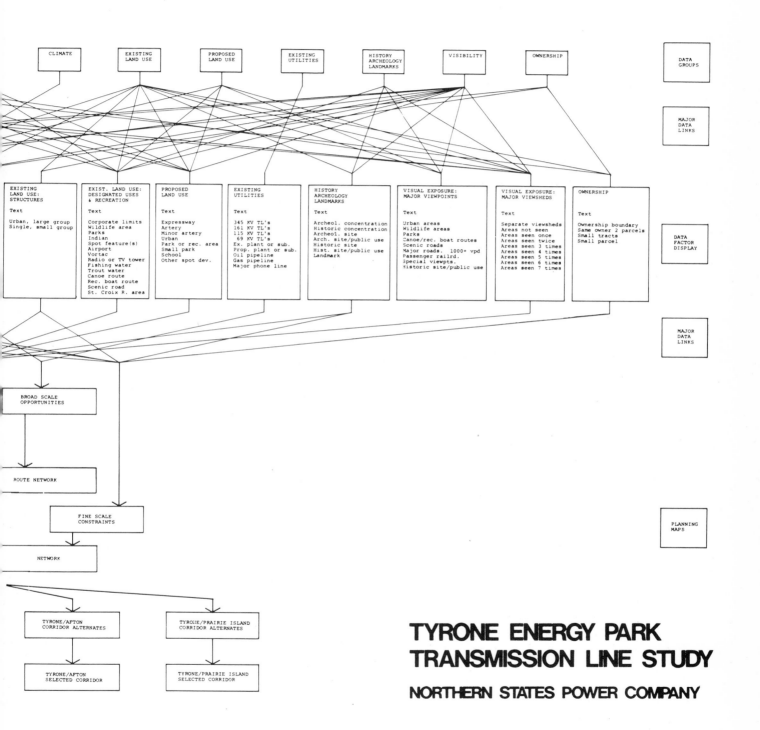

TYRONE ENERGY PARK
TRANSMISSION LINE STUDY

NORTHERN STATES POWER COMPANY

CORRIDOR SELECTION PROCESS DIAGRAM

· Structure erection

· Access-road construction

· Conductor stringing

· Removal of vegetation or buildings for construction and line clearance

· Periodic vegetation control and transmission line maintenance

· Repair as needed

· Substation location with attendant site preparation, construction, and landscaping

The relative degree of constraint of each of the major data factors is shown in Exhibit 2-3. Degrees of constraint were defined according to the potential of a factor to have a short- or long-term adverse effect on environmental conditions or the design and economics of transmis-

sion lines. To identify the broad-scale constraints and opportunities shown in Exhibit 2-4, the areal features of the data factor maps were colored (using translucent color to allow overlaying of the maps on a light table) to represent graphically the approximate constraint values. For example, slopes of 25 percent or more were colored dark red, 12 to 25 percent slopes were pale orange, and 0 to 12 percent slopes were uncolored. The three major vegetation types—riparian forest, upland forest, and savanna—ranged from dark green through midgreen to pale yellow to represent decreasing levels of constraint. Spot and linear features such as towns and roads were represented with symbols or line weights roughly corresponding to their relative constraint values.

The broad-scale constraints map was then examined with the benefit of extensive inspection of the study area to formulate a generalized landforms map. This showed

EXHIBIT 2-3 Relative degree of constraint of major data factor categories.

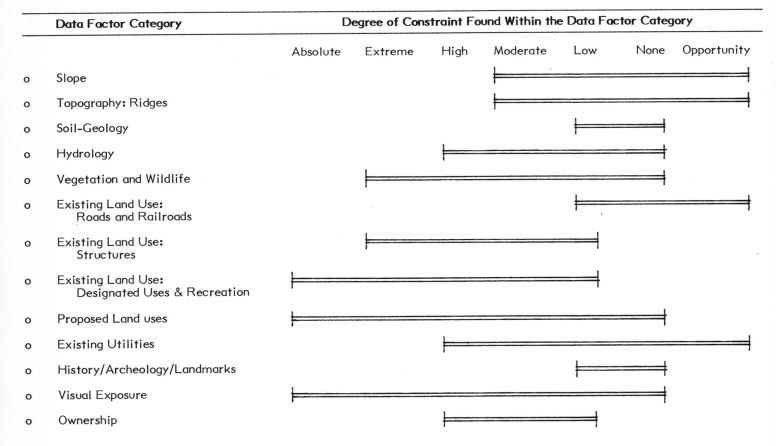

Data Factor Category	Degree of Constraint Found Within the Data Factor Category						
	Absolute	Extreme	High	Moderate	Low	None	Opportunity
o Slope				⊢————————————————————————⊣			
o Topography: Ridges				⊢————————————————————————⊣			
o Soil-Geology					⊢————————⊣		
o Hydrology			⊢————————————————⊣				
o Vegetation and Wildlife		⊢————————————————————————⊣					
o Existing Land Use: Roads and Railroads					⊢————————————————⊣		
o Existing Land Use: Structures		⊢————————————————————⊣					
o Existing Land Use: Designated Uses & Recreation	⊢————————————————————————⊣						
o Proposed Land uses	⊢————————————————⊣						
o Existing Utilities			⊢————————————————————————————⊣				
o History/Archeology/Landmarks					⊢————⊣		
o Visual Exposure	⊢————————————————————⊣						
o Ownership			⊢————————⊣				

the major constraint barriers with drainages which had to be crossed, the major constraint areas to be avoided, scarp slopes to be paralleled, moderate topography where lines should follow natural landforms, and level topography where lines should run north-south or east-west. Existing transmission lines which represented right-of-way opportunities in the western part of the study area were also identified.

With these tools, it was possible to arrive at a rough preliminary route network, using several major design criteria. Examples of these criteria, to be applied again later in a more detailed manner during corridor refinement and evaluation, are shown in Exhibit 2-5.

Finally, a fine-scale constraints map (Exhibit 2-6) with which to refine the rough preliminary route network by a more detailed application of the design criteria was developed. The fine-scale constraints map was produced by overlaying and correlating the following subfactors from six of the data factor maps.

1 Topography: ridges

· Major ridges
· Major saddles in major ridges
· Minor saddles in major ridges
· Minor ridges in rolling terrain

2 Hydrology

· Lakes and reservoirs
· Major rivers and streams
· Perennial streams
· Intermittent streams

3 Vegetation

· Marshes
· Riparian forests
· Upland forests
· Savanna
· Orchard and conifer

4 Existing land use: structures

· Individual structures or small groups of structures

5 History, archaeology, and landmarks

· Historical or archaeological sites with potential for public use

6 Ownership pattern

· Small parcels in individual ownership, boundaries of large holdings

Environmental Data and the Data Factor Maps

To illustrate the degree of detail of data required to meet the environmental and functional objectives and design criteria, we include below a description of the treatment of a single environmental data factor: slope. The discussion also illustrates the manner in which constraint weightings were applied. It should be noted that slope is a relatively simple factor and that substantially greater information was required for other factors, such as vegetation and wildlife.

GENERAL CONCERN   Here the concern was to maintain, as far as possible, the existing slope conditions in the study area. If alteration of existing slopes because of route configuration had to occur, the concern was to minimize the impact of that alteration.

SLOPES 25 PERCENT OR GREATER Erosion is the major issue raised by slopes of this class. The rate of erosion has been found by the U.S. Department of Agriculture to be proportional to 1.35 power of land slope. If, for example, land slopes of 5 and 10 percent are compared, the doubling of the slope would increase the erosion rate by 2.3 times. Thus the location of towers and access roads or the removal of vegetation for conductor clearance on steep slopes (those 25 percent or greater) can initiate erosion which has far-reaching effects.

Erosion removes topsoil from the affected area, which directly changes the area's ability to support vegetation (discussed under the "Vegetation" factor). Because the topsoil is often transported by water, erosion tends to lower water quality (discussed under "Hydrology and Soils"). These impacts, in turn, result in the reduction of existing visual quality. Fortunately slopes of this steepness, though frequent within the study area, are generally short enough that structures can be located below the bottom and above the top of the steep land. Conductors can be strung above steep areas with little or no environmental change.

The spanning of even short, steep slopes can contribute to the reduction of existing visual quality. In such cases, the inclined plane of the slope emphasizes areas where vegetation must be removed for conductor clearance by offering a larger profile of the cleared area for observation than would occur on a flatter location.

Careful location of transmission structures above and below the slope can minimize the need for clearing. The location of a tower above the slope crossed would increase its apparent height and thus also contribute to a reduction of visual quality. By contrast, a steep slope can offer an opportunity for reduced visual impact if a route configuration is established along the base. (This point

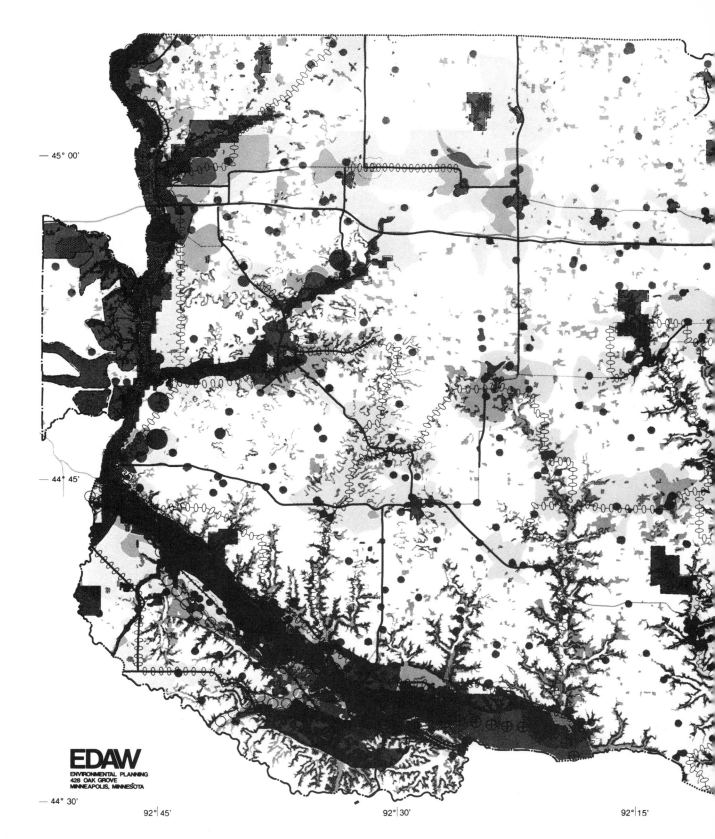

92°|45' 92°|30' 92°|15'

— 45° 00'

— 44° 45'

EDAW
ENVIRONMENTAL PLANNING
428 OAK GROVE
MINNEAPOLIS, MINNESOTA

— 44° 30'

92°|45' 92°|30' 92°|15'

EXHIBIT 2-4 Broad-scale constraints map.

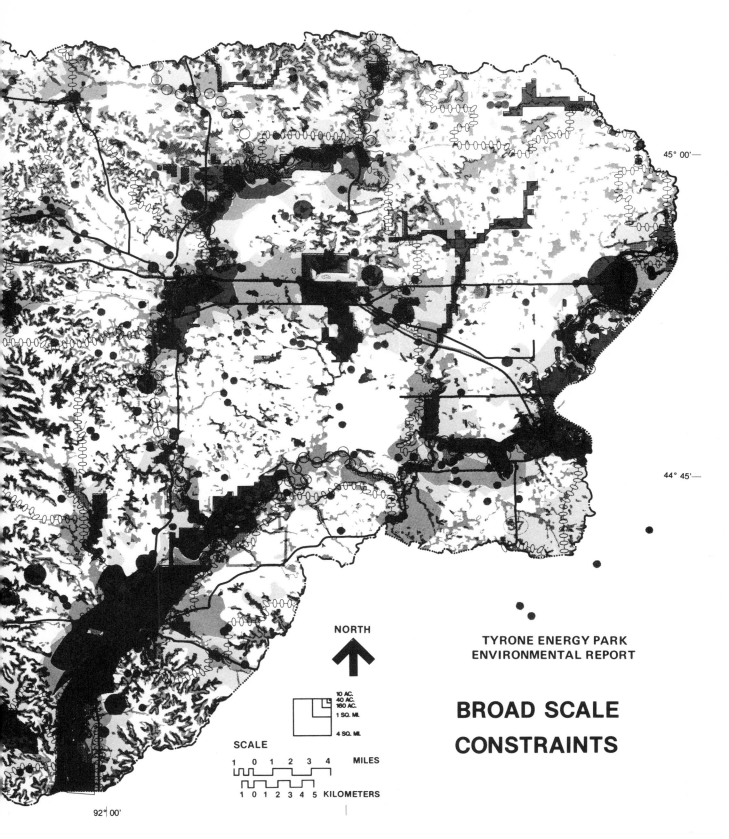

45° 00'—

44° 45'—

NORTH

TYRONE ENERGY PARK
ENVIRONMENTAL REPORT

10 AC.
40 AC.
160 AC.
1 SQ. MI.

4 SQ. MI.

SCALE

1 0 1 2 3 4   MILES

1 0 1 2 3 4 5   KILOMETERS

BROAD SCALE
CONSTRAINTS

92°|00'

For constituents see text.

MINIMIZE SILHOUETTING OF TOWERS

Avoid locating a transmission line parallel to and at the same time close to a bluff top. Therefore avoid locating along a ridge narrower than about 3/4 mile. See Chapter 5 TOPOGRAPHY: RIDGES. This has implications for the choice of approaches to valley crossings when the valley has many tributaries.

FOLLOW LANDSCAPE EDGES

° The edges of the woods.
° The bottoms of slopes.
The above in combination are a particularly suitable location for a transmission line since the line has a backdrop of trees.

AVOID SCALE CONFLICTS

Avoid routing a transmission line up a very small valley (of which there are many on the study area) where the scale of the transmission line would be enough to completely dominate the valley as observed either from within or from the outside looking in.

EXHIBIT 2-5 Some major design criteria used in determining a preliminary route network.

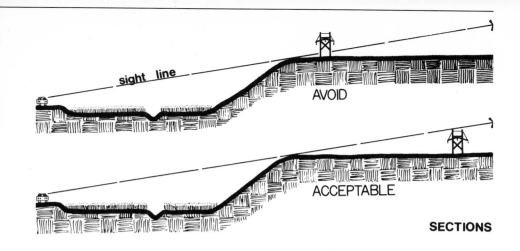

sight line

AVOID

ACCEPTABLE

SECTIONS

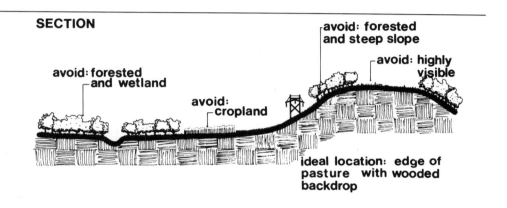

SECTION

avoid: forested
and wetland

avoid: cropland

avoid: forested
and steep slope

avoid: highly
visible

ideal location: edge of
pasture with wooded
backdrop

AVOID

SECTIONS

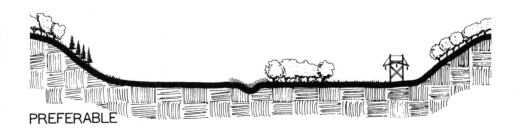

PREFERABLE

215

92° 45'   92° 30'   92° 15'

— 45° 00'

— 44° 45'

EDAW
ENVIRONMENTAL PLANNING
428 OAK GROVE
MINNEAPOLIS, MINNESOTA

— 44° 30'
92° 45'   92° 30'   92° 15'

EXHIBIT 2-6 Fine-scale constraints map.

216

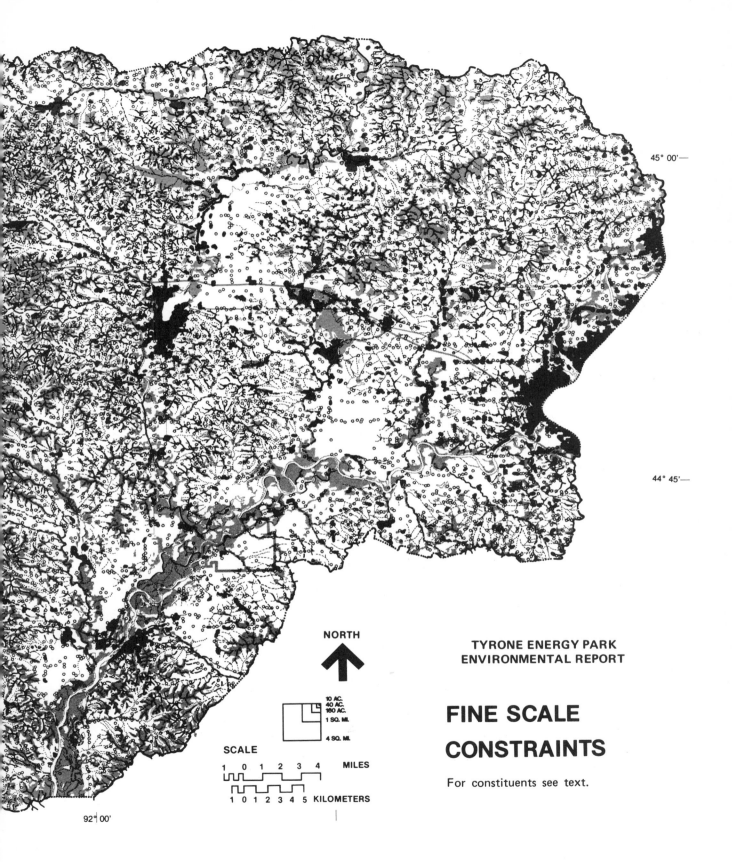

92° 00'　　　　　　　91° 45'　　　　　　　91° 30'

45° 00'—

44° 45'—

NORTH

10 AC.
40 AC.
160 AC.
1 SQ. MI.
4 SQ. MI.

SCALE

1 0 1 2 3 4　　MILES

1 0 1 2 3 4 5　KILOMETERS

92° 00'

TYRONE ENERGY PARK
ENVIRONMENTAL REPORT

FINE SCALE
CONSTRAINTS

For constituents see text.

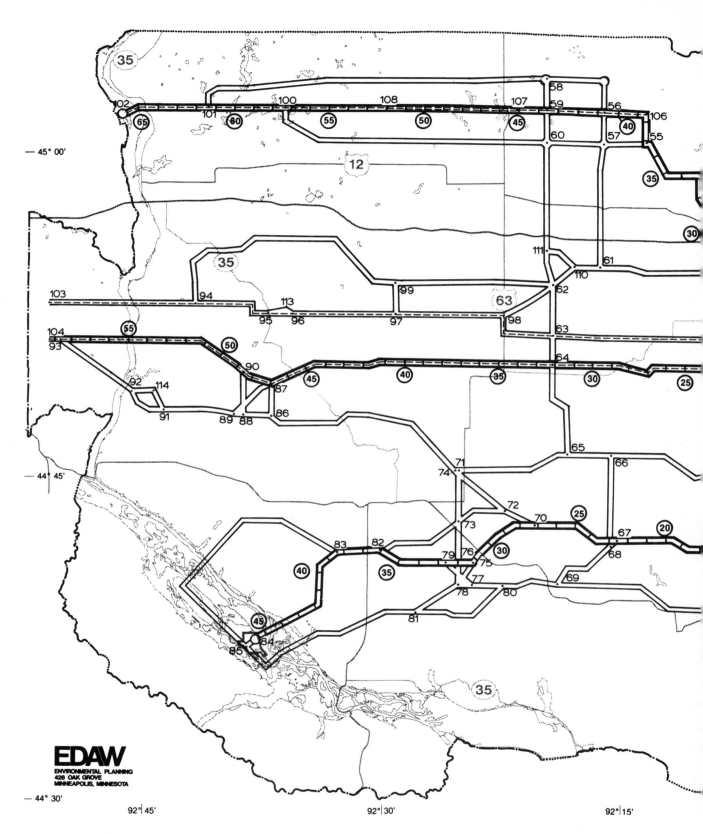

EXHIBIT 2-7 Corridors identified from broad- and fine-scale constraints mapping and application of design criteria.

218

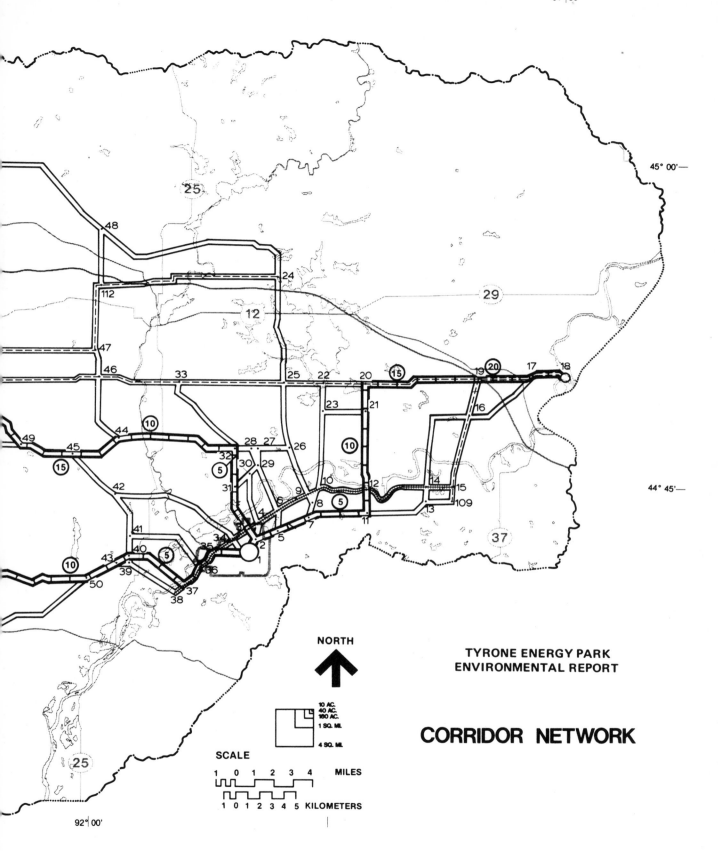

NORTH

TYRONE ENERGY PARK
ENVIRONMENTAL REPORT

10 AC.
40 AC.
160 AC.
1 SQ. MI.
4 SQ. MI.

CORRIDOR NETWORK

SCALE

1 0 1 2 3 4   MILES

1 0 1 2 3 4 5 KILOMETERS

LEGEND

X — Environmental Condition Included in Constraint Value

Constraint Values Assuming Mitigation

A — Absolute
E — Extreme
H — High
M — Moderate
L — Low
N — None

ENVIRONMENTAL DATA FACTORS	Units	Economics	Water Quality	Soil Resources	Unique Nat./Cult. Resources	Wildlife Habitat	Visual Quality	Forest Resources	Agricultural Resources	Recreation Resources	Other Existing Land Uses	Other Potential Land Uses	Public Safety/Comfort	Continued Use/Occupancy	Extractive Activities	Constraint Value
1.0 SLOPE																
1.01 Crossings of Spanable Slopes 25% & Steeper (1,200 ft or Less in Length)	Number		X	X			X									L
1.02 Length thru Non-Spanable Slopes 25% & Steeper	Miles	X	X	X			X									M
1.03 Length thru 0-12% with corridor not Parallel to Grid Pattern of Ownerships	Miles						X		X					X		L
2.0 TOPOGRAPHY: RIDGES																
2.01 Crossing of Major Ridges not at Major Saddles	Number						X									M
2.02 Crossings of Major Ridges at Major Saddles	Number						X									L
3.0 SOIL – GEOLOGY																
3.01 Length thru Moderate Erosion Potential when Disturbed	Miles		X	X												L
3.02 Length thru Instability Hazard when Disturbed	Miles	X	X	X												L
3.03 Length thru Shallowest Watertable (0 ft - 5 ft)	Miles	X	X	X		X										L
3.04 Length thru "Variable" Watertable (> than 5 ft. with Seasonal Change to < 5 ft.)	Miles															N
3.05 Length thru Shallowest Bedrock (0 ft - 6 ft)	Miles	X														L
3.06 Length thru Variable Bedrock (1 ft to Greater than 6 ft.)	Miles	X														N
3.07 Length thru Severe Erosion Potential when Distrubed	Miles	Constraint included in Environmental Factors 1.01 and 1.02														
4.0 HYDROLOGY																
4.01 Crossing of Lakes and Reservoirs	Number	X	X		X	X										E
4.02 Crossings of Major Rivers and Streams	Number	X	X		X	X										E
4.03 Crossings of 3rd and 4th Order Perennial Streams	Number		X		X	X										M
4.04 Crossings of 1st and 2nd Order Perennial Streams	Number		X		X	X										L
4.05 Total Crossings of Lakes, Reservoirs, Rivers and Perennial Streams		See Environmental Factors 4.01, 4.02, 4.03 and 4.04														
4.06 Length thru Floodplains	Miles	X														N
4.07 Length thru Marsh	Miles	See Environmental Factors 5.02 and 5.04														

EXHIBIT 2-8 Constraint values and unit measures to be applied to environmental factor impact evaluation for transmission lines.

EXHIBIT 2-9 Constraint value multipliers for various circuit–structure–right-of-way combinations.

CIRCUIT/TOWER/ RIGHT-OF-WAY COMBINATION	FACTORS DEALING WITH VISUAL QUALITY ONLY[a]	FACTORS DEALING PRIMARILY WITH AREAL CONDITIONS[b]	FACTORS DEALING WITH CONSTRUCTION PERIOD CONSTRAINTS OR PRESENCE OF TRANSMISSION LINE[c]
CONSTRAINT VALUE MULTIPLIERS FOR VARIOUS CIRCUIT/STRUCTURE/RIGHT-OF-WAY COMBINATIONS			
A. New Right-Of-Way			
A.1 Single circuit (S)	1.0 (Base condition)	1.0 (Base condition)	1.0 (Base Condition)
A.2 Two single circuits (SS)	1.5	1.25	1.25
A.3 Double circuit (D)	1.5	1.0	1.0
A.4 Three single circuits (SSS)	2.0	1.5	1.5
A.5 Double and single circuit (DS)	2.0	1.25	1.25
B. Existing Railroad Right-of-Way			
B.1 Single circuit (S)	Same as A.1 – A.5	50% of A.1[d]	Same as A.1 – A.5
B.2 Two single circuits (SS)		50% of A.2[d]	
B.3 Double circuit (D)		50% of A.3[d]	
B.4 Three single circuits (SSS)		50% of A.4[d]	
B.5 Double and single circuit		50% of A.5[d]	
C. Existing Transmission Right-of Way			
C.1 Single circuit added to existing Single circuit	0.5	50% of A.2	Same as A.1 – A.5
C.2 Two single circuits added to existing single circuit	1.0	50% of A.4	
C.3 Double circuit added to existing single circuit	1.0	50% of A.5	
C.4 Existing single circuit removed and rebuilt as double circuit with one new circuit	0.5	25% of A.3	

NOTES:

[a] Visual Quality Factors are 2.01, 2.02, 6.13, 6.14, 6.15, 7.01, 9.01, 9.02, 9.04 9.05, 10.01, 10.04, 11.04, 12.01 through 12.09.

[b] Areal Condition Factors are 1.01, 1.02, 1.03, 5.03, 5.05, 5.06, 5.07, 5.08, 10.02, 13.02.

[c] Construction Period or Presence of Transmission Line Factors are 3.01, 3.02, 3.03, 3.05, 4.01 through 4.04, 5.01, 5.02, 5.04, 5.09, 7.02, 7.03, 8.01 through 8.24, 9.06 through 9.12, 11.01, 11.02, 11.03, 13.03.

[d] Except factors 1.03 (length through 0.12% slope where not parallel to existing ownerships) and 13.02 (number of parcel splits), which are zero.

was addressed further in the discussion of design criteria.)

When these steep slopes cannot be spanned, there is an erosion hazard resulting from the actual construction on the slope (covered under "Soils") as well as an additional impact on costs. Higher costs result from the need for more inconvenient construction procedures mainly stemming from difficulty of access and the need to minimize erosion.

SLOPES FROM 13 TO 25 PERCENT These were covered in the discussion of the conceptual landforms map.

SLOPES FROM 0 TO 12 PERCENT These were considered under "Other Issues."

OTHER ISSUES The location of the origin and destinations for the transmission lines considered in this study required an alignment diagonal (in some areas) to the

ALTERNATE CORRIDOR COMPARISONS
PROJECT 1: TYRONE – EAU CLAIRE
Corridors Between Nodes 1 (Tyrone) And 18

Corridor Number	Corridor Nodes														Corridor Length (Miles)	Sum of Weighted Constraints (Points)
1	1	2	5	7	11	12	14	15	16	17	18				22.7	180.
2	1	2	5	7	11	13	14	15	16	17	18				21.6	183.
3	1	2	5	7	11	13	109	15	16	17	18				21.6	177.
4	1	2	4	6	9	10	12	11	13	14	15	16	17	18	24.1	207.
5	1	2	5	7	11	12	21	20	19	17	18				23.6	153.
6	1	2	5	7	11	13	14	16	17	18					21.9	168.
7	1	2	5	7	11	13	14	16	19	17	18				22.7	176.
8	1	2	5	7	8	10	23	21	20	19	17	18			23.1	141.
9	1	2	5	7	11	12	14	16	17	18					22.9	164.
10	1	2	5	7	11	13	109	15	16	19	17	18			22.4	185.
11	1	2	4	6	9	10	23	21	20	19	17	18			23.0	141.
12	1	2	5	7	8	10	23	22	20	19	17	18			23.2	160.
13	1	2	5	7	11	12	14	16	19	17	18				23.8	172.
14	1	2	4	6	9	10	23	22	20	19	17	18			23.1	160.
15	1	2	5	6	9	10	23	21	20	19	17	16			23.2	144.
16	1	2	5	7	8	0	12	14	15	16	17	18			22.6	177.
17	1	2	5	7	8	10	12	21	20	19	17	18			23.6	151.
18	1	2	5	7	11	13	14	15	16	19	17	18			22.5	192.
19	1	2	4	6	9	10	12	14	15	16	17	18			22.5	177.
20	1	2	4	6	9	10	12	21	20	19	17	18			23.5	151.
21	1	2	5	6	9	0	12	11	10	9	17	18			23.3	163.
22	1	2	5	7	8	10	12	14	16	17	18				22.9	161.
23	1	2	4	6	9	10	12	14	16	17	18				22.8	162.
24	1	2	5	7	8	10	12	14	16	19	17	18			23.7	169.
25	1	2	4	6	9	10	12	14	16	19	17	18			23.6	170.
26	1	2	5	6	9	0	12	14	15	16	17	18			22.7	180.
27	1	2	5	6	9	10	12	21	20	19	17	18			23.7	154.
28	1	2	5	7	11	12	14	15	16	19	17	18			23.5	188.
29	1	2	3	4	6	9	10	23	21	20	19	17	18		23.3	151.
30	1	2	5	6	9	10	12	14	16	17	18				23.0	164.
31	1	2	3	4	6	9	10	23	22	20	19	17	18		23.4	170.
32	1	2	5	6	9	10	12	14	16	19	17	18			23.8	173.
33	1	2	4	6	9	10	12	11	13	109	15	16	17	18	24.1	200.
34	1	2	3	4	6	9	10	12	14	15	16	17	18		22.8	187.
35	1	2	3	4	6	9	10	12	21	20	19	17	16		23.8	161.
36	1	2	5	7	8	10	12	14	15	16	19	17	18		23.5	185.
37	1	2	4	6	9	10	12	14	15	16	19	17	18		23.4	186.
38	1	2	3	4	6	9	10	12	14	16	17	18			23.1	172.
39	1	2	3	4	6	9	0	12	14	16	19	17	18		24.0	180.
40	1	2	5	6	9	10	12	14	15	16	19	17	18		23.6	189.
41	1	2	4	6	9	10	12	11	13	14	16	19	17	18	25.2	199.
42	1	2	3	4	6	5	7	11	13	14	16	19	17	18	25.0	199.
43	1	2	5	6	9	10	12	11	13	14	16	17	18		24.5	194.
44	1	2	3	4	6	9	10	12	14	15	16	19	17	18	23.7	196.

EXHIBIT 2-10   Alternative corridor identification and comparison of total weighted constraints.

TEP EAU CLAIRE
PROJECT I

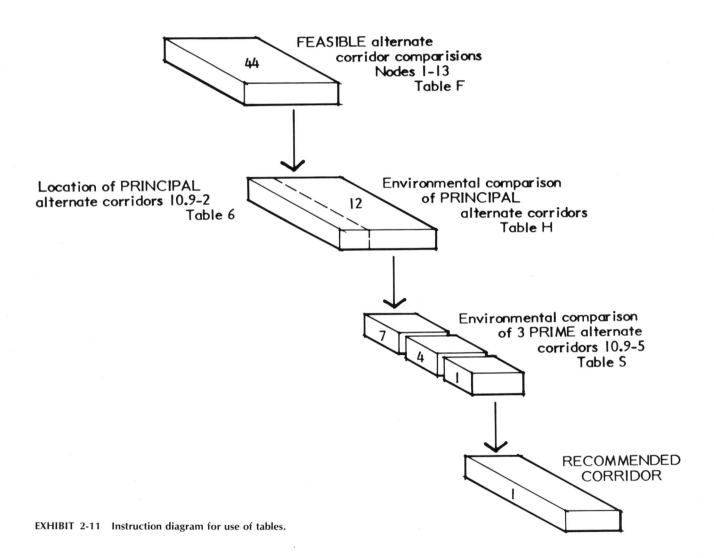

FEASIBLE alternate
corridor comparisions
Nodes 1-13
Table F

Location of PRINCIPAL
alternate corridors 10.9-2
Table 6

Environmental comparison
of PRINCIPAL
alternate corridors
Table H

Environmental comparison
of 3 PRIME alternate
corridors 10.9-5
Table S

RECOMMENDED
CORRIDOR

EXHIBIT 2-11   Instruction diagram for use of tables.

View Looking West
Existing conditions on hill immediately west of the Eau Claire substation. View from left to right: 161-kV single circuit, 345-kV double circuit, and two 115-kV single circuits.

Alternate One
Replace 345-kV single-circuit line with a double-circuit metal pole structure, H-frame style. Construct as far north as possible.

TYRONE ENERGY PARK TRANSMISSION LINE STUDY
NORTHERN STATES POWER COMPANY

EXHIBIT 2-12   Recommended alternative solutions: Eau Claire problem area.

Alternate Two
Remove existing 161-kV line. Add 345-kV single circuit. Minimize distance from existing 345-kV line to avoid need for additional right-of-way.

Alternate Three
Remove 161-kV line and 345-kV line. Construct a metal pole structure (345-kV double circuit) as far north as possible.

PROPOSED ALTERNATES: EAU CLAIRE

EDAW
ENVIRONMENTAL PLANNING
428 OAK GROVE
MINNEAPOLIS, MINNESOTA

sectional grid pattern of the study area. Examination in the field suggested that the landscape could be divided into two classes as far as this grid pattern was concerned:

· Flat, level land (slopes of 0 to 12 percent) where section lines dominate, resulting from rectangular cultivation and fencing patterns. In these areas, a north-south or east-west alignment along or parallel to sectional lines would be desirable. This would minimize the disruption of agricultural use of divided parcels (discussed further under "Ownership") and reduce the impact on visual quality.

· Rolling or hilly land where the natural topography tends to dominate the landscape. In these areas the diagonal alignment, if it followed natural landforms, would have less impact on land use and the condition of visual quality. Thus areas where slopes of 12 to 25 percent predominate might offer opportunities for a diagonal route configuration.

From examination of soils data it was also noted:
"Steep rock areas," one of the soil associations shown on the soils map, falls within the areas of over 25 percent slope on the slope map; and

· Soils defined as having "moderate erosion potential when disturbed" in the "Soils" section owing to their sandy nature will erode under low-slope conditions (0 to 25 percent).

DATA SOURCES   U.S. Geological Survey topographic maps at 1:62500 and 1:24000.

CONSTRAINTS AND WEIGHTING   A 25 percent plus slope was taken as a constraint in the corridor-identification process. In the weighting process, clear span crossings of slopes were given a *low* constraint value, crossings of nonspannable slopes were given a *moderate* value, and corridors passing through flat land (0 to 12 percent slope) not parallel to the section lines were given a *low* constraint value.

Corridor Identification

Exhibit 2-7, the corridor network map, shows all potential corridors connecting Tyrone with the four terminal points at Prairie Island, Afton, King, and Eau Claire. The corridor network contains a large number of interconnected corridors since portions of corridors could be combined differently to reach each terminal point or used to reach any one of several terminal points. Each point of intersection of corridors is called a *node,* and each portion of corridor between two nodes is called a *link.*

These potential corridors were identified by computerizing all links and nodes in a corridor subnetwork (the

portion of the network connecting Tyrone to any *one* terminal point) and having the computer search the network for all potential paths. These corridors, defined by the sequence of nodes from Tyrone to the terminal point, were listed in the first two columns of a series of tables, one of which is shown as Exhibit 2-10.

Corridor Comparison

Because of the large number of potential corridors, a procedure was developed to compare and screen the full list in order to identify a smaller number of prime alternatives for more detailed study. The procedure included measurement of data factors along each corridor and constraint weighting of those data factors to determine a total environmental constraint number for each corridor.

MEASUREMENT OF DATA FACTORS   Data factors for each potential corridor were measured by overlaying the corridor network on each factor map and measuring the extent to which it passed through each data factor. The length of the corridor centerline through each areal factor (for example, riparian forest, urban areas, or steep slopes) was measured in miles. The number of spot features (such as churches, archaeological sites, and structures) within approximately ¼ mile of the centerline and the number of linear-feature crossings (of highways, railroads, other utilities, and perennial streams) were counted. Approximately 110 specific environmental data factors were measured or counted and were coded for computer processing. A partial listing of the environmental factors appears in the first column of Exhibit 2-8. The table illustrates how the subfactors were related to environmental conditions to determine constraint values as described below.

CONSTRAINT WEIGHTING   Each of the 110 environmental data factors which could be encountered was evaluated independently to determine the degree of constraint of the factor, using the constraint definitions in Exhibit 2-3. In establishing weights for each data factor, it was assumed that mitigation measures would be used to reduce adverse changes in environmental conditions to the lowest reasonable level. For example, if a corridor passed through a marsh (data factor 5.04), construction would take place during the winter season with the ground frozen so that unavoidable ground disturbance and changes in water quality would be minimized, or if it was routed through an agricultural field (data factor 5.08), the owner would be compensated for any crop damage.

Constraint values for the individual data factors are given in Exhibit 2-8, together with the environmental conditions that were considered in establishing the constraint values. For example, crossing a large lake or reservoir (data factor 4.01) was given an extreme constraint value because of the potential adverse effect on construction economics, water quality, wildlife habitat, and visual quality.

Numerical weights were assigned to each degree of constraint as follows:

Constraint value	Numerical weight per unit of measure
Extreme	6.0
High	4.0
Moderate	2.0
Low	1.0
None	0.0

These numerical weights applied to a unit length of measured data (e.g., 1 mile of forest). For most spot features and linear feature crossings, the numerical weight was reduced by one-half. Adjustments were also made to the numerical weights for some data factors under the following situations:

1 When more than one circuit was to be located on a new right-of-way, weights on data factors concerning visual quality were increased.

2 When the new corridor paralleled an existing railroad right-of-way, weights on data factors concerning the establishment of new rights-of-way through areal features were decreased.

3 When the new corridor paralleled an existing transmission line right-of-way, weights on data factors concerning the establishment of new rights-of-way through areal features were decreased and weights on data factors concerning visual quality were also decreased. These adjustments are defined in Exhibit 2-9.

The numerical constraint weights for each data factor multiplied by the measured extent of the data factors were then summed to give a total environmental constraint number for each corridor:

Total environmental constraint number for Corridor X
= (weight of data factor 1.01)
× (measured amount of data factor 1.01)
+ (weight of data factor 1.02)
× (measured amount of data factor 1.02) + etc.

Corridor Selection

The sum of weighted constraints represented by each corridor can be found (for the Tyrone to Eau Claire subnetwork only) in the last column of Exhibit 2-10. For each subnetwork those corridors with the lowest total weighted constraint numbers, together with others representing the geographic range of available alternatives, were selected for further analysis and comparison. Total corridor length in miles, a rough indicator of construction cost, was also considered in the selection.

By using this procedure, over 700 *feasible* alternatives were reduced to 49 *principal* alternatives. The principal alternatives were once again compared by measuring or counting the spot and linear features encountered. The process permitted selection of *prime* alternatives. Recommended corridors in each subnetwork were selected from among these prime alternatives in a final comparison (see Exhibit 2-11).

Structure Design and Treatment of Problem Areas

Final steps in the study involved the presentation of general guidelines and locational criteria for use in detailed alignment studies within each recommended corridor. The guidelines dealt with the use of alternative structure styles and their application in particularly sensitive areas. An example of recommended solutions to problems identified with the assistance of computer visibility studies is presented in Exhibit 2-12.

Case Study 3 | PROJECT SEAFARER

History and Scope of This Study

As we indicated in Chapter 1, in the late 1960s the U.S. Navy began its continuing search for a site for the controversial communications grid known first as Project Sanguine, later as Project Seafarer, and currently as the ELF system.

After rejection of the site in Wisconsin that had been the first choice, EDAW was retained by the Navy to assist with selection of another site. The objective was a site that would meet Project Sanguine's siting criteria with the least possible environmental harm. EDAW, of course, was not in a position to address either the political issues or the issue of possible public health hazards associated with the project and was not requested to do so. Ideally, these issues would be handled within the site-selection process we have described, but questions of national security have a habit of creating exceptions.

What we will describe is the technical process which was followed to evaluate site conditions as the search widened and narrowed.

Evaluation of Preselected Sites in Texas and Michigan

The first task involved an intensive environmental inventory in two areas that had been identified by the Navy: Llano, Texas, and the Upper Michigan Peninsula. These were considered because they offered extensive sparsely developed areas which appeared to be geologically appropriate to the system.

Exhibits 3-1 and 3-2 illustrate the level of detail involved in these regional investigations. Despite the apparent suitability of the Michigan site, political objections again arose. Political objections were also voiced in Texas. There, however, the site was found to require very widely spaced antennae because of the high conductivity of the rock and was deemed undesirable.

Comparative Evaluation of Sites on Public Lands

The difficulties encountered in Wisconsin, Michigan, and Texas prompted the Navy to expand its search to lands in federal ownership. Fifteen regions in Colorado, Wyoming, Idaho, Utah, Nevada, Arizona, New Mexico, and California were identified as candidates for comparison with the three earlier regions. These candidates included national forest and other public lands, Air Force ranges, and weapons and atomic energy test ranges.

EDAW was asked to make surveys of each region to determine the suitability of conditions for efficient construction and operation of the system. Exhibit 3-3 shows how conditions within each region were displayed. Some of the regional summary sheets were quite long and had to be printed in a foldout format. The land area extended in some cases to as much as 13,000 square miles owing to the need to place transmitters at wide intervals in areas of high rock conductivity.

Detailed Site Surveys: New Mexico and Nevada

Through comparison of survey findings, two regions in Nevada and New Mexico were selected for further study. Except for the previously studied northern Michigan region, these two regions appeared to offer the only technically feasible locations for the project, now known as Seafarer. This time a more thorough examination was made, including all the factors that could be affected by the system. Data on the factors listed below were collected and presented in map and narrative form. Investigations were restricted to on-site conditions, except as noted. Exhibits 3-4 and 3-5 illustrate the level of detail achieved.

· Land use (on-site and regional)

Facilities and range use by federal agencies
Radiation or ordnance hazard
Air use, existing and proposed

PROJECT SANGUINE – Site Study
LLANO, TEXAS REGION

ECKBO
DEAN
AUSTIN &
WILLIAMS

landscape architecture
environmental planning
urban design

san francisco, los angeles,
honolulu, minneapolis

145 mission st., san francisco, calif. 94105

NORTHERN
DIVISION

department of the navy
naval facilities engineering command
naval base, philadelphia, pa.

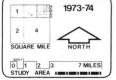

EXHIBIT 3-1 Project Sanguine, Llano, Texas, region: bedrock geologic data. The Llano region was deemed unsuited to the Sanguine system because of high-conductivity rock.

BEDROCK GEOLOGIC DATA

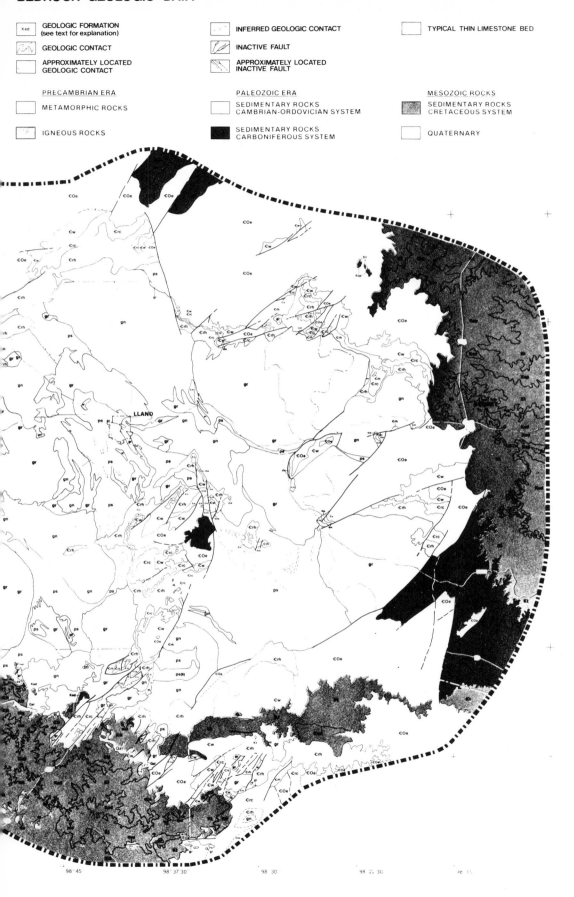

PROJECT SANGUINE – Site Study
UPPER MICHIGAN REGION

ECKBO DEAN AUSTIN & WILLIAMS
landscape architecture
environmental planning
urban design
san francisco, los angeles,
honolulu, minneapolis
145 mission st., san francisco, calif. 94105

NORTHERN DIVISION
department of the navy
naval facilities engineering command
naval base, philadelphia, pa.

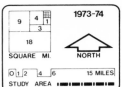

1973-74

SQUARE MI.

NORTH

0 1 2 4 6 15 MILES

STUDY AREA

OWNERSHIP DA

PRIVATE LAND

GOVERNMENT LAN

CORPORATE LAND

90°30'   90°15'   90°00'   89°45'   89°30'   89°15'   89°00'   88°45'   88°30

BESSEMER   WAKEFIELD
IRONWOOD

IRON RIVE

EXHIBIT 3-2   Project Sanguine, Upper Michigan region: owner-ship data. An example of basic data mapping developed for one of two candidate regions originally selected by the U.S. Navy for an underground communications system. While the region was environmentally suitable, political objections led to its rejection.

FORT IRWIN
CALIFORNIA
COMPARATIVE SUMMARY
EDAW inc.

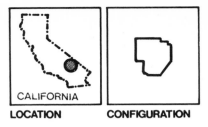

CALIFORNIA
LOCATION

CONFIGURATION

SQUARE MILES

980 | 1000 |

2000 |

REAL ESTATE [1]
Other
Federal
Military

SOIL CHARACTERISTICS
Drill & Blast
Rip
Plow

CAPSULE SITES
Wet soil
Dry soil
Fractured rock
Competent rock

TOPOGRAPHY
Mountainous
Hilly
Gently rolling
Flat

WATER SOURCES
Low
Intermediate
High

LAND USE
Built up
Special
Open

VEGETATION
Heavily wooded
Lightly wooded
Brush
Other

LINEAR MILES / SQUARE MILE .2 | .4 |

SURFACE WATER
Perennial
Intermittent

ROADS
Primary
Secondary

CLIMATE Precipitation 4.8" Lowest temperature 4° Highest temperature 117° Normal annual temperature 63°

CONSTRUCTION UNIT COST DATA Construction index 182

CULTURAL/HISTORICAL Number of sites 0   Number of endangered species 0

NOTES:
1. For map, see appendix.

LEGEND:

Distribution — Colors indicate distribution by heading

Reliability — Shaded areas indicate data uncertain

Qualification — ✳ — Asterisk indicates significant qualification – see narrative

EXHIBIT 3-3   Data used to screen fifteen regions in federal ownership following rejection of Texas and Michigan sites.

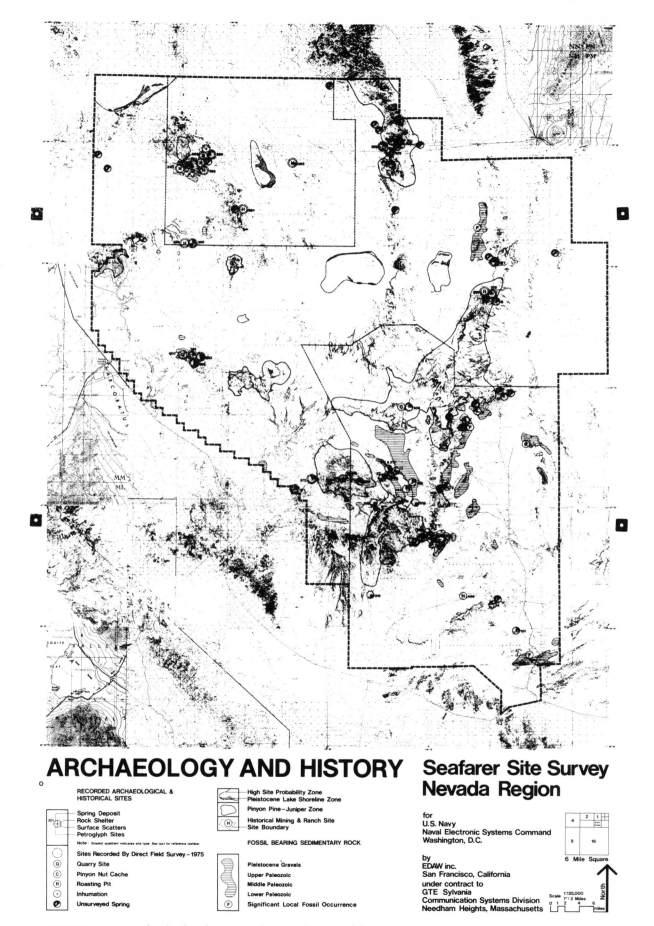

ARCHAEOLOGY AND HISTORY

Seafarer Site Survey
Nevada Region

**RECORDED ARCHAEOLOGICAL &
HISTORICAL SITES**

- Spring Deposit
- Rock Shelter
- Surface Scatters
- Petroglyph Sites

Note: Shaded quadrant indicates site type. See text for reference number.

Sites Recorded By Direct Field Survey – 1975

- Ⓠ Quarry Site
- Ⓒ Pinyon Nut Cache
- Ⓡ Roasting Pit
- Inhumation
- Unsurveyed Spring

- High Site Probability Zone
- Pleistocene Lake Shoreline Zone
- Pinyon Pine – Juniper Zone
- Ⓗ Historical Mining & Ranch Site
- Site Boundary

FOSSIL BEARING SEDIMENTARY ROCK

- Pleistocene Gravels
- Upper Paleozoic
- Middle Paleozoic
- Lower Paleozoic
- Ⓕ Significant Local Fossil Occurrence

for
U.S. Navy
Naval Electronic Systems Command
Washington, D.C.

by
EDAW inc.
San Francisco, California
under contract to
GTE Sylvania
Communication Systems Division
Needham Heights, Massachusetts

4	2	1
8	16	

6 Mile Square

Scale 1:125,000
1" 2 Miles
0 1 2 4 6 miles

North

EXHIBIT 3-4 Example of a data factor map for one of two candidate regions.

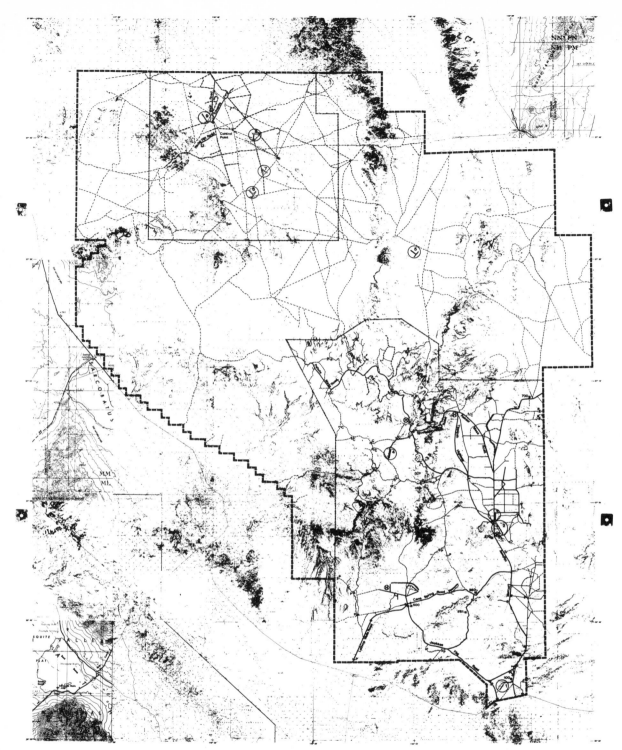

TRANSPORTATION

- ——— Primary Paved Road
- ——— Secondary Paved Road
- ——— Primary Unpaved Road
- ——— Secondary Unpaved Road
- ——— Railroad
- Guard Station
- Barricade
  Refer to Text for Reference Letter

- Abandoned Airstrip (see text)
- Operating Airstrip (see text)
- Helicopter Pad

Seafarer Site Survey
Nevada Region

for
U.S. Navy
Naval Electronic Systems Command
Washington, D.C.

by
EDAW inc.
San Francisco, California
under contract to
GTE Sylvania
Communication Systems Division
Needham Heights, Massachusetts

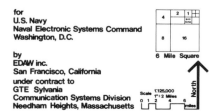

Scale 1:125,000
1" = 2 Miles

6 Mile Square

North

EXHIBIT 3-5 Transportation data map.

Regional land control
Regional land use (federal and other)

· Transportation (on-site and regional)

· Socioeconomic characteristics (regional)

Population, existing and projected
Employment, existing and projected
Economic activity
Services
Governmental functions and policies

· Slope and terrain

· Bedrock geology

· Mineral resources

· Surficial geology

· Soils

· Subsurface water

· Surface water

· Climate (on-site and regional)

· Air quality and noise

· Vegetation

· Wildlife

· Archaeology and history

· Utilities

As a result of these studies, it was concluded that neither the Nevada nor the New Mexico location offered a suitable site.

THE UPPER MICHIGAN SITE-SELECTION STUDY

A further political decision focused the search for a Project Seafarer site once more on northern Michigan. A site-screening effort was undertaken to identify suitable corridors within which to locate detailed alignments.

The specific area of study was approximately 4700 square miles in extent, located in the western section of Michigan's Upper Peninsula and containing all or part of eight counties. The boundaries of the area were defined by the Ottawa National Forest to the west, Lake Superior to the north, and the Menominee River to the south. The eastern boundary related to the extent of geologic units usually associated with low electrical conductivity.

Identification of System Design and Environmental Relationships

This step involved a review of previously identified system goals and objectives, project definition, and environ-

mental relationships. It was also reaffirmed that the primary objectives of the siting study were to maximize performance while minimizing construction, operating, and environmental costs.

The performance requirements for the Seafarer system were set forth in the Navy's system specifications. To achieve the best performance on the Upper Michigan site, approximately 2400 miles of antenna were required. The antenna ideally needed to be spaced at uniform intervals in a north-south, east-west grid configuration over an area of low electrical conductivity. To minimize cost and environmental disturbance it was desirable to select existing rights-of-way (ROWs) wherever possible, developing new ROWs only when necessary to interconnect sections of antenna route.

Project-environmental relationships were expressed in terms of costs.

CONSTRUCTION COSTS These would be incurred through all activities from the acquisition and preparation of ROWs to putting the system into operation. It was recognized that few activities were unique to the Seafarer system. Site conditions would have the most influence on the type of construction activities required and on their environmental conditions. The most important factors determining methods and relative ease of construction were:

· Ownership and ROW acquisition

· Terrain

· Number of water crossings

· Vegetation type

· Access-road locations

· Bedrock conditions

· Waste disposal

· Equipment movement and field testing

· Environmental restoration.

MITIGATION COSTS These would be incurred in precluding electrical interference in telephone and other utility systems and also with induced coupling with long wire conductors such as metal fences and guardrails.

OPERATION AND MAINTENANCE COSTS These included costs for repairs, preventive maintenance, and surveillance.

PHYSICAL AND BIOLOGICAL COSTS These were identified as any alteration of environmental features with potential for loss of wildlife habitat, vegetation destruction, or landform changes.

SOCIAL AND CULTURAL COSTS Potential restrictions on any existing or planned land uses and effects on land values, local services, public health and safety, schools, recreation areas, and historic or archaeological sites were treated as social or cultural costs.

It was recognized that avoidance of environmental constraints might necessitate departures from the ideal antenna configuration. However, achievement of the goals of maximizing construction and operating cost required that any deviations meet the following criteria:

· The electrical axis of each physical antenna line should be kept as close to the nominal axis of the ideal line as possible.

· Maximum practical use should be made of areas of lowest conductivity.

· The number of close approaches of nominally parallel segments should be minimized.

· The orthogonality of the grid should be maintained by minimizing both the number and the length of lines crossing at other than 90° angles.

Determination of Constraints and Opportunities

The preceding step led to identification of the siting factors to be used in the site-screening program. These required reference to twelve of the twenty data reports and maps prepared for the region in the Project Sanguine study. These data categories are listed below, and two examples of factor maps are shown in Exhibits 3-6 and 3-7:

· Governmental data
· Land ownership
· Land use
· Transportation
· Utilities
· Mineral extraction
· Surficial geology
· Slope and terrain
· Surface water
· Cultural and recreation data
· Vegetation
· Wildlife

The next task was to categorize each site condition on the factor maps as an avoidance feature, a constraint, or an opportunity. Representatives of the U.S. Navy, GTE

Sylvania (the system designers), and other consultants participated in workshop sessions with EDAW staff to arrive at these categorizations, using a simple worksheet, examples of which can be seen in Tables 7-6 and 7-7 in Chapter 7, "The Screening Process." The categories were assigned according to the following definitions:

AVOIDANCE FEATURE Feature or area which would not be considered for system development; highest environmental, social, or engineering cost.

CONSTRAINT AREA

· *High constraint.* Area which might be considered for system development only when alternative locations were not possible or feasible; high level of environmental, social, or engineering cost.

· *Moderate constraint.* Area which might be considered for system development only after evaluation against alternative locations of lower impact but less efficient system configuration; moderate level of environmental, social, or engineering cost.

· *Low constraint.* Area which would be considered for system development whenever existing ROWs could not be utilized; low level of environmental, social, or engineering cost.

RIGHT-OF-WAY OPPORTUNITY Existing ROWs such as roads, transmission lines, telephone lines, and abandoned railroads that represented opportunities for siting with the lowest level of environmental, social, or engineering cost. These ROWs might exist within any of the above three constraint areas.

Several key assumptions were made as part of the opportunities and constraints analysis.

· The wilderness character of the Upper Peninsula region could be significantly altered or degraded with substantial amounts of cleared ROWs. For this reason, existing serviceable roads, trails, and ROWs would be used in siting the antenna system whenever possible.

· Since the final detailed alignment phase would afford additional opportunity for siting, a 1-mile corridor width was considered optimum for this phase of the study. This would provide ample latitude for selection of detailed 25-foot alignments

· Because the avoidance features ranged in size from large areas (towns and reservoirs) to small "point" data (historic sites, nesting sites, and recorded viewpoints), it was assumed that the mile-wide corridor could include some small avoidance features. At the detailed alignment phase, when finer-scale information would be available, these features would be avoided.

At this point each data map was being considered on

Seafarer Corridor Analysis
Upper Michigan Region

by EDAW inc.
San Francisco, California

under contract to
GTE Sylvania
Communication Systems Division
Needham Heights, Massachusetts

for
U.S. Navy
Naval Electronic Systems Command
Washington, D.C.

UTILITY BUFFERS
One Mile Buffer Around:
Electrical Substations
Electrical Switching Stations
Electrical Generating Stations
Telephone Central Exchanges

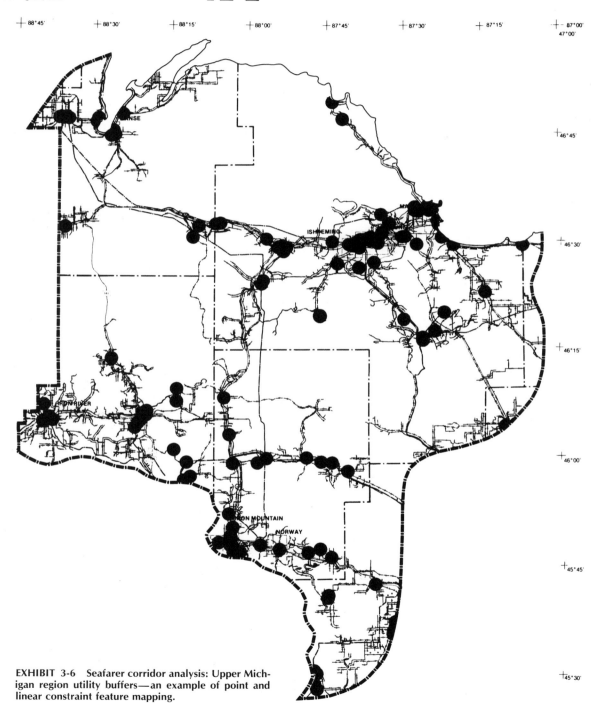

EXHIBIT 3-6 Seafarer corridor analysis: Upper Michigan region utility buffers—an example of point and linear constraint feature mapping.

Seafarer Corridor Analysis
Upper Michigan Region

VEGETATION I
Wetlands Dominant

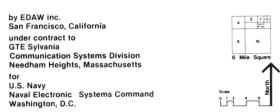

by EDAW inc.
San Francisco, California

under contract to
GTE Sylvania
Communication Systems Division
Needham Heights, Massachusetts

for
U.S. Navy
Naval Electronic Systems Command
Washington, D.C.

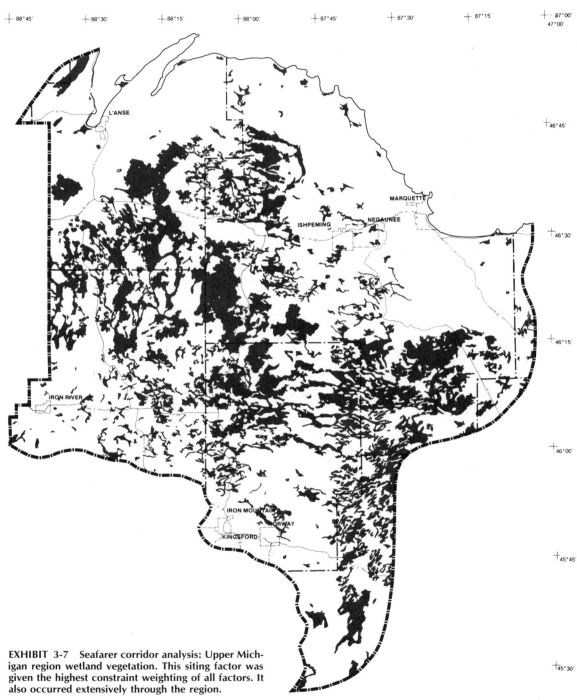

EXHIBIT 3-7 Seafarer corridor analysis: Upper Michigan region wetland vegetation. This siting factor was given the highest constraint weighting of all factors. It also occurred extensively through the region.

its own merits, with no attempt to compare and relate parameters from different data maps. The next problem was to decide how to composite all the identified constraints.

The graphic complexity of preparing a composite map involving three levels of constraint (high, medium, and low) for each data category led to the decision to exclude low-constraint features. Exhibits 3-6 and 3-7 provide examples of constraint maps for single data categories. The avoidance features and ROW opportunities maps appear as Exhibits 3-8 and 3-9.

Weighting and Compositing of Constraints

As in virtually all site-screening efforts, it was recognized that not all constraint categories merited equal consideration in siting. The weights to be assigned to each one were decided during lengthy discussions between the Navy, the system designers, and the EDAW team.

The wetlands constraint category, which Exhibit 3-6 shows was very extensive, was agreed to be more sensitive to the effects of the construction of the system than any other category. It was therefore ranked highest. The least important category was judged to be slope because of the gently rolling nature of most of the study area. The remaining categories could then be ranked and grouped according to their importance relative to slope and wetlands, using a simple weighting index of 1 to 4.

A new and valuable approach to compositing constraint maps, which was discussed in Chapter 7, was produced for this study. It has the advantage of allowing the weights assigned to each parameter to be reassessed easily. A clear film overlay with a yellow tint on the area of constraint was made for each parameter.

When all thirty film sheets were stacked, it was still possible to read the underlying base maps (avoidance and ROW opportunities) and to photograph the stack. The resulting composite constraint map, which appears in Figure 7-16, shows the gradations of value produced by the varying number of tinted layers across the study area. An area which contains several low-weighted constraining factors may appear darker than one containing only one high-weight constraint. The special value of this approach is that in a workshop situation the participants can see the patterns created by the sum of all the weighted constraints very rapidly and make any appropriate adjustments to the weightings very easily by inserting or removing sheets. This flexibility has particular value in handling fairly small study areas with finely detailed data.

Corridor Selection

The composite constraint map provided the basis for identifying and comparing a number of alternative configurations for the Seafarer system. It will be recalled that project goals called for locating corridors as far as possible along existing roads, trails, or utility ROWs. This would have been relatively easy with a small system. However, performance requirements in this area called for a rather large system. Exhibit 3-10 illustrates the selected alternative 1-mile corridors adapted to meet both goals and performance requirements. The corridors shown either follow existing ROWs or cross open areas. Whenever an existing ROW could not be followed, every attempt was made to minimize intrusion into high-constraint areas. In fact, over 60 percent of alternative corridor miles could be located along existing ROWs.

Preliminary Evaluation of Corridors

To gain a more thorough understanding of the relative effects of the Seafarer system on each environmental factor, the corridor plan was spot-checked against key uncomposited constraint maps. This procedure provided an understanding of the conflicts which might occur in siting the antenna and the environmental factors to be used in the subsequent detailed siting and alignment work. The emphasis in this sampling exercise was on off-road areas, where it was assumed that conflicts would be greatest.

Ten environmental conditions were used in this exercise as representative indicators of effect. Tabulations were made of total corridor miles sited within:

· Off-road areas within buffers around existing settlements and other important land uses (state park and experimental forest)
· Privately owned land
· Areas of diverse vegetation (and therefore habitat types)
· Wetland areas
· Forested areas
· Steep slopes with forest vegetation near perennial streams, lakes, or wetlands
· Areas of exposed or near-surface bedrock

In addition, tabulations were made of the total number of point avoidance features within the corridors, of stream crossings, and of utility stations.

The locations, relative distribution and frequency of these indicators were tabulated and mapped to ensure

Seafarer Site Survey
Upper Michigan Region

by
EDAW inc.
San Francisco, California

under contract to
GTE Sylvania
Communication Systems Division
Needham Heights, Massachusetts

for
U.S. Navy
Naval Electronic Systems Command
Washington, D.C.

6 Mile Square

Scale
0 1 2   4   6
miles

North

AVOIDANCE FEATURES

■	Corporate Boundaries, Planned Developments or Special Preserve Areas
●	Urban and Rural Settlements
	Railroads
	Pipelines
	Lakes and Reservoirs

Q	Quarries and Pits
CG	Park Sites with Campgrounds
P	Small Parks and Picnic Areas
S	Ski Areas
V	Recorded View Points
AS	Archaeological Sites
HS	Historic Sites
N	Nesting Sites
WF	Wildlife Flooding Areas

A	Airports
H	Harbors
C	Cemeteries
PF	Prison Facilities
M	Mines

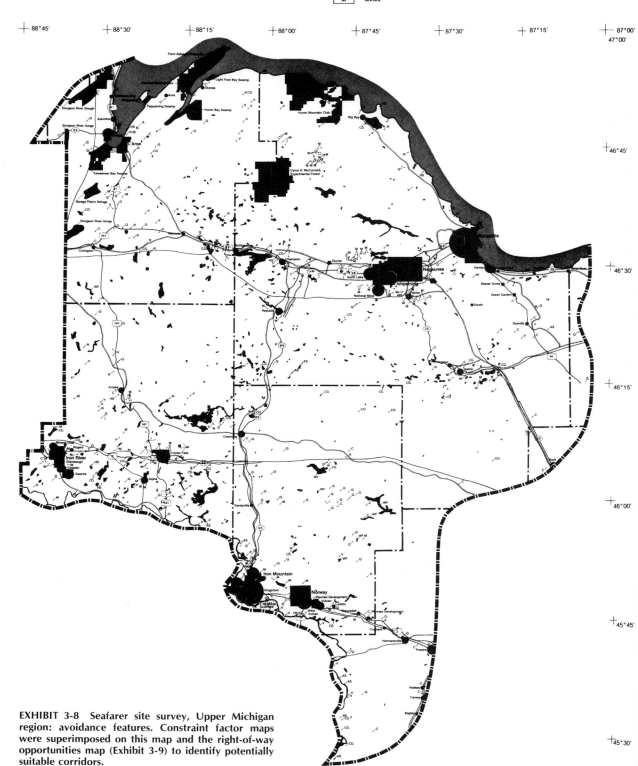

EXHIBIT 3-8 Seafarer site survey, Upper Michigan region: avoidance features. Constraint factor maps were superimposed on this map and the right-of-way opportunities map (Exhibit 3-9) to identify potentially suitable corridors.

242

Seafarer Site Survey
Upper Michigan Region

by
EDAW inc.
San Francisco, California

under contract to
GTE Sylvania
Communication Systems Division
Needham Heights, Massachusetts

for
U.S. Navy
Naval Electronic Systems Command
Washington, D.C.

6 Mile Square

Scale
0 1 2   4   6
miles

North

R.O.W. OPPORTUNITIES

ELECTRICAL TRANSMISSION AND DISTRIBUTION SYSTEM
Transmission Line (69kV-138kV)
Three Phase Distribution Line (12.5kV-33kV)
Single Phase Distribution Line
Underground Cable
Substation
Switching Station
Generation Station

TELEPHONE SYSTEM
Underground Cable
Open Wire
Aerial Cable
Central Office

TRANSPORTATION
U.S. and State Highways
Other Paved Roads
Gravel Road
Good Dirt Road
Poor Dirt Road
Abandoned Railroad

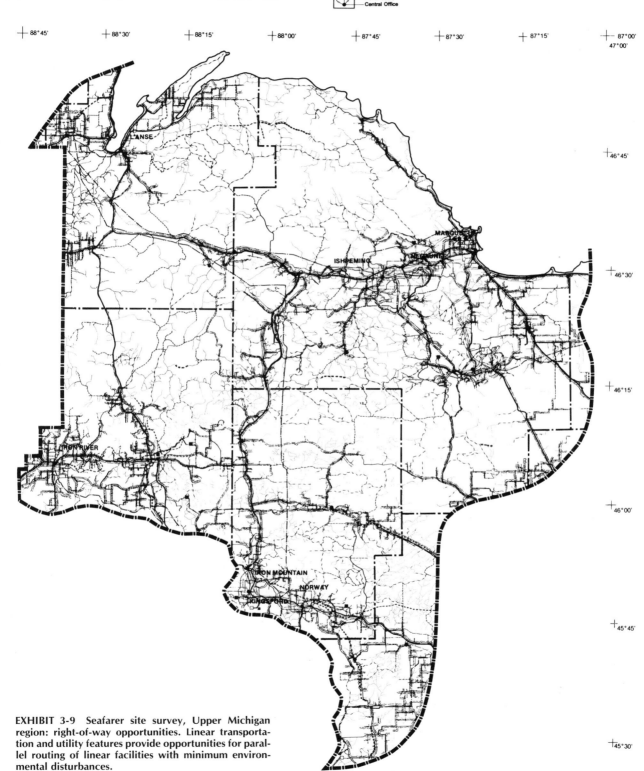

EXHIBIT 3-9 Seafarer site survey, Upper Michigan region: right-of-way opportunities. Linear transportation and utility features provide opportunities for parallel routing of linear facilities with minimum environmental disturbances.

243

Seafarer Corridor Analysis
Upper Michigan Region

by EDAW inc.
San Francisco, California

under contract to
GTE Sylvania
Communication Systems Division
Needham Heights, Massachusetts

for
U.S. Navy
Naval Electronic Systems Command
Washington, D.C.

CORRIDOR PLAN C

Areas on Existing Roads or Rights-of-Way

Off-Road Areas

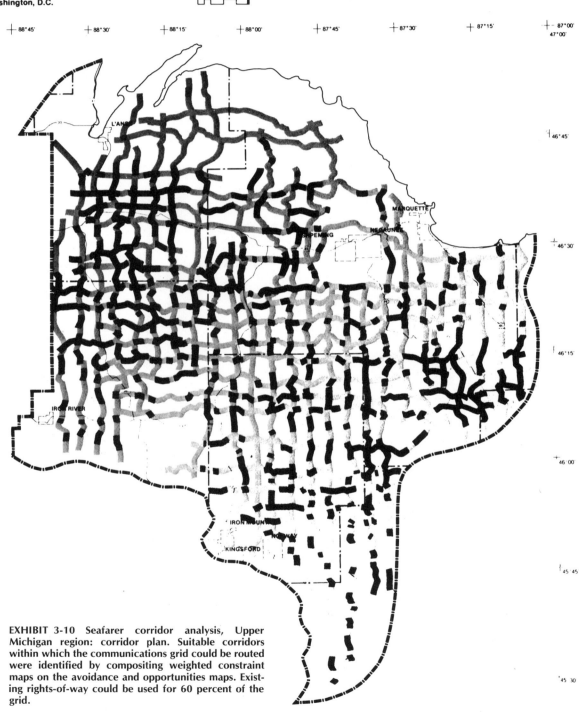

EXHIBIT 3-10 Seafarer corridor analysis, Upper Michigan region: corridor plan. Suitable corridors within which the communications grid could be routed were identified by compositing weighted constraint maps on the avoidance and opportunities maps. Existing rights-of-way could be used for 60 percent of the grid.

244

that each condition would be addressed in the route-evaluation phase. It was known that a time lag would occur between phases.

The Seafarer Test-Bed Alignment Studies

After approval of the recommended network of milewide corridors EDAW was asked to assist the Navy by selecting detailed alignments within each corridor. The objective was to determine minimum-constraint ROWs within each corridor where short sections of test bed could be laid, prior to final detailed design and construction of the full system.

The process of defining the test-bed alignments involved six steps:

· Corridor review

· Data collection and interpretation

· Data mapping

· Constraint (criteria) weighting

· Review of siting objectives

· Constraint analysis and selection of detailed alignment within each corridor

The first step required a brief on-site study, principally of landownership patterns and public road ROWs.

Next, detailed data from which to prepare the following four sets of maps for each corridor were collected:

1 Surficial geology and slope

2 Surface water, vegetation, and wildlife

3 Ownership and jurisdiction

4 Land use

· Roads
· Railroads
· Pipelines (restricted to underground obstructions or transmission lines that might offer ROW opportunities)
· Transmission lines
· Mining features
· Developed areas
· Recreation features
· Experimental forest
· Historic sites
· Archaeological sites

A fifth set of maps showed the selected alignment alone.

The constraint weightings employed in this process of detailed evaluation were those already evolved at work sessions by EDAW, the system designers, and the U.S. Navy for use in corridor selection. However, in some cases new constraining environmental conditions emerged from the more detailed examination of each corridor.

None of these more detailed factors was found to warrant changing prior weighting, although in some cases a very localized factor had to be assessed on its merits. Although new constraint weightings were not developed at this stage, it was necessary to identify more refined siting objectives:

· Minimize siting on steep slopes.

· Minimize siting on areas of rock (where blasting would be required).

· Minimize siting on wetland vegetation and boggy organic soils.

· Minimize siting across open surface water; cross as few streams as possible; use existing bridges whenever possible.

· Minimize siting across critical wildlife areas.

· Minimize siting across privately owned land.

· Minimize paralleling operating railroads whenever possible, especially for long distances.

· Minimize paralleling buried pipelines, especially for long distances.

· Minimize siting on existing or proposed mining features.

· Minimize siting adjacent to developed areas.

· Minimize siting adjacent to recreation features.

· Minimize siting adjacent to historic, archaeologic, and special features.

The following is a brief listing of the major reasons for using these environmental conditions as siting constraints for the test-bed alignment:

· *Slope.* Siting on steep slopes may increase the erosion or sedimentation hazard, the visibility of constructed works, and the cost of construction.

· *Surficial geology.* Siting on areas with hard rock near the surface increases construction costs and causes temporary noise from blasting.

· *Vegetation.* Areas of wetland vegetation are environmentally fragile and may be altered by construction activities. Siting in wetland areas increases construction costs.

· *Surface water.* These features may be altered by construction activity. Siting across surface-water features increases construction costs.

· *Wildlife.* Construction or human activity in the vicinity of critical areas at certain periods of the year may drive away the protected species or alter the habitat on which they depend.

· *Ownership.* Acquiring easements across private land may be time-consuming. Costs may be difficult to estimate.

· *Railroads.* Operation of the Seafarer antenna may require special mitigation efforts to avoid interference with the railroads' electrical systems. Interference mitigation may be defined as the design and implementation of techniques and devices which will eliminate or reduce to tolerable levels interferences or effects which the Seafarer electromagnetic fields could impose on long metallic structures.

· *Pipelines.* Any necessary mitigation of electrical interference with buried pipelines will increase costs.

· *Mining features.* Siting across existing or proposed mining features may require eventual removal and resiting of the antenna.

· *Developed areas.* Siting adjacent to developed areas increases social and construction costs.

· *Recreation features.* The value of certain recreation features may be reduced by adjacent construction activity.

· *Historic, archaeologic, and special features.* These features may be liable to damage from construction or associated human activities.

Whenever possible, according to the refined siting objectives, existing ROWs or easements contained within the selected corridors were followed in the detailed alignments. It was assumed that co-use could be negotiated.

As each corridor in the selected grid was found to be at least more suitable than those not selected, the objectives of the corridor evaluation and alignment selections were to minimize physical-biological and social-cultural impacts as well as direct financial costs of constructing, operating, and maintaining the system.

The analysis process consisted of defining required cable lengths and disposition of the grounds at each end of the line on the basis of conductivity and then threading the alignment through and, where necessary, across the various constraining conditions, keeping the defined constraint values in mind.

In this study the prime 25-foot ROW (and in a few locations an alternate ROW) could be identified directly on a set of aerial-photograph base maps, without the need for narrative description or tabular or matrix display. This was possible because the most desirable alignment in each case was clearly apparent as a result of the data mapping and visual inspection tasks. Had it been necessary to score a number of alternative alignments according to their satisfaction of the siting criteria and subsequently to rank them, other site-evaluation techniques, described in Chapter 8, would have been used.

Conclusion

The numerous hearings held in Upper Michigan did not reduce the apprehension of local residents and others regarding the project. However, the results of these extensive studies are now somewhat academic in light of the President's decision of October 1981, as discussed in Chapter 1.

Regardless of the final political decision, the environmental studies achieved two things. First, in the event that the full system were installed, they identified a location and an alignment that appeared technically and in most cases environmentally feasible. Thus they helped to reduce the system's potential impacts. Second, whether or not the project becomes a reality in any form, the siting process allowed the political debate to occur with a greater appreciation of the true environmental conditions and consequences.

Case Study 4 | THE DAVENPORT SITING STUDIES

History and Scope of These Studies

These pioneering studies were conducted in 1971 and 1972 for the Pacific Gas and Electric Company (PG&E). The company was contemplating construction of a nuclear power plant on its site near the town of Davenport on the coast of Santa Cruz County, California, some 80 miles south of San Francisco. The studies were conducted in three major phases:

1 *A land-use study.* A study of the 7000 acres of land in PG&E ownership to develop land-use options and a plan for the location of various use options.

2 *A power plant siting study.* A detailed siting study of the power plant itself and the accompanying switchyards, considering the relative visibility of alternative sites and the resulting impact on adjacent land uses.

3 *A transmission line study.* Route selection; right-of-way treatment and design for the transmission lines required as part of the proposed power plant installation.

The studies thus provide examples both of detailed site evaluation within a previously selected site and of broader-scale route selection and evaluation. Many new conceptual approaches and analytical techniques of facility siting and routing were developed by EDAW during the studies. We should note here that in 1971 nuclear power generation was viewed in a relatively optimistic light. The case is described here for its general approach rather than its subject matter.

LAND-USE STUDY

Scope

The scope of the land-use phase of this project recognized the following objectives:

· That the plan be compatible with overall land-use planning for the north coast area of Santa Cruz County

· That the plan be based on the determination of and respect for social, economic, and environmental values and implications

· That the plan be mindful of PG&E's interest in exploring the potential of locating a power plant on a portion of the site

The data base was prepared in accordance with the following assumptions:

· That the utility's actions at Davenport would be subject to considerable scrutiny and therefore should have thorough documentation

· That the utility might reject the consultants' recommendations and thus should have the data with which to support another course of action

· That if the study process were to be valid and viable, the basic data must be available and adaptable in the face of changing needs, technologies, and values, as discussed below in the subsection "Process"

· That no preliminary assumptions or intuitions regarding land use should alter the process, which was equipped to handle the range of potential uses from heavy development to open space

Process

The planning process, illustrated in Exhibit 4-1, consisted of four basic parts: information gathering, interpretation, planning and design, and evaluation.

INFORMATION GATHERING   This was to provide an inventory of resources, acquiring, sorting, storing, and combining the data which identified and defined the peculiar qualities of the site in such a way that rational and objective decisions could be reached in determining its use potential. The collection and grouping of site data were based on the concept of landscape causality levels.

The term *landscape causality* refers to the dynamic interdependencies that exist between environmental variables, helping to reveal both the more sensitive and the more constant of the variables to be considered in the

247

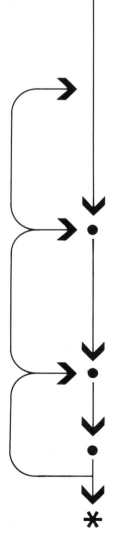

Information Gathering

Data
Natural: Climate, geology, topography, soils, hydrology, vegetation, and wildlife. Aesthetic: visual and noise considerations. Governmental: tax base, services, county planning. Economic: growth projections, market demands, land values.

Data Bank
Translation of data to common terms in grid cells on base map for storage in data bank.

Analysis of Data Bank
Review of data for accuracy, completeness, and relative importance.

Interpretation

Selection and mapping of specific information relating to landscape modification; combining and weighting of related groups of information to indicate general limitations and potentials of landscape modification; combining and weighting of limitations and potentials to indicate suitability for specific land uses.

Planning & Design Development

Program quantification, identification, and selection of land use types, densities, and spatial arrangements.

Evaluation

Testing of land use proposals for social, environmental, political, and economic consequences.

Recommended Plan

EXHIBIT 4-1   Planning process.

land-use study. The concept provides a useful commentary on the way in which the simple organization of environmental conditions and impact matrices that were presented in Chapter 6 may be adapted to a specific study requirement.

In Exhibit 4-2 arrows illustrate a flow of interactions that are both horizontal and vertical, with the more constant, stable, and determining environmental factors generally to the top and left and the more dependent and sensitive generally to the bottom and right.

The most constant conditions on the highest level represent patterns which have been established over great periods of time. They are less dependent on other factors than other variables and are not so subject to alteration by land use. Climate and historical geology interact to form their own timeless and relatively unyielding system.

Surface geology, landforms, water and drainage patterns, and finally soils have occurred in response to the interaction of climate and historical geology. On this level land-use policies can cause significant alterations, ranging from the more conscious modifications required through the use of heavy machinery on surface geology and landforms to the unexpected havoc that can occur within water and soils in the form of pollution, flooding, depletion, or erosion.

Vegetation is more sensitive in that it is dependent on

the level above and is thus subject to ready alteration in both direct and indirect ways. Moreover, the system is reactive in that disturbance of vegetation can act in reverse, producing unfavorable alterations to the water and soils systems.

Most sensitive of all is wildlife, whose dependencies run back through all levels of landscape causality, in addition to being in many cases subject to disturbance and alteration by noise and even by the mere presence of human activities.

The information-gathering phase involved a number of consultants and took many forms: *governmental*, including an investigation of the tax base, services, and county planning policies and guidelines; *economic*, including growth projections and market demands; *natural factors*, including topography, soils, hydrology, vegetation, and wildlife; and *aesthetic*, including visual and noise considerations. The information was obtained from interviews with local public and private individuals and agencies, official publications and documents, various published data and literature, and on-site investigations. Specific mappable on-site information was recorded at a scale of 1 inch = 500 feet. Because of the utility's need for a permanent data bank, maps were computerized. Human forces and regional trends were presented in an accompanying narrative.

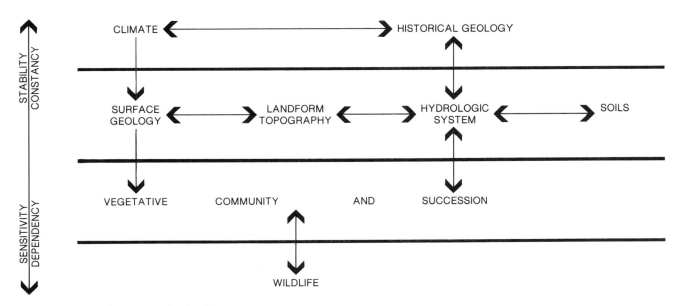

EXHIBIT 4-2 Landscape causality levels.

LAND USABILITY
FLOW DIAGRAM OF PROCESS

TOPOGRAPHY
TOPOGRAPHIC ELEVATION
TOPOGRAPHIC SLOPE
TOPOGRAPHIC ASPECT
VISUAL EXPOSURE
HORIZONTAL DISTANCE
DISTANCE TO SHORELINE
TERRAIN UNITS
GEOLOGY
SOILS
SUBWATERSHEDS
STREAM FLOW-QUANTITY
OFF-SITE WATERSHED CONTROL
PONDS, RESERVOIRS
MARSHES, MARSHY PONDS
CHEMICAL AND SILTATION PONDS
WATER QUALITY
AQUIFER POTENTIAL
FLOODING HAZARD
VEGETATION TYPE
VEGETATION DENSITY
WILDLIFE AND HABITAT
WIND EXPOSURE-DIRECTION AND SEASON
SUN EXPOSURE-TIME AND SEASON
SUN INTENSITY-TIME AND SEASON
SUMMER FOG PATTERNS

TOPOGRAPHY [1]

TOPOGRAPHIC ELEVATION [2A]

HORIZONTAL DISTANCE mapped as DISTANCE TO SHORELINE [2B]

COLD AIR POCKETS
PRECIPITATION
COASTAL CLIMATIC INFLUENCE
TEMPERATURE AND HUMIDITY
SEQUENTIAL SPACES-LINEAR
UNIQUE SPACES
SPECIAL VIEWPOINTS
SPECIAL FEATURES-GEOLOGIC
SPECIAL FEATURES-VEGETATION
BEACH QUALITY
TIDE POOL AREAS
VIEWSHED-OCEAN
VIEWSHED-SCENIC HIGHWAY
VIEWSHED-VARIOUS P.C. & A. OPERATIONS
NOISESHED-SCENIC HIGHWAY
NOISESHED-VARIOUS P.C. & A. OPERATIONS
EXISTING LAND USE
EXISTING LEASE
EXISTING MANMADE STRUCTURES
UTILITY INFORMATION
RAILROADS
ROADS
HIGHWAYSIDE PARKING
AUTO ACCESS-BEACHSIDE
PEDESTRIAN ACCESS-BEACH

DATA BANK

GEOLOGY [4AB]

TOPOGRAPHIC SLOPE [3]

TOPOGRAPHIC ASPECT [11]

WIND DIRECTION

SPRING-FALL SUN EXPOSURE 10:00 AM
SPRING-FALL SUN EXPOSURE 2:00 PM
SUMMER SUN EXPOSURE 10:00 AM
SUMMER SUN EXPOSURE 2:00 PM
WINTER SUN EXPOSURE 10:00 AM
WINTER SUN EXPOSURE 2:00 PM
[20]

TERRAIN UNITS [5AB]

NORTHEAST WIND EXPOSURE [12]
NORTHWEST WIND EXPOSURE [13]
SOUTHEAST WIND EXPOSURE [14]
SOUTHWEST WIND EXPOSURE [15]

SPRING-FALL SUN INTENSITY 10:00 AM [21]
SPRING-FALL SUN INTENSITY 2:00 PM [22]
SUMMER SUN INTENSITY 10:00 AM [23]
SUMMER SUN INTENSITY 2:00 PM [24]
WINTER SUN INTENSITY 10:00 AM [25]
WINTER SUN INTENSITY 2:00 PM [26]

* DATA HAS BEEN ENCODED BUT MAPS
NOT PRINTED FOR THIS REPORT

DATA BANK MAPS

NORTHEAST WIND EXPOSURE [12]
NORTHWEST WIND EXPOSURE [13]
TOPOGRAPHIC SLOPE [3]

VEGETATION TYPE [7]
VEGETATION DENSITY [8]

NORTHWEST WIND EXPOSURE [13]
WILDLIFE INVENTORY [9]
SUBWATERSHEDS AND SURFACE WATER [10]

RAINFALL [27]

SOILS [6]

TOPOGRAPHIC SLOPE [3]
DEPTH OF SOIL
SOIL WATER HOLDING CAPACITY
SOIL SURFACE PERMEABILITY
SOIL SUBSURFACE PERMEABILITY

SPRING WIND EXPOSURE [16]
FALL WIND EXPOSURE [17]
SUMMER WIND EXPOSURE [18]
WINTER WIND EXPOSURE [19]

SUMMER FOG COLD AIR POCKETS RAINFALL SALT AIR EFFECT [27]
SPRING-FALL DAILY SUN INTENSITY [28]
SUMMER DAILY SUN INTENSITY [29]
WINTER DAILY SUN INTENSITY [30]

NOISESHED (TRACTORS WITHOUT MUFFLERS) [31]

VIEWSHED - LIMESTONE QUARRY (GROUND LEVEL + 5 FEET) [32]
VIEWSHED - LIMESTONE QUARRY (GROUND LEVEL + 100 FEET) [33]
VIEWSHED - LIMESTONE QUARRY (GROUND LEVEL + 200 FEET) [34]
VIEWSHED - LIMESTONE QUARRY (STORAGE STRUCTURE) [35]
VIEWSHED - SHALE QUARRY (GROUND LEVEL + 5 FEET) [36]
VIEWSHED - SHALE QUARRY (GROUND LEVEL + 100 FEET) [37]
VIEWSHED - CONVEYOR SYSTEM [38]
VIEWSHED - CEMENT PLANT (TOP OF BUILDINGS) [39]
VIEWSHED - CEMENT PLANT (TOP OF STACK) [40]
VIEWSHED - CEMENT PLANT (OVERBURDEN AREA) [41]
VIEWSHED - SCENIC HIGHWAY [42]

EXHIBIT 4-3 Land viability flow diagram.

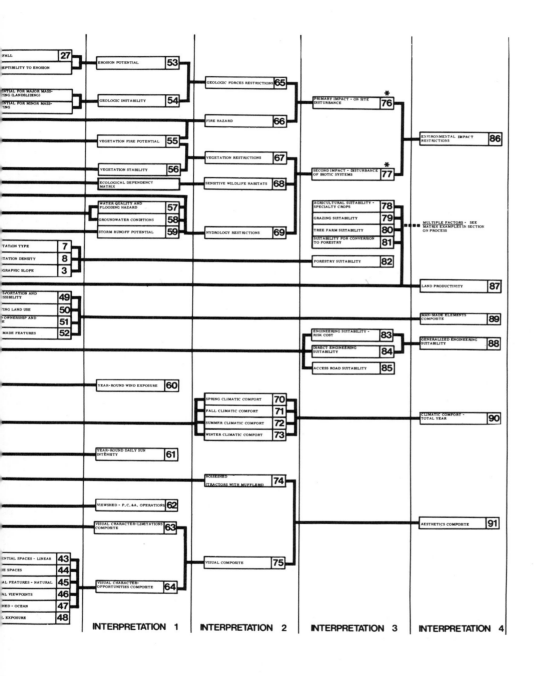

INTERPRETATION 1	**INTERPRETATION 2**	**INTERPRETATION 3**	**INTERPRETATION 4**

EXHIBIT 4-4 Sample evaluation matrix. Ratings based on a 0–10 scale indicate for each terrain unit its suitability for engineering, its potential productivity, and its susceptibility to environmental impact if developed.

LAND USE OR LAND USE ACTION

TERRAIN UNITS — DATA	Excavability-mass grading	Trenchability	Trench wall stability	Erosion potential-cut slope	Stability-cut slope	Compromise-reduce cut slope	Erosion potential-fill slope	Stability-fill slope	Compromise-reduce fill slope	Suitability for fill	Tunneling conditions	Bearing capacity-light loads	Bearing capacity-heavy loads	Shrink-swell potential
Embankment fill	8	8	5	5	5	67 to 50	4	6	67 to 50	8	4	6	3	1
Quarry spoil	4	4 to 9	2	8 to 1	1	67 to 50	3 to 1	7	100 to 67	5	1	4	2	1
Tailings	2	10	1	4	1	<20	5	2	50 to 20	2	1	2	1	5
Beach sand	8	10	2	10	1	67 to 50	10	6	67 to 50	4	1	5	3	1
Wind-blown sand	9	10	2	9	2	67 to 50	7	6	50	5	1	7	3	1
Canyon bottom soil	8	8	5	8	5	<50	3	4	50 to 40	5 to 6	2	9	5	2
Slope wash	8	8	7	4	4	50	3	4	50 to 40	7	3	8	5	3
Earth flows	8	9	4	5	1	<38	3	7	50	6	1	6	3	3
Landslide: relatively flat bench	5	5	4 to 3	3	3	33 to 67	3	5	50	9	3	9	4	2
Landslide: closed depression	7	7	3 to 8	4	2	33 to 67	2	7	50	6	2	6	2	4
Landslide: remainder of slide (incl. face & toe)	5	4	2 to 8	3	2	33 to 67	7	7	50	9	3	8	2	2
Terrace deposits	10	8	8	7	8	200 to 50	2	8	67 to 50	8	5	9	7	2
Mudstone-flat bench (< than 20%)	4	2	10	1	8	vert. to 50	2	8	67 to 50	9	10	10	9	1
Mudstone-predom. steep canyon walls (>than 20%)	5	4	9	2	7	200 to 67	3	7	50	9	10	9	7	1
Mudstone-same as above but heavily forested	6	6	6 to 3	3	6	100 to 50	9	7	50	8	9	8	5	1
Sandstone-canyon wall exposure	8	7	7	8	6	200 to 67	9	8	50	8	5	8	6	
Sandstone-canyon bottom areas	9	9	3	8	5	100 to 50	9	8	50	7	3	7	6	2
Sandstone-ridge capping exposure	8	8	8	8	6	200 to 67	9	7	7 to 30	8	5	10	7	1
Decomposed granite	9	8	9	6	7	200 to 67	9	7	67 to 30	8	8	10	8	
Marble	2	1	9	1	9	vert. 280	2	10	67	2	7	10	10 to 1	1

ENGINEERING

ENVIRONMENTAL CONDITIONS, PROPERTIES ACTIONS, AND IMPLICATIONS

252

LAND PRODUCTIVITY

ENVIRONMENTAL IMPACT

Action ■ Reaction

Septic tank suitability	Dustiness	Trafficability-muddiness	Hardness when dry	Depth to water table	Aquifer recharge potential	Groundwater availability (major source)	Groundwater availability (minor source)	Spring location potential	Soil permeability-subsurface	Soil permeability-surface	Soil water holding capacity	Soil depth	Cutting-unloading	Filling-loading	Spraying-chemicals, oils	Fertilizing	Surface water addition-irrigation, septic, pond	Surface water removal	Planting	Grazing	Clearing	Burning	Runoff potential	Erosion potential	Minor mass wasting potential	Landslide potential	Vegetation stability-elimination potential	Stream flow reduction	Stream pollution potential	Groundwater pollution potential	Flood potential	Wildlife sensitivity-destruction potential
	RELATIVE WEIGHT																															
3	6	6	4	9		1	1	1	8	5	6	10											4	2	2					4	0	
7	4to3	10to3	7	10to4		1	3	3	9	10to8	5to1	8to10											0to10	9to10	2to10					8	0	
1	10	10	9	1		1	1	1	1	1	10	8to10											4	4	4to0					3	0	
8	1	7	1	1		1	1	1	10	9	3	1to8											10	0	0					6	10	
0	3	6	1	8		1	2	2	10	9	4	10											8	6	6					4	2to8	
6	8	9	3	2		7	10	7	8	7	10	10											8	4	0					9	8	
3	3	7	8	4		1	6	6	3	2	8	10											4	6	4					4	4	
4	3	8	7	3	Summarized under 'Groundwater availability'	2	8	8	4	2	8	10											4	6	10					8	2	
3	3	5	8	5		3	5	4	9	6	3	8											2	2	4to0					8	2	
6	7	10	7	4		3	5	5	8	5	7	10											0	4	4to10					8	8	
3	3	6	8	5		5	10	8	9	6	3	8											2	8	4to0					8	2	
9	6	8	2	7		3	8	4to10	10to2	7	8	3											6	4	2					8	2	
2	1	10	10			2	3	2	3	1	1	1											2	0	2					3	2	
2	3	3	10	8		2	4	5	3	3	3	3											2	4	2					4	2	
2	6	9	6			2	6	5	5	5	8	8											2	2	4					5	2	
7	3	3	2	8		4	8	8	8	8	8	8											6	6	4					9	2	
4	5	7	4	2		9	10	8	8	7	10	10											6	4	0					10	8	
3	3	3	2	9		1	2	2	8	7	8	3											4	6	4					4	0	
2	2	2	2	8		2	4	0	3	5	7	3											4	6	4					4	7to8	
3	1	1to7	10	8to1		10	10	10	10	3	1	2to1											0	2	2					10	7to8	

253

INTERPRETATION Interpretation required the data to be combined and weighted according to their relative importance and interdependence, which varied when considered from the six standpoints described below.

1 *Environmental impact.* This level of approach was an attempt to identify the problem areas most immediately sensitive to development and so to avoid or mitigate the potential chain reaction of environmental degradation. The analysis grew out of landscape causality considerations and treated the land as a system which could either be affected or affect land-use modifications. It formed the basis for development guidelines as well as for siting recommendations.

2 *Land productivity.* This approach to the site dealt with its potential "growing power" for commercial plantings of any kind, an especially important consideration for a landscape whose primary existing uses are agriculture, grazing, and timber production. The influencing variables mainly included slope, coastal climatic influence, and soil properties.

3 *Generalized engineering suitability.* This rather loose term was an attempt to describe the land's workability—its ease of modification. Data synthesis was approached by way of a classification system of *terrain units,* areas of land with associated properties and conditions (suitability). The system was directed at indicating the potential of each unit for virtually any land use and the public costs which might derive from these units for various land uses in response to the indicated market demand.

4 *Constructed features.* This component of the approach was a simple composite of physical features such as roads and buildings and legal or political areas including districts, property lines, and other boundaries.

5 *Climatic considerations.* This was a compilation of data relating to wind, sun exposure, rainfall, fog, and coastal influence directed primarily at identifying *comfort zones* but having application to land productivity and other factors as well.

6 *Aesthetic considerations.* Finally, this effort combined subjective visual site analysis with considerations of ocean view potential and of visual and noise limitations presented by the existence of the coast highway and various cement and aggregates operations.

The information and interrelationships involved in each interpretation are expressed in Exhibit 4-3.

PLANNING AND DESIGN Planning and design included determination of appropriate land-use types, densities, and spatial arrangements. This task was based on the information interpretations described above and on an understanding of market demand.

EVALUATION Evaluation included the testing of land-use proposals in terms of their social, environmental, political, and economic consequences and their response to aesthetic, climatic, and engineering values established for the land. Matrices were developed to aid in analyzing the relationship between data and the proposed actions. Exhibit 4-4 presents one of these matrices, relating terrain units to engineering, land productivity, and environmental impact considerations associated with or affecting the proposed land-use actions.

Conclusions

Land-use evaluation led to identification of areas most suitable for forestry, housing, recreation, agriculture, and other uses. It also resulted in selection of a general location, but not a specific site, for the utility's power plant. These recommendations are shown in the development and open-space plans (Exhibit 4-5). In addition, PG&E was provided with the means of interpreting and, if necessary, modifying those recommendations.

Although this phase of the Davenport studies was not related solely to major-facilities siting, it provides a valuable example of a permanent data bank and decision-making process which may be readily applied to site selection and evaluation.

In developing the tools for a continuing series of siting and land-use decisions it is important to build in flexibility. The process should be quickly responsive at any time and at any level both initially and as long as practicable thereafter. This study illustrates that an organization of the data into meaningful categories of like kind and of like implications helps in achieving flexibility and dynamism.

The process must regard the landscape as a source of determinants on a lasting scale but must draw also from probable and potential land uses with their attendant demands and potential for land modification. Finally, a decision on approach requires a close look at constructed features and determinants to see what physical or aesthetic opportunities and limitations they present.

POWER PLANT SITING STUDY

In the next phase of the Davenport study, EDAW was asked to examine the previously selected general location for the proposed nuclear power plant in terms of aesthetic and terrestrial environmental impacts. Other investigations, mainly of geologic engineering feasibility, were being conducted concurrently by the utility.

The purpose of this phase was to integrate aesthetic and environmental evaluations with cost, feasibility, geologic, seismologic, and marine ecological studies in determining the optimum site for the power generation facilities.

Process

Again, we should remind readers that the range of concerns relative to nuclear power in 1971 was still rather limited. The following steps were taken in the site-evaluation process:

· Identify and understand the basic elements of the problem by visiting other nuclear power plants, relating them to the Davenport site, and preparing aesthetic descriptions or inventories of power plants and their related facilities; describing and recording the visual-physical qualities to the Davenport site; and developing basic conformation and size assumptions for the Davenport plant.

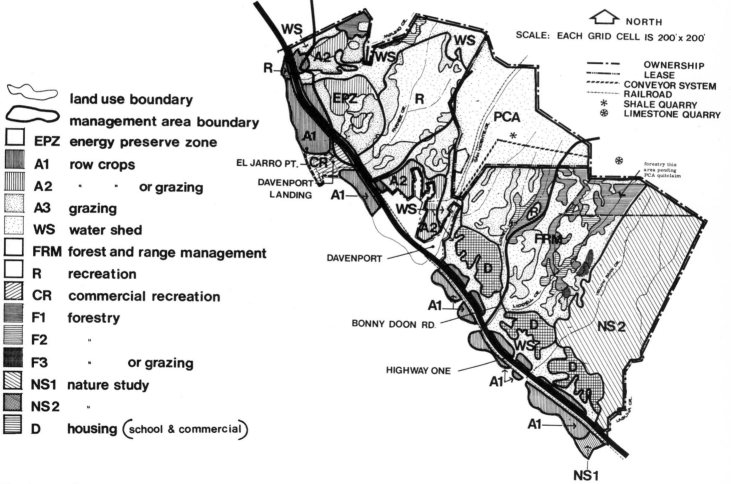

land use boundary
management area boundary
EPZ energy preserve zone
A1 row crops
A2 "   "   or grazing
A3 grazing
WS water shed
FRM forest and range management
R recreation
CR commercial recreation
F1 forestry
F2 "
F3 "   or grazing
NS1 nature study
NS2 "
D housing (school & commercial)

DEVELOPMENT PLAN

NORTH
SCALE: EACH GRID CELL IS 200' x 200'

—————— OWNERSHIP
— — — — LEASE
- - - - - - - CONVEYOR SYSTEM
||||||||| RAILROAD
* SHALE QUARRY
⊛ LIMESTONE QUARRY

forestry this area pending PCA quitclaim

EXHIBIT 4-5 Recommended development plan for the Davenport site.

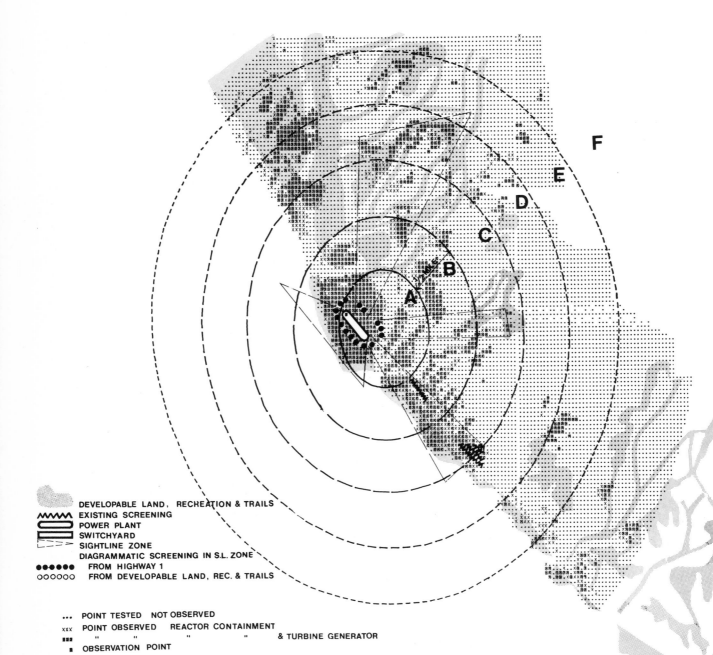

F

E

D

C

B

A

DEVELOPABLE LAND, RECREATION & TRAILS
EXISTING SCREENING
POWER PLANT
SWITCHYARD
SIGHTLINE ZONE
DIAGRAMMATIC SCREENING IN S.L. ZONE
●●●●●● FROM HIGHWAY 1
○○○○○○ FROM DEVELOPABLE LAND, REC. & TRAILS

••• POINT TESTED NOT OBSERVED
xxx POINT OBSERVED REACTOR CONTAINMENT
▪▪▪ " " " " & TURBINE GENERATOR
▪ OBSERVATION POINT

POWER PLANT SITE PLAN 5 UNIT 1

VISIBILITY STUDY

EXHIBIT 4-6 Visibility study.

· Determine the importance of the degree and nature of visibility of the proposed power plant by examining the preceding element descriptions within the regional social and political context.

· Identify populated or frequented areas within the study area, which was not limited to the utility's property, in order to establish the critical viewpoints.

· Test six representative alternative site plans to determine the areas from which they would be visible.

· Evaluate the visibility impact in terms of the distance of the viewer from the plant (Exhibit 4-6).

· Identify problems of access, screening, and protection of natural and historic resources in the six alternative site plans, and propose design solutions to these problems.

· Make final recommendations regarding the specific schemes tested, and from these establish general guidelines for future power plant site evaluation and selection.

FINDINGS AND RECOMMENDATIONS

A fundamental assumption of the study was that the rural landscape of the coast was and would remain valuable as a needed contrast to the built-up environment. The Davenport area and the small town of Davenport were representative of this kind of coastal landscape, a cement plant being the only urban intrusion. Political and social concern for the preservation of rural land along the coast had been indicated by such actions as the designation of the coast road, State Highway 1, as a scenic highway. The plant-siting arrangement had to respect and preserve the rural quality of the area. The most important factor in establishing the aesthetic and environmental compatibility of the power plant was found to be the degree of visibility from Highway 1, from potentially developable areas, and from recreation and trail areas.

A second assumption central to the study approach was that although nuclear power plants and related appurtenances are urban and industrial in character, they need not be visually unattractive in themselves. It was recognized that the power plant in particular had a good deal of design potential and could become a handsome structure.

It was also believed that the proposed installation could become a tourist attraction. It should be treated to emphasize its design possibilities, including construction of appropriate visitor facilities. However, the great size and urban-industrial quality of a nuclear power plant and its related components could easily disturb the rural quality of the landscape at Davenport. Site arrangement

and design therefore should emphasize harmony with existing landforms, vegetation, wildlife, and historical and cultural features.

Each of the six power plant and switchyard site plans was rated in terms of level of visibility, assuming only natural screening and using the computerized visibility study process illustrated in Exhibit 4-6. (The data for this component of the study were derived from the data base developed for the land-use study.) Results were as follows:

Power Plants	Visibility from Highway 1
Site Plan 1	Moderate
Site Plan 2	High
Site Plan 3	Moderate
Site Plan 4	Low
Site Plan 5	High
Site Plan 6	High

Power plants	Visibility from development and recreation areas
Site Plan 1	Moderate
Site Plan 2	High
Site Plan 3	Moderate
Site Plan 4	Low
Site Plan 5	High
Site Plan 6	High

230-kilovolt switchyards	Visibility from Highway 1
Site Plan 1	Low
Site Plan 2	High
Site Plan 3	High
Site Plan 4	Moderate
Site Plan 5	Low
Site Plan 6	Moderate

230-kilovolt switchyards	Visibility from development and recreation areas
Site Plan 1	Low
Site Plan 2	High
Site Plan 3	High
Site Plan 4	Moderate
Site Plan 5	High
Site Plan 6	Moderate

115-kilovolt switchyards	Visibility from Highway 1
Site Plan 1	Low
Site Plan 2	Moderate

Site Plan 3	Moderate
Site Plan 4	Moderate
Site Plan 5	Moderate
Site Plan 6	Moderate
115-kilovolt switchyards	**Visibility from development and recreation areas**
Site Plan 1	Low
Site Plan 2	High
Site Plan 3	High
Site Plan 4	High
Site Plan 5	Moderate
Site Plan 6	High

The degree of visibility of the power plant was found to be generally a function of relationship to the topography. The lowest potential for visibility would result from locating at higher elevations (the second marine terrace). Moderate potential for visibility would result from locating in the gullies behind the Davenport landing. A potential for high visibility would result from locating at lower elevations (the first terrace).

Power plant and switchyard visibility could be reduced by earth forming and planting. Additional potential existed to improve aesthetic and environmental compatibility with the site by raising or lowering the plant relative to the data considered in the study.

The study revealed additional factors requiring special design consideration. These included:

- Highway and rail access
- Potential harbor development if a breakwater were required for plant construction
- Location of visitor facilities
- Transmission line visibility

Environmental and Aesthetic Guidelines Related to Siting

The goal of siting the power plant and its related facilities was to preserve the rural coastal atmosphere of the site. Studies of the six representative site arrangements, including the degree of visibility, led to the general guidelines for aesthetic considerations relating to siting nuclear power plants on the Davenport site described below.

The less visible the power plant, switchyards, and construction yards, the more likely they were to be visually acceptable in the context of the site. Visibility of the power plant could be reduced by locating it in areas of higher elevation and/or by lowering the profile of the structures. The site arrangement should be in harmony with existing landforms, vegetation, wildlife, and historical and cultural features.

Constructed and natural elements on the site were to be left undisturbed unless change, relocation, or removal resulted in an overall environmental and aesthetic benefit.

- Highway 1 appeared to require relocation in Site Plan 5. In Site Plans 1, 2, and 3 the facilities could be screened as effectively with or without a relocated road. Any necessary relocation should be accomplished with minimum inconvenience and change in natural or constructed features.
- Rail access to the plant should allow for preservation of existing eucalyptus trees, historic farm buildings, and other natural and constructed features to the greatest extent possible.
- Highway access to the plant should be accomplished in a manner resulting in minimum disruption of travel along Highway 1 and making use of existing roadways when possible.
- Planting and earth forms used for screening should be harmonious additions to existing vegetation and landforms.
- Location of construction yards should be accomplished to minimize impact on existing views and natural and constructed features.
- Potential harbor development should preserve the existing rural coastal quality of the site.

The entire power plant zone, including switchyards, construction yards, and related facilities, should be considered a single design problem. All the elements and adjacent land uses needed to be related in terms of function and aesthetics:

- The power plant should be designed to emphasize sculptural qualities and to express the functions of major elements of the plant to the visitor. If lower-profile plants were to become technologically feasible, they should be used to help reduce visual impact.
- Visitor facilities should be located so that they present an informative and attractive view of the plant and related structures. These facilities should be located so that the plant receives front lighting most of the day. Access roads should be convenient, not interfere with plant operations, and present interesting sequential views of the whole operating area.
- Construction yards and other temporary facilities should be screened with earth mounds and planting.
- Switchyards should be constructed in the location having the lowest visibility (Site Plan 1) and should be carefully sited to be in harmony with existing landforms. Switchyards should

be screened to reduce visibility as indicated in the design critiques.

· The possibility of using low-profile or underground transmission lines between the power plant and the switchyards should be vigorously explored.

Ratings of Site Plans

The six site plans tested, Exhibits 4-7, 4-8, and 4-9, for which only environmental and aesthetic guidelines were considered, were rated as to general level of acceptability. Site Plans 1 and 3 appeared to offer the best solutions of the six tested. The natural gullies in which they were located offered considerable natural screening and provided a good framework of topography for additional screening.

Site Plan 4, although it achieved the least visibility, was less acceptable. It would cause a massive excavation scar in the second terrace, which would generate a huge amount of excess material requiring disposal.

Site Plans 2 and 5, located on the first terrace, were also less acceptable than Site Plans 1 and 3. The facilities would be highly visible and difficult to screen. Their profiles would appear above the horizon, emphasizing their visual domination of the Davenport landscape.

Site Plan 5 had two desirable features. The switchyards were located in the same excavation as the power plant. This eliminated overhead transmission between plant and switchyard and helped to screen the switchyard. The plan permitted low-profile power transmission from the switchyard to a creek where conventional transmission towers could be more easily hidden. It was recommended that consideration be given to incorporating these ideas in Site Plans 1, 2, and 3.

Site Plan 6 was the least acceptable. The facilities occupied the most prominent location in the immediate area and could not be effectively screened. Views to the ocean from the highway and from surrounding areas would be blocked, and access to the ocean frontage would be restricted.

In summary, the following acceptability ratings were assigned to the three basic locational options for the plant, switchyards, and construction yards:

· Most acceptable   Gullies behind Davenport landing

Second terrace and first terrace on inland side of highway

· Least acceptable   First terrace on ocean side of highway

It was recommended that any further site planning observe these ratings.

TRANSMISSION ROUTING STUDY

Scope

The scope of this study consisted of the analysis necessary to determine feasibility, routing, right-of-way treatment, and design of transmission lines associated with the proposed power plant. Power demand, location of origin and destination points, transmission voltage, and structural engineering requirements (that is, project goals and definition) were determined by the sponsoring utility company. Requirements consisted of two 230-kilovolt lines from Davenport to Monte Vista, one 230-kilovolt line from Davenport to Mount Hermon, and one 230-kilovolt line from Mount Hermon to an existing line from Monte Vista to Metcalf. These locations can be seen in Exhibit 4-10, which also shows the preferred alignments resulting from the study.

The study area was and still is largely undeveloped and mountainous. Much of it is forested, and several state parks lie within its boundaries. Extreme care was required in routing and development guidelines to ensure that, once installed, the lines would become incidental elements of generally minor impact on the mountains.

Process

The route-selection process was guided by a number of premises regarding the potential impacts of overhead transmission lines on the Santa Cruz Mountains. Since the study area was largely undeveloped, social constraints were expected to be relatively low. Visual, physical, and economic constraints in the rugged, forested, and visually impressive mountains would be high and very numerous.

Objectives relating to physical and economic feasibility and to limitation of visual and sociocultural impact were established. Of these the visual objectives proved to be the most influential in route selection.

The process was one of identifying areas of relative sensitivity to landscape modification in order to follow the path of least sensitivity and to develop special criteria for traversing unavoidable highly sensitive areas.

Two important assumptions were made regarding visual impact and landscape modification. First, it was assumed that when routed and developed to minimize visibility and clearing and in accordance with detailed design and environmental guidelines, conventional 230-kilovolt overhead transmission lines could become incidental elements of mostly minor impact on the mountain landscape. Exhibit 4-10 indicates that the study area was se-

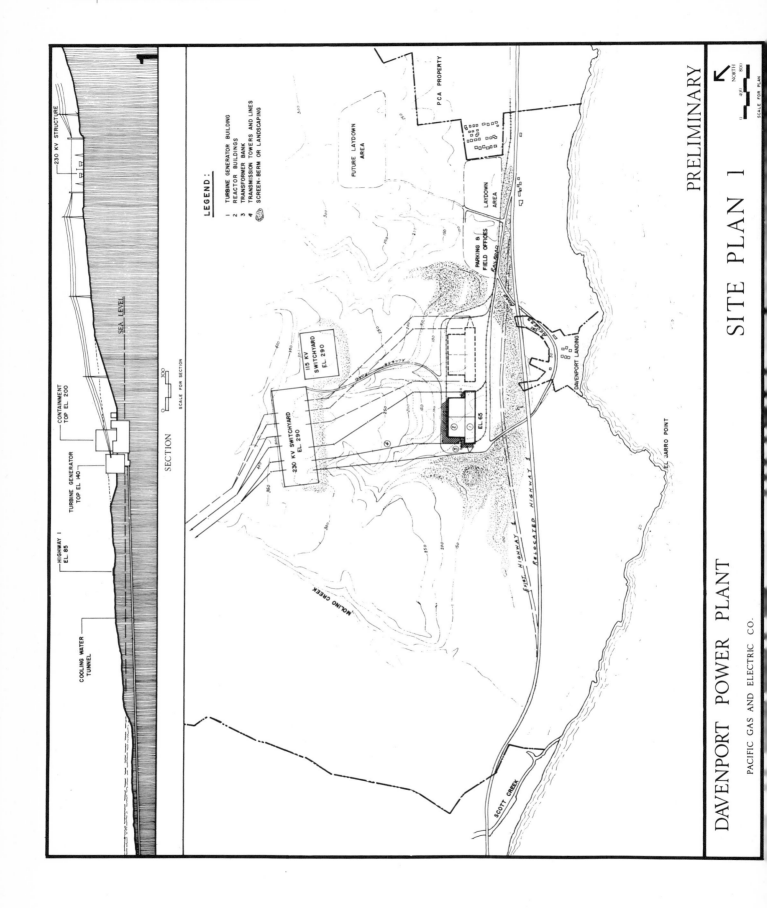

PRELIMINARY

SITE PLAN 1

DAVENPORT POWER PLANT

PACIFIC GAS AND ELECTRIC CO.

LEGEND:

1 TURBINE GENERATOR BUILDING
2 REACTOR BUILDINGS
3 TRANSFORMER BANK
4 TRANSMISSION TOWERS AND LINES
   SCREEN-BERM OR LANDSCAPING

SECTION

SCALE FOR SECTION

NORTH

SCALE FOR PLAN

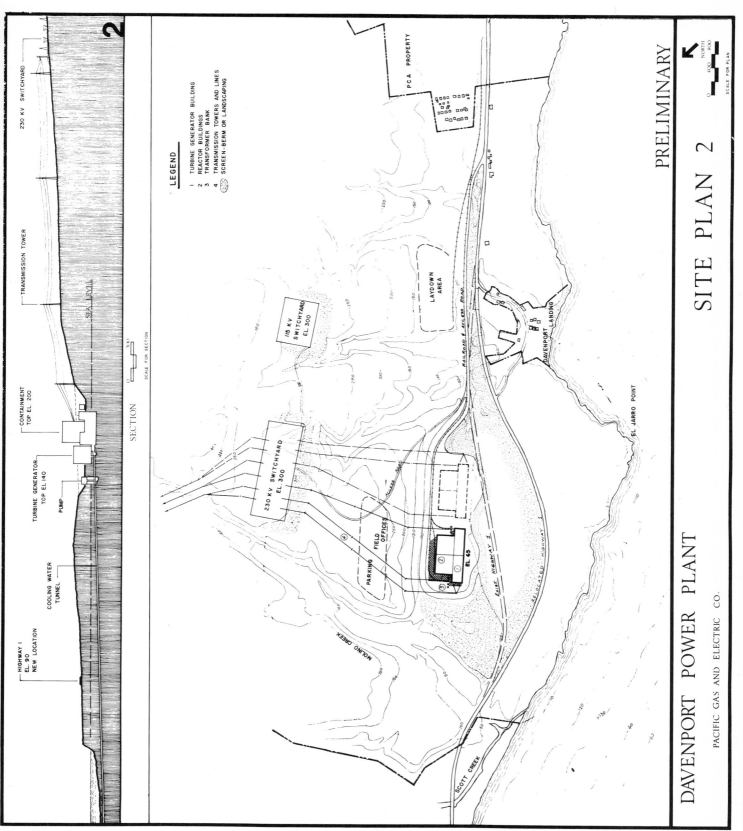

LEGEND

1 TURBINE GENERATOR BUILDING
2 REACTOR BUILDINGS
3 TRANSFORMER BANK
4 TRANSMISSION TOWERS AND LINES
SCREEN-BERM OR LANDSCAPING

PRELIMINARY

SITE PLAN 2

DAVENPORT POWER PLANT

PACIFIC GAS AND ELECTRIC CO.

EXHIBIT 4-7 Davenport power plant: alternative Site Plans 1 and 2.

3

230 KV SWITCHYARD
EL. 320

CONTAINMENT
TOP EL. 235

TURBINE GENERATOR
TOP EL. 140

SEA LEVEL

EXISTING HIGHWAY I
EL. 85

COOLING WATER
TUNNEL

SECTION

0   300

SCALE FOR SECTION

LEGEND:

1   TURBINE GENERATOR BUILDING
2   REACTOR BUILDINGS
3   TRANSFORMER BANK
4   TRANSMISSION TOWERS AND LINES
     SCREEN-BERM OR LANDSCAPING

PCA PROPERTY

LAYDOWN
AREA

FIELD
OFFICES

PARKING

115 KV
SWITCHYARD
EL. 300

EL. 65

230 KV SWITCHYARD
EL. 300

DAVENPORT
LANDING

EL JARRO POINT

MOLINO CREEK

HIGHWAY 1

SCOTT CREEK

PRELIMINARY

NORTH

0   400   800

SCALE FOR PLAN

SITE PLAN 3

DAVENPORT POWER PLANT

PACIFIC GAS AND ELECTRIC CO.

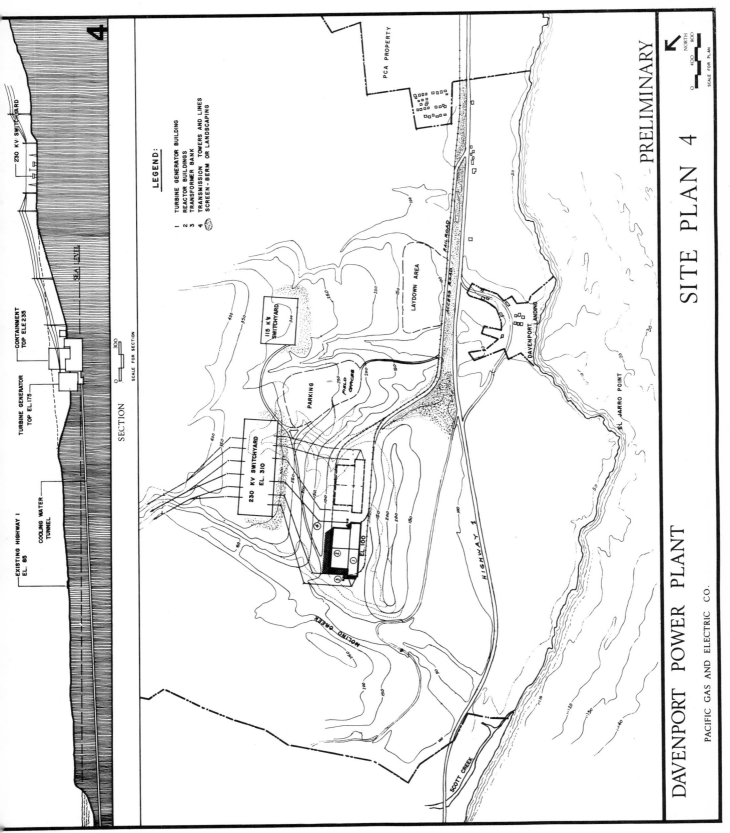

SECTION

SITE PLAN 4 — PRELIMINARY

DAVENPORT POWER PLANT

PACIFIC GAS AND ELECTRIC CO.

LEGEND:

1 TURBINE GENERATOR BUILDING
2 REACTOR BUILDINGS
3 TRANSFORMER BANK
4 TRANSMISSION TOWERS AND LINES
SCREEN - BERM OR LANDSCAPING

EXHIBIT 4-8 Davenport power plant: alternative Site Plans 3 and 4.

DAVENPORT POWER PLANT

PACIFIC GAS AND ELECTRIC CO.

SITE PLAN 5

PRELIMINARY

NORTH

0 400 800
SCALE FOR PLAN

LEGEND:

1 TURBINE GENERATOR BUILDING
2 REACTOR BUILDINGS
3 TRANSFORMER BANK
4 TRANSMISSION TOWERS AND LINES
5 SCREEN - BERM OR LANDSCAPING

SECTION

0 300
SCALE FOR SECTION

HIGHWAY 1
EL. 70

COOLING WATER
TUNNEL

TURBINE GENERATOR
TOP EL. 140

CONTAINMENT
TOP EL. 200

230 KV SWITCHYARD

SEA LEVEL

5

PCA PROPERTY

RAILROAD & ACCESS ROAD

LAYDOWN AREA

PARKING

FIELD OFFICES

DAVENPORT LANDING

EL. JARRO POINT

115 KV SWITCHYARD

230 KV SWITCHYARD
EL. 100

EL. 65

MOLINO CREEK

RELOCATED HIGHWAY 1

EXIST. HIGHWAY 1

SCOTT CREEK

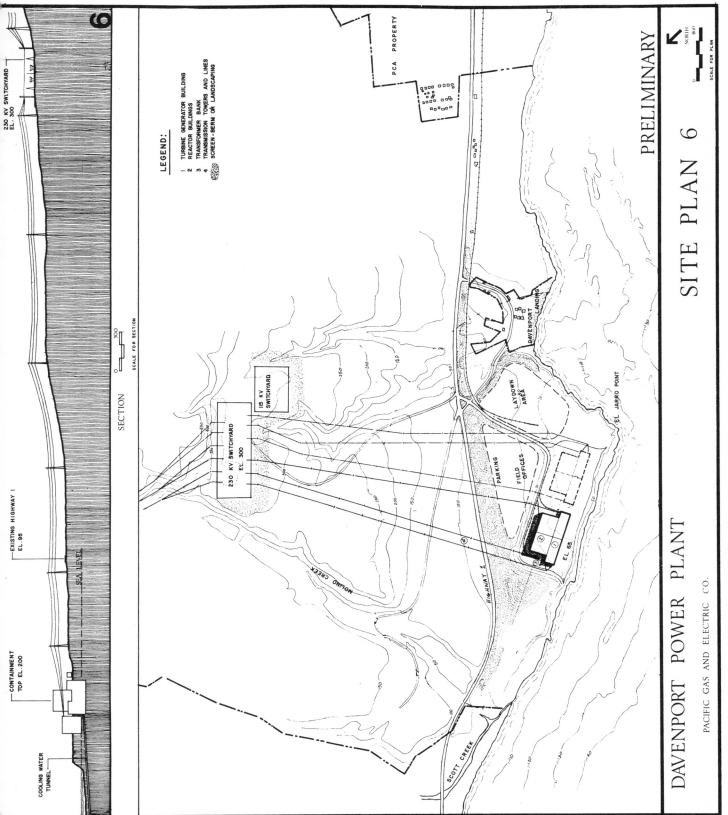

DAVENPORT POWER PLANT

PACIFIC GAS AND ELECTRIC CO.

PRELIMINARY

SITE PLAN 6

EXHIBIT 4-9 Davenport power plant: alternative Site Plans 5 and 6.

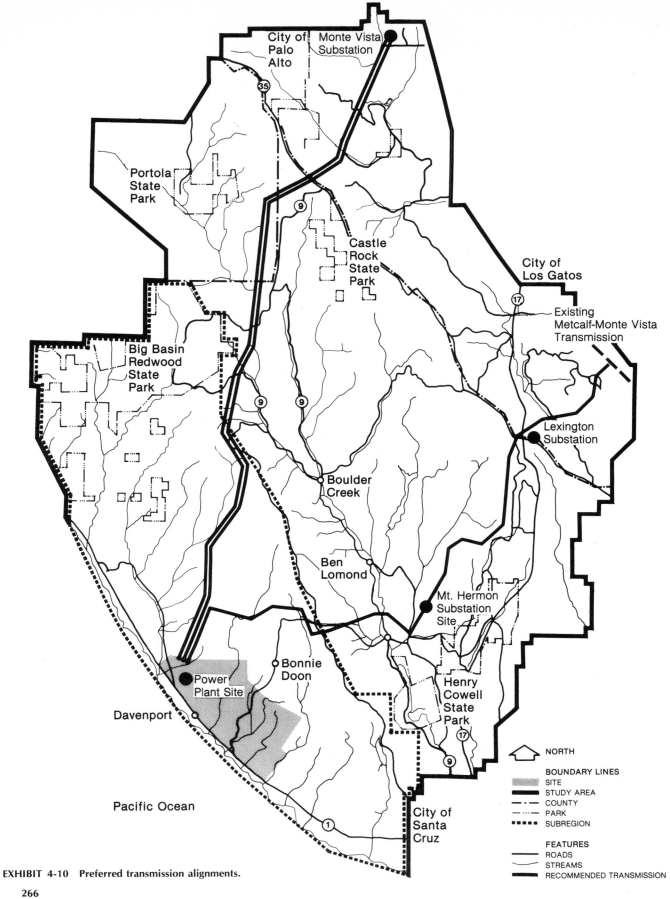

NORTH

BOUNDARY LINES
SITE
STUDY AREA
COUNTY
PARK
SUBREGION

FEATURES
ROADS
STREAMS
RECOMMENDED TRANSMISSION

EXHIBIT 4-10 Preferred transmission alignments.

266

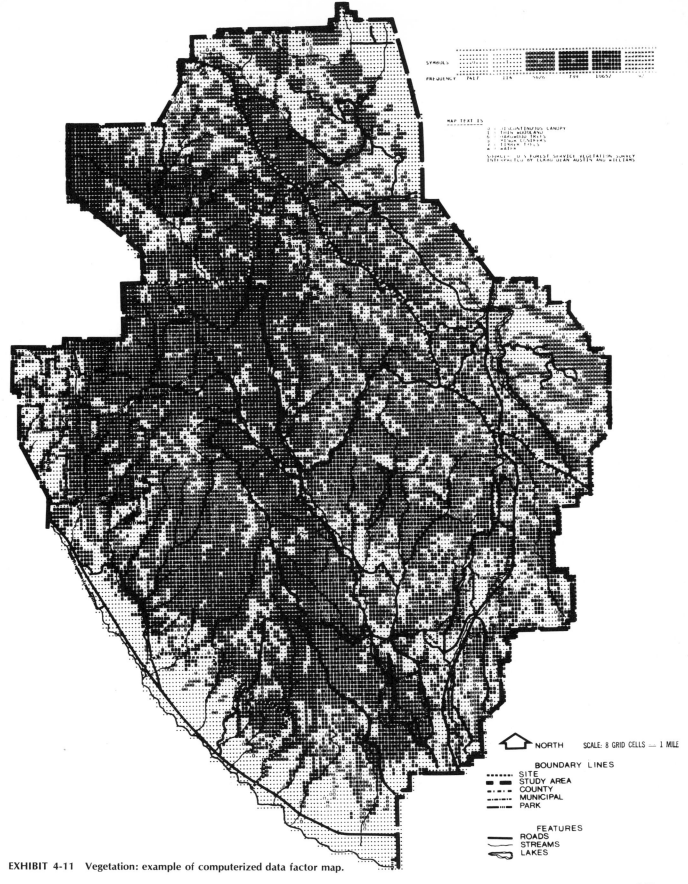

EXHIBIT 4-11 Vegetation: example of computerized data factor map.

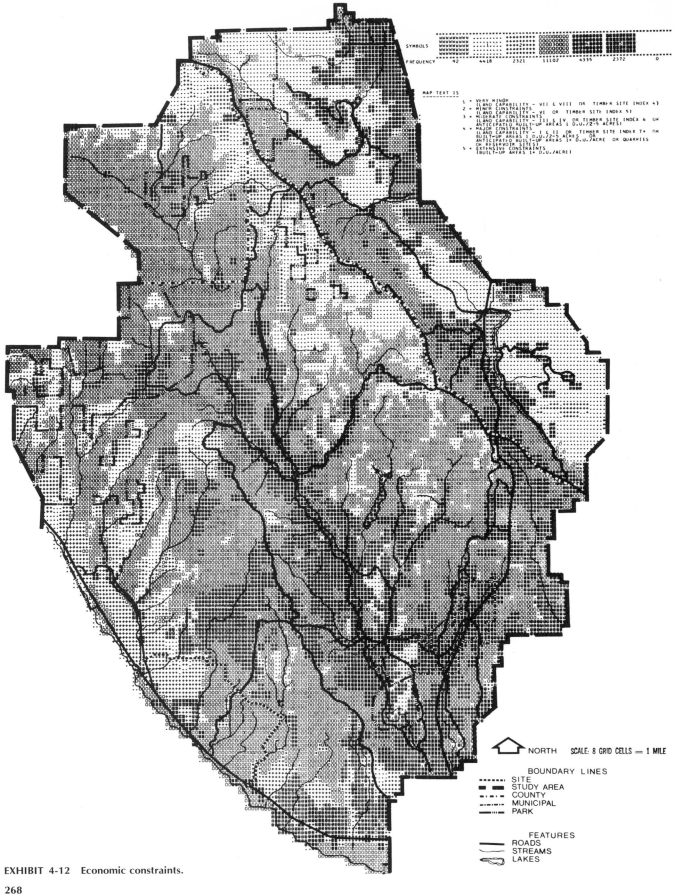

SYMBOLS

FREQUENCY   92   4418   2321   11102   4335   2372   0

MAP TEXT IS

1 = VERY MINOR
    (LAND CAPABILITY - VII & VIII OR TIMBER SITE INDEX 4)
2 = MINOR CONSTRAINTS
    (LAND CAPABILITY - VI OR TIMBER SITE INDEX 5)
3 = MODERATE CONSTRAINTS
    (LAND CAPABILITY - III & IV OR TIMBER SITE INDEX 6 OR
    ANTICIPATED BUILT-UP AREAS 1 D.U./2-5 ACRES)
4 = MAJOR CONSTRAINTS
    (LAND CAPABILITY - I & II OR TIMBER SITE INDEX 7+ OR
    BUILT-UP AREAS 1 D.U./2-5 ACRES OR
    ANTICIPATED BUILT-UP AREAS 1+ D.U./ACRE OR QUARRIES
    OR RESERVOIR SITES)
5 = EXTENSIVE CONSTRAINTS
    (BUILT-UP AREAS 1+ D.U./ACRE)

NORTH   SCALE: 8 GRID CELLS = 1 MILE

BOUNDARY LINES

SITE
STUDY AREA
COUNTY
MUNICIPAL
PARK

FEATURES
ROADS
STREAMS
LAKES

EXHIBIT 4-12 Economic constraints.

268

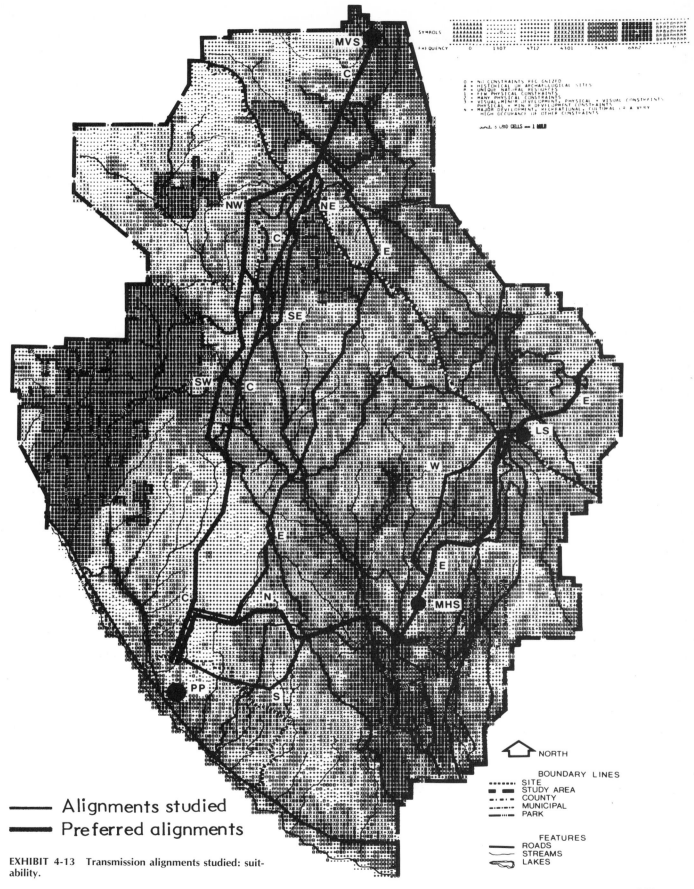

SYMBOLS

FREQUENCY   0   1307   4712   4301   7458   6862

0 = NO CONSTRAINTS RECOGNIZED
A = HISTORICAL OR ARCHAEOLOGICAL SITES
R = UNIQUE NATURAL RESOURCES
1 = FEW PHYSICAL CONSTRAINTS
2 = MANY PHYSICAL CONSTRAINTS
3 = VISUAL+MINOR DEVELOPMENT, PHYSICAL + VISUAL CONSTRAINTS
   PHYSICAL + MIN.R DEVELOPMENT CONSTRAINTS
4 = MAJOR DEVELOPMENT, RECREATIONAL, CULTURAL OR A VERY
   HIGH OCCURANCE OF OTHER CONSTRAINTS

3 GRID CELLS = 1 MILE

NORTH

BOUNDARY LINES
SITE
STUDY AREA
COUNTY
MUNICIPAL
PARK

FEATURES
ROADS
STREAMS
LAKES

——— Alignments studied
━━━ Preferred alignments

EXHIBIT 4-13 Transmission alignments studied: suitability.

269

lected to define an area beyond which transmission lines were impractical. It was large enough to allow the major effects of transmission line routes to be evaluated. It therefore included all of two state parks but excluded highly built-up areas on the eastern boundary.

Second, while desirable land-use opportunities such as trails and parks can be made possible by the construction of conventional overhead transmission lines, they can seldom be enhanced by their presence.

Existing regional data relevant to determination of physical and economic feasibility and landscape modification were collected from various county, state, and federal agencies. The data were encoded for computer use at a scale of ½ inch = 1 mile or at a grid cell scale of ⅛ mile by ⅛ mile and stored in the data bank. Computer maps produced directly from the basic data covered vegetation, geologic formations, existing development and recreation, historical and archaeological sites, natural resources of special interest, general plans, and topography.

The information contained on most of these maps was interpreted, sorted, and combined to produce maps specifically relating to key landscape modification factors. The factors were determined by the study team from field observation, examination of planning documents for Santa Cruz County, and U.S. Geological Survey topographic maps. The factor maps covered slope instability, soil color, soil-vegetation contrast, physiography, land capability for cultivation, timber trees, discontinuous canopy, unique vegetation forms, timber productivity, general visibility, and existing and anticipated development and recreation. An example of a factor map, on vegetation, is shown in Exhibit 4-11.

Further interpretive mapping was produced by grouping related elements in the first level of map interpretation. This second level of interpretation produced generalized maps showing physical, economic, visual, and sociocultural constraints to landscape modification. The economic constraints map is shown in Exhibit 4-12.

Visual impacts of transmission development were described as major (readily apparent and conspicuous), moderate (readily apparent but not conspicuous), and minor (not readily apparent). Terms used to relate the effectiveness of concealment were *substantially* (90 percent to completely concealed) and *partially* (50 to 90 percent concealed).

To facilitate selection of the best overall transmission corridors, a map of suitability for transmission lines was developed by weighting and combining all the foregoing

constraint information. This composite map may be found in Chapter 7 (Figure 7-17). It was compiled by using the following constraint definitions and weightings:

Weighting	Constraints
9	Existing and proposed parks
9	Existing and proposed scenic highways
9	Existing, future, and potential reservoirs
9	Built-up areas, one or more dwelling units per acre
9	Public institutions
5	Potential recreation areas
5	Private recreation areas
5	Built-up areas, one dwelling unit per 2 to 5 acres
5	Scenic areas within 4 miles of viewpoint
4	Anticipated built-up areas, one dwelling unit per acre
3	Scenic areas beyond 4 miles from viewpoint
2	Anticipated built-up areas, one dwelling unit per 2 to 5 acres
2	Timber tree areas
1	Course line and lowlands
1	Ridge lines and uplands
1	Soil-vegetation contrast areas
1	Areas of high risk of slope instability
1	Slopes of greater than 50 percent in discontinuous canopy
½	Visually degraded areas

Accumulated weighting	Suitability	Constraints
0	Very high	None recognized
1–2	High	Physical
3–4	Moderate	Major physical
5–8	Low	Visual or social, or physical and visual, or physical and social
9+	Very low	Extensive social or visual, or high occurrence of other constraints

Highly constraining point features (historic or archaeological sites and unique natural resources) were incorporated by the use of separately identifiable symbols.

Test alignments were drawn on clear acetate overlays following the routes of least constraint (see Exhibit 4-13). The test overlays were checked in the field and against all basic data maps for correctness and details. Further feasibility and alignment studies were conducted in those areas identified as highly sensitive. Visual impacts were studied by simulation at critical or typical points. Finally, a narrative and graphic description of each preferred alignment was prepared, recommending special design, land-use, and construction treatment in sensitive areas.

Case Study 5 | SWAN FALLS—GUFFEY

HYDROELECTRIC PROJECT

History of This Project

EDAW was contracted by the Idaho Power Company and the Idaho Water Resources Board in August 1978 to prepare the required Federal Energy Regulatory Commission (FERC) Exhibit W environmental report as part of the power license application for the proposed Swan Falls—Guffey hydroelectric project located on the Snake River southwest of Boise, Idaho.

The unique aspects of this case lie not in the process of site selection but in the final evaluation of an already selected site. The project sponsors proposed to raise an existing earth-fill dam to 82 feet and to construct another dam rising 75 feet, impounding 40 miles of river. The hydroelectric potential of the Grand View—Guffey reach of the Snake River had been studied for almost 30 years. Reconstruction of the existing Swan Falls Dam and construction of a new dam and power plant in the Guffey area had been proposed in the mid-1960s. Alternative plans had been evaluated in 1970.

Issues and Approach

The proposed Swan Falls—Guffey project represented the development of the hydroelectric potential of a reach of the Snake River with competing environmental interests. The principal competing use was the Snake River Birds of Prey Natural Area (BPNA). This area had received national prominence through a Bureau of Land Management protective withdrawal as well as through media exposure and visits by prominent governmental and public figures. There was also an unusually high concentration of archaeological and historic sites within the BPNA.

Preparation of the environmental report, which is similar in scope to an environmental impact statement, required analysis of many controversial environmental issues. The studies differed from the majority of environmental impact studies in that EDAW was asked specifi-

cally for its professional opinion on whether the project should be pursued through the FERC application for power license. Thus the environmental report was preceded by a *decision document* discussing key issues, identifying areas of likely opposition to the proposed project, and recommending a course of action for resolving conflict or opposition.

The publicized uniqueness of the BPNA led to the active involvement of national and international conservation organizations and state and local environmental groups. The interests of a number of federal, state, and local governmental agencies with regulatory or management responsibilities for lands within the Grand View—Guffey reach of the Snake River were also directly affected.

A 3-month investigation into the environmental issues associated with the development of the Swan Falls—Guffey project focused on the documentation of existing environmental conditions in the project area. This investigation provided the basis for identification of both positive and negative impacts and the development and assessment of mitigation opportunities.

In the course of the study, it became evident that the concerns expressed by the agencies and conservation groups would be the ones carrying the greatest weight in terms of possible administrative delay or legal obstacles which the client might encounter in the licensing process. The EDAW team therefore chose to:

· Document and report the concerns and potential environmental impacts of the project as seen by various governmental agencies

· Document and report the concerns and position of each conservation organization and, when possible, determine the probable course of action that various organizations might pursue should the project proceed

It was difficult initially to obtain written statements from most agencies and conservation groups before the official FERC review period.

However, in pointing out the importance of viewing a written statement as constructive input to the planning and environmental assessment process, EDAW was able to secure a representative cross section of most agency and conservation group concerns.

The concerns and opinions expressed on the potential impacts of the project were in most instances very general. The concerns of the government agencies were based primarily on their management objectives and regulatory responsibilities. The conservation group concerns stemmed from a common goal of protection and preservation of natural areas for use and enjoyment by existing and future generations.

The concerns identified by the agencies and conservation groups corresponded closely to five major issue areas identified and analyzed independently by the EDAW team. These were:

· Impacts on the raptor populations and other wildlife found in the Snake River BPNA

· Impacts on historical and archaeological resources known to exist in the canyon

· Impacts on the river fish, especially white sturgeon

· Impacts on free-flowing river recreational opportunities, including educational programs and tours of the BPNA

· Areawide growth-inducing impacts associated with the potential of future implementation of project irrigation features

Because conservation groups and indirectly affected agencies often are not involved during the planning of major facilities, their energies must be concentrated on responding to proposals during the review period after extensive environmental documentation and perhaps also in court proceedings. In the case of the Swan Falls–Guffey project, the formal opportunity for review would not have occurred until some months later, after extensive expenditure of effort and money. By pointing out the importance of viewing a written statement as constructive input to the planning and environmental assessment process, EDAW was able to secure the response of a representative cross section of agencies and conservation groups. The majority were surprised and pleased to be contacted early in the process.

In the final analysis, the concerns expressed by the agencies and conservation groups would be the ones carrying the greatest weight in terms of possible administrative delay or legal obstacles that could be encountered in the licensing process. The conclusions they drew differ from the findings of the EDAW team mainly in terms of the magnitude of adverse impacts. The fundamental question, regardless of the anticipated magnitude of impacts, was: "Could these differences of opinion relative to impacts be resolved between the parties to the point at which the project had a reasonable chance of surviving the environmental review process and obtaining a FERC license?"

The agency and conservation group positions seemed clear. If the project was pursued through the FERC application process, a very strong, influential, and experienced opposition would likely challenge the project on the basis of need, severity of impact, and unacceptable resource loss. This, coupled with a fundamental opposition to the project by conservation groups (i.e., the project in itself was in conflict with the goals of the organizations), suggested that no amount of technical data or offering of mitigation measures would be likely to reduce the opposition to the project. Differences of opinion on precise levels of impact are at best professional judgments and typically are subject to lengthy debate and challenge. This process is often extremely time-consuming and expensive, especially for the project proponent. Moreover, the environmental process as initiated by the National Environmental Policy Act of 1969 appears to have conditioned state and federal agencies to expect mitigation measures either to offset or to minimize *any* unavoidable adverse impacts. A significant adverse impact with no possible mitigation opportunity presents an almost intolerable situation.

The Swan Falls–Guffey project would have caused several unavoidable as well as *nonmitigable* impacts such as inundation of the riparian edge and its associated wildlife habitat, loss of white sturgeon habitat, and disruption (although the level of impact was debatable) of the habitat and population of birds of prey. The project would also have had a major impact on archaeological resources and would have resulted in a nonmitigable loss of recreation opportunities such as float boating. Few acceptable mitigation measures existed for these impacts, and therefore the question became: "Does the need for the project override the unavoidable adverse environmental effects?"

The need for additional energy generation capability for projected population growth in the state of Idaho was well documented and appeared defensible even under the most conservative of projections. However, the ability to overcome the likely environmental opposition, even in the face of demonstrated need, was questionable. As with all proposed energy projects regardless of fuel type, the question of pursuing other alternatives was raised and would be important in justifying the need for the Swan Falls–Guffey project.

It appeared, at least at the time when the study was conducted, that the only way to overcome the anticipated strong environmental opposition would be to show that *no other* reasonable alternative project location or equivalent energy source could be found. This could not be established since the client was simultaneously pursuing licenses for two other hydroelectric projects on the Snake River in less environmentally sensitive areas.

Conclusions and Final Decision

The EDAW team concluded that while the precise levels of impact on such resources as the birds of prey or the stream fishery were debatable, the findings were such that agency and conservation group concerns could not be entirely resolved and certainly not dismissed. Regardless of attempts to quantify and minimize adverse effects, many groups felt that absolutely no development was compatible with the existing environmental setting, and therefore no amount of technical analysis would appreciably limit the opposition.

EDAW further concluded that in light of many unresolvable issues pursuing an FERC license for the Swan Falls–Guffey project was likely to be an extremely lengthy and costly process with significant public relations risks to the Idaho Power Company and with no assurance that a license was even obtainable.

Idaho Power concurred with the findings and conclusions of the study and jointly with the Idaho Water Resources Board elected not to pursue the Swan Falls–Guffey project for the immediate future. The client felt that the *decision report process* was valuable in saving the considerable time and money that would have been committed on a project which had a low probability of success.

The use of the decision report process was generally seen *not* as negative input but as a constructive tool. It addressed the realities of a controversial project and resulted in a decision based on weighing environmental concerns against the long-range goals of developing alternative hydroelectric power sites in the state of Idaho.

Normally, as we have recommended repeatedly, the examination of issues and the involvement of affected interests would be incorporated in the process of site selection. When previous studies have not considered all potential issues and objections, the decision report can provide a delayed substitute.

Case Study 6 | DULUTH FREEWAY ROUTING STUDY

History of This Project

Duluth, located at the westernmost point of Lake Superior, is a city well known for the beauty of its setting. It is a long, narrow city, being built mainly on the steep northern slope of the lake.

Like many other cities in the United States, Duluth experienced problems of traffic congestion during the 1950s and 1960s as population and automobile use increased beyond the capacity of the local street system. In many cities, freeways were pushed through close-knit neighborhoods, often with regrettable consequences from a later vantage point. In other cities, freeway extension proposals were stopped dead by public opposition. The case of Interstate 35 in Duluth provides an example of cooperation between the project sponsors and the local public in developing a successful solution.

Interstate 35 links Duluth with the twin cities of Minneapolis and St. Paul. Extension of this highway through Duluth's central business district from its western edge was first proposed by the Minnesota Department of Highways in 1958. In 1965, the department proposed relocating the Duluth Missabe and Iron Range (DM&IR) Railroad so that the highway facilities could occupy the railroad corridor. The freeway was extended from the west as far as Mesaba Avenue (see Exhibit 6-1), and an arena complex, connecting ramps, and a bridge were constructed at Fifth Avenue West in anticipation of further extension to Tenth Avenue East. However, the final extension was delayed owing to environmental objections to the proposed design, concern over the future of the area between Tenth and Sixty-eighth Avenues East, and the inability of the highway department and the railroad to agree on relocation plans and costs.

In 1970, a group known as Citizens for the Integration of Highway and Environment (CIHE) was formed. CIHE advocated halting the freeway at Mesaba Avenue until a complete analysis could be performed. Such an analysis should indicate both the need for a new facility and the proper location and type of facility or facilities which could solve east-west traffic problems with minimum environmental disruption. As a result, a multidisciplinary consulting team headed by Eckbo, Dean, Austin & Williams was retained by the Minnesota Department of Highways to perform the Duluth Corridor Study.

Scope

The study was required to produce a documented recommendation as to what, if any, additional road traffic facilities should be developed beyond the existing terminus of Interstate 35. This requirement meant that carefully recorded assumptions about future transportation demand against which to test the sensitivity of the recommendation were needed. It was felt that it ought to be possible to adjust the assumptions should the future differ from them.

It was recognized that with sufficient time and budget a large number of projections and alternatives might be developed and tested. With limited time and budget the detailed research that would have been required to reduce uncertainty had to be traded for a methodology that was less precise but still practical.

Citizen Participation

This was a case in which, in order to arrive at an acceptable recommendation, it was clearly essential to involve the potentially affected citizens in the study from its very beginning. Before we discuss the scope, procedures, and findings of the study, we will therefore devote our attention to the manner in which highly effective citizen participation was achieved.

The study team structured the participation program on several levels to ensure direct community involvement. Continuous and intensive participation occurred at the citizens' advisory committee level. More general con-

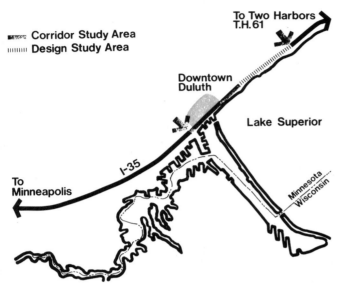

Corridor Study Area
Design Study Area

To Two Harbors
T.H. 61

Downtown
Duluth

Lake Superior

I-35

To
Minneapolis

Minnesota
Wisconsin

EXHIBIT 6-1   The Duluth Corridor Study area.

At the citizens' office set up by the study team, study materials, maps, and data were available several hours a day for review by the public. In addition, the study team was personally represented 1 day a week. Citizen forums were scheduled at those points in the project when major subjects were being considered and substantial input from the community was necessary.

Because of the extent of community involvement there were, in effect, two study projects progressing in parallel. The first was the technically oriented planning process, which proceeded through a sequence of steps that we will discuss later. That project was closely guided and reviewed by a technical advisory committee representing federal, state, and local transportation departments. The second project was the citizen participation program, which required almost every step in the technical process and almost all technical data to be presented and interpreted by the study team. To obtain the necessary citizen input to the study team's work, it was important to ensure that uninitiated lay persons could understand the process.

Background Studies

To help determine a project goal, studies of the role of road transportation and of population growth were undertaken first. The role of the automobile had come under increasing attack during the 1960s throughout the United States. However, the trend was toward greater per capita use of the automobile. The study team believed that alternative transportation modes would eventually become attractive but that this would occur first in those areas with the most severe problems of environmental pollution, the greatest concern for environmental health, and the most feasible commuter travel patterns. Duluth was among those urban areas which had suffered least severely from the environmental and social costs associated with automobile use. It was assumed that the automobile would remain the primary mode of transportation and that the trend to increased per capita automobile use would continue in the Duluth area. It was believed, however, that thinking about standards of service would change, allowing alternatives to freeway or expressway standards with less community impact to be developed and tested.

On the basis of both the trend toward increased per capita automobile use and the expectation of declining rates of population growth in the area, the study team established reasonable upper and lower bounds to the probable growth in traffic demand by 1995. Within these

tact was maintained via the newspaper, radio, and television media and a citizens' office. In addition, although it was a time-consuming effort, the team endeavored to answer every letter from the community.

The citizens' advisory committee was formed at the outset of the study. Its members represented over thirty community, environmental, labor, and commercial organizations, businesses, local government offices, and educational and cultural institutions. The major purposes of the committee were:

· To provide the consultant team with data, background information, guidance, and opinion
· To review the study process and findings as the study progressed
· To pass information back to groups represented by the committee members

While the singular task of the citizens' advisory committee was to consider transportation questions and how they related to the region, other community concerns such as parks, urban growth, and tourist facilities were naturally raised and discussed.

The committee elected cochairpersons, established criteria by which additional organizations would be accepted into membership, and set up six subcommittees. The subcommittees covered environmental, historical and cultural, economic, traffic and urban growth, legislative, and resource concerns.

limits it then developed more detailed alternative forecasts.

Next, consideration was given to the social and environmental effects of a transportation facility. Owing to increased awareness of the impact that a highway could have, consideration was directed well beyond the factors of traffic demand and cost which had dominated many previous freeway projects. The positive and negative aspects of social, economic, environmental, and visual factors were to be addressed.

Establishment of Objectives

The study team recognized that while standards for certain environmental conditions were generally accepted, community viewpoints on others were likely to vary widely. To ensure study results that conformed as closely as possible to the needs and wishes of Duluth, several meetings of the citizens' advisory committee and an open citizens' forum were devoted to establishing a goal and specific objectives for the study.

The fundamental community goal for the study was stated as "the determination of need for a traffic facility and, if needed, the selection of the necessary alignment and facilities of maximum social and physical value and least social and physical cost" (Eckbo, Dean, Austin & Williams, 1972:32).

To guide discussion, five groups of objectives were suggested to the committee and the citizens' forum. These have been presented previously in Chapter 4 (refer to Table 4-1). The study team found that these "seed" objectives corresponded very closely to those of the citizen participants. Criteria or "tests" by which to evaluate the ability of an alternative to meet these objectives were developed. Exhibit 6-2 provides an example of criteria in one impact cluster and shows both the underlying objective to which they were directed and the specific measures used to evaluate compliance with the objective.

The Duluth Corridor Study differed from most of the cases we describe in its approach to treatment of facility cost. Cost is generally a fundamental project objective, accompanied by cost criteria against which alternatives are measured concurrently with other performance and impact criteria. In the Duluth case, preliminary tests of financial realism were imposed during the first screening process to eliminate any clearly infeasible alternatives. The sequence involved the evaluation of transportation alternatives first in terms of their total effectiveness or total community impact without regard to costs. Next, the total impact of the alternatives on social and environmental conditions was evaluated relative to direct facility investment and maintenance cost. Finally, consideration was given to the fact that the costs of different transportation alternatives would fall on different funding sources. This allowed a composite selection, considering not only the cost but who would bear that cost, to be made.

Methodology and Process

The Duluth Corridor Study differs in its methodology from the sequence we have described in Part One in that the facility type was not selected until relatively late in the corridor-screening process. Also, detailed evaluation criteria were applied relatively early in the process. Two important considerations explain the difference in approach. First, as the discussion of the study framework has indicated, the study was conducted in an atmosphere of uncertainty regarding future demand for automobile travel. Second, owing to the already well defined study area, potential corridors were clearly evident. Thus the study largely omitted the site-screening phase of the site-selection process. It can be seen as roughly the equivalent of the site-evaluation phase, described in Chapter 8.

The evaluation process was composed of five *screens,* which, in keeping with our overall process, ascended in level of detail as the scope was narrowed. The sequence of screens is presented in Exhibit 6-3.

Corridor Identification and Selection

The first step in the process was to generate a complete list of the corridors within which transportation facilities could be built. This list was intended to be complete, within practical limits, and to include all realistic alternatives that had been discussed within the community. Several possible routes were identified by citizens and the study team within some of the corridors as shown in Exhibit 6-4. It was also recognized explicitly, as we have noted previously, that a transportation alternative might consist of an alternative cross section or an alternative standard of service, such as an arterial highway or an expressway rather than a freeway. Finally, the *null alternative* (to build no new major transportation facility at this time) was included in the list because no initial presumption could be made that a facility was needed. The null alternative was to be evaluated by the same process as all other project alternatives.

CRITERIA GROUP G: Economic Factors

Objective: Minimize long- and short-term adverse impact on the economy of Duluth and, wherever possible, contribute to increased economic activity in the metropolitan region.

CRITERIA	MEASURES USED DURING EVALUATION		
	INITIAL SCREENING	DETAILED EVALUATION	FINAL DOCUMENTATION
Provide for expansion of business activity, particularly retail sales.	Identify areas where decreased congestion will increase or relocate retail sales.	Estimate retail activity. Determine capability of areas with decreased traffic congestion to handle increased retail sales and/or other business transactions.	Estimate increase in gross retail sales in the central business district and elsewhere.
Provide for expansion of business community by means of joint development.	Briefly identify any commercial multiple-use opportunity.	Estimate financial feasibility and gross volume of joint developments.	Analyze detailed financial feasibility and rate of return for potential joint development.
Minimize short-term disruption to and relocation of established businesses.	Estimate number and gross sales of businesses to be relocated.	Estimate impact on gross receipts for all businesses affected (either by relocation or by changes in sales).	Estimate impact on gross receipts by block group and by sector of Duluth economy.
Provide for increased employment. (a) during construction	(a) Estimate gross differences in employment potential.	(a) Estimate gross employment differences by skill and duration.	(a) Estimate construction payroll by type and origin of workers.
(b) after construction	(b) Indicate factors fostering the location of new industry and business.	(b) Compare types of new industry or business most likely to be affected with available labor supply.	(b) Estimate gross receipts of new industry, its impact on tax revenues, and desirability on other than economic grounds.

EXHIBIT 6-2 Evaluation criteria and measurements. For a single factor group, economic impact, this table illustrates the criteria and measures used to evaluate the ability of each alternative to meet a stated objective.

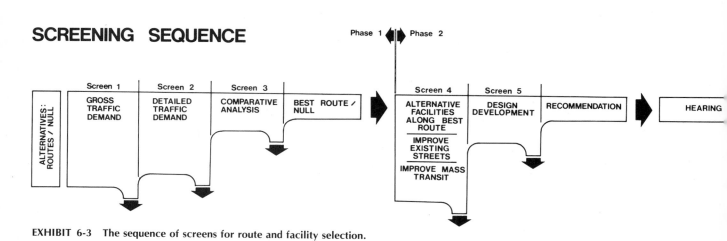

EXHIBIT 6-3 The sequence of screens for route and facility selection.

EXHIBIT 6-4 **Preliminary identification of corridor alternatives.**

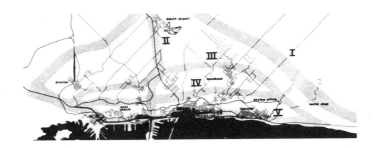

Corridors

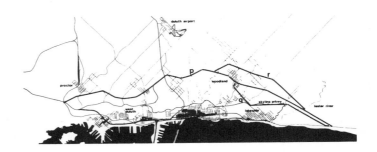

Citizen-Suggested Routes

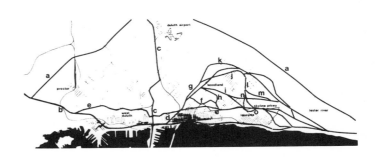

Routes Considered

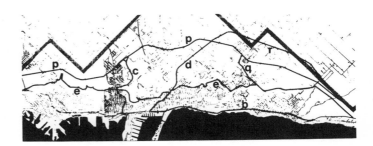

Routes Surviving Screen

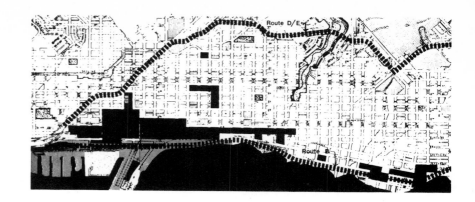

Existing Land Use

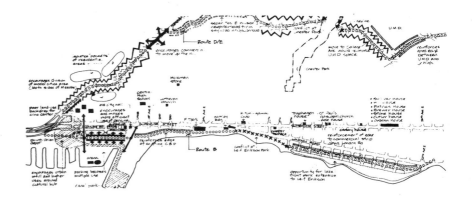

Land Use Analysis

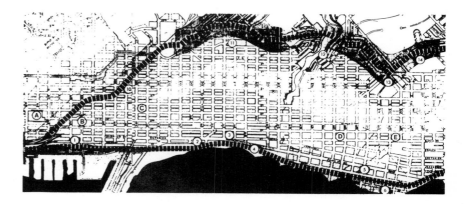

Social Impact

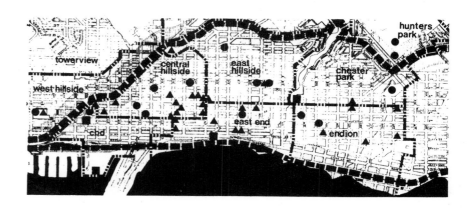

Noise Pollution

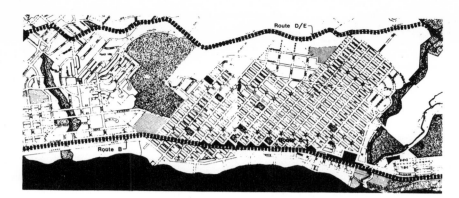

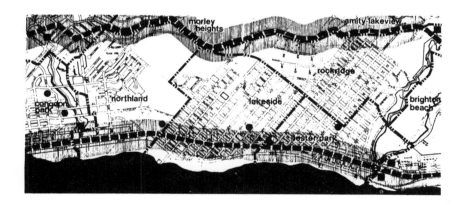

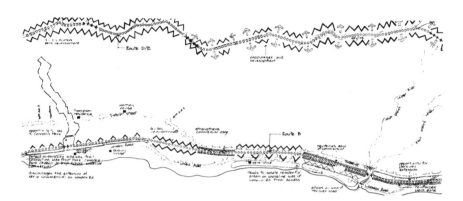

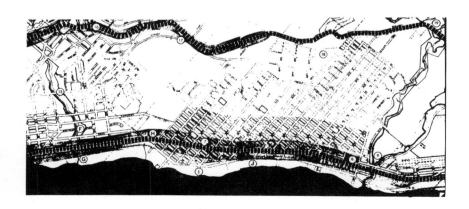

EXHIBIT 6-6 Data mapping and analysis of corridor conditions for Screen III evaluation (continued).

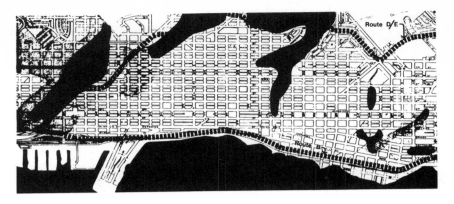

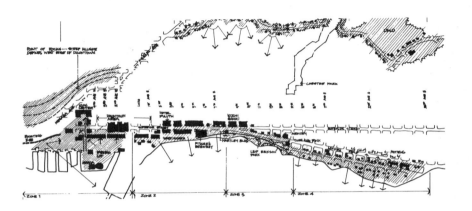

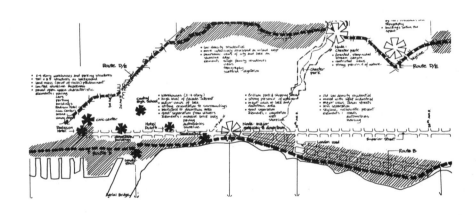

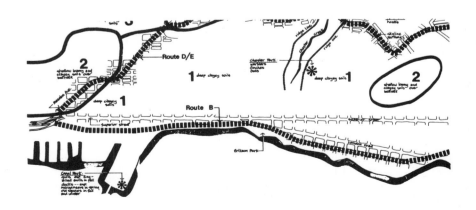

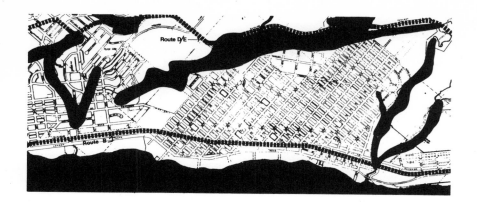

Land Slope

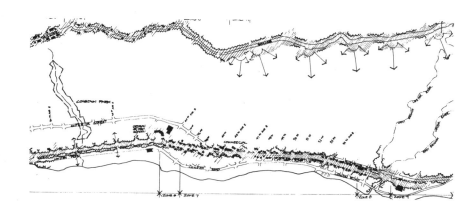

Spatial Definition/Views/ Elements

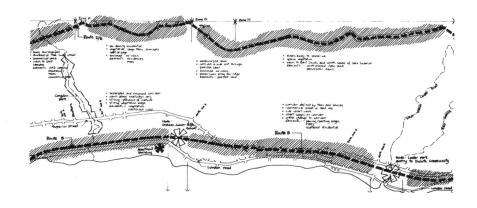

Visual Character

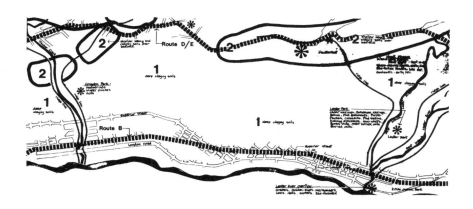

Wildlife Habitats and Soil Types

SCREEN I The corridor alternatives were first evaluated solely in terms of their effectiveness from the standpoint of transportation. Exhibit 6-4 shows that a large number of alternative routes, including all of Corridor I, were eliminated because trip generation studies did not indicate sufficient traffic to justify construction of more than a two-lane city street.

SCREEN II Screen II was essentially a refinement of Screen I, this time using sophisticated traffic assignment and 1995 computer projection techniques. Corridor II, a north-south route, was eliminated because its improvement would not affect downtown congestion. Corridor III was eliminated because of insufficient traffic generation.

SCREEN III The surviving alternatives, Corridor IV (Route D/E), Corridor V (Route B), and the null alternative, were evaluated individually and comparatively in terms of their total impact on a broad range of environmental and community conditions in Screen III (see Exhibits 6-5 and 6-6). These impact factors were grouped into ten clusters:

· Natural features
· Air, noise, and water pollution
· Land use
· Historical-cultural
· Visual
· Social
· Economic
· Road traffic movement
· Facility costs and financing
· Transportation benefit-cost relationship

Table 7-5 in Chapter 7 should be consulted for detailed subfactors in each cluster.

Screen III thus included for the first time the benefits directly associated with traffic flow, such as reduced travel times. This screen also considered facility investment and maintenance (based on an assumption of unit construction and maintenance costs for surface grade alignments) so that conventional but preliminary benefit-cost comparisons could be made. This stage also involved the first evaluation of alternatives according to factors not related to transportation.

Evaluation of the alternatives at this stage used the concept of *pure dominance*. That is, two alternatives are compared on every standard of judgment (whether trans-portation, economic, or environmental). If one is clearly inferior to or "dominated by" the other, that alternative is eliminated from further consideration. Considerable judgment is usually involved, and cases of pure dominance rarely occur. But even in the absence of what can rigorously be described as pure dominance, one alternative may be seen as so superior to its competitor that no further resources should be devoted to the latter alternative.

Use of the pure-dominance approach eliminated Corridor IV, leaving alternatives within Corridor V and the null alternative to be considered in the next screen.

SCREEN IV In Screen IV, feasible alternative facility types and combinations of types were generated for comparison with the null alternative. Nine alternative facility types, including freeway, parkway, expressway, and arterial facilities, were generated. The null alternative involved mass transit, street upgrading, and do-nothing subalternatives.

A multiple-criteria ranking, weighting, and scoring process was then applied to each alternative and subalternative. The first step in this process was to use expert judgment as well as factual estimates to rank all the alternatives separately according to each criterion. Then the alternatives were scored numerically on an arbitrary scale to provide a subjective indication of "distance" between the alternatives according to each criterion. Finally, an evaluation of the criteria themselves was made, and a composite evaluation of each surviving alternative was prepared.

The procedure differs in detail, although not in essence, from other ranking, weighting, and scoring procedures described in previous chapters. The particular approach used for preparing the rankings on each separate criterion was the so-called partial-pair comparison. One alternative was compared with another according to a subjective evaluation that involved all the elements of a particular criterion. A subjective decision was made that the alternative was "better" or "worse" than the alternative with which it was compared, according to that particular criterion. Then a third alternative was compared with the poorer of the previous pair. If it was deemed subjectively to be better, it was compared with the better of the previous two. At the conclusion of this process, the alternatives were placed, by consensus of an expert panel assembled from the study team, on a numerical scale, relative distance between alternatives expressing a subjectively valid measure of relative ability to satisfy each criterion. Alternatives were eliminated if they clearly

EXHIBIT 6-7   The proposed Ericson Park Tunnel. This design solution was recommended to maintain a pedestrian link between the park and Lake Superior.

scored so low on one or more criteria that on that basis alone they fell below the level of performance necessary to meet project and community goals and objectives.

In the final step at the end of Screen IV, the expert panel assigned a policy weight to each major criterion and prepared a composite numerical score for each surviving alternative. These composite scores were subjected to a test of intuitive plausibility. Then the discounted present value of the capital investment and maintenance cost of each alternative was recalculated, carefully applying average or unit costs for facility and right-of-way to each segment of the routes. The remaining alternatives were compared on the basis of their composite scores relative to their costs, ready for final selection of a recommended alternative in Screen V.

The particular characteristic of this procedure that distinguishes it from that described in Chapters 7 and 8 of Part One is that criteria can be weighed *after* considering the factual estimate of the impact of an alternative on conditions governed by each criterion. This is not often feasible because of the effort involved. In the majority of site-evaluation studies, in which a single facility type has already been established, the efforts are not justified by

improved results. It is an appropriate approach to matching a number of alternative facilities with a small number of alternative sites or routes. The column titled "Final Documentation" in Exhibit 6-2 indicates that a clear record of the comparison is available for those who would question the outcome of the evaluation or wish to consider alternative assumptions about the relative importance of various criteria.

On the basis primarily of considerations of traffic demand and route continuity, Screen IV resulted in elimination of all but three facility type alternatives, four design variations on these alternatives, and the null alternative.

SCREEN V   Screen V tested twenty-nine facility type and design combinations and the null alternative, using the same nine criteria groups employed in Screen III. The best of these facility type and design components were combined to make up the recommended alternative displayed in Exhibit 6-7.

Exhibit 6-4 showed a straight-line process from screen to screen and continuing after Screen V. However, the actual sequence applied during the Duluth Corridor Study recognized explicitly the possibility of a revised

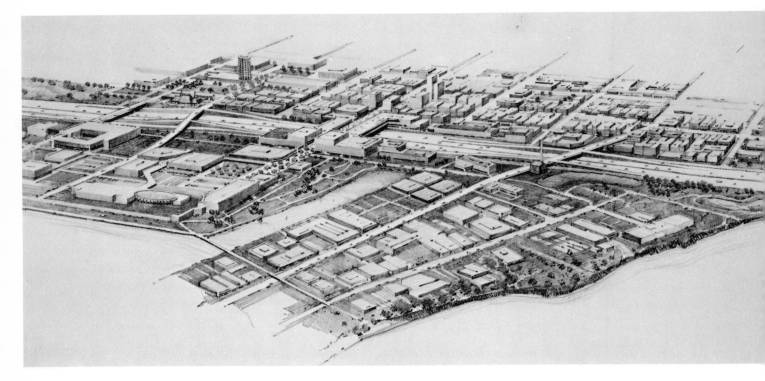

EXHIBIT 6-8   Model showing the recommended alternative.

recommendation after a sensitivity analysis had been carried out. If the recommendation had proved to be highly sensitive to an assumption that was clearly subject to change, it might have been necessary to consider an alternative that was less sensitive to assumptions. The objective was to find a robust design solution that would remain practical and acceptable to the community in the face of a number of alternative future states for such variables as population, regional economy, and community attitudes. In fact, the recommended alternative was determined to meet the test of robustness, and no revision was necessary.

The Recommended Alternative

The final recommendation was for a 3.6-mile extension of Interstate 35 eastward as a four-lane freeway from Mesaba Avenue to Twenty-sixth Avenue East. It was also recommended that Two Harbors Expressway be connected from its westerly terminus at Sixty-eighth Avenue East to the proposed Interstate 35 terminus at Twenty-Sixth Avenue East by a 4.0-mile four-lane parkway.

The interstate portion would parallel the railroad rights-of-way, with only minor track relocations. The parkway portion required right-of-way acquisition throughout its length. Access points were identified and design guidelines were established to promote both the successful integration of the facility with its surroundings and the revitalization of the core area traversed by the facility. For example, a 1300-foot tunnel was recommended in order to preserve a lakeshore park, maintaining a vital pedestrian connection with the lake and increasing the effective size of the park (see Exhibit 6-8).

The environmental impact statement prepared for the project concluded that the proposed solution was superior to other alternatives in terms of traffic movement and visual and community impact. The solution took relatively few buildings, had excellent access, respected the existing infrastructure of the city, and was at the same time sensitive to the shoreline of Lake Superior and adjacent park areas.

Case Study 7 | COAL-FIRED POWER PLANT SITING STUDY

HISTORY AND SCOPE OF THIS STUDY

The California Department of Water Resources (DWR) contracted with a consulting team under the direction of EDAW, in conjunction with Earth Sciences Associates (ESA), in November 1978 to examine the feasibility of locating a coal-fired power plant in California. The goal of the project was the identification of three sites suitable for further analysis as locations for such a plant. The new plant would have a capacity of approximately 1000 megawatts electric generated either by three units of 350-megawatt electric nominal size or by two units of 500-megawatt electric nominal size.

As an initial step to the siting study, DWR and the EDAW-ESA consulting team met to decide upon a set of project and environmental objectives. These are enumerated in the "Defining Project Objectives" section of Chapter 4.

THE SITING PROCESS

The major objective in developing the siting process was to provide a well-documented record of the decision making that led to the selection of three sites. The overall process was divided into three sequential phases:

1 *Statewide analysis* to identify *candidate areas*

2 *Candidate area analyses* to identify *candidate sites*

3 *Candidate site analyses* to identify tentative *plant locations* and to select three sites for further analysis

See Figure 7-1 for a graphic breakdown of these three analysis levels.

Common Procedures Used in the Siting Process

The site screening involved two activities: (1) data collection and analysis and (2) group decision making. These were repeated at several points during the process.

The statewide analysis concentrated on siting issues, constraints, and opportunities of statewide magnitude and importance. These factors of major importance were translated into geographic terms when possible and recorded on maps of California at a scale of 1:1,000,000 (1 centimeter = 10 kilometers). Subsequent analyses concentrated on smaller geographic areas and considered more factors in greater detail. The candidate area analysis was conducted at a scale of 1:125,000 (1 centimeter = 1.25 kilometer) and the site area analysis at a scale of 1:24,000 (1 centimeter = 0.24 kilometer).

STATEWIDE ANALYSIS PHASE

Four objectives guided the derivation of statewide data base categories:

1 Technical feasibility

2 Environmental compatibility

3 Economic feasibility

4 Social acceptability

These were further broken down into eight *data base categories* for ranking candidate areas and sites:

· Land use

· Environmental resources

· Air quality and meteorology

· Socioeconomics

· Electrical energy systems and DWR facilities

· Site-dependent costs

· Water supply

These data base categories were translated into a series of constraints, or *data factors*, of state and national significance which could exclude portions of the state from consideration and provide a basis for ranking areas not excluded.

Group Consensus Selection of Exclusion Factors

A multidisciplinary group of eleven professionals representing the major environmental and technical disciplines considered in the statewide analysis and DWR selected the exclusion factors used in the study. These were based upon the presentations made by the discipline specialists in each of the eight data base categories and also included the recommendations of the discipline specialists for exclusion factors. After all the presentations and discussions had been completed, a ballot listing all the identified data factors was given to each group member. Members were asked to vote on whether a factor should be (1) an exclusion factor, (2) an evaluation factor, or (3) a factor to be deferred until the site-analysis phase of the study. See Chapter 7, "Exclusion Factors" subsection, and Table 7-2 for methods and results of the balloting in one category, land use.

Overlay maps of exclusion factors were prepared and assembled to form a composite map of all exclusion factors (Figure 7-8). On the basis of exclusion factors alone approximately 75 percent of the state was eliminated from further consideration, primarily in the interests of air quality preservation.

All unexcluded areas in the state were then identified as candidate areas. A total of thirty-one candidate siting areas, ranging in size from 40 to 2850 square kilometers, remained. To focus attention on the most promising, the decision-making group devised a system for ranking the candidate areas thus determined. In this system evaluation categories were defined and assigned *importance ratios* (see Chapter 7, "Numerical Weighting" subsection, for further definition of this process). Nine-point rating scales were established for each evaluation category, as in Figure 7-18, and applied to each candidate siting area. The results were tabulated in a ranking matrix, such as that shown in Table 7-8.

A set of candidate areas was chosen for further study both for its high rankings and for its ability to satisfy state DWR goals and objectives. For example, consideration was given to ensuring that the set of candidate areas selected for continuing study covered a diversity of geographic settings including coastal, desert, Central Valley, and urban areas. Nine of the thirty-one candidate areas were eventually selected for further study.

STATEWIDE SITING DATA BASE BREAKDOWN

The following breakdown by data base category at the state level generally follows the six-part analysis format

shown in the "Data Analysis and Organization" section of Chapter 9.

Land Use

SUMMARY AND ASSUMPTIONS Major land-use areas and land management units were identified, categorized, and evaluated to determine their importance to the statewide screening process. Exhibit 7-1 summarizes the determination of evaluation and exclusion factors based on land use and management considerations.

Land uses which for legal or administrative reasons were plainly not compatible with coal-fired power plant facilities were assumed to be exclusion factors, as were areas in which a power plant would constitute a hazard to the continuation of present land uses or inhibit the best use of lands determined to have other critical value (e.g., prime agricultural lands).

APPROACH The term *land management units* describes areas in which construction of a coal-fired power plant would not necessarily be incompatible with present land use but within which such construction is strongly discouraged or inhibited by management policy. For example, the U.S. Bureau of Land Management was then studying roadless areas under its jurisdiction to recommend to Congress whether they should be managed as wilderness or nonwilderness areas. Nonwilderness areas would be eligible for consideration as power plant candidate areas; however, until completion of reclassification, all roadless areas were to be managed in a manner not to reduce their wilderness potential, effectively excluding them from siting consideration. In order to have the proposed plant operational in 1987, it was judged impractical to wait for reclassification.

RESULTS AND SITING INTERPRETATION Ten land uses were identified as power plant siting constraints, either exclusion or evaluation factors (see Exhibit 7-1 for listing).

Environmental Resources

SUMMARY At the state level of screening, only those water and wildlife resources designated by law or by existing policy as critical environmental resources were considered. Consideration of special botanical communities was deferred until later. In almost all cases, the wildlife and water resources identified were recommended as exclusion factors.

EXHIBIT 7-1   Summary of recommendations for land use and management factors.

Land Use/ Management	Component	Buffer	Recommendation
Forests	National Forests;	None	Exclusion factor
	State Forests	None	Exclusion factor
Parks and Recreation Areas	National Parks, Monuments,& Recreation Areas;	8 km.	Exclusion factor
	State Parks	8 km.	Exclusion factor
Wilderness Areas	Federal Wilderness Areas	8 km.	Exclusion factor
	USFS 7 BLM Roadless Areas	None	Exclusion factor
Military Reservations	Military Reservations	None	Evaluation factor
Airports	Civil & Military Airports with Instrument Approach Systems;	4.8 km.	Exclusion factor
	Airports without Instrument Approach Systems	--	Evaluation factor
Urban Areas	Urban Areas	None	Exclusion factor
California Highways designated or eligible for designation as State Scenic Highways	Same	8 km.	Exclusion factor
Indian Reservations	Indian Reservations	None	Exclusion factor
Agricultural Lands	Lands in USDA SCS Class I & II	None	Exclusion factor
	Irrigated Lands	None	Exclusion factor
	Irrigable Lands	None	Evaluation factor
Archaeological Sites	--	--	Evaluation factor

APPROACH   The environmental resources reviewed in the statewide screening phase fell into two important categories:

1   "Areas of specific biological significance, critical habitat, and protected areas," designated by the California Department of Fish and Game.

2   Coastal lands and environmental resources under the jurisdiction of the California Coastal Commission.

These categories were reviewed to determine their applicability to statewide mapping for candidate area identification and selection.

"Areas of special biological significance" at the statewide scale have been mapped by the California Department of Fish and Game and are therefore quite specific. However, the statewide data on most endangered species are incomplete. They therefore required thorough examination in the site-evaluation phase.

The California Coastal Commission staff has issued a "Final Staff Recommendation of the Designation of Coastal Zone Areas Where Construction of an Electric Power Plant Would Prevent Achievement of the Objectives of the California Coastal Act of 1976." It was assumed that the commission had accounted for all critical environmental resources within the coastal zone and that for this study their subject designations could therefore be adopted as exclusion factors.

RESULTS AND SITING INTERPRETATIONS   In general, encroachment upon specific endangered or rare fish or wildlife habitats was treated as an exclusion factor, while proximity to these regions (within 8 kilometers) was determined to be a factor for evaluation at the site-specific level.

Natural Hazards and Terrain

SUMMARY Natural hazards such as earthquakes, faulting, landslides, floods, and areas of steep or rough terrain can impose serious constraints upon the siting and design of coal-fired power plants. Most of these constraints can be avoided in local siting decisions or accommodated in plant design. All require site-specific investigations. Of the hazards and terrain conditions considered, only surface faults with historic or major Quaternary displacements and areas of steep terrain were recommended as exclusion factors for the statewide analysis because (1) engineering judgment and power plant design limitations for accommodating sudden ground surface displacements suggest that plant facilities should not be located on major faults and (2) the extensive earth movement required to build on steep terrain would have undesirable environmental and economic consequences.

Natural hazards are important factors in the economic evaluation of power plant candidate areas because the cost of development is directly related to the degree of hazard mitigation required. This is particularly true for strong ground motion since seismic design requirements vary widely in the state and are a major determinant of plant cost.

APPROACH   Natural hazard and terrain constraints to coal-fired power plant siting include:

· Ground rupture and foundation hazards caused by faulting
· Ground motion hazards caused by earthquakes
· Flooding hazards
· Areas of steep or rough terrain

Each of these constraints was further analyzed to determine its importance to the statewide phase of the siting process and to decide whether or not data were available to illustrate the constraint adequately. No state or federal regulations have been identified to define the influence of these hazards on the siting of coal-fired power plants.

RESULTS AND SITING INTERPRETATIONS   The results were focused on earthquake fault activity potentials. For purposes of the statewide screening process, a 0.8-kilometer buffer zone was shown on each side of known Quaternary fault traces. This is the narrowest band that could be mapped at the statewide scale.

Contours of effective peak acceleration (EPA), a measurement related to the damage potential of an earthquake, were obtained by using various seismic risk procedures. Although the values of acceleration were adequate for preliminary studies, more detailed site-specific studies, considering the effects of local and regional geology and seismology and the effects of local soil conditions on ground motion characteristics, were deemed necessary for final site selection.

Air Quality and Meteorology

SUMMARY Compliance with myriad federal, state, and local laws and regulations in the preservation of air quality was a matter of prime concern in siting this coal-fired facility. Laws and regulations imposed at all governmental levels may be divided into two classes: (1) those defining allowable emissions from a source and (2) those setting standards for ambient-air quality. The latter excluded plant construction in regions where the net effect of plant emission could produce pollutants exceeding allowable prevention of significant deterioration (PSD) increments in downwind areas. To date, PSD increments have been specified only for sulfur dioxide and particulate matter (TSP); that is, the plant must be sufficiently remote from sensitive areas to ensure compliance with PSD in those areas.

The need for obtaining appropriate offsets (compensating reductions in emissions from existing sources when a new source is permitted in or near areas not in attainment of state or national ambient standards) presented another severe siting problem. When the statewide analysis was first carried out, no rules or methods were specified in any existing regulations for the determination of necessary or sufficient offsets. Therefore an arbitrarily defined offset potential was used as an evaluation factor. Additional identified and analyzed constraints included the following:

· The requirement to comply with local, state, or National Ambient Air Quality Standards (S/NAAQS) for any criteria pollutant. Criteria pollutants include SO_2 (sulfur dioxide), NO_2 (nitrogen dioxide), CO (carbon monoxide), O_3 (ozone), TSP (particulates), and lead and nonmethane hydrocarbons.

· The requirement to obtain emission reductions for existing sources (offsets) in areas currently not in attainment.

APPROACH To analyze air quality aspects of potential candidate siting areas, the following steps were carried out:

1 Identify, characterize, and quantify air quality constraints in federal, state, and local regulations applicable to the proposed DWR coal project, and review anticipated changes in these regulations and the potential effects of such changes on power plant siting.

2 Specify typical source parameters to characterize the expected emissions in order to perform dispersion modeling estimates.

3 Postulate critical worst-case dispersion conditions for the plant taken by itself and prevailing climatological transport patterns for offset availability analyses.

4 Determine zones where potential violations of air quality constraints might be expected from plant emissions, on the basis of the plant parameters and worst-case dispersion conditions.

5 Identify potential offset availability for those areas where ambient constraints could not be satisfied.

At the date of this study, all PSD attainment regions were included in one of two categories. The most stringent PSD goals were applied to Class I areas, a designation given to particularly pristine areas such as national parks and wilderness areas. All attainment areas not labeled as Class I were considered Class II.

In addition to PSD federal emissions limitations, a new source must comply with state and local emissions standards. In California the legal authority for setting such standards rests with the 49 local air pollution control districts (APCDs). Some of these districts have adopted a so-called Rule 67–type emissions limitation, written as a specified pounds-per-hour limitation rather than scaled according to source size. In districts where these limitations have been imposed, a large source such as a power plant would find it difficult, if not impossible, to comply. An emissions map was prepared to show those regions of the state where the postulated plant would exceed these local standards.

However, the California Air Resources Board (CARB) has prepared a new rule which would essentially negate

the need for Rule 67–type emissions limitations expressed in absolute terms and eliminate them from state regulations. For this reason projected violations of these rules could not be sufficient cause to eliminate a potential siting area from further consideration. However, it could represent a serious potential obstacle to siting in some areas if these emissions limitations were not rescinded as anticipated.

In no circumstances, either in attainment or nonattainment regions, may a new source be permitted that would cause the federal or state ambient-air quality standards to be exceeded. Consequently, plant emissions together with ambient concentrations from all other sources must be kept below these limits.

If the proposed plant were to be sited too close to a PSD Class I area, the concentration resulting from its emissions could exceed the allowable increment within that area during those times when the wind blows toward the area.

Dispersion calculations based on the worst-case conditions and the assumed SO_2 emission rate indicated that a buffer distance of 33 kilometers would be adequate in all parts of the state to avoid exceeding the PSD Class I increment. Similar methods found a 16-kilometer buffer for Class II areas.

It should be noted that this analysis assumed that the full PSD increment would be available for the power plant. In the event that the maximum increment were not available because of some regulatory mandate, greater buffer distance would be necessary.

Offsets may be required by state rules for any and all pollutants emitted by the project in areas which cause or contribute to a violation of the S/NAAQS. Potential offset availability was analyzed (1) to identify areas within the PSD buffer zones that potentially could afford necessary offsets for mitigation of potential impacts and (2) to assist in evaluating all other areas where site-specific background concentrations combined with potential plant emissions might cause a violation of standards and therefore necessitate obtaining the requisite offsets.

ASSUMPTIONS The regulatory environment of the power plant siting process changes rapidly. The assumptions used in carrying out this phase of the study were mainly related to anticipating the regulations that would be in effect at the time of the notification of intention (NOI) reviews.

RESULTS AND SITING INTERPRETATIONS To ensure that emissions from the proposed project would not cause a violation of the PSD increment in air quality attainment areas, the 33- and 16-kilometer buffer zone esti-mates around PSD Class I and II areas were accepted as exclusion areas unless sufficient potential offsets could be identified to mitigate plant impacts.

Socioeconomics

SUMMARY *Socioeconomics,* as defined for statewide screening, included no exclusion categories and one evaluation category: distance to labor pools from candi-date areas. A discussion of socioeconomic factors is therefore deferred until the preferred candidate area analysis.

Electrical Energy Systems and DWR Resource Facilities

SUMMARY Transmission corridors of 115 kilovolts or greater, existing and proposed power plants, the energy demand center of the state water project, and areas which maintain service agreements with DWR were all seen as factors to be considered in evaluating candidate areas.

APPROACH Transmission corridors and existing and proposed power plants were mapped at the statewide scale of 1:1,000,000, using existing data sources. These factors represented a generalized configuration of the electrical network and were based on the assumption that they would be used for evaluation purposes only.

ASSUMPTIONS Use of existing transmission corridors would increase the likelihood of environmental compati-bility and social acceptability, as would candidate areas located within existing DWR service areas. Proximity to areas of high energy demand and/or the electric utilities network would enhance the economic feasibility of the project.

RESULTS AND SITING INTERPRETATIONS It was recom-mended that candidate areas containing transmission corridors be given preference and that the distance of a candidate area to the nearest transmission corridor be calculated as a site-dependent cost.

Site-Dependent Costs

SUMMARY Only generalized information was available for identifying relative cost differences among candidate areas on a statewide basis.

Evaluation factors used were as follows:

· Distance from mine to siting area
· Proximity of rail to area
· Proximity of water to area
· Seismic risks
· Distance to an existing transmission corridor
· Distance to nearest DWR pumping facility
· DWR service area

APPROACH Each of these site-dependent cost factors was analyzed to determine the amount and type of work necessary. Cooling system and water transport costs were broken down into a number of variables, which are discussed in detail in the subsection "Water Supply."

ASSUMPTIONS It was assumed that transmission lines could be routed from any place in the state if environ-mental impacts could be mitigated. A number of cost es-timates on seismic design features and coal transport were made, given certain assumptions on peak accelera-tion values, existing state capacities for rail traffic, etc.

RESULTS AND SITING INTERPRETATIONS Site-depen-dent costs were determined to be important evaluation factors on a statewide as well as a site-specific basis. It did not appear appropriate to exclude any areas in the state because of costs alone since the combined effects of all site-dependent costs were not known and no upper limit on project costs had been established.

Water Supply

SUMMARY Potential water supplies for a coal-fired plant include ocean water for once-through cooling and inland fresh water or wastewater for closed-cycle cooling. Use of ocean water and inland wastewater were emphasized in the statewide analysis. The following discussion ex-cludes ocean waters, as these were considered only for the coastal areas.

Sources of inland wastewater include municipal wastewater, agricultural wastewater, and brackish groundwater. In conducting this study, the use of these wastewaters for power plant cooling was assumed to be feasible. Verification of this assumption would require extensive site-specific studies.

APPROACH Inland supplies of water for closed-cycle cooling systems might be obtained from surface and/or underground sources of either fresh or poor-quality water. It was assumed in this study that freshwater sources would not be considered as long as poor-quality waters were available and suitable for use in closed-cycle cooling systems.

ASSUMPTIONS For the purpose of the statewide analysis, the following assumptions were made:

1 Water could be delivered with a pipeline and pumping system to siting areas at a considerable distance from the water source. There should be no technical distance limit for a pipeline, provided that the costs of building and operating the delivery system were included in the computation of site-dependent costs.

2 Poor-quality waters from more than one source might be used to supply a project.

3 Legal, environmental, and technical problems associated with the development and use of specific water sources would be considered in the site anlaysis.

4 Effluent from closed-cycle cooling systems using poor-quality waters would not be discharged off site.

RESULTS AND SITING INTERPRETATIONS Sources were identified and maps and tables prepared for municipal-industrial wastewaters, agricultural wastewaters, and poor-quality groundwaters. The identification and evaluation of potential wastewater sources was essentially independent of the scale of the evaluation, as most of the sources of water were outside the boundaries of the candidate areas. All water sources within 150 kilometers of candidate areas were identified in the evaluation process.

Candidate Area Identification

Following the map overlay process of exclusion factors described previously, a total of twenty-seven candidate siting areas were identified (Figure 7-8). While the statewide analysis was in progress, the CARB issued proposed new regulations concerning their new source review rules and held a hearing on the subject. As a result of these activities, DWR and the consulting team concluded that some revision in the air quality exclusion factors used in the first ranking session was necessary. As a result of this second iteration in response to changing data, four new candidate areas were added, making a final total of thirty-one candidate areas.

Candidate Area Ranking and Selection

Many of the thirty-one identified candidate areas were quite large, so the consulting team expected to find an average of at least two or three sites in each candidate area. This would have resulted in the identification of far more alternative site areas than necessary for DWR's project, so DWR and the consulting team decided to concentrate on only a portion of the candidate areas, assuming that (1) the selection of areas to be studied would focus on those that appeared best to satisfy the study objectives, (2) the selection would provide a diversity of alternatives (i.e., coast, valley, desert, urban), and (3) the remainder of the candidate areas were still available for study if the first group selected did not yield adequate site areas.

The selection of candidate areas to be studied was made by using the group decision-making process previously discussed. The candidate areas were ranked by using this two-part process and then examined to see that the better-ranked areas provided an adequate diversity of alternatives.

Relative-Importance Ratios for Evaluation Categories

Information was grouped into eight *evaluation categories* corresponding to the eight data base categories used in the preceding analysis to identify the candidate areas. The decision-making group reviewed the eight evaluation categories and established importance ratios for each. The numerical values assigned by each participant to each factor were normalized to a scale of 10. The group average was then computed and tabulated for each evaluation category. Air quality, with a value of 1.93, was voted almost three times as important as socioeconomics, with a value of 0.67. From this result it was apparent that certain compensations would be necessary in later phases of the study to produce valid, weightable results.

Rating of Candidate Areas

After establishing the relative importance of each evaluation category, the group rated each candidate area on its suitability as a site for a coal-fired power plant with respect to each of the evaluation categories. A common rating scale was used for all categories, as defined in Figure 7-18.

Since all thirty-one candidate areas had to be rated on each of the eight categories, a total of 248 ratings was necessary. Results of the 248 ratings were tabulated in a candidate area evaluation matrix.

Selection of Candidate Areas for Further Analysis

The ranking process was designed so that the candidate areas with the lowest weighted total scores were the most suitable for siting. Half of the candidate areas that scored best were located in the Central Valley and southeastern desert areas. On the basis of these results, a strict reliance on the numerical ranking would not be acceptable since the decision-making group felt that a coastal area and an area in the southern California urban region were also desirable. Other factors, such as pending legislation which could render an area unsuitable, were taken into account to modify the numerical-ranking results. In all, nine candidate areas were selected for further study.

PREFERRED CANDIDATE AREA ANALYSIS PHASE

Derivation and Structure of the Candidate Area Data Base

The preferred candidate area analysis identified specific sites suitable for power plant siting within the candidate areas. The EDAW/ESA-DWR team expected that twenty to thirty sites, of at least 13 square kilometers, would be identified in the nine preferred candidate areas.

The first step of the preferred candidate area analysis was to develop new base maps of each candidate area at a scale of 1:125,000. This enabled much more precise mapping of data factors already identified in the statewide analysis as well as some which were too small to be seen in the statewide analysis. Each new base map covered a region somewhat larger than the candidate area so that siting decisions within the candidate area could be made with an awareness of the regional setting.

To identify specific sites within the candidate areas, a transparent color overlay procedure similar to the one used in statewide analysis was employed. In the case of some candidate areas, the overlay procedure revealed five or six candidate sites. In other cases, only one or two sites were identified. A minimum of one site was chosen from each preferred candidate area in order to provide the greatest geographic diversity of sites for the final ranking.

PREFERRED CANDIDATE AREA DATA BASE BREAKDOWN

While the broad data categories used for the candidate area analysis were basically the same as those used in the statewide analysis, many additional data factors within each category were assessed by the discipline specialists. The following discussions focus mainly on additional constraint factors and siting opportunities identified for the preferred candidate areas.

Preferred Candidate Area Constraint Analysis

The constraints were generalized graphically into four categories:

1 Environmental resource constraints
2 Land-use constraints
3 Terrain and natural-hazards constraints
4 Air quality constraints

Because not all constraints within the first two categories were equally limiting, those categories were divided into *constraints* and *critical constraints*.

Land Use

The ten land uses identified at the statewide scale as power plant siting constraints, either exclusion or evaluation factors, were joined by additional constraint factors for the preferred candidate areas which refined the original exclusion and buffer zones. Additional existing land uses that could not reasonably coexist with the power plant and were thus designated as constraint factors included county and regional parks with a 4.8-kilometer visual buffer and cemeteries with a visual buffer zone.

Environmental Resources

Additional constraint factors identified at the candidate area scale included further delineation of potentially affected wildlife and plant refuges and protected animal species. In addition to areas designated as "natural" or "special" by a government agency, over 2000 additional natural areas having no legal status or protection have been inventoried by private concerns in California. These areas also were considered in the evaluation process.

No siting opportunities were identified in conjunction with the environmental resource analysis at this stage.

Natural Hazards and Terrain

The more accurate topographic details available at the candidate area mapping scale showed that many relatively uniformly sloping areas as steep as 15 percent were probably economically feasible for development. It was also apparent that some relatively gently sloping areas of less than 10 percent slope were not feasible for development because of the dissected and irregular nature of the ground surface.

When a choice of several sites within one preferred candidate area existed, the following conditions or factors were judged to represent siting opportunities:

· Level terrain

· Absence of minor faults

· Absence of recorded earthquake epicenter locations

· Safety from flood zones

· Greatest distance from active or major faults

· Absence of landslide-prone terrain

· Great depths to or absence of groundwater

· Strong foundation materials

Air Quality

To identify specific sites within the preferred candidate areas, the PSD Class I and II buffers were replotted at the scale of 1:125,000. The Class II buffer distance was recomputed to 8 kilometers (versus 16 kilometers in the statewide analysis). However, this was deemed acceptable because at the larger map scale the elevation contours show more terrain details so that impingement can be predicted with greater accuracy.

Socioeconomics

During the statewide screening process, socioeconomics played a small role in the determination and evaluation of candidate areas. No exclusion factors from this category were noted. The sole evaluation factor was distance of the candidate area from construction labor pools of sufficient size to avoid undesirable impacts on the present populations. During the preferred candidate area analysis, socioeconomic considerations were limited to evaluation factors. No constraint factors from this category were included in the determination of sites within candidate areas.

No siting opportunities were identified for the pre-ferred candidate areas in this phase of the study, and socioeconomic input was deferred to the site-evaluation stage.

Site-Dependent Costs

On a 1:125,000 scale, actual rail, highway, and water pipeline routing could be closely identified and restrictions to site access from these facilities used as a constraint. Also, existing transmission lines and corridors were more clearly pinpointed.

If several sites existed in one area, all the statewide evaluation factors were considered. No siting opportunities were identified at this stage.

Water Supply

The only additional constraint in the evaluation of possible sources was to limit the size of wastewater sources evaluated.

The factors considered that influence the availability of municipal and industrial wastewaters, agricultural drainage waters, and brackish groundwaters in the vicinity of each preferred candidate area include geographic relationship to the candidate area, chemical quality of the water source and associated treatment requirements, development and transport costs, environmental problems with developing the source and with use of the waters in the power plant cooling system, willingness of local wastewater agencies to supply the water, and competing uses for the source. Although some of these factors are of economic as well as technical and environmental significance, the actual costs of developing adequate water supplies are included in the "Site-Dependent Costs" subsection.

MUNICIPAL AND INDUSTRIAL WASTEWATERS Each significant municipal and industrial waste discharge within 100 kilometers of a preferred candidate area was reexamined in the candidate area analysis. The statewide analysis used published data which were somewhat out of date, so the appropriate wastewater agencies and regional water control boards were contacted during the candidate area analysis to obtain more recent unpublished information.

Much of the municipal and industrial wastewater has a relatively low level of total dissolved solids (TDS) and can be used for irrigation, groundwater recharge, streamflow augmentation, and other beneficial uses.

Use of these low-TDS wastewaters from any of the municipal or industrial sources in the state where the wastewater is not discharged to the ocean may reduce downstream flows, groundwater recharge, and/or delta outflow. All these impacts may reduce the quality of existing freshwater supplies downstream of the existing discharges.

The availability of reasonably inexpensive agricultural drainage water for power plant cooling was dependent upon the development of a master agricultural drain, which, if constructed, would make usage much more convenient than if it were necessary to collect the drainage from existing small drains and drainage sumps. For the purposes of this study, the construction of the proposed drain was considered to be uncertain, and the usefulness of agricultural drainage water was discounted accordingly.

BRACKISH GROUNDWATER   Brackish groundwater occurs in most of the major groundwater basins of the state and is available to some extent to all the candidate sites. However, this resource is undeveloped, and the basins are largely unexplored, resulting in varying degrees of uncertainty for different areas with regard to usable quantities available for development.

Limited information in the statewide analysis phase necessitated a more detailed analysis to refine the estimates of the usable quantity of brackish groundwater in storage. Each inland groundwater basin within a 48-kilometer distance of the boundaries of the preferred candidate areas was reexamined.

PREFERRED CANDIDATE SITE IDENTIFICATION AND ANALYSIS PHASE

The candidate sites were identified by using overlays of the constraints, which revealed areas of least constraint. All areas of least constraint were identified as candidate sites provided that the areas were reasonably close to the opportunities. At least one candidate site was identified in each candidate area even though some of the candidate areas were relatively highly constrained. Small areas of less than 1 or 2 square miles were ignored. The decision-making process to identify candidate sites used a workshop format with a group of specialists from the study team representing all the environmental and technical disciplines. A total of twenty-three candidate sites were thus identified.

The final phase of the siting process was to evaluate and rank the twenty-three sites selected in the candidate area analysis. The data categories used to evaluate the sites were the same as those used to identify sites in the candidate area analysis, with the exception of the electrical energy systems and DWR resource facilities category, which was absorbed into site-dependent costs. With the exception of power plant layouts, the scale of data collection and mapping remained the same.

The first step of the site analysis was to select the most promising location within each site for the proposed power plant. U.S. Geological Survey topographic maps at scales of 1:62,500 and 1:24,000 were used as base maps. Schematic layouts showing the generating facilities, the switchyard, the cooling towers, and links to transmission corridors, railroad lines, and roads were developed by the engineering discipline specialists for each site. Sites with two equally good locations for the plant were divided into two separate sites for evaluation and ranking.

A series of general criteria was developed by the engineering specialists in selecting individual plant locations within large site areas.

Once a plant location within each site was tentatively identified, it was possible for each consultant to evaluate more accurately the sites for any constraints not avoided previously. For example, a candidate site identified in the candidate area analysis may have partially overlapped the range of a protected animal species. Once a plant location was specified within the site, that location could be determined more precisely relative to the animal's range and could be rated accordingly.

CANDIDATE SITE DATA SUMMARIES

A candidate site data summary was prepared for each site in the preferred candidate areas, including information on the location, size, and physiography of the site. Photographs were included to provide a better idea of the terrain.

Federal, state, and local regulatory agencies having jurisdiction or responsibility for the development of a coal-fired generating plant in these sites were identified and listed in a separate index.

Site Ranking and Selection

The ranking of the sites used a two-step decision-making process. First, the decision-making group employed the importance-ratio rating process to develop a single weight total score for each site. Although that process provided valuable results, the numerical results alone did not provide a conclusive and defensible basis for selection of sites. The second part of the process thus involved a final review by the consulting team and a recommendation of sites for further study in DWR's NOI preparation. The details of each factor had changed considerably since the candidate area ranking because of the more detailed scale of mapping and analysis. The decision-making group concluded after hearing briefings from each discipline specialist that the evaluation categories were still appropriate for the site ranking. Importance-ratio ballots were completed by each participant, and the results were examined.

A few shifts in importance had occurred since the balloting for the candidate area ranking, but in general the results were relatively consistent. As before, air quality issues were considered by far the most important factor, with water supply ranking second.

Ratings of Site Areas

An extensive tabulation was made by site of data factors within each evaluation category. This descriptive information was used to rate the suitability of each site. Before assigning the ratings, the decision-making group heard how the data factors were developed, how the data were collected, and how the discipline specialist would recommend establishing a rating scale. These presentations were summarized for each evaluation category.

Land Use

To evaluate the candidate sites, six land-use criteria were employed:

1 *Development compatibility* concerns the relationship of the proposed power plants to existing cities, towns, settlements, and rural residential development.

2 *Scenic-recreational-cultural compatibility* concerns the relationship of the proposed facility to areas used for these purposes.

3 *Agricultural compatibility* focuses on the potential conflict between the proposed power plant and lands currently in, or with the potential for, agricultural use.

4 *Military-institutional compatibility* covers the relationship of a coal-fired power plant to certain facilities and activities associated with the operations of military and institutional lands. Issues of compatibility focus on three areas of concern: (a) direct conflicts with facilities or activities, (b) indirect conflicts created by reduced visibility, and (c) potential interference with the electromagnetic spectrum needed

to operate highly sophisticated electronic communications equipment.

5 *Site flexibility* describes the ability of the candidate site to entertain various plant locations and arrangements which might lessen the impact on current and future land use.

6 *Industrial proximity* was considered an opportunity as it implies both conformance with existing land use and visual patterns and availability of existing support facilities.

Environmental Resources

The analysis of environmental resources did not readily lend itself to quantification or ranking since (1) existing data on protected wildlife species differ qualitatively from species to species; (2) some animal species have been mapped by range, others by nesting sites, and still others by sitings; (3) numerical counts exist for some populations but not for others; (4) habitat requirements are not fully understood for all species, and attempts to transplant species have been few and largely unsuccessful; and (5) the effects of a coal-fired power plant on wildlife species and their habitats, specifically vegetation, are largely unknown. The same problems apply to protected plants.

In addition to the on-site impacts of the power plant on environmental resources, new off-site facilities were assessed for their impacts on habitat areas. Secondary effects, such as increased human population in currently unpopulated spots and increased recreational use of areas important to wildlife, were also assessed.

Natural Hazards and Terrain

Each candidate area was analyzed once more to confirm the location of historically active and major Quaternary faults and of dissected terrain or areas with more than 15 percent slopes. The candidate sites identified during the workshop were then evaluated by reference to maps, aerial-reconnaissance photographs, flood hazard information, and personal knowledge of geographic conditions throughout the area.

The EPA range developed for the candidate area screening was refined during candidate site evaluation by measuring the distance from the suggested plant location to the nearest seismogenic source and scaling the EPA value, on the assumption that the acceleration decreases linearly from the source.

The EPA provided only a relative comparison between sites, since the actual strong ground shaking for which the plant would be designed depends upon a variety of factors. Seismic design cost implications were thus considered in the site-dependent cost category, while general engineering difficulty, operational reliability, and licensability implications were considered in this category.

Air Quality

Sites were evaluated by criteria related to statutory, physical, and perceived air quality goals as well as by offset criteria. A scale by which the criteria were applied to the sites was developed. Although this scale had a certain merit for a given criterion, the relative importance of the criteria could not be judged objectively. In the absence of such judgment, the factors were all weighted equally, and site ratings were obtained by averaging the scores given for each factor.

Socioeconomics

The socioeconomic factors needed to determine community absorption capability and suitability have been discussed in Chapter 8. A construction worker in-migration estimator was developed by EDAW for this project. A value for *percentage local*, the percentage of workers already living in the immediate radius and expected to work on the construction project, was also calculated by the estimator for each site, using the criteria specified in Chapter 8.

Three quantifiable factors for each site were determined: construction period community stress, operation period community stress, and unemployment. A rating scale reflecting impact intensities for community stress values and unemployment rates was developed, on the assumption that a larger ratio of increase in population results in greater community stress.

Site-Dependent Costs

Six factors were determined to contribute significantly to the differential cost between individual sites and were considered for the engineering evaluation:

1 *Access,* including construction of an access road and a railroad from existing facilities to the plant.

2 *Site development,* including site grading and drainage, foundation costs, and development of storage areas.

3 *Transmission,* including the capital cost of constructing transmission lines to carry the power generated by the plant to the nearest 500-kilovolt substation and from there to the DWR load center.

4 *Fuel transportation,* measured along existing major railroad main lines.

5 *Water supply,* including the cost of bringing water to meet plant demands from a known source to the site.

6 *Seismic effects,* including the additional costs required to strengthen the plant structurally to resist the forces created by peak acceleration.

Unit costs were computed and used to translate the significant factors into differential quantities.

Water Supply: Wastewater and Brackish-Water Sources

For brackish-water sources, usable storage capacities, possible contamination of freshwater aquifers in the same basin, and subsidence of the basin ground surface from brackish-water withdrawal were considered for each source. The different evaluation criteria were then rated and tabulated for each site.

Final Recommendation of Sites for the DWR Notification of Intention

It was apparent from the weighted scores that sites in the Central Valley and southeast desert were superior to those in southern California and on the coast. It was also clear that the top seven sites were so closely grouped that a small change in the rating of even the least important of the evaluation categories was sufficient to shift any of them by at least one position. As a result, the decision-making group made a final comparison of the top seven sites and of the best southern California and coastal sites.

The best southern California site ranked sixteenth overall, while the coastal site ranked twenty-second overall. It was recognized, however, that these low-ranking sites might still be acceptable and that they represented important opportunities for a diversity of alternatives in the final recommendations.

It was in fact necessary to exploit this degree of diversity when, following preliminary completion of the candidate site analyses and rankings, it became apparent to the study team and DWR that the sites identified in the southern California candidate areas were unacceptable owing to the difficulties in locating adequate space for power plant facilities. This unexpected result eliminated the only candidate sites under consideration that could utilize emissions trade-offs from the southern California urban areas. These emissions trade-offs represented an important siting opportunity for compliance with CARB's regulations, so a search was initiated by the study team and DWR to locate an alternative area.

The search immediately focused on a region which was part of a candidate area identified earlier in the candidate area ranking and rejected in favor of the now unsuitable southern California area. DWR requested that the study team examine this region to determine whether power plant locations could be found to take advantage of the emissions trade-off opportunities.

The process employed by the study team generally paralleled that used to examine the other candidate areas and sites. Siting constraints and opportunities were inventoried and mapped to identify a site area in which one potential plant location was then evaluated and ranked. Since the decision-making process, criteria, and weighting used to rank the new-area site were based on those used to rank the other twenty-three sites, the results were comparable. The product of the study was thus the required defensible set of three alternative sites.

REFERENCES CITED

Appleby, M.: "Methods for Achieving Productive Citizen Participation," Virginia Polytechnic Institute, Urban and Regional Planning Department, unpublished, 1978.

Arthur D. Little, Inc.: *Effective Citizen Participation in Highway Planning,* vol. 1: *Community Involvement Processes,* U.S. Department of Transportation, Federal Highway Administration, 1976.

Belknap Data Solutions Ltd.: "Facility Location Decisions: A Fortune Market Research Survey," *Fortune,* New York, 1977.

Blackwelder, B.: "Water Resources Development," in James Ratilesberger (ed.), *Nixon and the Environment: The Politics of Devastation,* Village Voice/Taurus Communications, Inc., New York, 1972, pp. 59–79.

Bosselman, F., and D. Callies: *The Quiet Revolution in Land Use Control,* Council on Environmental Quality, Washington, 1971.

Brooks, M. E.: *Housing Equity and Environmental Protection: The Needless Conflict,* American Institute of Planners Books, Washington, 1976.

California Department of Water Resources: "Objectives for Power Generation," prepared in association with EDAW Inc., unpublished, 1978.

Comstock, R. W., Vice President, Communications, Northern States Power Company: Talk given before the Westinghouse International School of Environmental Management, July 1975.

Crowe, S.: *The Landscape of Power,* The Architectural Press, Ltd., London, 1958.

Eckbo, Dean, Austin & Williams: "The Duluth Corridor Study," prepared for the State of Minnesota Department of Highways, unpublished, 1972.

———: "West Oahu College: Summary Report of Site Evaluations," prepared for the University of Hawaii, unpublished, October 1972.

EDAW Inc.: *Study of Environmental Impact of Underground Electric Power Transmission Systems,* prepared for the U.S. Energy Research and Development Administration and the Electric Power Research Institute, National Technical Information Service, 1975a.

———: "Inventory 1975: Candidate Areas for Large Electric Power Generating Plants," prepared for the State of Minnesota Environmental Quality Council, Power Plant Siting Program, unpublished, 1975b.

———: "Seafarer Site Survey, Upper Michigan Region," prepared for the U.S. Navy under contract to GTE Sylvania, unpublished, April 1976.

———: "Power Plant Feasibility Study," Phases 1 and 2, prepared for the Platte River Power Authority, unpublished, June–September 1976.

———: *Siting Manual—Thermal Power Plant Site Screening and Site Evaluation,* prepared for the California Energy Resources Conservation and Development Commission, printed by California Department of General Services, Office Services Division, February 1977.

———: "Rawhide Power Plant Siting Studies," prepared for the Platte River Power Authority, unpublished, 1978.

———: "Swan Falls–Guffey Hydroelectric Project: A Decision Paper," prepared for the Idaho Power Commission and the Boise Project Board of Control, unpublished, 1979a.

———: "Las Virgenes Areawide Wastewater Treatment Plan," environmental impact statement prepared for the U.S. Environmental Protection Agency, unpublished, 1979b.

———: "Statewide Coal-Fired Power Plant Siting Studies," prepared for the State of California Department of Water Resources, unpublished, 1980.

Frieden, B. J.: *The Environmental Protection Hustle,* The M.I.T. Press, Cambridge, Mass., 1979.

Hamilton, F. E. I. (ed.): *Spatial Perspectives on Industrial Organization and Decision-Making,* John Wiley & Sons, Inc., London, 1974.

Hunker, H.: *Industrial Development,* Lexington Books, Lexington, Mass., 1974.

Industrial Development, May–June 1978.

Isard, W. J.: *Methods of Regional Analysis,* The M.I.T. Press, Cambridge, Mass., 1960.

Mathey, C. J.: "Facility Planning with Screening Forms," *Industrial Development,* Conway Publications, Inc., Atlanta, March–April 1979.

Minnesota Environmental Quality Council: *Visual Sensitivity of River Recreation to Power Plants,* prepared with EDAW Inc., April 1978.

National Coal Policy Project: *Where We Agree: Report of the National Coal Policy Project, Summary and Synthesis,* Georgetown University, Center for Strategic and International Studies, Washington, 1977.

Rivkin, M.: *Negotiated Development: A Breakthrough in Environmental Controversies,* The Conservation Foundation, Inc., Washington, 1977.

Seelig, D.: "Visions of the 1980's: Downtown Rebirth, Energy Parks," *Industrial Development,* Conway Publications, Inc., Atlanta, March–April 1976, pp. 13–14.

Site Selection Handbook, prepared by editors of *Industrial Development,* Conway Publications, Inc., Atlanta, 1978.

Smith, D. M.: *Industrial Location: An Economic Geographical Analysis,* John Wiley & Sons, Inc., New York, 1971.

Soderman, S.: *Industrial Location Planning: An Empirical Investigation of Company Approaches to the Problem of Locating New Plants,* John Wiley & Sons, Inc., New York, 1975.

Stafford, H. A.: *Principles of Industrial Facility Location,* Conway Publications, Inc., Atlanta, 1979.

U.S. Department of the Interior, National Park Service: *Workbook for Yosemite National Park: Master Plan,* National Park Service, San Francisco, 1975.

SELECTED BIBLIOGRAPHY

Anderson, W.: "What Ever Became of the Dow Plant?" *Cry California,* San Francisco, vol. 14, no. 3, summer 1979.

Boise Project Board of Control: "Lucky Peak Power Plant Project, Exhibit W—Environmental Report," prepared by EDAW Inc., for the Federal Energy Regulatory Commission license application, unpublished, 1978.

Brown, J. E.: "Step Progression Makes Site Selection Simple," *Electric Light and Power: Energy Generation Edition,* vol. 52, no. 9, 1974, pp. 26–27.

Brubaker, R. I., Jr.: "A Rocky Road Awaits Industry on Its Way through the Environmental Obstacle Course," *Industrial Development,* Conway Publications, Inc., Atlanta, March–April 1978, pp. 2–5.

Calvert, J. D., Jr.: *New Siting Techniques for Nuclear Power Plants,* presented for the Joint Committee on Atomic Development and Space, California Legislature, Sacramento, Calif., Commonwealth Associates, Inc., Jackson, Mich., 1972.

Carter, L. J.: *The Florida Experience,* published for *Resources for the Future* by The Johns Hopkins Press, Baltimore, 1974.

Coffey, J. B., Jr.: "Area Developers Take Their Case to the Top," *Industrial Development,* Conway Publications, Inc., Atlanta, July–August 1977, p. 8.

Conservation Foundation: *Three Approaches to Environmental Resource Analysis,* prepared by the Landscape Architecture Research Office, Harvard University, Cambridge, Mass., 1967.

Cormick, G. W., and L. K. Patton: "Environmental Mediation: Potentials and Limitations," *Environmental Comment,* Urban Land Institute, Washington, May 1977, p. 13.

Dasman, R. F.: *The Destruction of California,* The Macmillan Company, New York, 1965.

Delbecq, A. L., and A. H. Van de Ven: "A Group Process Model for Problem Identification and Program Planning, *Journal of Applied Behavioral Science,* vol. 7, no. 4, 1971, pp. 463–492.

——, ——, and D. H. Gustafson: *Group Techniques for Program Planning: A Guide to Nominal Group and Delphi Processes,* Scott, Foresman and Company, Glenview, Ill., 1975.

Eckenrode, R. T., and Dunpal and Associates, Inc.: "Weighting Multiple Criteria," *Management Science,* vol. 12, no. 3, 1956.

EDAW Inc.: *Visual Sensitivity of River Recreation to Power Plants,* prepared for the Minnesota Environmental Quality Council, April 1978.

Ellis, G.: "Radio with a Difference—Sanguine/Seafarer," *Sierra Club Bulletin,* April 1976, p. 41.

Fearey, Peter J.: "The Clean Air Act: Industry in Wonderland," *Industrial Development,* Conway Publications, Inc., Atlanta, March–April 1979.

Fisher, J. L.: " 'Frivolous' Environmentalists vs. 'Paranoid' Developers: An Unproductive Stand-Off," *Industrial Development,* Conway Publications, Inc., Atlanta, July–August 1977, pp. 9–10.

Fort, T.: "Westinghouse Lists Key Factors in Labor, Community, Services and Taxes," *Industrial Facilities Planning,* Conway Publications, Inc., Atlanta, 1976, pp. 127–129.

Fulton, Maurice: "New Factors in Plant Location," *Harvard Business Review,* May–June 1971.

Gilliam, H.: "The Fallacy of Single-Purpose Planning." in Hans H. Landsberg (ed.), *America's Changing Environment,* Houghton Mifflin Company, Boston, and the American Academy of Arts and Sciences, 1970.

Gobar, A. J., and C. B. Coman: "Reserving Too Much Land in Industry Restricts Prospects for Broad-Based Development," *Industrial Development,* Conway Publications, Inc., Atlanta, May–June 1977, pp. 13–15.

Gramm, W. P., and R. B. Ekelund, Jr.: "Land Use Planning: The Free Market," *Industrial Development,* Conway Publications, Inc., Atlanta, November–December 1977, pp. 10–14.

Greenberg, M. R., and D. B. Straus: "Up-Front Resolution of Environmental and Economic Disputes," *Environmental Comment,* Urban Land Institute, Washington, May 1977, p. 16.

Haynes, W. W., and J. L. Massie: *Management: Analysis Concepts and Cases,* Prentice-Hall, Inc., Englewood Cliffs, N.J., 1961.

Heberlein, T. A.: "Principles of Public Involvement for National Park Service Planners and Managers," prepared for the National Park Service, Park Planning Task Force, Department of Rural Sociology, University of Wisconsin, Madison, unpublished mimeograph, 1975.

Hopkins, L. D.: "Methods of Generating Land Suitability Maps: A Comparative Evaluation." *Journal of the American Institute of Planners,* vol. 43, no. 4, October 1977, pp. 386–400.

Hornback, K. E.: "Overcoming Obstacles to Agency and Public Involvement: A Program and Its Methods," U.S. National Park Service Center, Washington, unpublished mimeograph, 1975.

Koleda, M. S.: "White House Conference Plots New Directions for Natural Growth," *Industrial Development,* Conway Publications, Inc., Atlanta, July–August 1978, pp. 5–7.

Lehman, G. H.: "Applications of Computer Technique to Specific Site Selection Programs," *Industrial Facilities Planning,* Conway Publications, Inc., Atlanta, 1976, p. 134.

Linstone, H., and Turoff, M.: *The Delphi Method: Technique and Applications,* Addison–Wesley Publishing Company, Inc., Reading, Mass., 1975.

McGuire, M., K. Chander, and P. Lonett: "Land Has to Be Kept Ready for Site-Seeking Industry," *Industrial Development,* Conway Publications, Inc., Atlanta, May–June 1977, pp. 16–19.

Mathey, C. J.: "A 'Cornerstone' for Facility Strategy," *Industrial Development,* Conway Publications, Inc., Atlanta, May–June 1978, pp. 2–4.

Miner, J. B.: *Management Theory,* The MacMillan Company, New York; Collier-Macmillan Ltd., London, 1971.

Nair, K., and R. Keeney: *Selecting Nuclear Power Plant Sites Using Decision Analysis,* Woodward-Clyde Consultants, San Francisco, December 1975.

Olsson, D. E.: *Management by Objectives,* Pacific Books Publishers, Palo Alto, Calif., 1968.

O'Neil, M. G.: "A Coordinated Program for Facility Planning," *Industrial Facilities Planning,* Conway Publications, Inc., Atlanta, 1976, pp. 60–61.

Paparian, M., Sierra Club, Sacramento: Personal communication.

Parten, M.: *Surveys, Polls and Samples: Practical Procedures,* Harper & Brothers, New York, 1950.

Pearlman, K.: "State Environmental Policy Acts," *A.I.P. Journal,* vol. 43, no. 1, January 1977, p. 42.

Popper, F. J.: "Siting Lulus (Locally Unwanted Land Uses)," *Planning,* April 1981.

Reich, Michael: "The Tocks Island Dam Is Dead, But the Delaware Gap Widens," *Planning,* December 1976.

Reiquam, H., N. Dee, and P. Choi: "Assessing Cross-Media Impacts," *Environmental Science and Technology,* February 1975, pp. 118–120.

Reynolds, J. Z.: "Power Plant Cooling Systems: Policy Alternatives," *Science,* vol. 207, no. 4429, Jan. 25, 1980.

Roberts, Jerry: "Dow's Plan to Clevelandize the Delta," *San Francisco Bay Guardian,* Sept. 27, 1977.

Russell, F., former director, U.S. Environmental Protection Agency, Region IX: Personal communication.

Russell, J. A.: "Geography of Industrial Costs," *Industrial Facilities Planning,* Conway Publications, Inc., Atlanta, 1976, pp. 102–105.

Sanoff, H. (ed.): *Designing with Community Participation,* Dowden, Hutchinson & Ross, Inc., Stroudsburg, Pa., and McGraw-Hill Book Company, New York, 1978.

Schaal, H. R.: "Consultant Maps," *Transmission and Distribution,* April 1972.

Scott, C. B.: "Clean Air Act Amendment to Loom as Threat to Industrial Expansion," *Industrial Development,* Conway Publications, Inc., Atlanta, July–August 1978, pp. 9–12.

Shepherd, P.: "Development Siting Decisions Must Not Be Left to Washington," *Industrial Development,* Conway Publications, Inc., Atlanta, July–August 1978, pp. 5–7.

Silcox, John H.: "The Regulatory Maze: Has Government Gone Loco?" *Industrial Development,* Conway Publications, Inc., Atlanta, March–April 1979.

Smith, D. C., R. C. Stuart, and R. Hansen: *Manual for Community Involvement in Highway Planning and Design,* Virginia Polytechnic Institute, Center for Urban and Regional Studies, for the Federal Highway Administration, U.S. Department of Transportation, 1975.

Smith, F. J., and R. T. Hester, Jr., *Community Goal Setting,* Hutchinson Ross Publishing Company, Stroudsburg, Pa., 1982.

Solano County Planning Department, Contra Costa County Planning Department, and J. B. Gilbert & Associates: *Final Environmental Impact Report, Petrochemical Project,* Solano County Planning Department, Fairfield, Calif., October 1975.

Steinitz, C., P. Parker, and L. Jordan: "Hand Drawn Overlays: Their History and Prospective Uses," *Landscape Architecture,* vol. 66, no. 5, September 1976, pp. 444–445.

Stelow, R.: "Industry & EPA Need Not Be at Odds," *Industrial Development,* Conway Publications, Inc., Atlanta, July–August 1976, pp. 11–12.

Stenger, A. J., and W. Cunningham: "Are You Misdirecting Your Distribution Dollar by Your Location Decisions?" *Industrial Development,* Conway Publications, Inc., Atlanta, September–October 1977, pp. 10–13.

Stephen, F. F., and P. J. McCarthy: *Sampling Opinions,* John Wiley & Sons, Inc., New York, 1958.

Talbot, Allan R.: *Power along the Hudson,* E. P. Dutton & Co., Inc., New York, 1972.

————: *Cornwall,* an information pamphlet, Consolidated Edison Company of New York, Inc., November 1973.

————: Public information releases, Consolidated Edison Company of New York, Inc., Mar. 1 and 5, 1977.

Tennessee Valley Authority, Division of Forestry, Fisheries, and

Wildlife Development: "Which Species Will Be Endangered?" *Industrial Development,* Conway Publications, Inc., Atlanta, May–June 1977, pp. 13–15.

Topping, C. H.: "How to Pick Process Sites," *Industrial Facilities Planning,* Conway Publications, Inc., Atlanta, 1976, pp. 116–118.

Udall, S. L.: *The Quiet Crisis,* Holt, Rinehart and Winston, Inc., New York, 1963.

Ueland and Junker Architects and Planners and Portfolio Associates, Inc.: *A Manual for Achieving Effective Community Participation in Transportation Planning,* Pennsylvania Department of Transportation, Harrisburg, 1974.

Viets, Victor F.: *Comprehensive Regional Land Use Studies to Identify Power Plant Sites,* presented to the Conference on Land Use Planning cosponsored by the Atomic Industrial Forum and the Edison Electric Institute, June 1974.

————: **and H. R. Schaal & Earth Sciences Associates:** "Coal Transport Planning Evaluation Process," *Minnesota Coal Transport Evaluations,* prepared for the Minnesota Environmental Quality Council, undated.

Winter, J. V., and D. A. Conner: *Power Plant Siting,* Van Nostrand Reinhold Company, New York, 1978.

————: "Business Climate Battle Moves to a New Arena," *Industrial Development,* Conway Publications, Inc., Atlanta, May–June 1978.

————: "Largest Costs of Saving Environment Lie Ahead," *Engineering News–Record,* June 29, 1978.

————: "Powerplant Size Studies Show Big Is No Bargain," *Engineering News–Record,* May 24, 1979.

Index

Absolute siting requirements, 51, 62–63
Absorption capability, 135
Accessibility, 55
Accountability to public, 24
Activity identification, 51, 55
Advisory committees, 185, 187–189
Aesthetics (see Visual objectives)
Agencies (see Governmental agencies)
Agriculture Department, U.S., 211
Air pollution (see Pollution)
Airports, 1, 4, 16–17, 23
Alternatives, facility, 51, 133
American Bar Association, 24
Analytical procedures for site evaluation, 136–137, 140–142
Appleby, M., 192
Archaeologic features, 246
Area identification, candidate, 83–84, 128
Area of study, geographic, 79–81, 83
Area requirements, 55
Army Corps of Engineers, U.S., 9, 21
Assessment approach, 60
Assumptions (see Project definition)
Attainment or prevention of significant deterioration areas, 71
Auburn dam (proposed), Calif., 3

BAAPCD (Bay Area Air Pollution Control District), 21
Ballots:
    screening factors classified by, 92
    screening factors weighted by, 120
Bay Area Air Pollution Control District (BAAPCD), 21
Big Cypress National Preserve, Fla., 16–17
Biological objectives, 39, 60
Birds of Prey Natural Area (BPNA), Idaho, 273
Bishop Estate, Hawaii, 18
Blackwelder, B., 1
Bodega Head nuclear power plant (proposed), Calif., 13–14, 23
Bonneville dam (proposed), Wash., 3

Bosselman, F., 1
Boston, Mass., Interstate 95 completion (proposed), 13
BPNA (Birds of Prey Natural Area), Idaho, 273
Brooks, M. E., 27
Bureau of Land Management, U.S., 273, 290

Cable systems (see Transmission lines)
Calaveras Water Master Plan in Calif., 169, 172
California:
    Bodega Head nuclear power plant (proposed), 13–14, 23
    coal-fired power plant siting study, 32, 41–42, 44, 83, 88, 91, 128–129, 165, 183, 187, 289–301
    data files in, 164–165
    Davenport siting studies, 179, 247–271
    Diablo Canyon nuclear power plant (proposed), 4, 14–15, 23
    environmental laws in, 20, 31–32, 60, 181
    Hetch Hetchy Valley Dam, 1, 9–11
    Humboldt Bay nuclear power plant (proposed), 4
    Los Angeles freeways (proposed), 13
    Montezuma Hills chemical plant (proposed), 4, 19–22, 24, 26, 181
    Nipomo Dunes nuclear power plant (proposed), 14
    Point Arenas nuclear power plant (proposed), 4
    San Francisco convention center (proposed), 4
    San Francisco freeways (proposed), 12–13
California Coastal Act (1976), 292
California Coastal Commission, 42, 292
California Department of Fish and Game, 291
California Department of Transportation, 36

California Department of Water Resources (DWR) Power Plant Siting Study, 32, 41–42, 44, 83, 88, 91, 128–129, 165, 183, 187, 289–301
California Energy Resources Conservation and Development Commission (ERCDC), 32, 41, 66, 116, 120, 165, 183, 187
California Public Utilities Commission, 14
California Resources Agency, 14
Callies, D., 1
Campbell Estate, Hawaii, 18, 202, 204
Candidate area identification, 83–84, 128
Candidate site identification, 125–129
Century Freeway (proposed), Calif., 13
CEQ (Council on Environmental Quality), 181
Checklist approach, 60–61
Chemical plants, 1–2, 4, 19–22, 49, 181
CIHE (Citizens for the Integration of Highway and Environment), 277
Citizen participation (see Public participation)
Citizens for the Integration of Highway and Environment (CIHE), 277
Clean Air Act (1970), 32, 71
Coal-fired power plants, 3, 41–42, 45–48, 53–55, 72–73, 76, 289–301
COGs (councils of government), 164
Collection methods, data, 161, 163–165, 168
College construction, 17–18, 24, 53, 55, 195–204
Collier County, Fla., 16
Colorado:
    Platte River Power Authority Study, 100–102, 111, 114, 116, 126–127, 169, 173–174
    Rawhide Transmission Line Siting Study, 32, 140–141, 144, 153–157, 160, 183, 190
Committees, advisory, 185, 187–189
Community service capacity analyses, 136–137

Composite mapping, 88, 90–91, 93, 96–102, 104–114, 117, 123, 169, 179
Comprehensive approach, 26
Comstock, R. W., 6, 16
Conceptual layouts, 131, 133, 137, 140–144, 146–147
Condition-impact matrices, 66, 70
Congress, U.S., 24
  Clean Air Act, 32, 71
  Everglades Jetport (proposed), 17
  Federal Power Act, 15
  Hetch Hetchy Valley Dam, 9
  National Environmental Policy Act, 1, 11, 16–17, 60, 274
  Project Seafarer, 19
Conservationists, 1, 4–5, 9–11, 23–24, 32
Consolidated Edison Company, 14–16, 24
Constraint composite mapping, 114–117
Constraint factor mapping, 97–99, 104–109
Constraint factors, 85, 89, 93–96, 120
Construction activities, impact of, 65–67
Cornwall, N.Y., Storm King Mountain nuclear power plant (proposed), 4, 14–16, 23–24
Corridor network maps, 226–227
Corridors, 205, 226–227
Cost estimates, 131, 133, 145, 169
Cost mapping, 103, 112–113
Council on Environmental Quality (CEQ), 181
Councils of government (COGs), 164
Court decisions, 4, 15–16
Criteria:
  site-evaluation, 133, 135
  site-screening: defined, 35
    refined, 71, 77
Critical siting requirements, 51, 62–63
Cross-Florida Barge Canal (proposed), 1, 4, 17
Crowe, S., 32
Cultural constraints (mapping), 106–107

Dade County, Fla., 16–17
Dade County Comprehensive Land Use Plan, 17
Dade County Port Authority, 16
Dams, 1, 3, 9–11, 32–33, 273–275
  (See also Power plants; Transmission lines)
Data base, 176–177, 179
Data collection methods, 161, 163–165, 168
Data needs and analyses, 33, 153–179
  collection methods, 161, 163–168
  data plans, 153, 161–163
  identification of, 153–155, 160–161
  mapped data, 168–179
  organization of, 168–179
  for project definition, 50–51, 154, 160
  for screening, 85, 160
  for site evaluation, 135–136, 138–139, 160–161
  sources, 161, 163–168
Data plans, 153, 161–163
Data records, 164, 166–167
Data sources, 164
Davenport Land-Use Study in Calif., 247–254, 257–259
Davenport Power Plant Siting Study in Calif., 247, 254–257
Davenport Transmission Routing Study in Calif., 179, 247, 259–271
Decision documents, 273

Decision making:
  Delphi procedure, 88, 128, 188
  groups, 82–83
Definition, project (see Project definition)
Delphi decision-making procedure, 88, 128, 188
Demographic analyses, 55, 136
Developed areas, 246
Diablo Canyon nuclear power plant (proposed), Calif., 4, 14–15, 23
Diagrams, 27, 55–57
Dickey-Lincoln dam (proposed), Maine, 3
Direct impacts, 66, 68
DM&IR (Duluth Missabe and Iron Range) Railroad, 277
Dominance, pure, 286
Dow Chemical Company, 4, 19–22, 24, 26, 181
Duluth, Minn., Interstate 35 completion, 13, 37, 39, 49, 84, 151, 183, 277–288
Duluth Corridor Study, 32, 84, 151, 277–288
Duluth Freeway Routing Study, 32, 84, 151, 277–288
Duluth Missabe and Iron Range (DM&IR) Railroad, 277
DWR (see California Department of Water Resources Power Plant Siting Study)

Early site review (ESR) applications, 134
Earth Sciences Associates (ESA), 289, 296
Earthquake faults, 13–15
Eau Claire, Wis., Tyrone power plant (proposed), 205, 227
Economic factors (see Industrial and economic interests)
Economic objectives, 39
Economic studies, 136–137
Effects, identification of, 64–66, 69, 71
EIRs (environmental impact reports), 21
EISs (environmental impact statements), 1, 11, 21
Electric Power Research Institute (EPRI), 32, 60, 66
ELF, Project, 19, 229
  (See also Seafarer, Project)
Embarcadero Freeway, Calif., 13
Emissions controls, 71
Employment analyses, 136
Energy parks, 32, 164, 166–167, 205–227
Energy Research and Development Administration (ERDA), U.S., 32, 60
Environmental analyses, 59–61
Environmental and social interests, 1, 4–5, 9–11, 23–24, 32, 60, 181–182
Environmental Defense Fund, 4
Environmental impact reports (EIRs), 21
Environmental impact statements (EISs), 1, 11, 21
Environmental impacts, 60, 64–73
Environmental performance standards, 25–26
Environmental-project relationships (see Project-environmental relationships)
Environmental Protection Agency (EPA), U.S., 11, 21–22, 60, 135, 299–300
EPA (see Environmental Protection Agency)
EPRI (Electric Power Research Institute), 32, 60, 66
ERCDC (see California Energy Resources

ERCDC (Cont.)
  Conservation and Development Commission)
ERDA (Energy Research and Development Administration), 32, 60
ESA (Earth Sciences Associates), 289, 296
ESR (early site review) applications, 134
Evaluation (see Site evaluation)
Evaluation composite mapping, 93, 96–102, 104–114, 117
Evaluation factors, 92–103
Evaluation matrices, 124, 128
Everglades Coalition, 17
Everglades Jetport (proposed), Fla., 1, 16–17, 23
Everglades Jetport Pact (1970), 17
Everglades National Park, Fla., 16–17
Ewa campus (proposed), University of Hawaii, 195, 202–204
Exclusion composite mapping, 88, 90–91
Exclusion factors, 85, 88–93

Facilities:
  physical characteristics, 49–51, 55, 62–63
  types of, 50
Fact versus judgment, 27
Factor lists, 84–85
Factor mapping, 93, 96–113, 168–169
Factor overlay weighting, 103, 116
Factors:
  evaluation, 92–103
  exclusion, 85, 88–93
  project-environmental relationships, 59
  screening: classification of, 85, 88, 93, 96, 103
    identification of, 83–85
  weighting, 103, 116
Federal Aviation Administration, 16
Federal Energy Regulatory Commission (FERC), 24, 273, 275
Federal Power Act (1920), 15
Federal Power Commission (FPC), 14–16
FERC (see Federal Energy Regulatory Commission)
Flood control districts, 16–17
Florida:
  Cross-Florida Barge Canal (proposed), 1, 4, 17
  Everglades Jetport (proposed), 1, 16–17, 23
Florida Aviation System Plan, 17
Florida Board of Conservation, 16
Florida Game and Fresh Water Fish Commission, 16
Forest Service, U.S., 163
Formats:
  graphic, 27, 55–57, 168–169, 172–179
  photographic, 56
  for project definition, 50–51, 53, 55
  tabular, 51, 56
  written, 56
Fortune survey (1977), 181
Fossil-fuel power plants (see Coal-fired power plants)
Foundation geology maps, 93
FPC (Federal Power Commission), 14–16
Freeways, 1, 4, 11–13, 23, 40, 49, 84, 86–87, 277–288
Frieden, Bernard, 1

Geographic area of study, 79–81, 83
Geographic comprehensiveness, 26

Geological Survey, U.S. (USGS), 160–161, 169, 179, 270, 298
Geology:
  foundation, 93
  surficial, 245
Geology maps, foundation, 93
George Moscone Convention Center (proposed), Calif., 4
Goal identification, 25, 29, 35–42
  defined, 35
  need for, 35–36
  organizational goals, 36–37
  organizational missions, 36
  organizational objectives, 37
  project goals, 38
  project objectives, 38–39, 41
Golden Gate Freeway (proposed), Calif., 12–13
Government, councils of (COGs), 164
Governmental agencies:
  and councils of government, 164
  review of concerns, 133–135
Governmental policies, 71, 77, 96
Graphic presentation methods, 27, 55–57, 168–169, 172–179
Graphic weighting, 169, 179
Ground slope maps, 93
GTE Sylvania, 238

Hamilton, F. E. I., 39
Handbook approach, 60
Hawaii:
  higher education rulings, 18
  land-use laws, 10, 195, 204
  West Oahu College, 18, 24, 142, 195–204
Hawaii Department of Planning and Economic Development, 195
Hawaii Land Use Commission, 195, 204
Health risks, 1–2
Hearings, public, 190, 192
Hell's Canyon dam (proposed), Idaho, 3
Hetch Hetchy Valley Dam, Calif., 1, 9–11
Hickel, Walter J., 17
Highways (see Freeways)
Historic features, 246
Honouliuli campus (proposed), University of Hawaii, 195, 202–204
Housing and Urban Development Department, U.S., 135
Hudson River, N.Y.–N.J., 14–16
Hudson River Fishermen's Association, 15
Humboldt Bay nuclear power plant (proposed), Calif., 4
Hunker, H., 39
Hydroelectric power projects (see Dams)

Idaho, Swan Falls–Guffey dam (proposed), 32–33, 273–275
Idaho Power Company, 273, 275
Idaho Water Resources Board, 273, 275
Impact matrices, 66, 69–70
Impact reports, 21
Impact statements, 1, 11, 21
Impact variables, 66, 72–73
Impacts, environmental, 60, 64–70, 72–73
Indian reservations, 182
Indirect maps, 66, 68
Industrial and economic interests, 1, 4–5, 9–11, 23–24, 32, 60, 181–182
Information presentation, 26–27, 51, 55–57
Interior Department, U.S., 17, 184

Interstate highway system, 1, 11–13, 23, 277
Interviews, key-person, 190–191
Isard, W. J., 4
Issues, identification of, 77–78

Jackson, Henry M., 17
Judgment versus fact, 27

Kaiparowits nuclear power plant (proposed), Utah, 3–4
Kent, William, 9
Key-person interviews, 190–191

Labor force access, 96
Land costs, 96
Land-use controls, 1–5, 9–11
Land-use objectives, 39
Land values, 32
LANDSAT imagery, 179
Landscape causality, 247
Landscape edges, 214
League of Women Voters, 14
Legal regulations, 71, 77, 96
Links on corridor network maps, 226
Locational requirements, 50–51, 55
Logically sequenced approach, 24–25
Los Angeles, Calif., freeways (proposed), 13

Makakilo campus (proposed), University of Hawaii, 195
Manoa campus, University of Hawaii, 18
Manual compositing, 169, 179
Map scale, 168, 170–171, 214
Mapped data, organization of, 168–179
Mapping:
  composite, 88, 90–91, 93, 96–102, 104–114, 117, 123, 169, 179
  factor, 93, 96–113, 168–169
Market access, 96
Marketing objectives, 39
Master environmental assessments, 60
Mathey, C. J., 35, 38
Matrices:
  evaluation, 124, 128, 150–151
  impact, 66, 69–70
MEQC (see Minnesota Environmental Quality Council)
Miami Urban Area Transportation System Plan, 17
Michigan, Project Seafarer sites in, 18–19, 83, 97–99, 117, 128, 187, 229, 232–233, 237–246
Mililani campus (proposed), University of Hawaii, 18, 195
Mining operations, 33, 246
Minnesota:
  advisory committees in, 187, 189
  Duluth freeway studies, 32, 84, 151, 277–288
  environmental laws in, 32
Minnesota Department of Highways, 37, 277
Minnesota Department of Natural Resources, 187
Minnesota Environmental Quality Council (MEQC), 16, 41, 51, 88, 90, 111, 169, 175, 178, 183
Minnesota Power Plant Siting Program, 88, 90, 111, 169, 175, 178, 183
Missile site construction, 18–19, 187, 229,

Missile site construction (Cont.)
  237–238, 245
Missions, organizational, 36
Mitigation possibilities to overcome constraints, 96
Montezuma Hills chemical plant (proposed), Calif., 4, 19–22, 24, 26, 181
Muir, John, 9
Muir Woods National Monument, Calif., 9
MX missile sites (see Missile site construction)

National Coal Policy Project, 4, 187
National Environmental Policy Act (NEPA) (1969), 1, 11, 16–17, 60, 274
National Legal Center for the Public Interest, 4
National Park Service, 14, 16–17, 184
Natural Resources Defense Council, 4
Navy, U.S., Project Seafarer missile sites, 18–19, 187, 229, 237–238, 245
NEPA (see National Environmental Policy Act)
Nevada, Project Seafarer sites in (proposed), 229, 235–237
New Mexico, Project Seafarer sites in (proposed), 229, 237
New York (state):
  Storm King Mountain nuclear power plant (proposed), 4, 14–16, 23–24
  Westway (proposed), 13
New York, N.Y., Westway (proposed), 13
Nipomo Dunes nuclear power plant (proposed), Calif., 14
Nodes on corridor network maps, 226
NOIs (notifications of intentions), 133–134
Northern States Power Company (NSP), 16, 205
Notifications of intentions (NOIs), 133–134
NRC (Nuclear Regulatory Commission), 14
NSP (Northern States Power Company), 16, 205
Nuclear power plants, 2–4, 13–16, 23, 51, 76
Nuclear Regulatory Commission (NRC), U.S., 14
Null alternatives, 279
Numerical weighting, 115–124, 128

Oahu, college siting in (see West Oahu College site studies in Hawaii)
Objectives:
  defined, 35
  organizational, 37
  project, 38–39, 41
  refined, 71, 74–75, 77, 84
Oil refineries, 4
Opportunity composite mapping, 123
Opportunity factor mapping, 100–103, 110–113
Opportunity factors, 85, 89, 94–96, 103, 120
Optional siting requirements, 51, 62–63
Oregon, workshops in, 192
Organizational goals, 36–37
Organizational missions, 36
Organizational objectives, 37
Organized approach, 24–25
Ownership, 245

Pacific Gas and Electric Company (PG&E), 13–14, 247
Panhandle Freeway (proposed), Calif., 12
Pennsylvania, Three Mile Island nuclear power plant, 2–3, 14, 41
Performance standards, 25–26
Petrochemical plants (see Chemical plants)
PG&E (Pacific Gas and Electric Company), 13–14, 247
Photographs, 56
Physical characteristics of facility, 49–51, 55, 62–63
Physical constraints (mapping), 104–105
Physical objectives, 39, 60
Pipelines, 246
Pittsburg, Calif., Dow Chemical Company plant, 19–20
Plans, data, 153, 161–163
Platte River Power Authority Study in Colo., 100–102, 111, 114, 116, 126–127, 169, 173–174
Point Arena nuclear power plant (proposed), Calif., 4
Polling of public opinion, 181, 189–190
Pollution, 1–2, 21, 32, 71, 292–293
Population characteristics, 55, 136
Power plants, 2–4, 13–16, 23, 32, 41–42, 44–49, 51, 53–55, 72–73, 76, 289–301
    (See also Dams; Transmission lines)
Power supply access, 96
Preliminary specifications (see Project definition)
Process description, 50, 55
Profit objectives, 39
Program development (see Project definition)
Project definition, 29, 43–57
    data needs, 50–51, 154, 160
    format, 50–51, 53, 55
    graphic presentation methods, 27, 55–57
    physical characteristics of facility, 49–50
    purpose of, 43–44
    time for, 44, 49
Project-environmental relationships, 29, 59–78
    effect identification, 64–66, 69, 71
    environmental analyses, 59–61
    issue identification, 77–78
    objective and criteria refinement, 71, 77
    organization, 61–62
    purpose of, 59
    siting requirement identification, 62–63
Project goals, 38
Project objectives, 38–39, 41
Project publicity, 181, 185
Project Seafarer (see Seafarer, Project)
Public concerns, review of, 133–134
Public hearings, 190, 192
Public opinion surveys and polls, 181, 189–190
Public participation, 1–5, 9–11, 13, 16, 23, 181–192
    design of program, 182
    participant selection, 182–183
    purpose of, 181–182
    in screening, 183–192
    in site evaluation, 183–192
    timing of, 182–183
Public values, 71, 77, 103
Publicity, 181, 185

Pure dominance, 286
Puu Kapuai campus (proposed), University of Hawaii, 195

Railroads, 245–246
Rancho Seco nuclear power plant, Calif., 2
Ranking, site, 142, 149–151
Raw-material access, 96
Rawhide Transmission Line Siting Study in Colo., 32, 140–141, 144, 153–157, 160, 183, 190
Reactors (see Nuclear power plants)
Reagan, Ronald, 19, 246
Records, data, 164, 166–167
Recreational features, 246
Regional environmental assessments, 60
Residential location, 55
Rights-of-way (ROWs), 237–238, 241, 245–246
Rivkin, Malcolm, 5
Roosevelt, Theodore, 9
ROWs (see Rights-of-way)

Sacramento River, Calif., 20
Salt Lake City, Utah, West Valley Freeway (proposed), 13
San Andreas earthquake fault, 13–14
San Francisco, Calif.:
    Bay fill, 11
    convention center (proposed), 4
    freeways (proposed), 12–13
    water supply, 9
San Francisco Board of Supervisors, 12
San Joaquin River, Calif., 20
Sanguine, Project, 18, 229
    (See also Seafarer, Project)
Santa Cruz County, Calif., Davenport siting studies, 247, 270
Scale, map, 168, 170–171, 214
Scenic Hudson Preservation Conference, 15
Schedules, 51, 55
Schematic plan development (see Project definition)
Scoping, 181–182
Screening, 29, 79–129
    candidate area identification, 128
    candidate site identification, 128–129
    data needs, 85, 160
    design of process, 79, 82–83
    factor classification, 85, 88, 93, 96, 103
    factor identification, 83–85
    public participation in, 183–192
    purpose of, 79
    weighting systems, 78, 103, 116, 120, 128
Seafarer, Project, 18–19, 83, 97–99, 117, 128, 187, 229–246
Seattle, Wash., Interstate 90 completion, 13
Seelig, D., 1
Selection process (see Site-selection process)
Sewage treatment plants, 4
Shelf, Project, 18, 229
Sierra Club, 4, 9, 14, 21
Silhouetting, avoidance of, 214
Site evaluation, 29, 131–151
    agency and public concerns review, 133
    conceptual layout preparations, 131, 133

Site evaluation (Cont.)
    cost estimate preparations, 131, 133
    data needs, 135–136, 138–139, 160–161
    framework for, 133, 135–144, 146–147
    public participation in, 183–192
    purpose of, 131
    site verification, 131
    summaries, 142, 145, 148
Site-evaluation criteria, 133, 135
Site-evaluation summaries, 142, 145, 148
Site identification, candidate, 125–129
Site ranking, 142, 149–151
Site Selection Handbook, 26
Site-selection process:
    application, 31–33
    attributes, 30–31
    data needs and analyses, 33, 153–179
    evolution, 31–33
    goal identification, 25, 29, 35–42
    lessons from past, 23–24
    need for, 23–27
    overall, 29–33
    project definition, 29, 43–57
    project-environmental relationships (see Project-environmental relationships)
    public participation (see Public participation)
    requirements for, 24–27
    screening (see Screening)
    site evaluation (see Site evaluation)
    structure, 29–30
Site verification, 131
Siting requirements, identification of, 49–51, 55, 62–63
"Sliver zones," 168
Slope and slope maps, 93, 245
Smith, D. C., 39
Snake River, Idaho, 32–33, 273–275
Social constraints (mapping), 106–107
Social factors (see Environmental and social interests)
Social objectives, 39
Socioeconomic studies, 136–137
Soderman, S., 25
Soil Conservation Service, U.S., 201
Solano County, Calif., 4, 19–22
Solano County Board of Supervisors, 21
Solano County General Plan, 20
Sources, data, 164
Southern Freeway, Calif., 12
Stafford, H. A., 25, 37–39, 83
Standards, 71, 77
Storm King Mountain nuclear power plant (proposed), N.Y., 4, 14–16, 23–24
Studies:
    environmental impact, 60–61, 181–182
    for site evaluation, 136–137
Study areas, 79–81, 83
Suitability, 135
Summaries, site-evaluation, 142, 145, 148
Surface water, 245
Surficial geology, 245
Surveys of public opinion, 181, 189–190
Swan Falls–Guffey dam (proposed), Idaho, 32–33, 273–275
Symbolism, 169
System relationships, 51, 55

Tabular formats, 51, 56
Tax policies, 96
Technical langauge, avoidance of, 27
Tellico dam (proposed), Tenn., 3
Tennessee-Tombigbee Waterway, 4

Texas, Project Seafarer sites in (proposed), 229–231
Theory, site-selection, 4, 6
Three Mile Island nuclear power plant, Pa., 2–3, 14, 41
Time-related objectives, 39
Tocks Island dam (proposed), N.J.–Pa., 3
Trade-off decisions, 103
Transmission access cost mapping, 103, 112–113
Transmission lines, 32, 49, 52, 60, 65–67, 69, 104–109, 123, 140–141, 144, 153–157, 160, 205–227, 247–271
    (*See also* Dams; Power plants)
Transportation Department, U.S., 17, 135
Tuolumne River, Calif., 1, 9–11
Tyrone Energy Park Transmission Line Study in Wis., 164, 166–167, 205–227

United States Government Manual, The, 164
University construction (*see* College construction)
University of Hawaii Academic Plan, 18
University of Hawaii Board of Regents, 18, 24, 195, 199, 204
University of Washington Office of Environmental Mediation, 13

Upper Mississippi River Basin Commission, 187
Urban projects, 4
USGS (*see* Geological Survey, U.S.)
Utah:
    Kaiparowits nuclear power plant (proposed), 3–4
    West Valley Freeway (proposed), 13
Utilities and services, 55

Values, public, 71, 77, 103
Vegetation, 245
Verification, site, 131
Visual analyses, 137, 140–142
Visual constraints (mapping), 108–109
Visual objectives, 39, 77, 135

Waiawa-area campus (proposed), University of Hawaii, 195
Waipahu campus (proposed), University of Hawaii, 195, 202–204
Warm Springs dam (proposed), Oreg., 3
Washington:
    Indian reservations in, 182
    Seattle Interstate 90 completion, 13
Waterways, 1, 4
Weighting:
    graphic, 169, 179

Weighting (*Cont.*)
    for screening, 78, 103, 116, 120, 128
    for site evaluation, 149–151
    worksheets for, 118–122, 150
Wellington, Colo., Rawhide energy project, 190
West Oahu College site studies in Hawaii, 18, 24, 142, 195–204
West Valley Freeway (proposed), Utah, 13
Westinghouse International School of Environmental Management, 16
Westway (proposed), N.Y., 13
Wildlife, 245
Wisconsin:
    Project Seafarer sites in (proposed), 19, 229
    Tyrone energy park (proposed), 164, 166–167, 205–227
Worksheets and workbooks:
    data, 160
    for public participation, 184–185
    for weighting, 118–122, 150
Workshops, 190, 192
Written formats, 56

Yerba Buena Convention Center (proposed), Calif., 4
Yolo County, Calif., 2
Yosemite National Park, Calif., 9–11, 184

ABOUT THE AUTHORS

Edward A. Williams

One of the founders of EDAW Inc., Mr. Williams is a graduate of the University of California. He has had extensive experience in all phases of landscape architecture, from city parks and schools to large-scale development planning and the formulation of policy for the use of public lands. His works range from the finely detailed gardens of the Karatsu, Japan, City Hall to direction of EDAW's pioneering Urban-Metropolitan Open-Space Study for the state of California. A member of the American Planning Association and a fellow of the American Society of Landscape Architects, he has lectured widely in the United States, Japan, and other countries.

Alison K. Massa

Educated at Cambridge University (M.A. honors in geography) and the London School of Economics (graduate degree in economics and social policy planning), Mrs. Massa came to the United States on a Ford Foundation fellowship at the University of Wisconsin, Milwaukee, in 1965. After working as a planner with the city of Chicago and other consulting firms, she joined EDAW in 1973. A principal in the firm, Mrs. Massa has been involved in numerous site- and route-selection studies for rapid transit systems, transmission lines, power plants, and military installations. She has also been responsible for precedent-setting land-use management plans.

David H. Blau

A principal of EDAW, Inc., Mr. Blau was educated at Pennsylvania State University (B.S., with honors, in landscape architecture) and the Georgia Institute of Technology (master of city planning, with honors). He served as a coordinator and project manager for the Northern Division of the Naval Facilities Engineering Command, and he also was responsible for a planning study of the problems of Georgia cities. As a project manager for EDAW, he has directed the preparation of environmental impact analyses for major California hydroelectric projects and other comprehensive environmental studies.

Herbert R. Schaal

Mr. Schaal received a B.S. degree in landscape architecture from California State Polytechnic College and an M.L.A. degree from the State University of New York at Syracuse. A principal of EDAW, which he joined in 1970, he has directed three major transmission line routing projects that have received national awards. He has also been responsible for a diverse range of interdisciplinary team projects. Mr. Schaal has lectured at a number of universities and presented papers to the Institute of Electrical and Electronic Engineers and other professional societies.